MW01001922

Karma and Punishment

Harvard East Asian Monographs 443

Karma and Punishment

Prison Chaplaincy in Japan

Adam J. Lyons

Published by the Harvard University Asia Center
Distributed by Harvard University Press
Cambridge (Massachusetts) and London 2021

The Harvard University Asia Center publishes a monograph series and, in coordination with the Fairbank Center for Chinese Studies, the Korea Institute, the Reischauer Institute of Japanese Studies, and other facilities and institutes, administers research projects designed to further scholarly understanding of China, Japan, Korea, Vietnam, and other Asian countries. The Center also sponsors projects addressing multidisciplinary, transnational, and regional issues in Asia.

Library of Congress Cataloging-in-Publication Data

Names: Lyons, Adam J., author.
Title: Karma and punishment : prison chaplaincy in Japan / Adam J. Lyons.
Description: Cambridge, Massachusetts : Harvard University Asia Center, [2021] |
    Series: Harvard East Asian monographs ; 443 | Includes bibliographical references and index. |
Identifiers: LCCN 2021010250 (print) | LCCN 2021010251 (ebook) |
    ISBN 9780674260153 (hardcover acid-free paper) | ISBN 9781684176335 (pdf)
Subjects: LCSH: Religious work with prisoners—Japan. | Justice—Religious aspects—
    Buddhism. | Prison chaplains—Buddhism. | Karma. | Dharma (Buddhism)
    Interpretation and construction. | Capital punishment—Japan.
Classification: LCC HV8865 .L96 2021 (print) | LCC HV8865 (ebook) | DDC 294.3/61—dc23
LC record available at https://lccn.loc.gov/2021010250
LC ebook record available at https://lccn.loc.gov/2021010251

Index by EdIndex

⊛ Printed on acid-free paper

Last figure below indicates year of this printing
30 29 28 27 26 25 24 23 22 21

For Kyoko and Lisa

Contents

Figures and Tables

Figures

Tables

Preface

The Heart Sutra in the Prison Chapel

> People commit crimes because their hearts are turned toward the darkness. The job of the prison chaplain is to turn a person's heart back toward the light . . . but in reality, that is a difficult thing to do.
>
> —*Interview with a prison chaplain, November 2015*

In a small chapel inside Tokyo Jail, a female prison chaplain led a group of incarcerated women through a sutra-copying workshop. Ten women in pink uniforms were seated at a row of tables, each one focused intently. Their brushes moved in silence, tracing the characters of the *Heart Sutra*: "form is emptiness, emptiness is form." The chaplain was a Buddhist priest, clad in the black clerical vestments of the Shingon sect. She paced the aisles, stopping periodically to examine the brushwork. A guard sat on a folding chair in the corner, silently overlooking the room.

After about forty minutes, the chaplain instructed the inmates to finish their work. She said, "As you were writing, what happened to your consciousness?" One by one, the women responded to her question: "I felt concentrated," "My heart was at ease," "I couldn't understand the words, but as I wrote them down the sutra started to speak to me." After each shared a parting thought, the chaplain thanked them all for participating. The guard instructed the inmates to rise and bow, and the chaplain bowed in return.

After the chaplaincy session, the chaplain and I returned to the warden's office for a brief conversation. *What was the point of the sutra copying?* The chaplain said she hoped that the women would be able to concentrate and to calm themselves. The warden, an older man just months away from retirement, said he believed that those who interact regularly with chaplains are generally more relaxed. "We haven't conducted a survey, but it is my hope that these activities are good for the inmates." He was careful to note that the prison did not regard sutra copying as a religious activity. It was "general chaplaincy," but not "religious chaplaincy."[1] Officially, it was not a sutra-copying session at all, but a calligraphy workshop. The Postwar Constitution's guarantee of religious freedom and separation of religion from state prevent the prison from requiring inmates to participate in religious activity. Not sutra copying, but "calligraphy" was included in the prison's mandatory schedule. In this case, all female inmates were required to attend.[2]

Why only the women? The chaplain said, "I am one of the few female chaplains in Japan, so it is important for me to connect with female inmates. Many of the people in prison come from families that have fallen apart, but I think that women have what we call 'the heart of compassion' (*jihi no kokoro*). I try to bring this out—the sense that we are connected to others. I hope that the women will think of their families and their children. If they pay attention to the love they have received from others, maybe they will be able to reconnect with their families." A moment later, a guard appeared at the door with another matter for the warden, and our brief interview came to an end.

I left with more questions than answers. What does sutra copying have to do with correctional rehabilitation? Is it really constitutional to have inmates do this? The warden seemed to say that chaplaincy keeps inmates docile. Was that his personal opinion or the official policy of the Corrections Office? What did the chaplain mean when she said she tries to bring out "the heart of compassion?" Was the chaplain saying that Buddhist teachings about the importance of family can serve as a bulwark against recidivism? On the train home, I looked over my field notes, trying to extract coherent themes. I wrote three words: *conscience, control, community*. What ties these themes together?

In the chapel, the chaplain did not explain the doctrines of her Shingon sect at all. There was no sermon, and the connection between the ritual and any underlying doctrinal or correctional framework was opaque. Was this a result of Shingon esotericism, or a case of a traditional rite secularized and put to a new purpose? It seemed ironic that the Shingon tradition of concealed meanings had been maintained in the prison chapel as the sutra-copying exercise was passed off as a secular calligraphy workshop. And yet it also seemed obvious that the activity was intended to be meaningful, that it was somehow connected both to the prison's ostensible purpose of reform and to a Buddhist understanding of ritual performance as a means of self-cultivation. Was the most important idea hidden? The only clue for a doctrinal framework was the chaplain's ambiguous question: "What happened to your consciousness?" Where did this come from?

When I returned to my office, I opened my copy of the *Shingon Chaplain's Manual*. Upon appointment, each chaplain is issued a copy of the standard, nonsectarian *Chaplain's Manual* and, if their sect has one, a sectarian manual. These provide scripts for chaplaincy sessions as well as an overview of the correctional system and the official doctrines and history of the chaplaincy. I turned to the Shingon manual's chapter on sutra copying to find that it specifically recommends having inmates copy the *Heart Sutra*.[3] The rationale for this exercise suggested a missing link: *the purpose of copying the sutra is to purify an individual's heart and to produce karmic merit.* A constellation of doctrinal ideas follows: people commit crime because their hearts are disordered. Committing a crime is bad karma, and incarceration is the painful fruit born of evil action. Prison is a place of purification, and religious instruction contributes to change of heart and correctional rehabilitation. Religious people are less likely to commit crimes.

As I read the chaplains' manuals, I started to see a recurring pattern bringing the three themes together. The genre-defining exercise of the chaplains' manuals is to draw functional connections between the promotion of religious commitments and the formation of a healthy *conscience*, the capacity for *self-control*, and the maintenance of a stable *community*. The Japanese term *kyōkaishi* 教誨師 is typically translated as "prison chaplain," but the characters mean more literally "doctrinal admonition instructor." The official discourse of doctrinal admonition is predicated on finding the source of crime within the individual's heart and treating it there with a prescription of religious instruction.

Yet the Shingon chaplain's statements did not easily conform to the framework of admonition. She hadn't even remonstrated with anybody. After the warden indicated his desire to use chaplains to pacify inmates, she seemed eager to emphasize that she thinks there is more to her work. She mentioned cultivating "the sense that we are connected to others." In Japanese, the ubiquitous phrase for expressing relationships *"goen ga aru"* literally means "to have a karmic connection to someone." If the official body of chaplaincy literature emphasizes karma as a moral law necessitating individual responsibility, then the chaplain's words suggest a more fluid concept: karma as a field of intersubjectivity, messy relationships that have to be managed, a web of interconnected causes and conditions molding the course of a person's life and shaping their horizons. The chaplain's comments imply that interconnection—or its absence—is relevant to the problem of crime and rehabilitation: many inmates come from broken homes, but she hopes they "will be able to reconnect with their families." But then, like the manual, the chaplain, too, invoked the heart—a woman's "heart of compassion" as a factor in rehabilitation.

I struggled to make sense of the apparent disconnect between the warden and the chaplain as well as the gap between her words and the doctrinal orthodoxy laid out in the manuals. Was the chaplain caught between her official duty to correct individual behavior and her own desire to alleviate suffering by promoting strong family relationships? Or was her understanding structured by the logic of correctional reform and its focus on molding the individual psyche? How did she negotiate a tenable position for herself between the expectations of the Corrections Office and those of her own sect? How had she come into this role in the first place? Behind these personal questions loom historical and political issues: where did prison chaplaincy in Japan come from? How and why has it developed around the concept of doctrinal admonition? If prison chaplaincy is taken as a reflection of broader patterns in religion and state relations, what does it reveal?

As of 2020, chaplaincy sessions similar to the one described above are conducted every day in prison chapels throughout Japan. There are a variety of perspectives about the provision of chaplaincy services to the incarcerated. Japanese law holds that inmates may exercise their religious freedom by electing to meet with volunteer chaplains from a variety of sects. Prison regulations maintain that chaplains are dispatched to cater to the "religious needs" of the incarcerated. Wardens hope that chaplains will contribute to the work of correctional reform by providing moral instruction. Sectarian authorities view chaplaincy as exemplifying religions' work for the public good. Individual chaplains and inmates express a broad range of opinions about the role of religion in prisons. Nonetheless, despite the diversity of interpretations, there appears to be a shared assumption that religion has a natural role to play in prisons. This fact is noteworthy because 150 years ago Japan had yet to develop a carceral system and lacked a universalized concept of religion in either law or popular discourse. Despite this, modern conceptions of religion and the prison system grew up together in such a way that the existence of prison chaplains in Japan is taken for granted today. How did this happen?

This book investigates the history and present conditions of prison religion in Japan by exploring the prison chaplaincy's origins and development. The quotation that opens this preface represents one chaplain's explanation of the aims of the job. The chaplain maintains that crime arises from problems of the heart. This idea is in fact the guiding principle of the contemporary Japanese prison chaplaincy. Though beguiling in its simplicity, the claim is loaded with historical baggage. It is not merely an assertion of individual moral and legal responsibility. As a student of religion, what is of most interest to me is that this claim appears in chaplaincy discourse always paired with the subsequent statement that the job of the chaplain (as the representative of religion) is somehow *to rectify the errant heart*.

The question is, Why is that a job for religion at all? In the pages that follow, I argue that over the last century and a half, religious organizations and the Japanese state have negotiated their relationship in a way that assigns religious groups some responsibility for and authority over the management of crime. Both religions and prisons are expected to elevate the morals of the populace to benefit the nation.

In Japan, religions have long been expected to yield a public benefit. Since the nineteenth century, religious organizations have coordinated with the state to identify and respond to crime as a religious issue. In doing so, they have developed a model of prison chaplaincy centered on the goals of moral education. As we will see, this orientation makes Japanese prison chaplaincy distinct from the varieties of chaplaincy that scholars of European and North American religions recognize under the rubric of "spiritual care." Historically, the Japanese prison chaplains' mandate to "admonish" offenders has not always gone hand in hand with the expectation to offer comfort that characterizes fields like hospital chaplaincy. This particularity also means that chaplains working in Japanese prisons today inherit a complex legacy that leaves them in a difficult situation. After all: "The job of the prison chaplain is to turn a person's heart back towards the light . . . but in reality, that is a difficult thing to do." This book provides an account of how and why a Japanese prison chaplaincy developed and what this history means for those who take up the mantle today.

Acknowledgments

En is the Japanese term for the karmic bonds of relation that shape the course of our lives and our horizon of possibilities. I begin by acknowledging that I would not have been able to complete (or even begin) this book without the help of so many people who made it possible for me to research and to write. Though only my name appears on the cover, the truth is that this work and even the mind I used to produce it are products of collective efforts.

My dissertation advisor Helen Hardacre shepherded this project from its infancy to completion. For the better part of a decade, she encouraged my independent curiosity and provided the discipline and structure that enabled me to grow into the academic vocation. Her exemplary scholarship garners much-deserved public recognition, but that she brought equal attention and care to graduate student advising and teaching was the greatest fortune of my education. My dissertation committee members Ryūichi Abé and Mark Rowe offered insightful comments and constructive criticisms of my work, and the enthusiasm and collegiality of the whole committee helped me to see things through.

Anne Monius was my adviser while I was in the master's program at Harvard Divinity School, and she provided practical help as well as moral support throughout my student years and beyond. She tragically passed away in the summer of 2019 shortly before I sent this manuscript out for review, but in one of her last acts, she commented on my drafts with her characteristic mix of gratuitous benevolence and academic rigor. Anne supported my application to the PhD program in Religion in 2009, and she helped me to feel at home in Cambridge when I first arrived in the fall of 2007. I miss her greatly.

Classes with Michael Jackson inspired me to pursue anthropology in addition to history. He informally advised me for years and commented generously on drafts of my work. But in addition to vocational guidance, I sought him out to talk about fiction (I have lost track of how many times) as an escape from the grind of studies. He inspired me with his dedication to the craft of writing, and I can't thank him enough for helping me to hold on to the joy of reading and writing even when I felt buried in coursework.

This book was largely completed over the course of two postdoctoral positions. In the 2017–2018 academic year, I was a postdoctoral fellow at the Reischauer Institute of Japanese Studies, and during that time, the evolving manuscript benefited greatly from the insights of Ian Reader, Franziska Seraphim, and Richard Jaffe, who each provided incisive and detailed comments both in writing and in person at a book workshop in the winter of 2018. The book and the clarity of my own thinking were also improved by daily conversations with my postdoctoral "cellmates" (or was it partners in crime?), Colin Jones and Matthieu Felt. Katherine Matsuura, who arrived as the new librarian for the Japan Digital Research Center, was a dauntless comrade of boundless good cheer—and she also facilitated some much-needed library assistance in a pinch. Gavin Whitelaw and Stacie Matsumoto were constant sources of support. I also thank Daniel Botsman for inviting me to Yale to speak in the spring of 2018, for a helpful discussion of my research, and for words of encouragement at a critical juncture.

From the fall of 2018 to the spring of 2020 I was a postdoctoral fellow at the Kyoto Consortium for Japanese Studies (KCJS). During that time, I was privileged to work with wonderful students and colleagues, including two dedicated and supportive directors: Mark Lincicome in my first year and Matthew Stavros in my second. Mark helped me to get my bearings and to stay on for the second year; Matthew helped me to find myself as a teacher and exhorted me to press on with my research. Both encouraged me through the daunting job hunt. Matthew designed the maps for this book and did a far better job of it than I could have. KCJS assistant director Fusako Shore, the office staff, and the full-time faculty treated me with great kindness and allowed me to feel at home in Kyoto.

At later stages of writing, Ian Reader (for a second round), David Johnson, and Micah Auerback generously read and commented on drafts in ways that strengthened the manuscript and improved my writing. Orion Klautau and Shigeta Shinji of Tohoku University, Yijiang Zhong of the University of Tokyo, Sawai Makoto of Tenri University, Matthew McMullen of Nanzan University, Namiki Eiko and Stephen Eskildsen of International Christian University, and Inoue Yoshiyuki of Ryukoku University invited me to speak at their respective institutions, and the ensuing conversations enabled me to refine the work and rectify oversights. Shimazono Susumu and anonymous readers for the Harvard University Asia Center Press provided much-needed constructive criticism to improve every aspect of this work. In the spring of 2020, I had the good fortune to join the Faculty of Business and Commerce at Keio University. My colleagues Jeffrey Kurashige, Fukazawa Haruka, Yoshida Tomoko, Greg de St. Maurice, Moriyoshi Naoko, and Takeuchi Mikako went out of their way to make me feel welcome and created a superlative working environment even as we faced the challenges of the COVID-19 pandemic.

In the six years that I have lived with this project, I have benefited from the kindness of many people in more ways than I can count. I would like to acknowledge Carol Lawson, Dan Joseph, Edwin Cranston, Eric Swanson, Erik Schiketanz, Fujimoto Yorio, Hashizume Daisaburō, Hirayama Mari, Hoshino Seiji, Hosoi Yōko, Inoue Nobutaka, James Mark Shields, Kasai Kenta, Konagai Kayo, Kurita Hidehiko, Kenneth Tanaka, Kondō Shuntarō, Levi McLaughlin, Max Ward, Miyake Hitoshi, Morishita Saburō, Niels van Steenpaal, Nishimura Akira, Ōsawa Ayako, Paride Stortini, Umemori Naoyuki, Sawai Jirō, Shigeta Shinji, Stefan Grace, Stephen Covell, Takeda Sachiya, Tamura Kanji, Tim Benedict, Victoria Montrose, Yasumaru Yoshio, and Yumiyama Tatsuya for discussing research with me, providing materials, and/or reading and commenting on drafts at various stages of development.

Without certain "karmic connections" (or rather personal introductions), this research would not have been possible. Ishizuka Shin'ichi of Ryukoku University introduced me to the National Chaplains' Union, arranged for me to have access to the Ryukoku libraries, and invited me to broaden my horizons at the Ryukoku University Corrections and Rehabilitation Center. Inoue Yoshiyuki invited me to participate in Ryukoku University's Religion and Corrections Research Group as they embarked on a study of the history of prison chaplaincy, and these meetings were a great boon to my project. Sawai Yoshitsugu and Sawai Yoshinori arranged for me to have access to the library collection at Tenri University, and at different times, each of them put me in contact with the Tenrikyō social welfare department, who in turn facilitated introductions to Tenrikyō prison chaplains. Daitō Takaaki of Kokugakuin University introduced me to the Union of Shinto Sects (Kyōha Shintō Rengōkai). Kuniko Yamada McVey of the Harvard-Yenching Library guided me to sources and even purchased a rare book for the library collection to aid in my research. The staff at the National Library of Corrections in Nakano also helped me with countless searches over the years. These supporters created the connections that made it possible for me to learn about Japanese prison chaplaincy as a living tradition and, to some extent, from the inside.

I would not have pursued the study of religion as a vocation had I not had the good fortune to study under Jonathan Herman, Timothy Renick, Kathryn McClymond, and Kenny Smith as an undergraduate student at Georgia State University from 2003 to 2007. They inspired me to ask big questions about society and history, introduced me to the methods and theories of humanities scholarship, and enabled me to see independent research both as an enjoyable way to spend one's days and a possible career. I would not have been able to continue with the study of Japanese religions without the support of many language teachers over many years, and I want to acknowledge in particular Akizawa Tomotaro of the Inter-University Center for Japanese Language Studies in Yokohama. He oversaw my work in the 2010–2011 academic year when I finally made the breakthrough from language learner to independent researcher. From my early days as a graduate student, Komamura Keigo of Keio University has been a steadfast ally and mentor. He helped me to find an apartment in Tokyo as a young language student, and in 2016 he recommended me for my first job as an adjunct lecturer at the Keio University Global Interdisciplinary Courses program, which was a supportive environment for a junior scholar. Ethan Bushelle introduced me to Shimizu Yūshō of Taisho University, and Shimizu Sensei helped me to secure housing during my studies in Japan; I am grateful to him and his family for their kindness and hospitality.

I would like to thank the prison chaplains who helped me to understand their world and provided many hours of good company. The members of the committee responsible for updating the *Chaplain's Manual* allowed me to participate in their meetings for two years, and through these meetings, I was able to gain an understanding of the history, doctrines, and present conditions of the prison chaplaincy. Rev. Kondō Tetsujō of Honganji served as the chairman of the National Chaplains' Union during my stay in Japan, and he opened many doors for me and treated me with unfailing kindness. Former chairman Rev. Hirano Shunkō (also of Honganji) shared his time and his thoughts with me, and conversations with him fundamentally shaped my thinking about prison chaplaincy and Shin Buddhism in general. Rev. Dōyama Yoshio of Tenrikyō went above and beyond the call of duty in more ways than one, and he arranged for me to speak about my work with the Tenrikyō Chaplains' Union in Tenri. The staff at the National Chaplains' Union Office in Tokyo were always supportive of my work. The correctional officers I had the chance to meet were courteous and helpful, and they worked to accommodate my prison visits when they could have stonewalled me. I appreciate their efforts to work with me.

This work was made possible by generous financial support from Harvard University, the Reischauer Institute of Japanese Studies, the Harvard Asia Center, the Japan Foundation, Waseda University, the Kyoto Consortium for Japanese Studies, and Keio University. A Foreign Language and Area Studies scholarship, two Satoh-Tsuchiya Japanese studies scholarships, and a grant from the Religion and Diversity Project helped me to get started during the early stages of research. I gratefully acknowledge their contributions, and I am pleased to be able to return some of their investment at last in the form of this book.

I also acknowledge with gratitude the permission I have received to include in this book revised versions of work published previously. Chapter 4, "Thought Crimes and the Opium of the Masses," was originally published as "From Marxism to Religion: Thought Crimes and Forced Conversions in Imperial Japan" in the *Japanese Journal of Religious Studies* 46, no. 2 (2019): 193–218. Chapter 2, "The Way of Repentance and the Great Promulgation Campaign," was originally published as "Meiji Prison

Religion: Benevolent Punishments and the National Creed" in the *Journal of Religion in Japan* 7, no. 3 (2018): 219–49. At the end of the line, Bob Graham at the Harvard University Asia Center and Akiko Yamagata of Graphite Editing helped me to refine the manuscript for publication.

Last but not least, I would like to express my gratitude toward my friends and family in Japan and the United States. Simon Hull of Nagasaki Junshin Catholic University aided me at every stage with the study of the underground Christians and provided insightful comments on the manuscript. Koike Akio has helped me to get by in Tokyo in more ways than I can count. Peter Durigon as well as Axel and Kim Oaks-Takács rallied to help me cross the dissertation finish line back in Cambridge in 2017. Reaching farther back in time, my parents, Teresa and Peter Lyons, gave me the gift of a stable and happy childhood, invested in my education, and encouraged my curiosity from the beginning. They both read this manuscript and provided helpful comments on substance and style. My brother Matthew's good humor and his gift for understanding people made life feel more hopeful. My wife, Kyoko, painstakingly proofread all of my Japanese writings (letters, presentations, publications) and helped me to conduct interviews. We shared this struggle together as we welcomed our daughter, Lisa, to the world. Prison is not a happy place, but in the midst of conducting research into what is, in all honesty, a grim subset of the human experience, Kyoko and Lisa showed me the brightness of life, and for that and more, I am grateful.

Note to the Reader

A handful of Japanese characters appear in the text, but only when the etymology of a key term is relevant to the argument. Otherwise, Japanese terms are italicized and romanized according to the modified Hepburn system, with macrons for long vowel sounds. Italics for Japanese terms are omitted only in proper names and in quotations from English-language sources where they are originally absent. Japanese names are given with the surname first, with the exception of D. T. Suzuki, who is well known. This study refers to many people whose dates of birth and death are not readily discoverable; I give dates at the first reference when I can, but otherwise I have foregone writing "dates unknown." Place names and words found in English-language dictionaries are not italicized and are given without macrons: Shinto, shogun, Tokyo, Kyoto. Terms for major deities and supernatural beings are capitalized: Buddha(s), Kami. Doctrinal and political concepts like karma and *kokutai* appear in lowercase.

The Japanese government implemented the Gregorian calendar on January 1, 1873. I adhere to the convention typical in Japanese sources, so dates given before 1873 follow the lunar calendar. Thus, "April 1868" refers to the fourth lunar month of 1868. Dates from 1873 on correspond to the Gregorian calendar.

The postwar governing body of the prison chaplaincy is Zenkoku Kyōkaishi Renmei, which I translate as the National Chaplains' Union. Throughout this study, I refer to the two major sects of the True Pure

Land school of Buddhism (Jōdo Shinshū, or simply Shin). These are the sects most invested in prison chaplaincy, and their headquarters are located at Nishi (West) Honganji and Higashi (East) Honganji in Kyoto. It is typical in Japanese to refer to the former as the Honganji sect and the latter as the Ōtani sect, and I conform to this standard usage. Acronyms for the following appear repeatedly in the text: the Japanese Association of Religious Organizations (JARO); the National Association of Shinto Shrines (NASS); the Supreme Commander for the Allied Powers (SCAP); and volunteer probation officers (VPOs). Abbreviations used in citations are given in the bibliography.

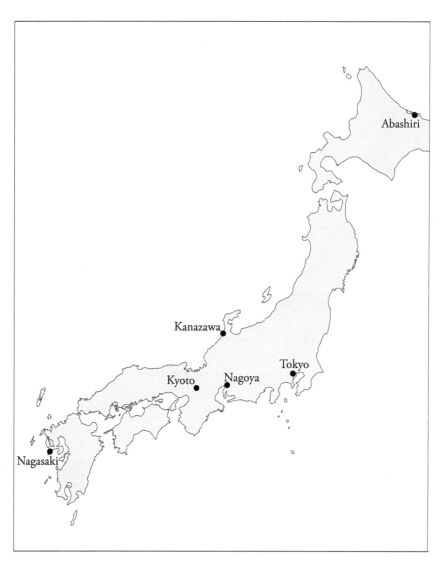

FIGURE I.I   Map of Japan. Prepared by Matthew Stavros.

INTRODUCTION

Finding a Connection to the Prison Chaplaincy

Karma is a difficult idea to pin down. In one sense, it can refer to the moral law of cause and effect—the idea that good or bad actions each engender their own just deserts.[1] In another sense, frequently seen in Japanese popular usage today, karma refers to the karmic bonds (*en*) of relationships between people. These are intersubjective connections that come our way through happenstance—the paradigmatic example being our blood relations. The first usage seems to imply that we make our own destiny through our choices. The second appears to support the opposite conclusion: that much of our fate is predetermined by the web of relations into which we are born and where we come of age. Both of these ideas and the competing perspectives that they imply are essential to understanding prison chaplaincy in Japan. I begin by sharing the story of my own initial connection to the world of the prison chaplaincy because most of the questions I brought to this project and any insights I might have had were in some way catalyzed by a series of serendipitous encounters.

In the summer of 2012, an acquaintance from Keio University where I had been auditing courses on Japanese constitutional law offered to introduce me to his family friend who happened to be a prison chaplain.

He said that the chaplain worked at Fuchū Prison—Japan's largest correctional institution, located on the outskirts of Tokyo. "You might have some common interests," he said.

As a college student in Atlanta in the 2000s, I had majored in religious studies while working part-time as an assistant to lawyers at the Georgia Capital Defender's Office. Though I didn't realize it at the time, I believe now that it was the combination of my humanities education and the experience of working on death penalty trials that kindled my interest in topics related to religion and state. I remember one semester taking a course about Zen Buddhism, whose class meetings were immediately followed by shifts photocopying stacks of personal letters provided by our inmate clients and their families to be used as evidence for mitigation arguments at trial. In the classroom, I felt spellbound by the professor's eloquent descriptions of Buddhist philosophy. I walked to work imagining a hidden world undergirding our everyday reality—a luminous and peaceful dimension that could be seen by the cultivated mind's eye. But when I stood in front of the photocopier holding a pile of letters from a defendant's case file, I became distracted from these reveries, and I started to read. Among the papers, there were often pamphlets from various churches mailed to inmates and exhorting them to "Repent!," "Save your soul!," and "Donate now!" These struck me as shameless money grabs, but I also recognized that many of our clients were deeply religious, and I had often seen their personal letters refer to seeking solace through prayer.

One day I photocopied a collection of letters from an incarcerated father to his young child. These worn pages painted a clear picture of family tragedy. Here, too, was a hidden world—or at least, it felt like one to me—and it was neither luminous nor peaceful. In my own relatively middle-class upbringing, I had no direct exposure to the grim realities of the carceral system or the scourge of poverty. As a white person, I had no personal experience of the impact of structural inequalities rooted in racism. And as a child of thoroughly secular British émigré parents, I had virtually no exposure to American religions within my home. Yet the factors of poverty, race, and religion came up again and again in the files that I dutifully assembled for the lawyers out of the raw material of our clients' personal correspondences.

Among these letters, I found a picture that I have never forgotten. It appeared to be a child's rudimentary drawing of a red racing car affected with dark black lines suggesting a whooshing speed. When I looked closely, I saw that it was not a child's drawing at all. An incarcerated father had drawn this for his young son. One of the lawyers eventually confirmed my initial impression: this man, who was on death row, was intellectually disabled. Below the picture was the phrase "Keep on praying!" I looked at this image for a long time, and I started to think that these letters were like a lifeline to the outside world. I had been thinking about the experiences of the incarcerated, but spending hours hunched over a photocopier reproducing these correspondences, I also started to wonder about the people receiving them. What was life like for people who have personal connections to those on death row? And with a mix of genuine curiosity and skepticism, I wondered again what role religion was playing behind bars.

So it was that when I was first introduced to a Japanese prison chaplain by a casual acquaintance, I was curious to know if he had experiences similar to my own, and I hoped to learn more about his work. Though we met only briefly, I realized in the course of our conversation that I had found a dissertation topic. I could investigate prison chaplaincy as a way to understand religion-state relations. I could try to gain a clearer sense of religion's role in prison and its connections to both sovereign power on one hand and the capacity to sustain hope on the other. The only problem was that the world of Japan's prison chaplaincy was generally closed to outsiders. I thought I might be able to use archival resources, but without a more significant connection, I worried that no one would be willing to talk with me.

As it turned out, I got lucky again. On a subsequent trip to Japan in 2014, I had an affiliation at Ryukoku University where Professor Ishizuka Shin'ichi, a legal specialist on human rights and the death penalty, agreed to support my research. I asked Ishizuka if he could introduce me to prison chaplains who might be willing to speak on the record. He agreed to put me in touch with the former head of the National Chaplains' Union, Rev. Hirano Shunkō, a Shin Buddhist priest. "He is a chaplain working on death row. He may be willing to talk with you," Ishizuka said. Somehow, our conversation then turned to the topic of a certain death row inmate's appeal that Ishizuka was involved with. It was a difficult case—a woman convicted of a mass poisoning. "She didn't do it," he said. "She had no reason to do it. There was nothing to be gained. There was another lead. But they let it go. And the people in the neighborhood hated her because she was obnoxious." It was clear that this woman's story weighed on his mind, and it started to weigh on mine too. I wondered what I was getting into.

These thoughts were on my mind sometime later when I met Hirano at his family temple in Chiba. Hirano was a thin man in his seventies with a gentle manner, and he greeted me warmly and invited me inside to a sunny meeting room for tea and conversation. On the wall above the table hung a painted scroll of Rennyo (1415–1499), the eighth patriarch of the Jōdo Shin (True Pure Land) school. The painting depicted the priest who had orchestrated a compromise with the secular authorities in the fifteenth century and bequeathed the maxim that his followers should obey the law of the sovereign while honoring the dharma in their hearts.[2] Even at the time, I regarded the portrait as a powerful symbol of the issues I hoped to understand. We sat down together and shared green tea, and feeling somewhat daunted by Rennyo's imperious gaze, I tried to explain my interest in Hirano's line of work. He listened attentively to my story and then smiled and said, "This is a karmic connection" (*goen desu ne*).

Hirano then began to explain his role as a chaplain. Most people on death row have been abandoned by their families. Other than a lawyer, the prison chaplain is often the only person they speak to. He produced a collection of letters from his clients to show me. He wanted me to see a set of skillful drawings in colored pencil: grinning anime characters, a landscape with blossoming cherry trees, and a remarkably lifelike depiction of a sparrow perched on a twig and pecking at a deep red berry. Every letter was addressed to him, and Hirano looked at these pictures with great affection. "This one," he said, almost to himself, "she is very talented." As we sat silently looking at these pictures together, I wondered if he was talking about the same woman whose case Ishizuka had described.

Hirano volunteered that he had been involved in arranging a public exhibition of such works by death row inmates. All of this brought to mind my own experience with stacks of similar material, and I thought that Hirano's clients' letters, too, were like lifelines—each one an attempt at connection. And here was Hirano, receiving them all, and returning week after week to visit their authors on death row—unpaid voluntary work he had been doing for nearly forty years. *How does he feel about doing this?* At first, I was not sure how to ask. But it struck me as enormously significant that he was trying to make these works of art public.

"These also come to me," he said, next placing a stack of books on the table. Each title had something to do with abolishing the death penalty. "Supporters send them." I couldn't tell what he meant by this. *Whose supporters? His own? His clients?* If he had an opinion about the death penalty, he wasn't giving it away. At the time, I wasn't sure what to make of this reticence—if he was preserving a professional protocol or just being cautious. He came across at once as both open and circumspect. It was clear that he was carrying a heavy burden.

It wasn't until a year later that another death row chaplain shared with me the words that helped me to understand what I was seeing. *As a death row chaplain, one is in no position to have a personal opinion about the death penalty.* The chaplain is responsible for religious matters—not politics. The chaplain is responsible for the inmates' problems of the heart. One wonders what Rennyo would have thought of this arrangement.

What I couldn't see at first was that Hirano could have been protecting his clients by keeping his opinions to himself. Nonetheless, what was becoming clear to me even in these first meetings was that being a prison chaplain must be enormously hard work.

This is how my research began. Hirano offered me something without which this book would not have been possible. It turned out that the board of the National Chaplains' Union had just started holding regular meetings to write a new version of the standard *Chaplain's Manual*. At Ishizuka's request, Hirano and Rev. Kondō Tetsujō, his successor as head of the union and also a Shin Buddhist priest, invited me to attend the meetings held at the union offices in Nakano, a suburb of Tokyo. I could watch a religiously diverse committee of chaplains go about the work of writing their own doctrine, history, and regulations. I could meet the board members and interview anyone willing to participate. Some might even be willing to let me shadow them, if we could get permission from the host institutions.

Though I did not realize it at the time, recent changes in the legal framework governing the prisons created the possibility for me to visit. After a century, the Meiji-era Prison Act (Kangoku hō) of 1908 had been revised following public outcry over the deaths of inmates subjected to horrific abuse by Nagoya Prison guards in 2001 and 2002. This scandal catalyzed legislative reforms culminating in the Act on Penal Detention Facilities and Treatment of Inmates and Detainees (Keiji shūyō shisetsu oyobi hishūyōshatō no shogū ni kan suru hōritsu), which came into effect in 2007 with the purpose of enhancing human rights protections for the incarcerated and providing more oversight. It was these changes that made possible for the first time the ethnographic description of Japan's prisons by creating a greater degree of openness in what had previously been "a silent space."[3] The reforms did not fundamentally transform local prison culture, which remained steadfastly committed to the maintenance of order above all else, but they did require the National Chaplains' Union (Zenkoku Kyōkaishi Renmei) to revise its *Chaplain's Manual*—or at least, the sections dealing with the law. And so it was that I received the invitation to attend the revision committee's meetings.

Thus, through the combination of a random "connection" and recent legal reforms, the closed world of the Japanese prison chaplaincy became open to me. For two years between 2014 and 2016, I participated in their meetings, and week after week, more than a dozen appointed representatives from different religious groups brought in materials and discussed their work. My book is the product of archival research and fieldwork, but the *Chaplain's Manual* committee meetings were at the center of my research experience. It was through these interactions, watching the chaplains painstakingly attempt to piece together the authoritative guidebook for their vocation—and socializing with them afterwards—that I realized I was most interested in trying to understand the prison chaplaincy's present situation as a product of history. I came to this orientation in large part because of a slowly dawning realization that the *Chaplain's Manual* sections on doctrine and history were being reworded but not subjected to rethinking. I still recall the words uttered by the meeting chair when he opened a session on the chaplaincy's core principles: "The section on doctrine has not changed at all in thirty years." As I would learn, this was an understatement. The tradition they maintained was of much longer standing.

Religion, Problems of the Heart, and the Public Good

This book analyzes prison chaplaincy in Japan from the Meiji period (1868–1912) to the present day, focusing on the chaplaincy activities of Jōdo Shinshū (commonly referred to as Shin Buddhism), Christian sects, Shinto shrines, and several other Buddhist and Shinto groups as well as so-called new religions like Tenrikyō. The sources for this study are drawn from archival research, interviews with chaplains, and site visits to prisons and religious institutions.

This work engages with scholarship on prison religion, the varieties of chaplaincy, and religion-state relations in Japan. The narrative spans Japan's modern history—including the infrastructural changes associated with modernization as well as nation building, imperialism, war, occupation, rebuilding, the economic boom, and the post-bubble era. Over the course of these transformations, the religious landscape has shifted too: the anti-Buddhist movement, the ending of the ban on Christianity, the rise and fall of State Shinto, the explosive growth and subsequent decline of new religious movements, and a general shift from "salvation to spirituality" in the current marketplace of religions.[4] The 2012 and 2016 editions of the *Journal of Religion in Japan* reflect the master narrative of Japanese religions in the twenty-first century: Japan is a "post-secular society."[5] Prison chaplains have been present throughout all of these transformations, and their location—as agents of both religious organizations and the government—makes them an excellent subject for research into the history of religion and state in Japan.[6]

Studying interactions between religion and law is important for understanding modern Japanese religious life because all religions in Japan have been affected by state policies—most notably two separate constitutions. As a shorthand, one can divide the history of modern Japan into two periods, each inaugurated by a constitution. The emperor-centered Meiji Constitution of 1889 provided for a form of limited religious freedom.[7] Many scholars have argued that this system also enabled the subsequent legal, cultural, and ideological development of State Shinto (Kokka Shintō) and ultimately made possible an atmosphere of religious suppression.[8] The Postwar Constitution of 1947 is the basis of Japan's

current liberal democracy, and many consider it the foundation of *real* re-
ligious freedom (*shinkyō no jiyū*) and separation of religion from state (*seikyō bunri*).[9] More recently, Jolyon Thomas has cogently argued that religious freedom was not introduced to postwar Japan by the Allied Occupation (1945–1952) and that the fraught process of negotiating the boundaries of religion has been a common feature of both constitutional regimes.[10] Despite such diverse interpretations of constitutional history, there is no doubt that a concept of religion has played a major role in negotiating the public-private divide in modern Japan and under both constitutions.

Since the nineteenth century, the place of religious organizations and religious vocations in Japanese society has been negotiated around a central tension. Religion is supposed to be both a private affair and a public benefit. Ongoing debates about religious freedom and separation of religion from state have long been framed in terms of competing visions about how this balance ought to be achieved. On one hand, Occupation-era reforms introduced a new element to this dynamic as Japanese society embraced the conviction that citizens have private religious needs that must be protected by law under the rubric of human rights. So it is that, today, even the incarcerated have a right to meet with chaplains. On the other hand, religious organizations and their adherents are still expected to offer some form of social contribution. Whether through social welfare work, nonprofit activities, disaster relief efforts, or the promotion of civic virtues, religions are generally expected to contribute to the public good. In prisons, chaplains are expected to fulfill this role by promoting offenders' moral reform through religious instruction.

The chaplaincy's history and present conditions are worth investigating because the chaplain exemplifies the tension between the private and public aspects of religion in modern Japan. Today, the chaplain must attend to the private realm of beliefs, aspirations, conscience, and inner experience—an inmate's "problems of the heart" (*kokoro no mondai*), to use a chaplain's term. At the same time, the chaplain performs work for the public benefit in the name of a religious organization, offering a contribution to the state's goals of inmate docility and correctional reform. Chaplains may offer attentive care to inmates, but only within rigidly defined parameters. The designated role of religion in prisons reflects in microcosm the legally circumscribed (normative) role of religion in society.

At the first meeting of the *Chaplain's Manual* committee that I attended in 2014, the chair Rev. Kondō opened the session by introducing an interview from 1987 that cited the former head of the Ministry of Justice's Corrections Office (Kyōseikyoku) Nakao Bunsaku describing his view of chaplaincy: "The purpose of conducting chaplaincy in cases when the individual desires it is that, to the extent that a person is living in faith, the result is the reality of crime prevention."[11] As Nakao's view implies, in prison, religions are expected to serve as handmaidens of the state (gendered metaphors appear throughout primary sources introduced later). Even if "access" to prison chaplains is described as a human right, chaplains themselves are in fact expected to (and do) tailor their presentation to suit the prison institution's objectives. This coercive program is described as a "freedom" that the incarcerated may enjoy. One cannot help but wonder how both inmates and chaplains feel about this arrangement. How did things get to be this way?

I address this question by taking the figure of the prison chaplain as representative of the modernization of Japanese Buddhism. Pioneering scholar of modern Buddhism and social work Yoshida Kyūichi (1915–2005) inaugurated the study of this topic by investigating two complementary trends.[12] On the one hand, modern Japanese Buddhism developed via a centripetal movement: an inward turn that saw Buddhist thinkers produce nuanced, psychologized models of subjectivity by blending imported Western philosophy and scientific thought with indigenous Buddhist doctrine. This trend is represented by the well-known *seishinshugi* movement investigated by Yoshida and many of his successors.[13] On the other hand, a centrifugal push, from temples outward into society, led to the development of Buddhist social welfare work (*shakai fukushi*).[14] There is a great deal of scholarship in English about the former subject, but currently a dearth of literature about the latter and nothing about the relationship between the two trends.[15] In my view, the prison chaplaincy is a case where both centripetal and centrifugal movements manifested at once, as chaplains became religious social workers responsible for attending to the psychological cultivation of the incarcerated. This book about chaplaincy addresses a lacuna in the study of Japanese religions by analyzing a paradigmatic example of religion's social contribution and exploring its significance for the understanding of religion-state relations in modern Japan.

I advance two primary arguments. First, *I argue that the Japanese model of prison chaplaincy is rooted in the Pure Land Buddhist concept of "doctrinal admonition," or kyōkai* (教誨). That term, which is traditionally read as *kyōke* in sutra literature, is the word used to mean prison chaplaincy today.[16] This word in its original context refers to a teaching practice for purifying a transgressor's heart (*kokoro*) so as to bring that person's thoughts, words, and deeds into harmony with the law of karma (*gō*).[17] Historically, the dominant model of prison chaplaincy in Japan has relied on conceptions of the human and frameworks of moral responsibility drawn from Buddhist teachings. Karma—the law of cause and effect (*inga ōhō*)—frames the prison chaplaincy's ethical discourse (*kyōkairon*).[18] This body of doctrine rests on an interpretation of the existential meaning of crime. Chaplaincy doctrines conform roughly to what sociologist Peter Berger refers to as a theodicy: intellectual strategies for deriving meaning from the experience of evil (or suffering) to preserve a sense that the world (the prevailing social order) is just.[19] The doctrines invest crime and rehabilitation with an existential meaning in which crime is a moral transgression (evil) for which correctional rehabilitation and religious instruction offer a chance at redemption. Committing crime is bad karma, and prison is a place of purification. Teaching the dharma can promote a change of heart and encourage people to be good citizens. Chaplaincy doctrines present a rationalized Buddhist ethic molded to the correctional program. I contend that this functionalist application of a traditional doctrine to a strategy of governance is one dimension of Buddhist modernism.[20] The case of chaplaincy suggests that we expand the horizon for thinking about Buddhist modernism to consider how Buddhist traditions have adapted to new modes of governmentality characteristic of modern disciplinary institutions like the prison.[21] Buddhist modernism is not necessarily deinstitutionalized, romantic, and individualist—it is just as modern for Buddhism to become hyperinstitutionalized, didactic, and statist.

Two caveats are due here. First, I do not claim that Buddhism is the only religion to have influenced the prison chaplaincy's development in Japan. Rather, doctrinal admonition and the form of Japanese prison religion it underwrites are hybrids that developed as Buddhism became incorporated into the prison, an institution born of Christianity.[22] My point is that the Japanese prison chaplaincy was not imported wholesale based on Euro-American models. Its genealogy must be traced through Japanese Buddhism's nineteenth-century "marriage" to the nascent correctional system. One implication of this tale is that in the process of molding themselves to serve in the prison, Buddhists came to resemble the Christians whom they sought to bar from Japan. The same point applies to the postwar chaplaincy, which sees participation from a range of Japanese religions (Shinto, Buddhist, Christian, and others). All of these groups are important, but relatively speaking, Shin Buddhism has had the largest influence on the prison chaplaincy because most prison chaplains have come from the Shin sects. Over the course of this narrative, the Buddhist term *kyōkai* comes into general usage to mean simply "teaching religion to encourage people to be good." Hence, today Christian or Shinto prison chaplains also provide doctrinal admonition on the assumption that these religions can contribute to inmates' moral reform. One goal of this study is to provide an account of just why and how the Buddhist concept of doctrinal admonition became a universal feature of modern Japanese religious discourse.

The chief implication of my line of argument for an understanding of chaplaincy as a global phenomenon is that it is necessary to decenter assumed connections between the aims of chaplaincy and concepts of spiritual health.[23] Doctrinal admonition in Japan did not develop from an ideology of spiritual care focused on relieving suffering. What was probably the world's first Buddhist chaplaincy developed from an explicit doctrine of maintaining social order, with karma presented as a moral law undergirding the secular law of the state.

The second caveat is that I do not claim that the whole of Japanese prison chaplaincy can be reduced to "doctrinal admonition." Particularly in the fieldwork chapter, I emphasize that many chaplains today work to go beyond the limitations of their official duties. They often do so by invoking the concept of karmic bonds as shorthand for relationships and connections. This intersubjective idiom allows chaplains to shift focus from admonishing individuals for their perceived moral failings to a register more akin to existential counseling. Nonetheless, the dominant discourse of chaplaincy in past and present remains rooted in the tradition of doctrinal admonition. When chaplains succeed in connecting with inmates, they do so despite, rather than because of, the way their duties are officially defined.

I consider the gap between the perspective presented in official publications (which emphasize karma as moral law) and the private stories of
individual chaplains (who emphasize intersubjective bonds) to be a chief
reason for pairing historical methods with ethnographic research. Archival sources about prison chaplaincy (the public records of the vocation)
adopt the perspective of the state and sect authorities who commissioned
and published them. These materials present an account in which admonishing offenders is the chaplain's paramount responsibility. In the textual
record, there are precious few individual accounts that cut against the
grain, whereas interviews with chaplains made it immediately clear that
the perspectives on chaplaincy that have been written down and preserved
represent only a fraction of the range of opinions and experiences that
the people who make up the chaplaincy actually have. For this reason, I
rely on interviews to highlight the contrast between dominant and demotic
discourses about chaplaincy. In short, the dominant discourse of chaplaincy is tailored to the correctional system in which religion must attend
to matters of the heart but avoid discussing political problems. Demotic
discourses resist this top-down perspective. This arrangement presents its
own enigma: why is it that in prisons the religion-state settlement—or the
Buddhism-state settlement—takes the primary form of doctrinal admonition (as opposed to prioritizing existential counseling)?

My second primary argument addresses this historical question by
interpreting the political significance of the prison chaplaincy's expansion. An essential issue in negotiations between religions and the state
has been the question of what religions can contribute to society.[24] This
study identifies a general tendency of Japanese religious organizations to
press for close relations with the government by presenting themselves as
guardians of the public good.[25] From the nineteenth century, the leaders of the powerful Shin sects offered a consistent answer to the question of social contributions that was extremely influential in shaping the
place of religion in Japanese society. *I argue that the political ideal undergirding the prison chaplaincy is the notion that the right kind of religion can
harmonize private interests with the public good.* In the Shin Buddhist
political tradition, this position is formally known as the principle of
"complementarity between dharma and law" (*nitai sōshi* 二諦相資).[26]
Each chapter traces the ramifications of this ideal in three related registers: doctrinal, political, and personal. In the first register, the notion that

religion mediates between the private realm of the heart and the encompassing sphere of public duties dovetails with the understanding of crime as a private trouble of concern to religions. The principle of complementarity authorizes the production of an enormous amount of religious discourse about crime and rehabilitation. In the second register, I focus on negotiations between religions and state. Buddhist sects developed chaplaincy at the dawn of the modern period when Buddhism's place in Japanese society was cast into doubt. The Shin sects championed the principle of complementarity as a political strategy. It is just an ideal, not a reality, but nonetheless this principle promotes normative parameters for religion (the idea that religions should benefit the nation-state) and, by the same gesture, pushes the idea that the state has a vested interest in promoting the right kind of religion (Buddhism over Christianity). Each chapter situates the expansion of prison chaplaincy in the shifting historical context of sect-state negotiations. Finally, there are personal implications. Historical records suggest that involvement in the chaplaincy has left a lasting mark on both the incarcerated and the chaplains. Interviews reveal that many chaplains today feel ambivalent about the role they have inherited. What can a chaplain do if he feels that crime is not just a problem of the heart, but rooted in deep-seated social injustices? In sum, the prison chaplain's role reflects in microcosm the contested place of religion in contemporary Japan. Doctrinal innovations, political negotiations, and personal dilemmas surrounding prison chaplaincy may be said to flow from the politics of harmony between religions and state.

Tracing this thread of "harmony," the narrative engages with major historical changes as well as continuity. In the former category, I show that conceptions of "the right kind of religion" change over time and that there are broad shifts in dominant ideas about the public good. In the mid-nineteenth century, Christianity was illegal in Japan, and even into the early twentieth century, some new religious movements were violently suppressed by the state. Yet since the postwar period, there have been plenty of Christian prison chaplains and chaplains hailing from new religions.[27] The notion of the public good also shifted through the twentieth century, meaning one thing during World War II (Support the war!) and another under Allied Occupation (Promote peace!). However, this study demonstrates that despite these shifts, the essential justification for prison chaplaincy remains intact: religion is a force for harmony, and it contributes to the public benefit. In every decade of the modern period, many Japanese religious organizations have tried to ally themselves with a statist vision of the public good. The chaplaincy's dominant conception of crime sees a social problem that religions are both uniquely qualified and responsible to ameliorate. The ideal of sect-state harmony is written into the structure of the chaplain's role. The case of chaplaincy shows how some religious groups have tailored their services to the state's demands and, in the process, created demand for more of (the right kind of) religion.

To avoid misunderstanding at the outset, I stress that I do not maintain that religion is the only or the most significant factor that has influenced the development of correctional theory and practice in Japan. My primary interest is more in line with the reverse: the carceral system has had an impact on Japanese religions that deserves investigation. The Japanese prison chaplaincy's historical legacy is of particular relevance today because it provides the backbone to an alternative model of prison religion to those found in majority-Christian societies. This history invites us to consider the fact that even when religion has been regarded as a private affair, it has been expected to yield a public benefit. As a matter of description, the sociologist Émile Durkheim interpreted religion as a kind of social glue, but in the context of modern Japan's correctional program, the state appears to have prescriptively insisted upon it, and religious organizations themselves have eagerly sought to play the part.[28]

Scope, Sources, and Methods

This study relies on sociological and anthropological theories to make sense of data drawn equally from texts and fieldwork. Like many researchers who work on prisons, I draw inspiration from Michel Foucault's work on the birth of the prison and governmentality.[29] Reading the archive of prison chaplaincy materials, one finds any number of key normative terms like "heresy" (*jakyō*), "thought crimes" (*shisōhan*), "change of heart" (*kaishin*), and "conversion" (*tenkō*) that serve to authorize certain ways of living while rendering others the object of disciplinary interventions: imprisonment, admonition, and spiritual counseling. Prison management regards chaplains as specialists in matters of the heart and expects them to measure the degree of an inmate's progress toward reform. The chaplaincy has developed a body of literature, techniques, and jargon that constitutes its specialized field of knowledge and practice. Foucault refers to such a refined manner of "seeing the patient" as a "clinical gaze."[30] In these ways, the chaplaincy's history is permeated with the hallmark issues of Foucault's oeuvre: surveillance, discipline, and subject formation. Similarly, my reading of political history is informed by Talal Asad's application of the genealogical method to religion and state relations. Rather than taking religion as something essential, self-evident, or universal, Asad invites us to consider how religion has become an organizing category in modern social life—a legal and moral concept central to the fraught processes of dividing the private (religious) from the public (secular) spheres.[31] Under both of Japan's modern constitutions, religion's social responsibilities are delimited to the private realm of home and conscience, and this settlement underwrites the chaplaincy's dominant perspective on religion's role in the management of crime. It is in this sense that religion's prescribed role in prisons reflects in microcosm the way the law establishes a normative role for religion in society. For me, the most salient feature of the genealogical approach lies in its orientation to investigate the historical processes that generate the unequal power relations of the present (those between prisoners and chaplains; chaplains and wardens).

Although I draw inspiration from the genealogical studies of Foucault and Asad, my interest extends beyond the level of abstract discourse to include both individual biographies and specific institutions.[32] In this study, I have investigated the historical development of particular religious organizations and correctional facilities. The institutions in question are connected to chaplain lineages that continue today, and I have found it useful and important to connect the biographies of present-day chaplains (interview subjects) to those of their predecessors. It is also worth noting that whereas for Foucault human science–based statistics play an essential role in the development of the European carceral system and modern strategies of governance generally, Japanese prison chaplains never seem to have made much use of statistics. Prison chaplaincy discourse remains today firmly rooted in its nineteenth-century origins. My own study is not about an epistemic shift from premodern to modern forms of punishment.

This study's fieldwork component is guided by anthropologist Michael Jackson's analysis of the politics of storytelling. Drawing on Hannah Arendt, Jackson interprets storytelling as a process for mediating relations between the public and private realms.[33] This approach provides a way to interpret the contrast between the dominant and demotic discourses of the chaplaincy (the official doctrines vs. the personal views of chaplains).[34] Unequal power relations determine which stories and whose voices are admitted to public discourse as opposed to those relegated to the shadows of the private realm.[35] In the context of the prison, this arrangement can be attributed to the organization of the institution itself, which serves in part to conceal the process of judicial punishment from the public gaze. Japan's prisons are known to be something of a black box, with the correctional bureaucracy historically resistant to any outside oversight.[36] This discursive gap can also be indexed to the way the public-private division surrounding religious labor compounds the problems of secrecy inherent in the Japanese prison system. Prisons are secretive institutions, and within the prison, chaplains are expected to talk with inmates about private religious affairs. Trying to learn what goes on in a specific chaplaincy session is like trying to overhear a secret conversation in a sealed room locked away in a fortress behind a barbed wire fence.

Because there is so little secondary literature about prison chaplaincy in Japan, we must rely on official documents produced by chaplains, religious organizations, and government officials. Most of the archive presents the official perspectives of the Corrections Office and the Shin sects. Historical materials to corroborate the personal experiences of prior generations of chaplains and that might highlight their ambivalence or criticisms of sect and state are almost nonexistent. In the field, however, I observed that the official doctrines of various organizations and the actions and statements of individual chaplains often conflict. This tension suggests that the dominant discourse or the official story presented in most of the readily available archival materials provides only a limited perspective on chaplaincy. Interviews and a handful of privately published written records shed light on a demotic discourse, which is censored or suppressed and thus remains private.[37]

In Japan, the distinction between the public and private dimensions of an individual's life may be expressed in terms of the classical Confucian division between a person's public (*kō* 公) and private (*shi* 私) roles.[38] The public designates the responsibilities of official station, whereas the private may be regarded as the realm of personal life, family, and the home. Chaplains serve in their official capacities as representatives of both religious organizations and state institutions. The official records of the chaplaincy reflect the perspectives appropriate to public station. However, the reality is that some chaplains struggle with the tension between their public role and its institutional obligations on the one hand and their own private opinions on the other. In the world of the chaplaincy, the distinction between what is acceptable for public consumption and what must remain unspoken is mediated by prison regulations and an unwritten code. Death row, for example, is not to be discussed publicly. Those who talk will be relieved of their responsibilities.[39] Thus, when a death row chaplain spoke to the *Japan Times* in 2004, he could do so only under cover of anonymity: "The death penalty is legal murder, and as someone who has stood by and watched it being carried out, I am an accessory to murder."[40] By recognizing the moral dilemmas that chaplains encounter, I hope to provide a more accurate picture of the chaplaincy than is available through official records alone. Moreover, the shape of these dilemmas—the way they fracture around the public-private divide— reveals something of the cost of the religion-state settlement that prevails behind bars.

I add a note here about the parameters of this study. I make no assessment of whether or not chaplaincy programs have an impact on the recidivism rate in Japan. This book is more about chaplains' goals and motivations than about their methods. I do not deconstruct the concept of crime.[41] Similarly, this work does not take up the legal concept of moral agency. Finally, this is not a study of the religion of the incarcerated in Japan for two reasons. First, virtually every work that touches on prison religion in Japanese has been published by and for prison chaplains or correctional professionals. Second, it has not been possible to go through chaplains to access inmates because prisons treat religion as private information. Sometimes even chaplains are not permitted to see their clients' case files. My hope is that this book will be read as a study of the Japanese prison chaplaincy aiming to illuminate the connection between chaplains and the larger history of religion-state relations rather than as a skewed history of Japanese prisons or as a failed attempt to study the religion of incarcerated people in Japan.

Global Prison Religion and Chaplaincies: Spiritual Health and/or Social Control?

This study comes at a time when research on prisons and chaplaincy is increasingly global. The field of prison studies is vast, but most works respond to Michel Foucault's famous account of the birth of the prison, which takes the institution's goal of instilling discipline as a model for understanding how power operates in modern society.[42] For the study of religion, Foucault's argument that Christianity gave birth to the prison institution as a reformatory for troubled souls cannot be ignored. This genealogical thread entails that practices of repentance derived from monastery life and the value assumptions of Christian theology are somehow embedded in the DNA of prisons. Building on this insight, a growing body of literature addresses the connection between prisons and religion in Europe and America.[43] Winnifred Sullivan discusses the connection between prisons and American religion with reference to faith-based organizations and the establishment clause of the US Constitution.[44] Joshua Dubler's ethnographic account of a week in the life of the chapel at Pennsylvania's maximum-security Graterford Prison offers a moving picture of American religious pluralism behind bars.[45] A study of prison religion in Britain and France describes how the baseline assumptions for prison chaplaincy in these majority-Christian countries disadvantage the growing number of Muslim religious minorities who face incarceration.[46] Most of the research literature interrogates institutionalized religion in nations where Christianity is the majority tradition, sometimes questioning the possibility of equal protections for the religious freedom of minorities when the legal framework for understanding religion is based on Christianity.

The development of global prison studies complicates the picture of religion behind bars. A recent literature review divides the international contexts for the multiple "births of the prison" into three broad categories: prisons introduced by a colonial government (Vietnam, Africa), by indigenous rulers under imperialist pressure from colonial powers (China, Japan), and by postcolonial leaders (Peru).[47] In general, rather than looking for the place of religion in prisons, these accounts highlight the role of imperialist racism and/or national "civilizing" projects as guiding the global rise of incarceration. This study does not seek to overturn the prevailing consensus about the factors driving the rise of prisons globally. However, I submit that there is a story to be told about religions (not just Christianity) in prisons beyond the West. The most important fact to note is that the Japanese prison chaplaincy originated in a nineteenth-century political context hostile to Christianity. In a fundamental way, the basic model for Japanese prison chaplaincy differs from those seen in Europe and America. Thus, the study of Japanese prison religion offers to shed light on chaplaincy as a global phenomenon precisely because most extant literature on the topic focuses on predominantly Christian societies. Moreover, this study also contributes to the growing literature on global prison history by introducing a focus on religion as a key variable in a non-Western carceral system.

Today, the term *kyōkai* is translated into English simply as "prison chaplaincy," but this translation obscures both the history and doctrinal specificity of the concept. Each chapter of this study attempts to restore some aspect of the history and particularity of the prison chaplaincy in Japan. I noted above that the doctrinal term *kyōkai* which finds its way into correctional discourse is adapted from a Buddhist term that means "doctrinal admonition." The term is not simply a neologism derived to translate European notions of "chaplaincy" into the Japanese language. For this reason, the standard translation produces a false equivalence with Euro-American versions of chaplaincy. This is not to say that Euro-American forms of chaplaincy have not had an influence in Japan. The forms of prison chaplaincy found in Japan have always been hybrid practices built from the confluence of imported influences and native traditions. Indigenous traditions of religion-state relations are reflected in the history of chaplaincy most clearly in the form of variations on the Buddhist discourse of complementarity between the dharma and the law of the state. In what follows, I attempt to unpack these entangled elements to highlight similarities and differences between Japanese prison chaplaincy and other forms of chaplaincy.

The presence of chaplains in the Japanese correctional system reflects a global trend, and there are a wealth of studies of European and American chaplaincy that deserve attention. Chaplaincies share a host of common features, the most salient being their location in a secular host institution, which provides the context for chaplains' interactions with clients.[48] Around the world today, forms of chaplaincy—pastoral or spiritual care work—proliferate in hospitals, prisons, universities, the military, and other ostensibly secular institutions.[49] One factor contributing to the expansion of chaplaincy is an increasing concern with religious or spiritual health as part of a holistic conception of human well-being.[50] There is a widespread understanding that people are subject to spiritual needs, which must be met as a necessary condition for human flourishing.[51] Religion is taken to be a concern of governments globally, and many liberal democratic societies seek to promote "good" forms of religion (compatible with secular values and human rights) and to quash "bad" ones (incompatible).[52] In Japan and the United States, for example, the government and its institutions recognize that citizens have religious needs protected by constitutionally enshrined principles of religious freedom, and most governments share this commitment to some degree.[53] However, Japanese and American state institutions like prisons are obligated to meet these needs without overstepping the constitutionally mandated separation of religion from state. The legal framework governing religion delimits and structures its institutional forms like chaplaincy.

For my purposes, it is important to note that concomitant with the evident concern for spiritual health is a pervasive bureaucratic rationale undergirding the provision of chaplaincy services in secular institutions. This reasoning, which is frequently invoked in chaplaincy's vocational discourse, holds that chaplains can provide services—therapeutic care, for example—that will facilitate the smooth functioning of the host institution. According to this managerial logic, the chaplain's specialty (promoting spiritual health) can be seen as a strategic asset in combat readiness for the military or as a contributing factor in correctional reform in the prison system.[54] Many of the social scientific studies that examine chaplaincy in prisons (mostly focused on Europe and North America) adopt the same normative framework, seeking to identify how religion may contribute to prosocial behavior.[55] The key theme for understanding the role of chaplains today is not merely religion and health, but religious work for the public benefit. The question is, Who gets to define what constitutes a public benefit?

In an important study of the forms of chaplaincy in the United States, Winnifred Sullivan argues that although chaplains today hail from a diverse range of religious groups, American chaplains generally understand their practice as "ministry of presence," a form of "empathic spiritual care" and a "religion without metaphysics [yet] deeply rooted in a specific Christian theology of the Incarnation."[56] Sullivan continues: "The word 'presence' does the double work of suggesting nonimposition of a particular religious perspective while also expressing a very Christian understanding of the significance of suffering in the economy of salvation."[57] One implication of her study is that in the United States, despite the apparent diversity of religions represented in the various chaplaincies (Jewish hospital chaplaincy, humanist university chaplaincy, Buddhist prison chaplaincy, Protestant park service chaplaincy), the whole range of practices is structured by the inherited, dominant model of Christian chaplaincy. Sullivan argues that the various American chaplaincies have been shaped by common cultural and legal requirements so that they may all be understood as variations on the practice of "ministry of presence."[58] Taking Sullivan's argument as a departure point, we may well ask: What does the word *kyōkai* ("doctrinal admonition") suggest about the "imposition of a particular religious perspective"? Does it express a Buddhist understanding of the significance of suffering in an "economy of salvation"? If all forms of Japanese prison chaplaincy (including Tenrikyō, Shinto, and Christian) are structured by their inheritance of the Shin Buddhist model of *kyōkai* that was dominant from the origins of Japanese prison chaplaincy until the end of World War II, what does that mean for the understanding of chaplaincy as a global phenomenon?

Varieties of Chaplaincy in Japan

It is necessary to distinguish Japanese prison chaplaincy from Euro-American versions of chaplaincy. The easiest way to gesture to the scope of this difference is to note that Japanese prison chaplaincy cannot be understood as variations on the Christian theme of "ministry of presence" because the inherited, dominant model for prison chaplaincy is Buddhist. To grasp the significance of "doctrinal admonition," we must also distinguish Japanese prison chaplaincy from other forms of Japanese religious practice that are also translated into English as "chaplaincy." The other form of Japanese chaplaincy represents a broad cross section of emergent religious vocations that fall under the heading of spiritual care (*supirichuaru kea*). For convenience, I refer to these as forms of "spiritual care chaplaincy." To be clear, these are not forms of doctrinal admonition.

Spiritual care chaplaincy includes bedside religious caregivers (*rinshō shūkyōshi*), spiritual caregivers (*supirichuaru kea shi*), clinical attentive listeners (*rinshō keichōshi*), Buddhist hospice chaplains (*bihara sō*), and hospital workers dubbed simply "chaplains" with the *katakana* pronunciation *chapuren*.[59] These forms of chaplaincy are practiced by religious professionals from a variety of traditions, and they are a distinctly postwar phenomenon. Research into these chaplaincies is in a nascent stage, but the current data suggests that some practitioners of these forms of spiritual care emphasize the importance of "being present" with their clients.[60] It remains to be seen if this modality of religious practice bears more than a superficial resemblance to the "ministry of presence" Sullivan has identified in the United States.

Research on spiritual care work has developed in the wake of the Tōhoku 3.11 disaster. Scholars have examined the role of religionists (*shūkyōka*) in the recovery effort, and recently a body of literature has developed around the theme of "care for the heart" (*kokoro no kea*), a neologism that can be translated as "spiritual care."[61] Whether or not such work will enter the mainstream of religious life in twenty-first century Japan remains uncertain, but Sophia University and Tohoku University are at the forefront of establishing vocational programs to train practitioners in the emergent field of clinical pastoral education (CPE).[62] Takahashi Hara describes such efforts as the "redistribution of religious resources to the secular sections of society," thus enabling "religious agencies [to] play a newly discovered role in non-religious settings."[63] Many key questions remain to be answered: what, precisely, is this redistribution of religious resources thought to accomplish? Without a doubt, one important answer must be related to the problem of suffering.[64] At the same time, we may ask, Who wants spiritual care and why? Clients? Religious professionals themselves? Or secular host institutions? Although there is a growing body of scholarship about these forms of spiritual care, they remain a marginal phenomenon, their emergence is relatively recent, and historical scholarship has yet to suggest what relationship, if any, such phenomena may have with earlier modes of Japanese religious life.

Unlike these forms of spiritual care chaplaincy, the Japanese prison chaplaincy has received little scholarly attention from students of religion despite its historical priority and its structural parallels with more recent spiritual care chaplaincies. The study of prison chaplaincy may shed light on some of the many questions that remain to be answered about the history and significance of spiritual care movements in Japan.

There are a variety of forms of chaplaincy, including those forms of spiritual care chaplaincy that have developed in Japan in the postwar period and the "ministry of presence" forms of chaplaincy practiced by American chaplains. In translation, the differences between Japanese prison chaplaincy and other forms of spiritual care chaplaincy (for example, *chapuren*) are obscured, but the historical contexts in which these two types of chaplaincy developed are separated by more than a century. *Chapuren* are a contemporary phenomenon, only recently emerging in Japan. By contrast, prison chaplaincy activities have been conducted in Japanese prisons, jails, and forerunner facilities in some form since 1872. Prison chaplains are also far more numerous than spiritual care chaplains. For example, in 2012, only 176 hospice chaplains were estimated to work in 68 palliative care facilities in Japan, and hospital chaplains remain a rarity.[65] By contrast, as of the end of 2018, Japan had 1,848 prison chaplains serving a prison population over 53,233, distributed throughout 77 correctional institutions (62 prisons, 8 jails, and 7 juvenile detention houses).[66] The large majority (66 percent) of these prison chaplains hailed from Buddhist sects. The largest contingent belonged to the Jōdo Shin sects, followed by the Protestant sects, then Zen sects, and then Tenrikyō (table I.1).

Since 1995, there have been approximately 9,000 group chaplaincy sessions conducted nationwide in Japan each year. In 2008, 8,514 individual sessions were held.[67] Today, inmates can choose whether or not to attend group chaplaincy sessions or individual counseling sessions. Some types of group chaplaincy sessions (conducted by religious professionals) are officially secular, and inmate attendance is mandatory—as in the sutra copying workshop in the opening vignette. Almost all death row inmates do meet with chaplains for individual counseling sessions at some point,

Table I.1 Prison Chaplains by Sectarian Affiliation, 2018

	Number of Chaplains		Number of Chaplains
Shinto Sects	222	**Christian Sects**	264
Jinja Honchō (NASS)	141	Catholic	66
Konkōkyō	65	Protestant	198
Other	16		
Buddhist Sects	1,109	**Miscellaneous**	163
Nichiren	151	Tenrikyō	162
Pure Land[a]	662	Other	1
Shingon	156		
Tendai	42		
Zen	188	**Total**	1,848

Source: Zenkoku Kyōkaishi Renmei, http://kyoukaishi.server-shared.com/99_blank024.html, accessed April 4, 2018.

a Shin sects and the Jōdo sect are counted together.

and chaplains are present for nearly all executions in Japan.[68] In 2018, 56 women served as prison chaplains, and the remaining 1,792 were men.

In global context, the Japanese prison chaplaincy appears to be an outlier quantitatively. Peer-reviewed statistics documenting prison chaplaincies internationally are difficult to track down, but some available comparators suggest that Japan has a very high ratio of chaplains to prisoners.[69] For example, the total number of Japanese prison chaplains is roughly 25 percent greater than the Pew Research Center's estimated total number of American prison chaplains, which stood at 1,474 in 2012.[70] Situated in the context of prison populations, the contrast is outstanding. Because of mass incarceration, American chaplains serve an inmate population greater than 2.1 million spread throughout more than 1,000 correctional facilities. For every American prison chaplain, there are about 1,439 inmates. For every Japanese prison chaplain, there are approximately 30 inmates. And yet, by any statistical measure, Japan is a far less religious country than the United States.[71] The curious conclusion is that Japan has a fraction of the US prison population and a much smaller percentage of people who self-identify as religious, but Japan has more prison chaplains than the United States. The United States is an outlier due it its high incarceration rate, but comparison with the situation in the United Kingdom,

Table I.2   International Comparison of Prison Chaplain–to–Prisoner Ratios, 2010s

	Japan	United States	United Kingdom[a]	France	Sweden
Chaplains	1,848	1,474	461	1,200+	140+
Prisoners	53,233	2,121,600	83,618	74,244	5,979
Ratio	1:29	1:1,439	1:181	1:62	1:43

Sources: Incarceration statistics are available at World Prison Brief [website operated by the Institute for Criminal Policy Research of Birkbeck, University of London], www.prisonstudies .org, accessed April 23, 2019. Chaplaincy statistics are from Pew Research Center, "Religion in Prisons," Appendix A [US]; UK Freedom of Information Request 112352; Rostaing et al., "Religion, Reintegration and Rehabilitation in French Prisons" [data drawn from this source]; and Eurel Project, "Chaplaincy," accessed April 24, 2019 [Sweden].

a The number of UK chaplains combines full-time chaplains with part-time chaplains.

France, and Sweden reinforces the impression that Japan's chaplain to inmate ratio is high (table I.2). The question now is, Why does Japan have so many prison chaplains? What do they do?

From this general outline, it is clear that Japanese prison chaplaincy is of particular historical and cultural importance for understanding the subsequent development of spiritual care chaplaincies in Japan. Moreover, the fact that Japanese prison chaplaincy was founded on the basis of Japanese Buddhism suggests that its historical development and structural characteristics reflect a different arrangement of institutionalized religion than the "ministry of presence" model found in the United States. I turn now to two factors that contributed to the development of prison chaplaincy in Japan: (1) Japan's own tradition of temple-state relations; and (2) the impact of modernization processes on these arrangements.

Tradition: Dharma and Law in the Long Arc of Temple-State Relations

The relationship between Buddhism and the state has influenced Japanese culture in myriad ways, and the topic has been one of the most enduring themes in English-language studies of Japanese religious history since the 1980s.[72] Three facts about the history of temple-state relations are immediately relevant for understanding the origins of the prison chaplaincy in the broader context of political history. First, far from being focused exclusively on otherworldly concerns, Buddhist institutions have long played a role as a force for maintaining social order. Second, the particular form that role took under the Tokugawa was that temples contributed to the ideological monitoring and control of the population. Third, the 1868 Meiji Restoration disrupted temple-state relations, and temple institutions were forced to renegotiate their place in Japanese society, resulting in a new arrangement with the sovereign authorities. Prison chaplains inherit all of this history.

Since its introduction to Japan, Buddhism has been involved in political strategies, and prison chaplaincy represents a modern iteration of this pattern. A Buddhist vision of ideal rulership can be seen already in one of the Buddhist texts first transmitted to Japan, the *Sutra of Golden Light* (*Konkōmyō saishō ōkyō*). This text was translated into Chinese in the fifth century before being brought to Japan by the Nara period (710–794). Because of its promise of divine protection for rulers who support the dharma, the *Sutra of Golden Light* came to be used in courtly "rites to pacify and protect the state" (*chingo kokka*).[73] The sutra's claim for itself was that the promotion of the Buddhist teaching could contribute to the maintenance of peace in the realm and hold both human and natural disasters at bay. The subsequent history of Japanese Buddhism saw the tradition become incorporated into institutional, ideological, and ritual strategies for maintaining rule. Throughout history, Buddhist authorities presented themselves as a force against anomie.

During the Tokugawa period (1603–1868), Buddhist temples were incorporated into the apparatus of governance through the temple certification system (*terauke seido*). Fearing foreign encroachment and the growing influence of the Catholic missions that had arrived in the sixteenth century, the shogunate instituted a ban on Christianity in 1612. To uphold this prohibition, all Japanese were required to register with their local Buddhist temple and to submit to an annual sectarian investigation to prove that they were not members of the heretical Christian (Kirishitan) religion. By coordinating with temple administration, the shogunal government could both prevent the spread of the foreign church (perceived as socially disruptive) and maintain a form of census.[74] The system was in part "an apparatus for population surveillance."[75] Thus, Buddhism served as an ideological mechanism for influencing the populace and contributing to the legitimacy of rule. Temple institutions also served as the eyes of the authorities in day-to-day affairs. Ideologically and institutionally, Japanese Buddhism has been an integral component of rule throughout history.

The immediate background to the development of prison chaplaincy was a time marked by the disruption of these old institutional and ideological arrangements. When the Meiji Restoration deposed the shogun and a new government took power in 1868, the regime promoted its own ideological legitimation relying on the myths, symbols, and rhetoric of indigeneity associated with the Shinto tradition. The new rulers declared a separation of Buddhism from the state, and this break with tradition led to a wave of popular anti-Buddhist movements (*haibutsu kishaku*).[76] In the wake of this disruption, Buddhist sects were forced to reconsider and rework their relationships vis-à-vis the government. For this reason, the Meiji period was a time of great uncertainty and also of enormous doctrinal and institutional innovation, spurred on by both regime change and shifting popular consciousness. Neglecting the Buddhist temples, the state launched the Great Promulgation Campaign (*daikyō senpu undō*, 1870–1884), an ill-fated attempt to generate a new national creed with a decidedly Shinto character.[77] In a short span of time, the government also set into motion a host of modern institutions, including an administrative state modeled on Western systems of governance, hospitals, universities, public schools, mandatory conscription, and prisons.[78] In the midst of these currents, by drawing on the resources of their own past, Meiji Buddhist leaders invented their form of prison chaplaincy as one face of the new, modern Buddhism.

The prison chaplaincy developed at the same time that the category of religion (*shūkyō*) was being negotiated. Buddhists were eager to reject any state creed that prioritized Shinto over their own sectarian doctrines, and by the 1870s they were also becoming aware that the Western nations Japan sought to emulate generally embraced some form of religious freedom. Seizing the zeitgeist, Buddhist intellectuals like the Shin priest Shimaji Mokurai (1838–1911) called for separation of religion from state and a degree of freedom of religion, articulating the legal protection of this internal dimension as a necessary component of modernization and social progress.[79] The developing category of religion absorbed traditional ideas about the heart as the object of self-cultivation (*shūshin, shūyō*).[80] Religion was conceived in relation to a notion of a private space for belief (*shinkō*), defined as internal (*naishinteki*), and a "matter of the heart."[81] At the same time, the call for freedom of religion was accompanied by the assertion that the right kind of religion was connected to the promotion of social stability and therefore was of benefit to the state. In this way, the concept of religion was adapted into Japanese legal and popular discourse as a term for negotiating the public-private divide.

In the context of Shin Buddhism, ideas about religion were grounded in a doctrinal tradition recognizing two semi-independent domains of law: the ultimate law and the secular law (*shinzoku nitai* 真俗二諦).[82] Thus, Shimaji, for example, argued that while the secular law was the authority over conduct, the ultimate law was the dharma, the authority over the internal domain of a salvific faith.[83] In this way, the freedom to believe was distinguished from the freedom to take political action, such that claims for religious freedom were always subordinated to the necessity for loyalty to the sovereign. It was in the context of these institutional and doctrinal transformations and the attempt to articulate a concept of religion that the first Buddhist prison chaplains appeared.

The discourse of two domains of law should not be regarded as driving a wedge between religion and state. The tradition of Buddhist kingship in Japan has left a legacy of regarding the relationship between the dharma and the law of the sovereign as analogous to that between "two wheels on a cart" or "two horns on an ox."[84] It was along these lines that the Shin patriarch Rennyo called upon his followers to "place emphasis upon the *ōbō* [law of the sovereign] but cultivate the *buppō* [dharma] deep in one's heart."[85] In the context of the chaplaincy, one's conduct and the content of one's heart have been understood as existing in a mutual relationship and so, too, the dharma and the law of the sovereign. The mainstays of chaplaincy discourse are that violating the law of the state is also a violation of the cosmic moral order and that a person whose heart is harmonized with the dharma will also live in accordance with the law of the state. Some among the prewar and wartime chaplaincy went so far as to deny any distinction, asserting a unity between the law of the state and the dharma.[86] Rather than being abnormal in the history of Buddhism-state relations in Japan, this development fits into a broader pattern in Japanese religious history.⁸⁷ The fundamental issue has been how to conceive of the relationship between the sect and the government. This study of the chaplaincy sheds light on this long-standing problem in temple-state relations.

Modernization: Prisons, the Administration of Religion, and Social Welfare Work in Japan

The development of a prison chaplaincy in nineteenth-century Japan became possible when the traditional arrangement between temples and the government was disrupted by larger social trends associated with modernization. When the new Meiji government began importing knowledge, technology, and strategies of governance from the West, prison institutions as well as legal, academic, and popular discourses about religion were among the new acquisitions. At the same time, because of pressure from encroaching foreign powers, the Japanese state was forced to scrap the Tokugawa-era ban on Christianity and admit missionaries. These newcomers and a wave of Japanese converts introduced a tradition of social welfare work that inspired competition and catalyzed major changes in the operations of Buddhist temple institutions. Prior scholarship has investigated these three issues, and this study builds on earlier ones by bringing the topics together.

This study is informed by important English- and Japanese-language research on the history of prisons in Japan. In a groundbreaking study, Daniel Botsman shows that the Meiji government, in competition with Western colonial powers, adopted and adapted the carceral institution as part of a broader modernization drive for "civilization and enlightenment" (*bunmei kaika*).⁸⁸ The shogunate's power operated through the enforcement of status hierarchies, physical punishments, and public spectacles like executions or amnesties whereby the shogun's authority or benevolence was put on display. The transition to the Meiji era saw the operations of power transform. Punishments receded from the public square, and the state developed a carceral system grounded in the educative model of corrections and geared toward instilling discipline with the goal of producing reformed subjects. Recent Japanese scholarship highlights religion as another key variable in the history of Japan's prisons. Akashi Tomono-ri's work details the personal networks of the bureaucrats and reformers responsible for building and expanding Japan's prison system, focused in particular on their efforts to secure funding for the carceral proj-ect.[89] Akashi devotes three chapters to explaining the role of religions (Shin Buddhist sects and Protestant social welfare activists) in creating nineteenth-century prison education programs. Shigeta Shinji's study sit-uates the prison chaplaincy's development in the context of larger de-bates about the role for religions in Meiji society.[90] Shigeta shows that the overwhelming majority of early Buddhist prison chaplaincy discourse fo-cuses on "national ethics" (*kokumin dōtoku*). Prisons became a testing ground where chaplains could serve as proponents of civic virtues. These outreach efforts were in accord with the ideal social role for religions en-visioned by the influential conservative philosopher Inoue Tetsujirō (1855–1944). Shigeta also shows that some Christian chaplains in Hok-kaido frontier prisons broke this mold by advocating for prison reform, and a minority of Shin Buddhist chaplains left records indicating that they sought to offer comfort to the incarcerated. Shigeta maintains that these Buddhist minority reports suggest the influence of Kiyozawa Man-shi (1863–1903) and his individualist Buddhist reform movement. These three studies of the prison in Japan all take the institution as a microcosm of the larger social world, using prison history as a lens for understanding the civilizational projects of elites (Botsman), the political machinations behind investment in the carceral system as one factor in the centraliza-tion of the bureaucratic state (Akashi), and the impact of public debates about the role of religions in society as seen from their influence on cor-rectional education (Shigeta).

Recent Anglophone studies of religion and law in Japan emphasize how the creation of a legal framework for governing religion fundamen-tally reshaped public and private life in multifarious ways for millions of people. Trent Maxey investigates the context of international diplomacy in which the Japanese first developed a legal concept of religion for the purposes of negotiations with Western powers.[91] Jason Josephson maintains that the process of cultural exchange with the West led nineteenth-century Japanese to "invent" a concept of religion as a strategy for organizing local social life. Science and religion came to be accepted as modern and civi-lized, while the state and elites sought to tamp down on beliefs and practices deemed superstitious.[92] Richard Jaffe's study of the Meiji-period legalization of Buddhist clerical marriage indicates the scope of reforms that the state imposed on traditional Buddhist institutions.[93] Hans Martin Krämer's work on the influential Shin priest and lobbyist Shimaji Mokurai shows convincingly that, from the early days of Meiji, Japanese Buddhists themselves worked to advance their ideals about religion-state separation to benefit their own tradition.[94] Jolyon Thomas traces the long arc of constitutional history from Meiji to the postwar period, identifying a wide range of competing Japanese perspectives about the meaning of religious freedom both before and after the war.[95]

Two common denominators between the studies of the prison system and the works on religion and law are relevant to this study. First, both the carceral system and the framework for governing religion developed under the influence of a combination of external factors (diplomatic pressure from overseas powers and the threat of colonization) and internal ones (domestic lobbying including by adherents of religious groups). Second, the idea that moral edification is essential to good governance and social stability influenced both the correctional program and debates about the role of religion in society. In a nutshell, from the perspective of the architects of Meiji policy, religions and prisons were expected to serve similar ends: they should inculcate the values of good citizenship in the populace. Many religious leaders accepted these perspectives, and religious groups vied with one another to contribute to the public good along these lines.

The history of religious social welfare work in Japan is an enormous topic in Japanese scholarship. No doubt this is in part because so many of Japan's private religious universities feature strong social work programs with faculty who publish extensively on sectarian public benefit work. By contrast, one of the first and only extant English-language works to analyze the connection between religions and social work in Japan is historian Sheldon Garon's study of the state-backed moral suasion (*kyōka*) campaigns of the twentieth century. Garon shows that these campaigns were not merely a result of top-down strategies of ideological control. Rather, religious groups, social welfare activists, and the rising middle classes eagerly participated in state-sponsored efforts to "elevate" the morals of the populace. Garon refers to these patterns of collaboration between interconnected public and private sectors as "social management."[96]

In the Japanese literature, Nakanishi Naoki, a scholar of Shin Buddhist history, has studied early sectarian public benefit works aimed at uplift for the poor and found that they were interwoven with campaigns to promote the idea of a family state united under the emperor.[97] Ogawara Masamichi has published works that examine the extensive contributions of Japanese religions to support the military during the Sino-Japanese War (1894–1895), the Russo-Japanese War (1904–1905), and World War II (1939–1945), and these studies cover a range of issues, including the provision of military chaplains, blood drives, fundraising campaigns, the work of missionaries in colonial territories, and religions' rhetorical and practical support for war efforts.[98] Similarly, a classic study by Akazawa Shirō highlights the mobilization of religious resources (ideological and material) in support of prewar imperial ideology. In Akazawa's reading, mainstream religious organizations and civic groups coordinated with state agencies to pursue the dual aims of promoting poverty relief while suppressing leftist and reformist movements.[99]

The cumulative picture that emerges from these studies is that religious organizations have invested considerable money and effort into works for the public good, which has usually been conceived in relation to the political authorities' favored conception of the national interest.[100] The history of prison chaplaincy in Japan is part of this broader picture of religion and state relations. Though it is typical in the academic literature to discuss chaplaincies under the rubric of spiritual care, I take the position that the history of prison chaplaincy in Japan should be understood in the broader political context of religious work for the public benefit—a context in which tradition and modernization played equal parts in shaping the new vocation.

Structure of This Study

The architects of Meiji state policy desired and adopted Western science and techniques of governance, including prisons, but they wanted no part of the Western nations' religion. So even as the new leaders jettisoned the old regime, they initially maintained one shogunal policy—the prohibition on Christianity. There was originally no plan to introduce chaplains along with the prisons. How, then, did religion enter the Japanese prison system, and how did a prison chaplaincy develop? I have chosen to tell this story by focusing on seven moments in the history of the chaplaincy: 1870s precursors (chapter 1), 1880s origins (chapter 2), 1890s formalization (chapter 3), 1920s–1930s civil service prison chaplaincy (chapter 4), 1940s–1960s postwar restructuring (chapter 5), 1960s–2010 volunteer prison chaplaincy (chapter 6), and prison chaplaincy's recent situation, introduced through fieldwork conducted between 2014 and 2016 (chapter 7).

The Japanese prison chaplaincy arose primarily as priests from one indigenous Buddhist tradition invented a new vocational form to suit the prison's aims of reform. Chapter 1 argues that the forerunner to prison chaplaincy can be found in the last persecution of the underground Christians of Japan. In the wake of the Meiji Restoration, Buddhist sects themselves were imperiled as the new government turned to Shinto as the basis for a new national creed. Seeking to negotiate their own place in the emerging social order, some Buddhists joined the government's drive to forcibly convert the remnant of Japan's Christian minority. Shin Buddhist clerics admonished illegal Christians to make them renounce their foreign faith and thereby signal their loyalty to the emperor and the new regime. These Buddhists eagerly participated in the forced conversions to demonstrate their sect's capacity to contribute to the Meiji state. This campaign was the origin of remonstrating with detainees to solicit a change of heart. The episode reveals that Shin sects developed doctrines and practices for rectifying the hearts of prisoners as a political performance of Buddhism's capacity to contribute to the public good by inculcating loyalty to the sovereign.

Chapter 2 focuses on a strange case of synchronicity. Because of international pressure, the ban on Christianity was tacitly lifted in 1873—one year after Japan mainstreamed punishment by deprivation of liberty. This chapter describes the relationship between the Great Promulgation Campaign and the early Japanese prison system. The campaign was a short-lived attempt by the government to promote a national doctrine for the purposes of unifying the populace and preventing Christianization. I argue that prison ministry began en masse when the Great Promulgation Campaign entered newly opened detention facilities to teach a "Great Way" (*daidō*, a national doctrine) to the incarcerated beginning in 1872. It was in this year that one Buddhist priest involved in the anti-Christian conversion campaign applied for and received permission to conduct the first session of doctrinal admonition to a captive audience of newly incarcerated Japanese; the National Chaplains' Union and the Shin sects regard this event as the origin of prison chaplaincy. This chapter shows that many Buddhist priests working with the Great Promulgation Campaign pressed for access to the incarcerated absent any overarching government program. Thus, prison chaplaincy began as a grassroots movement propelled by sectarian activists who sought to unify the hearts of the Japanese people in service to the cause of the nationalist creed.

Chapter 3 investigates how Shin clerics established the fundamental doctrines and practices of the prison chaplaincy and how they achieved a monopoly over prison religion after the promulgation of the Meiji Constitution of 1889 (and despite constitutional provisions for a degree of religious freedom). The first Japanese Protestant prison chaplains were active in prison reform efforts in the frontier territory of Hokkaido, and the Shin sects competed with the newcomers by building a curriculum for prison chaplaincy and maneuvering to position themselves as rightful guardians of the public good. By the turn of the century, Shin sects developed a vocational discourse for their chaplaincy focused on crime as a form of social pathology in need of a religious (and specifically Buddhist) solution. Shin activists successfully forced Protestant chaplains out of the prisons by lobbying the Diet, and victorious Shin chaplains were appointed as civil servants. The state handed the Shin sects a monopoly that would last until the end of World War II. I argue that the interpretive key to understand Shin Buddhist mobilization surrounding the prison system lies in the Shin sects' shared ideal of complementarity between dharma and law—an ideal formalized by the Honganji sect's first modern charter of 1886. This vision of sect-state collaboration formed the basis for Buddhist prison chaplaincy theory and the rationale for the Shin sects' efforts to claim control of religion-based correctional reform programs. The Shin sects developed prison chaplaincy as part of a broad political strategy to maintain advantages over Christian missionaries by making themselves the established religion. Hostility to Christianity was a driving force behind Buddhist investment in prison chaplaincy.

Chapter 4 takes up the history of prison chaplaincy during the imperial period. Prewar public debates between Marxist atheists and representatives of religions framed an antagonism that continued in prisons as the state designated Marxist dissidents as "thought criminals," arrested the subversives, and assigned Buddhist prison chaplains to force conversions (*tenkō*) to imperialist ideology. In response to state demands, Shin Buddhists worked to convert Marxists and other thought criminals to a nationalist strand of religion on the grounds that nonreligious thinking was correlated with criminal behavior and contrary to the Japanese spirit. In the process, a body of Marxist conversion literature developed as a subgenre of the popular religious literature of the day. Like the rest of the mainstream religious world, chaplains worked to promote the imperial cause, and they saw their work as a contribution to the empire. I interpret this project as continuous with prior efforts to use doctrinal admonition to change the hearts of illegal Christians in the 1870s, and I show that the campaign of ongoing surveillance against paroled and ostensibly reformed former thought criminals catalyzed the creation of the Japanese probation system for all adult offenders.

Chapter 5 discusses the impact of the Allied Occupation of Japan on the prison chaplaincy. The Occupation abolished the Shin Buddhist civil service prison chaplaincy and encouraged a variety of sects to collaborate in building an ecumenical volunteer chaplaincy that would adhere to the principles of religion-state separation and religious freedom encoded in the 1947 Constitution. I argue that the chaplaincy was updated to reflect new understandings of the social role for religion, emphasizing human rights and contributions to keeping the peace. At the same time, the baseline assumption that religions should contribute to society by elevating the morals of the populace in the national interest was retained. The chapter begins with a case study of the Sugamo Prison chaplain Hanayama Shinshō (1898–1995) and his work with convicted war criminals. It highlights how the prison chaplaincy was transformed in line with the Occupation's goals by adopting both a universalist understanding of religion and the idea that religions create peace in the individual heart and in society at large. The second half of the chapter shows how the newly formed Japanese Association of Religious Organizations (JARO) adapted these same understandings of religion's social role to form an ecumenical volunteer chaplaincy. I show that despite the prison chaplaincy's expansion beyond the Shin sects, the various postwar forms of chaplaincy continued to rely on the tradition of doctrinal admonition and rectification of the heart. Prison outreach developed as one component of JARO's efforts to position its member religions as guardians of the public good.

Chapter 6 follows the history of prison chaplaincy from the 1960s until the 2010s. This chapter argues that the tradition of doctrinal admonition was handed down from the prewar civil service prison chaplaincy to their postwar volunteer successors in a way that preserved an anachronistic understanding of religion's social role and passed on burdensome responsibilities for which chaplains were uncompensated. There was ambiguity and much debate about religion's relationship to the public good in the late twentieth century, but religious organizations and government agencies shared the understanding that religions should contribute to the public benefit in the areas of social work. In accordance with this ideal, the prison chaplaincy was organized based on the principle of public service (*hōshi*). This arrangement allowed state agencies to harness religious organizations to government projects despite the legal separation of religions from state encoded in the constitution. Chaplains saw their responsibilities drawn between conflicting obligations: to protect the religious freedom of the incarcerated or to serve the state's goals for correctional reform? This chapter concludes with an examination of the diversification and limitations of the postwar chaplaincy. Though individual chaplains had greater discretion to decide how to do their job, there was no reorientation of prison chaplaincy as a whole toward the goal of comforting inmates in the style of spiritual care. Rather than adopting a psychologized or medicalized concept of religion and a concern for the well-being of incarcerated clients, the chaplaincy continued to be defined in a manner consistent with the tradition of doctrinal admonition even into the new millennium. The bulk of chaplaincy discourse continued to focus on religions' responsibility to fight crime in the interests of society.

Finally, chapter 7 explores the prison chaplain's role today by introducing stories uncovered through fieldwork and interviews with chaplains from a variety of religions, especially Buddhism, Shinto, and new religions. I argue that the experiences of prison chaplains reflect tensions inherent in the political processes whereby public and private spheres of life are divided in contemporary Japan. The personal narratives and opinions of individual chaplains and their struggles tend to remain private, but I introduce their voices to show that the postwar settlement places prison chaplains in an untenable position. Their responsibilities to the state, the sect, their own clients, and their loved ones lead inevitably to intractable dilemmas. The chapter concludes by looking to the place of chaplaincy in recent debates about capital punishment in Japan.

In sum, a Buddhist practice for forcing illegal Christians to renounce their faith developed into the contemporary form of prison chaplaincy, which is now tied to a universalist understanding of religion and framed by the constitutional principles of religious freedom and separation of religion from state. Today, there are Buddhist, Shinto, and Christian chaplains as well as those affiliated with the new religions. The basic mold by which their role has been shaped is structured by the prison's mission as a reformatory and also informed by the Buddhist legacy of doctrinal admonition—a practice that resonates more with a conception of public benefit than with individual spiritual health. This book tells the story of prison chaplaincy in Japan and investigates its implications for understanding religion and state relations.

In Japan, traditional religious life has transformed as successive legal systems have constructed religion as an object of governance and circumscribed it to the realm of private life and individual interiority. At the same time, religious organizations have influenced state policies such that government agencies take an interest in the religious commitments of citizens and seek to promote certain forms of religion as a public benefit. Prison chaplains stand at the intersection of these countervailing tendencies, and the official doctrines, political negotiations, and personal dilemmas of the chaplaincy reflect the contradictions of their position—a refraction of the contested place of religion in modern societies.

CHAPTER I

Defend the Dharma, Admonish
the Heretics

The Japanese prison chaplaincy has more than one origin story. The standard sectarian history is recorded in *One Hundred Years of Prison Chaplaincy* (*Kyōkai hyakunen*, 2 vols., published in 1973 and 1974), produced jointly by the Honganji and Ōtani sects of Shin Buddhism. This official account traces the chaplaincy's birth to 1872, when Shin priests first gained access to prisons to preach to the incarcerated. According to this narrative, the first prison proselytizers were motivated by altruism and a desire to match the civilizing model of Western prisons.[1] From the perspective of academic historians of the prison, a forerunner to prison chaplaincy can be seen in Sekimon Shingaku teachers who preached in the stockades for forced laborers (*ninsoku yoseba*) from the late Tokugawa period.[2]

However, one important thread missing from the sectarian story and unexplored in academic studies is the role that hostility to Christianity played in catalyzing Buddhist preaching to prisoners. A tradition of anti-Christianity and the Tokugawa-period institutional arrangements that this commitment underwrote shaped the Buddhist clerics' conviction that temples' rightful role was as defenders of the public good. When the Meiji government's rejection of Buddhism in favor of Shinto threatened the social standing of temples, Buddhist priests worked to prove their utility to the state. To these Buddhists, demonstrating their capacity to contribute to society must have seemed a matter of life and death for their tradition.

This chapter considers the role of Shin Buddhists in the persecution of illegal Christians discovered in Urakami Village (located in present-day Nagasaki City) in the years surrounding the Restoration. This campaign of suppression was only the last of a series of attempts to stamp out the remnant of a Christian minority who persisted in their forbidden faith after the Tokugawa ban was first instituted in 1612. Japanese scholars, including Anesaki Masaharu, Tokushige Asakichi, and Kataoka Yakichi, have unearthed numerous primary documents outlining the details of this persecution.[3] There is also a wealth of secondary literature in English outlining the event's diplomatic significance.[4] I focus here on a dimension of the domestic story that has received limited scholarly attention since the 1930s when Tokushige investigated the role of Shin Buddhist clerics in the crackdown. Shortly before the ban on Christianity was relaxed in 1873, Shin Buddhist agents undertook efforts to force the illegal Christians to convert. To describe the practice of remonstrating with the imprisoned Christians, period documents sometimes referred to "admonition" (*kyōkai*). This is the term that now means "prison chaplaincy," but the link between the incidents surrounding the Urakami Christians and the subsequent history of the prison chaplaincy is not merely linguistic. Biographical, structural, and political continuities support including Buddhist clerics' roles in the forced conversions of Christian detainees in the origin story of prison chaplaincy in Japan.

The admonition campaign against the Urakami Christians prefigured the prison chaplaincy's subsequent development in several important ways. First, Shin cleric Ugai Keitan (1832–1885), whom sectarian publications identify as the first prison chaplain, was responsible for forcibly converting detained Christians before he entered prisons to preach in 1872 (his story is told in chapter 2). Second, Shin cleric Ishikawa Shundai (1842–1931) was involved in handling illegal Christians in the 1870s before becoming the sect lobbyist responsible for evicting Protestant chaplains from the prison system in 1898—thereby securing the Shin monopoly (this story appears in chapter 3). Third, the prewar Ōtani seminary scholar Tokushige Asakichi's (1893–1946) interpretation of the last persecution of underground Christians—in his terminology, a "defense of the dharma"—posits that the whole endeavor was a matter of "doctrinal admonition."[5] Tokushige wrote during the 1930s, in the midst of campaigns against Marxist thought criminals (discussed in chapter 4), so the forced conversions of Marxists may have seemed to him obviously similar in structure to the forced conversions of Christians in the 1870s. Finally, whether the targets of admonition were Christian heretics, political dissidents, or people arrested for petty theft, the work was fundamentally motivated by Buddhist sects' attempts to maintain their position as defenders of the public good. In 1872, the Meiji government introduced punishment by deprivation of liberty, and one year later, under diplomatic pressure, the state tacitly permitted Christianity. This combination spurred Buddhist sects to scramble for other ways to maintain their tenuous position of moral authority. Their opposition to Christianity and the religion's subsequent legalization motivated Buddhist priests to enter the prisons to preach.

On the eve of the Meiji Restoration, as external pressure from foreign powers contributed to the shogunate's collapse, the discovery of a community of underground Christians (*senpuku Kirishitan*) near Nagasaki ignited a political crisis fueled by widespread fears of foreign encroachment. The political authorities perceived the resurfacing of the Japanese Christians as if it were an outbreak of a contagious heresy: the social order was seen to be under threat from within. The ensuing crisis outlasted the shogunate, and when the Meiji regime took power in 1868, it inherited the problem of the illegal Christians. Maintaining the ban on Christianity, the Meiji rulers sought to promote their own legitimating ideology through a coordinated campaign of proselytization based on the ideal of loyalty to the sovereign and a xenophobic brand of nativism. In the early days of the Meiji era, anti-foreignism was so powerful that even Buddhist temples—a fixture of Japanese life for more than a thousand years—came under threat.

The appearance of the illegal Christians was the first major ideological challenge to the Meiji government. Ultimately, the new rulers opted to detain and subsequently exile the Christians from Nagasaki to distant domains where they would be held in custody and forced to renounce their faith. As this plan was implemented, the traditional role of Buddhist temples as the ideological firewall against the perceived threat of Christianization and colonization created an opening for sect leaders eager to renegotiate their relationship to the new regime. Sensing an opportunity, Shin Buddhists lobbied for access to the illegal Christians on the grounds that they could convert the heretics into loyal subjects of the emperor and the state. Here was a chance for the embattled Buddhists to demonstrate their capacity to contribute to the society emerging in the Meiji Restoration's wake.

In this chapter, I show that the fundamental political commitments that would later motivate Buddhist priests to preach in prisons were already in place when Shin clerics petitioned for access to the illegal Christians. In the early 1870s, the Shin Buddhists had not yet formalized their political ideal of complementarity between sect and state, and they had yet to develop a robustly theorized concept of religion in a recognizably modern form. Nonetheless, the Shin Buddhists who targeted the Christian threat clearly relied on a principle of sect-state collaboration, and this notion was behind both their political mobilizations and the doctrinal logic they brought to bear on the Christian problem. When the necessity arose, the Shin sects were prepared to offer a teaching to support the social order. I present my argument in three parts. In the first section, I provide an overview of religion-state relations in the turbulent years surrounding the Meiji Restoration and its aftermath. I emphasize that the Shin sects saw opportunity in the political crisis instigated by the discovery of the (no-longer) underground Christians of Urakami Village. In the second section, I demonstrate how the Ōtani branch of Shin lobbied for a role in managing the illegal Christians. In the third section, I compare both Buddhist and Christian testimonies of the encounter between remonstrators and prisoners to analyze the logic of conversion, its relation to a concept of social order, and the effects of the forced conversion campaign on those involved. Though Buddhist accounts of the interaction present a united front against Christianity, the testimonies of some Christian detainees paint a more nuanced picture, suggesting that some Buddhist priests drawn into their sects' political maneuvering may have been ambivalent about the assignment.

Temple-State Relations and the Christian Enemy

Buddhism was thoroughly integrated into the fabric of social life in Tokugawa Japan. Temples served as quasi-governmental institutions, and they fulfilled a variety of roles necessary to maintain order. These functions included the operation of village schools (*terakoya*), the management of illness, the ritual cycles associated with death and dying, public proselytization, the performance of private rites to cater to the needs of individuals and families, and public rites in support of governmental authorities.[6] The most important point for the present argument is that many Buddhist institutions were required to keep watch for the spread of Christianity, which was considered a subversive, heretical doctrine. From the seventeenth century on, temples were central agents in enforcing the Tokugawa ban on Christianity. All Japanese under the shogun's dominion were compelled to register as parishioners (*danka*) of the local temple, and beginning with the annual investigation of sectarian affiliation (*shūmon aratame*), temples increasingly served as a means of monitoring the local population.[7] The involvement of Buddhism in the modern correctional system is thus contiguous with parishioner temples' role as defenders of the early modern social order.

The rationale for the temple certification system relied on the perceived threat of Christianity. By the late Tokugawa period, widespread perceptions of Christianity held it to be an "evil doctrine" (*jakyō*), a source of social disruption, and even a weapon of Western colonialism.[8] Despite the widespread prejudice against Christianity, throughout the Tokugawa period, there remained a small community of underground Christians, most of whom were concentrated in and around the Nagasaki area, where Catholic missionaries led by Francis Xavier (1506–1552) had established a foothold in the sixteenth century.[9]

Under Tokugawa rule, the harbor of Nagasaki was one of the only ports open for trade with foreign powers—"an open window in an otherwise closed country," in Kataoka's telling phrase.[10] Nagasaki was perhaps Japan's most international town. The man-made island of Dejima in its harbor was home to a Dutch trading post, and Nagasaki was also home to a community of Chinese sailors and merchants in addition to the local Japanese populace.[11] In the years leading up to the Restoration, Nagasaki became even more international after five foreign powers forced the shogunate to sign trade treaties in 1858. As a result, ships from France, the United States, Holland, Russia, and England gained access to treaty ports like Nagasaki.

Under what came to be known as the "unequal treaties," foreigners enjoyed extraterritoriality, avoiding prosecution under what Western powers viewed as Japan's "uncivilized" laws. The treaties also required Japan to permit foreigners to practice their own faith and to construct their own places of worship.[12] In line with these provisions, foreign missionaries began to arrive in Nagasaki in 1863, and the shogunate allowed for the construction of a Catholic church. When Ōura Church was completed in 1865, it became a spectacle. The Japanese residents of Nagasaki were amazed to see a "French temple" open its doors in their neighborhood (fig. 1.1).[13] Among those who came to see the church for themselves were some of Urakami's underground Christians; they were astonished to find that foreign priests had returned to Japan after seven generations.[14] Soon a group of these underground Christians revealed themselves to the French Catholic priest Fr. Bernard Petitjean (1829–1884), and they began to worship together with him in secret.[15]

The existence of the illegal Japanese Christians became widespread public knowledge in a dramatic fashion in 1867. Some of the Urakami Christians violated the law by conducting funerals independently, refusing to engage the services of Shōtokuji, the Jōdoshū temple with which they were registered.[16] This refusal amounted to a public rejection of the temple certification system, and the Nagasaki authorities moved quickly to identify and detain the Christian community leaders for questioning.[17] Because foreign priests were involved and the persecuted were Christians, the incident became the focus of international attention, implicating higher levels of government.[18]

By December 1867, however, the shogunate's days were numbered, and the matter of how to deal with the Urakami Christians was left unresolved. In January, rebellious samurai from the Satsuma and Chōshū domains seized control of Kyoto and the emperor who resided there. The rebels proclaimed themselves the rightful government and declared the "restoration of imperial rule" (*ōsei fukkō*). The restorationists overcame shogunate forces, and by April 1868, the last shogun, Tokugawa Yoshinobu (1837–1913), had surrendered his castle in Edo.

Popular support for the Meiji Restoration was drummed up by the ideological leadership of nativists who championed a return to an imagined golden age of direct imperial rule beyond the reach of foreign powers.[19] They rallied to the slogan "Revere the emperor, expel the barbarians" (*sonnō jōi*). The nativists envisioned Japan as a sacred "national polity" (*kokutai*), the land of the Kami (*shinkoku*), ruled by a divine emperor, and this conviction was coupled with rejection of everything deemed foreign as a potential source of corruption. The hostility to foreign influence

大浦天主堂 創業時代当初の立面

FIGURE I.I   Ōura Church, 1865. Courtesy of the Nagasaki Ōura Church Christian Museum.

underwrote widespread opposition to the Tokugawa policy of opening the country to foreign trade. It also entailed a rejection of Buddhism's favored status under the Tokugawa on the grounds that Buddhism, too, was a foreign imposition, responsible in part for the shogunate's evils. Thus, when the restorationists seized power, they quickly issued a series of edicts calling for the "separation of Buddhas from Kami."[20] With these gestures, the new regime unleashed a tide of popular anti-Buddhist sentiment, which led to the destruction of numerous temples and the defrocking of many Buddhist priests. This anti-Buddhist fervor came to be known as the "abolish the Buddha, destroy Shakyamuni" (*haibutsu kishaku*) movement.[21] The future of all Buddhist temples was thrown into uncertainty as a "cultural revolution" swept the country.[22] The sudden popularity of slogans like "smash the priests" left many Buddhists terrified.[23]

Amid this uncertainty, Buddhist leaders seeking to defend the dharma (*gohō*) looked for ways to adapt to the new regime and to prove Buddhism's utility to escape the threat of annihilation. Wealthy sects were able to ingratiate themselves with the state through financial contributions to the new government, which was in dire need of money for its ongoing military campaign against Tokugawa loyalist holdouts in eastern Japan (the Boshin War, 1868–1869). More broadly, the threat of Christianity provided Buddhists with an opportunity to reassert their position as the vanguard standing against the foreign menace. Even after the Meiji government came to power, popular anger at Buddhist institutions paled in comparison to fear of Christianity as an existential threat. In the spring of 1868, the new rulers reasserted the ban on Christianity through notice boards placed throughout the country.[24] To some Buddhist leaders, the appearance of the Urakami Christians looked like a golden opportunity.

Defend the Dharma by Fighting the Christian Menace

The highest levels of government deliberated the question of the Urakami Christians. On April 22, the newly formed Department of State (Dajōkan) made known their policy. They declared the Christians "a threat to the nation" and announced that the authorities would persuade them to

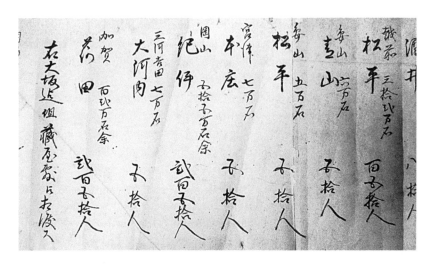

FIGURE 1.2   Instructions from the Department of State (Dajōkan) regarding the treatment of illegal Christians, seventeenth day of the intercalary fourth month of 1868. This photograph shows the order to exile an estimated "two hundred fifty" detainees to Kaga domain (present-day Kanazawa). Courtesy of the Nagasaki Ōura Church Christian Museum.

renounce their faith, destroy their objects of veneration, and make them "swear an oath before the Kami." If some refused to recant, a few of them would be executed as an example to the others; the rest would be scattered to various domains and put to work until they were ready to renounce Christianity.[25] On the seventeenth day of the following month (the intercalary fourth month on the lunar calendar), the Department of State ordered an estimated 4,010 Christians in Nagasaki to be rounded up and exiled to various domains for custody (fig. 1.2).[26]

As investigations continued, foreign powers became increasingly concerned about the treatment of Christians in Nagasaki. Nonetheless, the state proceeded with the Urakami Christians' mass internment in two phases. In May 1868, 114 leaders of the Urakami Christian community were exiled and transferred to custody in Hagi (66 persons), Tsuwano (28 persons), and Fukuyama (20 persons).[27] Then in the winter of 1869–1870, the rest of the Urakami Christian community, totaling approximately 3,400 persons, was uprooted and placed under the custody of authorities in various far-flung localities. Under the guard of provincial authorities far from home, the illegal Christians were to be subjected to interrogation, persuasion, and in many cases torture—all in an effort to force them to renounce the faith of their ancestors.

The mass internment of Christians has come to be known as the "Fourth Collapse of Urakami Village" (*Urakami yonban kuzure*). As the name suggests, there were three earlier crackdowns on the Urakami Christians, but these were relatively minor events.[28] The term "collapse" in this context refers to the political authorities' attempts to "break up" a perceived heresy. For that very purpose, the leaders of the Shin Buddhist sects petitioned the government in the summer of 1868, requesting permission to take responsibility for the Christians. It is in the context of the ensuing negotiations that "doctrinal admonition" first emerged as an issue of state policy at the dawn of the Meiji period. Originally, its aim was to bring about conversion (*kaishin* 改心, literally, "change of heart")—a renunciation of the forbidden sect of Christianity.

In June 1868, two months after the leaders of the Urakami Christians had been arrested, the Shin sects were granted some relief from the uncertainty caused by the anti-Buddhist movements sweeping the nation. They received official notice that the new government did not intend, after all, to "abolish the Buddha, destroy Shakyamuni" with its edict separating Buddhas from Kami: such unfortunate incidents were merely due to the excessive fervor of the lower classes.[29] Government representatives relayed to the Honganji sect a request from Obara Shigenori (1801–1879), the newly appointed head of the Department of Criminal Law (Keihōkan). Obara asked that the sect draft a government statement to condemn the excesses of the anti-Buddhist movements. As a result, Honganji officials drafted the following order permitting Buddhist temples to defend the dharma against the anti-Buddhist violence:

> Of late it has become apparent that a malicious faction has been seeking to fan the disturbance among the lower classes through baseless nonsense, claiming that the court supports "abolishing the Buddha, destroying Shakyamuni." We must return to our senses. Not only is this disturbing to the mind of the emperor, we must declare these factions the enemies of sect law.

For this reason, as you Buddhists are charged with the duty of influencing the populace, you must be deeply affected by this. In light of these
events, it will be necessary for the populace in all provinces to be instructed in the law and persuaded that [the Buddhist sects] will not be
diminished. The work to reassure the hearts of the people regarding this
matter must be encouraged. It is hereby decreed that no effort should be
spared to admonish [*kyōkai*] the populace to bear these principles in mind
so that the imperial influence may spread and so the people will not forget
their debt to the country.[30]

In the draft order, the term *kyōkai* appears in reference to the admonition of the populace at large and clearly refers to defending Buddhism
against violent upstarts. The import of this statement is that the benighted
populace must be reminded of the dharma's importance through a campaign of proselytization. The invocation of the emperor's will adds gravi-
tas to the message. Moreover, the defense of the dharma is linked to the
successful promotion of imperial influence. It is implied that teaching the
dharma promotes a sense of national duty among the people. Honganji
officials were making the case for reestablishing a close linkage between
temples and the state.

The immediate context necessary to understand this document cen-
ters on the two aforementioned political crises: the ongoing Boshin War
and the problem posed by the Urakami Christians.[31] The government and
the powerful Shin sects found common ground in their fear of the threat
posed by Christianity, and the government was, therefore, willing to authorize the Buddhist sects to invoke the emperor's name to denounce
anti-Buddhist activities. Moreover, the two major Shin sects, divided for
over two hundred years, now found themselves banding together in the
face of the double threat posed by the encroachment of Christianity from
without and the anti-Buddhist movements from within the nation. The
Honganji and Ōtani sects began to strategize together in their negotiations with state officials, thereby forging an alliance that would become
the basis for their political maneuvering through the Meiji period.[32]

On July 17, unified in their common cause, the Ōtani and Honganji
sects, together with the smaller Kōshō sect of Shin Buddhism, each wrote
to the Department of State to request permission to handle the underground Christians. The Honganji sect version of the text reads:

We are grateful for your decision to continue the just policy of strict prohibition against the Christian sect. At present, to support the advent of the
Restoration in government and doctrine, we wish to exert our every effort
to join our strength in service to the emperor. The responsibility of proselytizing to the populace falls with the followers of Shakyamuni. We wish
to be allowed to offer our assistance in managing the present situation by
joining in the effort to persuade the Christians who have infiltrated Nagasaki to return to their rightful place as good subjects. Of course, even
though we will work diligently with them, we anticipate that for some days
there will be difficulty in obtaining conversions, but we intend to do everything in our power to ensure success. Naturally, all Shin sects are united
in our desire to be permitted to join forces to support this cause. Each Shin
sect stands willing to offer dedicated service. We humbly request permission to take responsibility for the aforementioned matter.[33]

The wording of this request reproduces almost verbatim phrases from the
April 17 government circular announcing the plan to relocate the Christian leaders and "persuade them to return to their rightful place as good
subjects."[34] It appears that in light of the government's approval of their
attempts to stamp out the anti-Buddhist movements, the Shin sects hoped
to be granted permission to take custody of the captive Christian leadership in order to convert them into loyal subjects of the emperor.

The following week, on July 25, the Ōtani sect head temple issued a
circular to its seminary (*gakuryō*) in Kyoto, advising students and instructors that the sect had requested permission from the government to
handle the Christian menace. The sect leadership declared that preparations were to be made:

The Shin sects have reached a mutual settlement, and each sect has petitioned the government in defense of the dharma. We declared our support
for the ban on the Christian doctrine and offered to the Council of the
Department of State our services to persuade the Christians. If our petition should be accepted, lecturers [and other officials] at this seminary will
be among the first called into service. At that time, it will not do to be
unprepared with a general competence in the meaning of the heretical doctrine. By some chance, if, in the field, one encounters some question only
to be found incapable of reply, not only will this be a stain upon the reputation of our head temple, it will also make a bad name for our seminary's

instructors and officials, shaming us in front of the other sects and their instructors. Starting today, all lecturers in [Kyoto], along with [other qualified instructors] are ordered to prepare, first and foremost, the skills necessary to respond to the heretical doctrine. Research will commence at once, and, so that there will be no impediment to offering our services at any time, a list of [potential] investigators will be compiled. The rulers are gravely considering the present predicament, and more announcements will follow as the situation develops.[35]

This circular advised seminary faculty and staff that their own temples may be held responsible for converting Christians and set out a plan of action to defend the dharma.[36] It was announced that the seminary would initiate research into the Christian sect doctrines and introduce a curriculum preparing priests to persuade Christians to give up their faith and return to Buddhism. The Ōtani sect was preparing for an ideological struggle for the hearts and minds of the Japanese people.

Despite the Shin sects' enthusiasm in preparing to respond to the underground Christians, on August 23, the government issued a reply denying their requests for custody of the Urakami leadership. By this time, Restoration forces had secured major victories in their campaign against the Tokugawa loyalists in northeastern Japan, and one immediate existential threat to the nascent regime had been removed. The rejection was terse: "Although we have received your request to be permitted to persuade the open followers of Yaso [Jesus] in Kyushu, we have already dispersed their leaders to various domains for internment and investigation. Most of the others are to be placed under supervision in Hizen domain, so it has been decided that they are not to be admonished [*kyōkai*] based on the doctrine of your sect."[37]

At this time, the highest organ of state (at least in theory) was the Department of Divinities (Jingikan), an institution with a decidedly Shinto character. Although the new government may have disapproved of the anti-Buddhist movements' zealotry, it was not amenable to reinitiating the Tokugawa temple-state relationship. Under the new regime, Buddhism's position remained suspect, and the central government thus flatly rejected the Shin sects' offer to take responsibility for the Urakami Christian leaders. This responsibility was instead passed off to nativist scholars and Shinto priests.

This refusal did not convince the Shin sects to abandon the Christian problem to others. Anticipating the coming mass internment, the Ōtani sect took measures to prepare for a protracted conflict with Christianity. First, when the fall semester at the Ōtani sect seminary convened on September 15, 1868, the sect established additional courses of instruction based on the reading of Christian texts.[38] The emphasis was on the construction of polemics to overcome Christian doctrine. Second, without government approval, the Ōtani sect opted to follow the same course of action taken earlier in the year by Honganji: spies were dispatched from the Kyoto seminary to Nagasaki to investigate the Urakami Christians firsthand.[39] Even if the central government would not cooperate with the temple institutions, negotiations with regional authorities remained an option.

The Forced Relocation and Internment of the Urakami Christians

In part triggered by the sense of crisis arising from the presence of Christians in their midst, the Meiji government announced the initiation of the Great Promulgation Campaign on January 3, 1870. The campaign was an attempt to unite the populace through the promotion of a national doctrine with an explicitly Shinto character. Buddhists, too, were expected to conform to this framework. One of the first major tests conducted under the auspices of this campaign was the handling of the Urakami Christians.

It turned out that the preparatory work carried out by the Shin sects was not entirely in vain. By the beginning of 1870, the entire Urakami Christian community had been uprooted and exiled to scattered locations throughout western Japan.[40] All told, approximately 3,400 men, women, and children were transported by boat and over land to twenty-two places (in twenty domains): Kagoshima, Hagi, Tsuwano, Hiroshima, Fukuyama, Okayama, Himeji, Matsue, Tottori, Tokushima, Takamatsu, Matsuyama, Kōchi Tosa, Yamato Kōriyama, Yamato Furuichi, Wakayama, Iga Ueno, Ise Nihongi, Owari Nagoya, Kaga Kanazawa, Daishōji, Toyama.[41] Urakawa Wasaburō provides a statistical overview highlighting variances in the number of forced conversions by location as of 1873 when the Christianity ban was relaxed (table 1.1 and fig. 1.3).

Table 1.1 Detainment and Forced Conversion of Illegal Christians, 1873

				Detainees			
	Location	Total	Renounced Christianity	Refused to Renounce	Deaths	Births
1	Kagoshima	375	44	284	53	13
2	Hagi	300	162	104	43	11
3	Tsuwano	153	54	68	41	10
4	Hiroshima	179	105	39	40	5
5	Fukuyama	96	3	87	7	2
6	Okayama	117	55	48	18	4
7	Himeji	45	34	4	9	2
8	Matsue	84	81	0	10	7
9	Tottori	163	96	24	45	2
10	Tokushima	116	0	112	14	12
11	Takamatsu	54	0	47	14	7
12	Matsuyama	86	0	79	8	1
13	Kōchi Tosa	126	0	84	42	5
14	Yamato Kōriyama	86	0	107 (incl. Furuichi)[a]	9 (incl. Furuichi)	4 (incl. Furuichi)
15	Yamato Furuichi	28	2	–	–	–
16	Wakayama	289	152	52	96	11
17	Iga Ueno	59	3	49	11	4
18	Ise Nihongi	75	0	76	6	7
19	Owari Nagoya	375	195	113	82	17
20	Kaga Kanazawa	516	36	419	104	44
21	Daishōji	50	0	45	5	0
22	Toyama	42	0	42	7	7
	TOTAL	3,414	1,022	1,883	664	175

Source: Adapted from Urakawa KF 2: 752–53.
a Following Urakawa, the detainees at Yamato Furuichi are counted together with those held at Yamato Kōriyama.

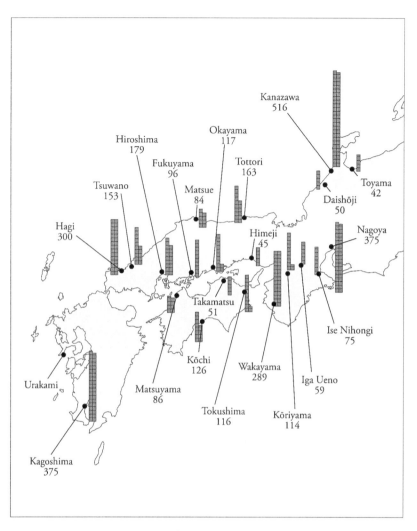

FIGURE 1.3   Detainment and exile of illegal Christians, 1870–1873. Prepared by Matthew Stavros.

In most of these locations, Shinto priests, nativist scholars, and local officials were charged with minding the Christians. However, Buddhist priests also took responsibility for admonishing the Christians in some locations: Nagoya, Daishōji, Kanazawa, Toyama, and Hiroshima.[42] Ōtani sect clerics Ishikawa Shundai (1842–1931) and Matsumoto Hakka (1838–1926) of

Kanazawa were among those charged with pressing Christians to renounce their faith. Yoshida Kyūichi notes that Ishikawa is said to have
regarded his experience admonishing Urakami Christians in Kanazawa
as a basis for his later work related to prison chaplaincy.[43] He was one of
a handful of Shin clerics who cultivated rhetorical skills with the captive
Christians before becoming invested in prison proselytization.

The treatment of the detainees appears to have varied with the
whims of their minders. Matsumoto Hakka reports that children under
seven were not separated from their parents, but those over fifteen were
chained with rings around their necks.[44] In some locations, captives
were treated relatively kindly and given sufficient food, but other minders
employed torture in addition to the techniques of persuasion. Tokushige
maintains that Kagoshima, Iga, and Ise appear to have been lenient compared with Hagi, Tsuwano, Tottori, Wakayama, Okayama, Hiroshima,
and Kanazawa.[45]

The most frequently cited scholar of the internment is Urakawa
Wasaburō (1876–1955), who served as priest of Ōura Church before being
appointed bishop of Sendai in 1941. Urakawa was himself the son of an
Urakami woman who had been exiled and interned at Kagoshima. Over
a period of years, he conducted interviews with the survivors of the internment, and these testimonies are recorded in his *Resurrection of the
Christians* (*Kirishitan no fukkatsu*, 1927).[46] Provided years after the events
in question, these testimonies often blur the lines between imagination
and reality. However, these accounts, traditionally known as "Stories of
the Journey" (*tabi no hanashi*), remain central to the collective memory
of the Nagasaki Catholic community, and they have even taken on something of the status of popular local legend.

Urakawa documents the survivors' testimonies from each point of exile. Rather than attempting to provide a comprehensive picture, I focus
here on the details of the internment and admonition of internees in locations where Buddhist priests oversaw the Christians. Various terms were
used to refer to the handling of the detainees, including persuasion (*kyōyu*),
remonstration (*setsuyu*), and admonition (*kyōkai*). I follow Tokushige by
referring to the whole enterprise as one of doctrinal admonition.

Kanazawa provides a useful case study, because accounts of the internment there survive from both the Christian and the Buddhist sides.

Urakawa reports that some 566 persons were exiled to Kanazawa (in Kaga domain), where 44 infants were born in detention, and the nearby Daishōji domain.[47] Of these, 464 eventually returned to Nagasaki after the ban on Christianity was lifted without ever surrendering their Christian faith; 109 died, 36 renounced Christianity, and 1 escaped.

The Christians were deported in phases, and officials from Kanazawa were dispatched to Nagasaki to transport one cohort of detainees. Before boarding a steamer at Ōhato port in Nagasaki, one of these officials, evidently never having seen a Christian before, is said to have asked the captives, "Is it true that the followers of the Christian sect practice magic or not?" One of the internees replied, "We absolutely cannot. If I could, would I be here right now? I would be flying like a bird over the sea or anywhere else. It's because we can't do anything of the sort that we have all been rounded up here so easily by you."[48] The detainees were shipped to Osaka, where they lodged overnight before transferring to another steamer for transport to Daishōji. From Daishōji, the detainees were eventually marched more than forty-six kilometers to Kanazawa. Urakawa writes that detainees recalled how their minders counted them like cattle (*ippiki, nihiki*) during the course of their journey.[49] When they arrived in Kanazawa, the detainees were housed in a large two-story building equipped with a fire and a bath, with no fence or guard posted. The Christians were periodically subjected to group lectures and individual persuasion sessions conducted by Shin Buddhist priests eager to participate in the Great Promulgation Campaign.

The Ōtani sect priest Matsumoto Hakka was one of those responsible for overseeing the internees at Kanazawa. He was only thirty-one years old at the time, but he produced a journal (*Bibōmanroku*, 1870) detailing his version of events.[50] Two years after the events described in this journal, Matsumoto would be appointed to a post in the Ministry of Doctrine (Kyōbushō) before being dispatched together with Ishikawa Shundai on the Ōtani sect expedition to Europe. After his return, he rose to prominence in the sect as a champion of reforms, and he is remembered today for raising money for the scholar Nanjō Bun'yū (1849–1927) and others to study Sanskrit in Europe.

Matsumoto's journal details how Shin Buddhists came to take charge of the internees in Kanazawa. In January 1870, Saigenji temple and Saishōji temple wrote to the town office requesting the chance to persuade (*kyōyu*) the captives starting on the fourteenth and fifteenth of the month.[51] The request was granted, and Shin priests from local temples received permission to proselytize to the Christians.[52] The Buddhist priests arranged to take turns sermonizing. It bears noting that the Buddhists took the initiative to gain access to the prisoners—nobody asked for their help. This was the first instance of a pattern that would recur when Shin priests started to request access to the incarcerated in 1872.

Abandon Heresy and Convert: Matsumoto Hakka's Record of Admonitions

For most of the Tokugawa period, Christianity was an abstract threat, but there was not a widespread practice of admonishing underground Christians. There was thus little precedent for a Buddhist priest to attempt to convert Christian detainees in the way that Shin priests did with the Christians who were interned, for at least two years, in Kanazawa. Tokushige presents a summary of one of the first admonition sessions, as described in Matsumoto Hakka's journal, and I analyze this text here. It is not clear which of the Buddhist priests delivered the admonition, but the speaker appears to have been familiar with anti-Christian polemics. Nonetheless, Matsumoto and his colleagues had certainly never done this kind of work before. This episode represents a missing link between temples' Tokugawa-period role in defending society against Christianity and the later development of Buddhist prison chaplains, whose job was to defend society against crime. There was not yet a formalized chaplaincy discourse. However, these admonitions present clear precedents for the subsequent development of prison chaplaincy in both political orientation (leaning toward sect-state collaboration) and in their focus on change of heart.

The remonstrator's thesis is simple: it is legally, logically, morally, and pragmatically necessary to abandon Christianity and convert to Shin Buddhism because Christianity is bad for the Japanese. His sermon consists of four primary themes: the illegality of Christianity, the falsehood of its teachings, the conflict between Christian teaching and the virtues of filial piety and loyalty, and the practical benefits of converting to Buddhism.[53]

First, he asserts that the Christian faith is illegal because it harms the nation. He does not specify the nature of the harm, instead explaining that for generations the penalty for following the forbidden sect has been death. It is only because of the emperor's compassion (*jihi*) that these Christians are to be persuaded to abandon their faith rather than killed. The emperor, he claims, hopes for the Christians to "return" to their rightful status as loyal subjects and to continue their work as good farmers. Matsumoto then explains that Japan is home to three Ways (*michi*): Shinto, Confucianism, and Buddhism. By contrast, the teaching (*kyō*) of Christianity does not amount to a Way for the Japanese people. The invocation of a Way reflects the rhetoric of the Great Promulgation Campaign and its drive to unite the Japanese people through a Great Way. Moreover, he invokes the emperor to sanctify the work of farming, implying that such labor is a sacred duty. His assertion is that the emperor does not want the Christians to be executed, but rather hopes that they will continue their labor for the sake of the realm. The reference to the sacred responsibility to work must not go unnoticed: prison chaplains engaged in similar exhortations to worldly labor in subsequent generations.

Second, the remonstrator argues that the Christian teachings are a mere fabrication. In support of this claim, he declares that although the biblical creation story places the age of the Earth at some 7,000 years, this is certainly false—the Japanese islands themselves have over 7,000 years of history, he proclaims, making them older than the age of the Earth according to Christianity. Thus, the Christian doctrine suffers from both logical and historical defects. It is notable that Matsumoto does not invoke either the truth of Buddhist doctrine or any information related to the history of Buddhism to support his argument. Rather, his argument assumes the historical veracity of ancient Japanese myths recorded in the *Kojiki* (712 CE), which trace the history of Japan back to the mythological Age of the Kami. Here, too, he tailors his presentation to the requirements of the Great Promulgation Campaign with its emphasis on Shinto symbols and mythology.

Third, the remonstrator maintains that the Christian prohibition against worshipping idols amounts to nothing less than a denial of the veneration of ancestors. He believes that Christianity is in conflict with the virtues of filial piety and its concomitant obligation to repay the kindness of one's lord with similar loyalty. He makes a series of rhetorical linkages: obedience to one's parents is connected to ancestor veneration; ancestor veneration is enacted through the veneration of Buddha images; and finally, these virtues are precisely mirrored in obedience to the emperor and his law.

There is a ritual context for understanding the remonstrator's attempt to link filial piety, ancestor veneration, veneration of Buddha images, and obedience to the law of the sovereign. Urakawa's accounts emphasize that the Urakami Christians being tended by Buddhist priests were pressured to perform obeisance before Buddha images to symbolize their renunciation.[54] Buddhist ritual was an essential means for actualizing their change of heart. The act of renunciation was understood as a matter of willingly performing this ritual under the minders' gaze. Doctrinal logic links the performance of this Buddhist ritual to the cultivation of the heart and the inculcation of loyalty.

It appears that the Buddhist priests did not consider that the parents of the Urakami Christians were themselves Christians who presumably desired for their children to continue the tradition. It is as if the remonstrator does not recognize the possibility that filial piety could take a form not approved by the public authorities. There is reason to believe that this is not merely an oversight: the doctrinal framework undergirding these admonitions does not allow for the possibility of conflict between filial piety and political obedience any more than a Platonic framework would admit that the true can be the enemy of the good. In this framing, both ancestors and the dharma (the good) are aligned with the law of the sovereign.

Finally, the remonstrator maintains that true doctrines must result in karmic rewards in this very life. But Christianity fails this test: "Are you getting enough to eat? Are you not deprived of your freedom? Are you not cold? This Christian doctrine does not produce karmic rewards even in this life, so the claim that believers will be reborn in Heaven must also be a lie."[55] The idea that a true doctrine must yield this-worldly benefits rests on an underlying circular premise: prisoners must be criminals because they are imprisoned. It is taken for granted that the imprisonment is just. It hardly needs stating that the guiding assumption throughout is that the Buddhist priest's role is to take the side of the public authorities, not that of the prisoners.

The speaker concludes by arguing that the Christians have an obligation to repay their debt (*on o hōji*) to the nation by converting to Shin, an accepted doctrine, and denying the forbidden teaching of Christianity. The invocation of a debt (*on*) to the nation is implicitly connected to this-worldly benefits, thereby implying that a relationship of reciprocity and mutual benefit exists between the subject and the nation. The term is connected to the conception of loyalty (to parents, to ancestors, and to the sovereign). The evil of Christianity, which is never explained, appears to be that it disrupts the ideal cycle of reciprocity between subject and sovereign by introducing an external loyalty. The remonstrator's proposed solution is for the prisoners to publicly perform the rejection of this external loyalty by venerating a Buddha image and signing a certificate of conversion (*kaishin shōmon*) to guarantee their change of heart. If they simply agree to fulfill these requirements, they will be allowed to go home.

It is clear that Matsumoto Hakka and his compatriots considered loyalty to the emperor and what modern observers might call "religious commitments" to be inseparable. In early Meiji Japan, there was not yet a robust discourse about religion as something that belongs to a (politically nonthreatening) private, internal realm of subjective beliefs, aspirations, and the conscience—such ideas did not become widespread or influential until later. In Matsumoto's framing, the threat posed by Christians amounted to a threat of subversion—the notion that Japanese subjects may reject their obligation (*on*) to the sovereign and the country and prioritize another loyalty. The language Buddhists used to describe the presence of Christians in Nagasaki provides a clue as to how and why Christianity was perceived as such an existential threat. Their expressions rely on the vocabulary of contagion: "the Christian doctrine is spreading like a disease" (*Kirishitan no oshie ga man'en shiteiru*).[56] The logic, it appears, is that the Other's presence within the polity threatens to corrupt the social fabric. The notion of Christian Japanese was threatening because it united two categories (Japanese and Christian) that were regarded as mutually exclusive, thereby revealing the contingency of the prevailing conservative conception of the community. This conjunction was doubly worrisome to Buddhists, for whom the threat of Christianization meant the end of their tradition.

The Captive Christians and the Stories of the Journey

Urakawa preserves the impression of one Christian detainee subjected to the remonstrations of Buddhist minders in Kanazawa. Aikawa Chūeimon, a leader of the Urakami Christians, recalled being summoned to a town magistrate's house on the pretext of an errand only to find "three or four Buddhist priests and five or six" officials awaiting him.[57] When he arrived, the priests pressured him to renounce his faith: "Convert!" (*kaishin shiro*). Chūeimon recalled challenging the priests: "If you want me to convert, then let me hear of a doctrine worth converting to!"

In Chūeimon's retelling, the Buddhist priests are bumbling and incompetent. His story rests on the amusing premise that the priests' hands were tied by the government's promotion of Shinto doctrine. Thus, rather than presenting him with arguments in favor of their own doctrines, the Buddhists were obliged (if not obligated) to pressure him to believe in a creed other than that of their own sect. Making his captors appear foolish, Chūeimon recasts in a humorous light an interaction that may have been traumatic, thereby preserving his own dignity:

The priest said, "In Japan, we have the divinities Izanagi and Izanami."

Chūeimon counted out "one" on his finger and said, "Great! I learned one new thing."

The priest continued, "These two divinities went into a Heavenly Rock Cave, and that's where the other Kami come from."

Chūeimon said, "Great! I have learned two new things." He counted out "two" on his fingers.

The priest said, "And these Kami were originally in a form like smoke."

Chūeimon said, "Good. I have learned three new things." He counted a third finger. "And what next?" [Urakawa adds the gloss: "We can only imagine how the priests must have been displeased."]

The priest said, "Nothing. That's all there is to it."

Chūeimon said, "That's it? This is precisely what we call a 'tobacco-shredding knife' back at home—it has no head or bottom to it. Even if I did convert to such a stupid doctrine, I would never be saved. No matter what you do to me, I absolutely cannot believe it."[58]

Chūeimon's story, like other Stories of the Journey, both emphasizes his commitment to the Christian faith and reflects the judgment that these Buddhist agents of the Great Promulgation Campaign were buffoons and their doctrine a preposterous hodgepodge. His story has a comic quality, buoyed by the redeeming power of Chūeimon's humor and his ability to laugh at his tormentors. However, many other testimonies paint a darker picture.

As a counterpoint to Chūeimon's story, Urakawa preserves the recollections of Fukahori Masa, a woman who was only twelve years old during her captivity in Toyama.[59] Masa describes a group of Buddhist priests, all young adult men, who bullied her, saying that all the water and food in the land belonged to the emperor. If she were to eat a grain of rice or drink so much as a drop, it would amount to a renunciation of Christianity. Despite the cruelty of her tormentors, Masa recalled the head priest of the temple where she was housed as a kindly old man who snuck her food and water when the younger men were not present. Unlike the others, the older priest never tried to coerce Masa to renounce her faith. When his compatriots returned and pressed Masa, the older priest even defended her by denying that she had eaten or had anything to drink. In Masa's story, her unlikely supporter was a sympathetic Buddhist priest willing to lie to his sect comrades to protect this stranger, a child of a scapegoated minority. As moving as this episode is, a lack of sources makes it impossible to know how representative this priest's actions were, nor is it possible to know his true motivations; but Masa's testimony gives no indication that she felt deceived by the man. This one man's kindness notwithstanding, eventually a gang of eighteen or nineteen Buddhist priests managed to separate young Masa from her protector, and they tormented her into the middle of the night, even going so far as to strike her face with an iron rod. The terrified child finally gave in, and she agreed to renounce Christianity and perform an obeisance before a Buddha image.[60] As with many persecuted Urakami Christians, her renunciation lasted only as long as the ban on Christianity prevailed.

The story of Moriuchi Ishi reflects a more positive experience. Ishi was twenty years old when she was exiled to the domain of Daishōji. At Daishōji, it appears that all relocated Christians were placed directly under the custody of Buddhist temples. (The Hokuriku area of northwestern Japan was and still is a stronghold of Shin Buddhism.) Ishi stayed with a Buddhist temple family, and she recalled that they treated her as one of their own. She developed a particularly close bond with the matriarch of the temple household. When the Christians were finally released in 1873, Ishi felt as if she were leaving her own parents behind.[61]

Masa's and Ishi's stories suggest that some agents of doctrinal admonition prioritized the duty to care over the duty to remonstrate. The sympathetic priests did not try to force the young women to convert. Even the partisan Urakawa admits: "Not all Buddhist priests were demons."[62] However, these instances of kindness amount to minority reports from what was otherwise a massive government-sponsored scapegoating project characterized by careless planning, haphazard execution, and petty cruelty. Nobody seems to have known exactly what to do with the Christians even if they did agree to convert, and multiple Christians reported encountering locals and even officials who seemed incredulous to learn that Japanese Christians were human beings like themselves as opposed to mythical beasts like *tengu*. Urakawa notes that many Christians under the custody of Daishōji priests ended up renouncing their faith. Even once back in Nagasaki, they worried about returning to the fold of Christianity, afraid that they might be rounded up and tortured again. Citing this fear, Urakawa concludes that many captives held by Buddhist temples must have been brutalized and abused (as were many of those under the authority of nativists and others).[63] Nonetheless, Urakawa's statistics indicate that all who survived the ordeal at Daishōji ultimately returned to the Catholic Church.[64]

Masa's and Ishi's recollections preserve minority reports from the very origins of doctrinal admonition. Although some Buddhist priests were enthusiastic in prosecuting the campaign against Christianity, these women's stories suggest that other priests may have felt conflicted or reluctant to be involved in admonishing the prisoners. Despite these moving personal accounts, contemporaneous Shin Buddhist records present the dominant perspective of the sect institution: Christians were the enemy and converting them was good work in defense of the dharma and the sovereign. The suggestion of ambivalence survives only in the testimony of Christian women incarcerated as youths. This hint of nuance on the part of those appointed as remonstrators merits inclusion in the origin story of prison chaplaincy because it resonates strongly with the situation of subsequent generations of chaplains. In my own interviews, I found that many contemporary chaplains feel conflicted about their assigned role but refrain from preserving these thoughts in writing. In this light, the general insight that these early-Meiji minority reports offer is that clerics assigned to work with the prisoners did not always have personal interests aligned with those of the sectarian hierarchies, for whom investment in doctrinal admonition formed part of a broader political strategy for negotiating the sect's relations with the state. "Frontline" clerics and sect elites were not necessarily on the same page when it came to dealing with the prisoners.

Urakawa's accounts present the difficulty of assessing the historical value of oral testimonies gathered years after the events in question. At the same time, these stories testify to the significance of individual memories as a way to shed light on the meaning historical events hold for the persons involved. Despite the difficulties in sifting historical fact from imagination, the testimonies still express clear judgments about the existential significance of the experiences they describe. Chūeimon and Masa both viewed their captivity as unjustifiable and as fundamentally ill-conceived. However, these Christians also shared with Matsumoto Hakka the understanding that the essential point of their ordeal revolved around the issue of conversion. In the Christian narratives, the refusal to convert amounts to a preservation of faith; from a sociological perspective, the stories of successful resistance entail a preservation of personal dignity that reinforces the connection between individual identity and group identity as mediated by a shared commitment to Christianity. To refuse to renounce one's faith and rather risk the possibility of martyrdom was seen as heroic; to surrender one's faith rather than suffer torture or worse was seen as a betrayal of the community and of God.

The statistics provided by Urakawa suggest that the effort to convert the Urakami Christians was largely a failed project.[65] Urakawa claims that of 3,414 exiled, only 1,022 persons agreed to convert while 1,883 refused to do so. (By Urakawa's count, 20 escaped, 664 died, and 175 children were born.)[66] The attempts to force the Urakami Christians to convert, therefore, did not lead them to take on new identities (whose primary loyalties were to the emperor); rather, these efforts appear to have back-fired, instead reinforcing their collective identity as Christians. The Sto-ries of the Journey testify to this solidarity.

On the other side of this relationship, the remonstrators tell a differ-ing story. Matsumoto Hakka claims to have succeeded in converting a number of Christians, counting those who signed certificates of conver-sion as successes. Reading the Buddhist and the Christian accounts to-gether, two things become clear. First, two competing value systems are in play. Second, the point of the conversion effort led by Matsumoto and others was precisely to bring the members of the targeted minority com-munity into line with the dominant values espoused by state ideology. From the Buddhist perspective, the project of admonishing illegal Chris-tians in the name of the political authorities might be regarded as a suc-cessful experiment: local activism proved to be an effective strategy for building bridges between sect and state. The dharma's traditional role as a form of protection for the realm appeared to have a potential appeal even after the Restoration.

Conclusions: "Changing Hearts" for Social Order

The Shin Buddhist response to the Urakami Christians set precedents for later participation in the development of the carceral system. In the fraught context of the anti-Buddhist movements, sect leaders and ordi-nary clerics capitalized on the appearance of the underground Christians. The perceived threat to society created an opportunity, and the sects mo-bilized by presenting themselves as guardians of the public good. They employed a combination of national and local negotiation strategies to take responsibility for some of the Urakami Christians. In so doing, Shin activists worked to create a space for Buddhism in the modern nation-state by drawing on anti-Christianity to assert their sect's efficacy as a force for social harmony. Buddhist priests charged with admonishing the illegal Christians performed the social contribution that the sect claimed as its sacred duty, and they thereby sought to secure their tradition's future at an uncertain time.

What of the individuals whose lives were shaped by the campaign to convert the illegal Christians? The Buddhist remonstrator Matsumoto Hakka was an eager proponent of the sectarian mission to "defend the dharma." Yet the case of the reluctant Buddhist priest who chose to care for the child Fukahori Masa and that of the Buddhist temple family who accepted Moriuchi Ishi as one of their own suggest that some clerics may have had misgivings about this project. Nonetheless, despite their disagreements about basic facts, both the Urakami Christian narratives and the Shin Buddhist account focus on rituals of conversion. The testimonies recorded by the Catholic priest Urakawa are structured around performances of resistance. Chūeimon, Masa, and others emphasize their unwillingness to submit to their captors and their solidarity with the Christian community.

The testimonies from Christian captives and Buddhist priests involved in this episode suggest that they shared the assumption that the public renunciation of faith amounted to a change of heart. For the Christians, this was a reversal from their position during the underground years when they were routinely required to publicly deny their faith and participate in the temple certification system.[67] No doubt the reconnection with foreign priests altered their understanding of the situation and catalyzed their commitment to practice Christianity in a public way: the persecuted Urakami Christians appear to have regarded public renunciation as a grave sin. From the perspective of Buddhist remonstrators, it appears that change of heart was imagined primarily in relation to loyalties and ritual performance. Rituals intended to cultivate the heart also made the heart visible to an external observer. All conversions were documented and reported to sect and political authorities. Tokushige provides an example of a certificate of conversion that indicates the general form:

Confirmation of Conversion

Regarding our failure to bear in mind obligations to the nation and our violation of an important prohibition by belonging to the heretical Christian sect: we have been under custody in your province, and gradually through your merciful consideration, we have received instruction. Immediately and without excuses, we performed a ritual of repentance and conversion [*kaishin kaigo*]. In the future, our children and descendants shall not wish to return to the heretical sect. We have been deeply stained by Christianity, but even one of the ten precepts [commandments] of that sect prohibits lying. Because it is a faith without benefit, there is none among us who would wish once again to practice it. Naturally, when called upon to trample a crucifix [*fumie*], we will do so without the slightest discomfort. From now on, because we have deep faith in the teachings of [Shin], we request permission to enshrine this sect's icon [*gohonzon*]. In the unlikely event that there is one among us who falls short of the provisions stated here, may that person suffer punishments from both imperial and divine authorities and for eternity slip through the invisible salvation of the Buddha to a future in hell.

Thus is it sworn.

Ninth day of June, Meiji 3 [1870], Hizen domain,
Urakami Mura Naka no Gō Village[68]

The written confirmation of conversion was important to sect and state authorities because it provided proof of repentance and submission as well as evidence of efficacy. The Shin Buddhists' claim to be capable guardians of the social order rested on their capacity to influence the hearts of the people by promoting loyalty to the sovereign. Moreover, the practice of making prisoners sign written documents to guarantee their change of heart did not disappear with the ban on Christianity. Directed writing exercises focused on repentance are a mainstay of the contemporary prison chaplain's repertoire.[69] These, too, are intended both to actualize and to demonstrate a change of heart.

All the Christian detainees were released by March 1873, regardless of whether they had abandoned their faith. The captives, now freed, made their way home to Nagasaki, where they gathered together to exchange tales of their ordeal. In doing so, the exiles developed the Stories of the Journey to preserve their collective memory. Some, like Aikawa Chūeimon, developed reputations as heroes of the faith based on their remarkable deeds during the persecution (fig. 1.4); others who renounced Christianity under duress struggled with a badge of shame.[70] The memory of exile became central to the identity of the Urakami Catholic community descended from the underground Christians, and the exiles' return from their journey has been commemorated for generations (fig. 1.5). Their stories continue to be passed down in the twenty-first century. On a

FIGURE 1.4   Aikawa Chūeimon, 1938. Source: Urakawa Wasaburō, *Tabi no hanashi*, front matter.

FIGURE 1.5   The surviving Urakami Christians assembled at Urakami Church on the sixty-fifth anniversary of their return from exile, 1938. Source: Urakawa Wasaburō, *Tabi no hanashi*, front matter.

May 2016 research trip to Urakami Cathedral (St. Mary's Cathedral) in Nagasaki, I saw floor-to-ceiling banners bearing the slogan "Do not forget our ancestors' Stories of the Journey."

In contrast, the involvement of Buddhist sects in the last persecution of the Christians has been all but forgotten—though this does not mean it was a genealogical dead end. The Tokugawa ban on Christianity and the role of Buddhist temples in enforcing that prohibition enabled the Shin sects to develop the practice of admonition as a form of Buddhist public benefit work to prove their utility to the Meiji state. Though the new regime scrapped the temple certification system, Buddhist sects— most notably Shin Buddhists—sought ways to retain their traditional involvement in the maintenance of social order. They did so by asserting their capacity to harmonize individual hearts with the public good. Japan's Buddhist form of prison chaplaincy is descended from temples' traditional role as defenders of society under the Tokugawa-era ban on Christianity.

CHAPTER 2

The Way of Repentance and the Great Promulgation Campaign

Benevolent Punishments and the National Creed

This chapter examines the origins of prison proselytization in Japan in relation to two of the Meiji government's enormous social engineering projects: the Great Promulgation Campaign and the development of a modern carceral system. Prison proselytization began as a grassroots movement in the 1870s before prison chaplains were officially incorporated as a fixture of the prison system in 1892. That year, to commemorate the state's adoption of prison chaplaincy nationwide, Honganji sponsored a week-long retreat at the Tsukiji Honganji Betsu-in temple in Tokyo. One of the speakers was the sixty-one-year-old priest Ōta Kenjū (1831–1910), the twenty-third abbot of the nearby Honganji branch temple Shinkōji and a member of the first generation of proselytizers who began preaching to the incarcerated in the early 1870s. In his speech, Ōta offered a retrospective to explain to the new cohort of junior prison chaplains that they were inheritors to a tradition with twenty years of history:

> In March of Meiji 5 [1872], [. . .] the office of national instructor [*kyōdōshoku*] was instituted for all sects of Shinto and Buddhism. We were to preach in accordance with the three principles of the Great Promulgation Campaign.
>
> After that, I believe it must have been in May of Meiji 6 [1873] that the Revised Penal Code was promulgated. In the same year, the old

penal grounds were reformed into labor camps. In short, the physical punishments—penalties like caning—were abandoned. As the saying goes, hate the sin, not the sinner.

It was then that the Shin sects petitioned the Great Teaching Institute to be permitted to enter the labor camps to preach. I was one of those who filed such a petition. After the deliberations, the director of the Great Teaching Institute conveyed the request to the Ministry of Doctrine, and in June of Meiji 7 [1874], we were officially granted permission to enter the prisons.

I went to preach at Tsukudajima labor camp, which is now Ishikawa-jima Jail. I believe this was the very beginning of prison chaplaincy [*kyōkai*]. At that time, lots of different sects were doing it at once. We had five people coming in from the Shin sects, and two from other sects as well. We were going in every Sunday. We went to the twenty-two separate group cells, and each of us conducted our own prison chaplaincy session. I suppose looking back on it today it was quite disorganized.[1]

This chapter traces the theme of sect-state complementarity as the backbone to both Buddhist doctrinal production and political mobilizations surrounding the Great Promulgation Campaign and the carceral system. In line with Ōta's narrative, I argue that the prison chaplain is the "spiritual successor" to the national instructor (*kyōdōshoku*) system initiated by the Great Promulgation Campaign for two reasons. First, all the earliest prison chaplains started out as national instructors. Second, chaplaincy's philosophy and ideals inherited concepts from the Great Promulgation Campaign even after that campaign collapsed. At the level of doctrine, Shin Buddhist national instructors wanted to teach a trans-sectarian form of Buddhist civil religion.[2] They developed a rationalized ethical teaching based on the theory of karma, and this doctrine became the basis for prison proselytization and laid the foundation for the subsequent development of chaplaincy discourse. One essential idea carried over from the national instructors to the chaplaincy was the notion that doctrinal instruction promotes "change of heart" in the individual and thereby contributes to character reform, good citizenship, and social harmony. At the level of politics, local activism on the part of Buddhists was the driving force behind the introduction of Buddhist teachings to the nascent prison system. Buddhist activism surrounding the prisons took off in part because embattled Buddhists found it politically advantageous to press for their sectarian interests by positioning themselves as rightful guardians of the public good, and they created the Buddhist national instructor doctrine to demonstrate this capacity. The Shin Buddhists' success in the field of prison proselytization during the Meiji period set a course for prison religion in Japan that has left a lasting influence on the carceral system for nearly 150 years.

The Great Promulgation Campaign and Public Order

The adoption of punishment by deprivation of liberty (*jiyūkei*) in the 1870s presented the Japanese with a conundrum. As part of the national drive for civilization and enlightenment, the Restoration government sought to modernize the institutions of governance to compete with Western powers. Along with the public education system and mandatory conscription, Japan introduced the educative model of punishment. Then as now, the goal of correctional rehabilitation was to produce reformed, law-abiding citizens. However, the importation of Western correctional theory and practice to late nineteenth-century Japan posed a problem because penology was deeply informed by the logic and values of the alien religion, Christianity.[3] The architects of state policy desired Western techniques of governance and science, but they wanted no part of the foreign religion. If not Christian values, what would be the basis for the educational content of Japanese correctional rehabilitation?

It so happened that at this time the Japanese were already busy orchestrating a national creed specifically intended to fight Christianization and to unify the populace through moral edification. Though short-lived, the Great Promulgation Campaign was a watershed moment in the development of modern religious vocations. The campaign was in the ascendant from 1870 to 1875 and formally ended in 1884, but its lasting impact came because it forced Buddhist and Shinto clergy to conform to the newly created role of national instructors in exchange for legal recognition. The campaign established the precedent that the social role for sects is to benefit the nation-state.

The Great Promulgation Campaign has been the subject of a great deal of scholarship in both Japanese and English.[4] I highlight here two aspects most relevant to the development of prison proselytization. First, from its inception, the campaign tasked its workforce with the promotion of public order—a goal that would align with the objectives of correctional rehabilitation. When the Meiji government was first established, it disavowed the connection between Buddhism and state and set out to disseminate its own ideology under the auspices of the newly formed Department of Divinities.[5] Under this department, the first iteration of the Great Promulgation Campaign saw the appointment of a corps of Shinto evangelists (*senkyōshi*) from the ranks of notable shrine priests and scholars in 1870.[6] The evangelists were issued nebulous instructions to promulgate the "Great Way of the Kami" (*kannagara no daidō*) and issued a handbook, *Guidelines for Evangelists* (*Senkyō kokoroe sho*, 1870). Although the handbook lacks a unifying doctrine, it evinces an underlying theory of governance through moral edification and community networks of population surveillance. The evangelists were charged with monitoring the conduct of the people, and they were expected to employ "persuasion" (*kyōyu*) to reform offenders:

> At your destinations, if you encounter filial children, righteous young men, faithful wives, or others distinguished by their virtuous conduct, talents, or capacities, you are to report this to the regional authorities. Furthermore, if you encounter those who oppose the good, who trouble the good people, who engage in licentious or violent conduct, or who otherwise engage in evil actions or harbor evil intentions, you are to inform the family and the neighborhood group, then the person in charge. Rely on personal connections [to the offender] and apply every means of persuasion [. . .] It shall be a meritorious deed for an instructor to lead a person to a change of heart [*kaishin*].[7]

The previous chapter noted that most Urakami Christians scattered throughout the various domains were subjected to the persuasion tactics of Shinto evangelists. From the *Guidelines for Evangelists*, it is clear that the concept of "change of heart" was not limited to Shin Buddhists and that it was not exclusively linked to the forced conversion of Christians. The concept presupposes an understanding of morality that locates the source of good or evil actions in the contents of a person's heart. "Evil intentions" are listed as a problem together with "evil actions." The heart is subject to conditioning through persuasion. The Department of Divinities expected the evangelists to improve the moral qualities of the population by integrating them more fully into the ideal of a harmonious, hierarchical community under the emperor—but the means of that integration presupposed the necessity of both moral instruction and community-based strategies for monitoring the people. The educative model of punishment being imported to early Meiji Japan was coherent with this indigenous notion of character reform through moral edification.[8]

It is perhaps not surprising that a pragmatic faction within the Department of State viewed the Department of Divinities as a failed experiment.[9] Even Tokoyo Nagatane (1832–1886), an evangelist with the campaign, recalled later that the evangelists had been at loggerheads with one another about what to teach.[10] Although the evangelists were responsible for the moral indoctrination of the people, they themselves had not been uniformly indoctrinated into any cohesive system. Thus, as Tokoyo reports, the Shinto evangelists' teachings were idiosyncratic. These problems did not go unnoticed by the public, the political authorities, or the resentful Buddhist sects.

Two Domains of Law and the Curriculum for Buddhist National Instructors

The second aspect of the Great Promulgation Campaign most relevant to the development of prison proselytization was the expansion of Buddhist activism and doctrinal production surrounding the state creed. I highlight specifically the efforts to craft a Buddhist curriculum to suit the needs of the campaign. The general narrative of the Great Promulgation Campaign's rise and fall is well known. Shin Buddhist sects, led by Shimaji Mokurai, actively sought to join the campaign from 1871 in the hope of carving out a place for Buddhism within it. These efforts were partially successful, and the campaign was restructured in 1872 in large part by assigning Buddhist priests along with Shintoists to serve as national instructors. However, the attempt to insert Buddhist content into the creed itself was stymied, much to the dissatisfaction of the Buddhist community. One of the first Japanese Buddhists to travel to Europe,

Shimaji studied religion-state relations there and came to the conclusion that separation of religion from state was preferable to a state creed. He led his faction in declaring its independence from the campaign, and the Shin sects dropped out in 1875, signaling the Great Promulgation Campaign's failure and initiating a national shift toward the separation of religion from state.[11] In what follows, I move away from the topic of high-level political negotiations surrounding the campaign and emphasize the lesser-known history of Buddhist curricular production intended to serve the state creed.

In the context of the Great Promulgation Campaign, the Shin sects authored a new form of Buddhist civil religion tailored for the Meiji era. They developed a Buddhist brand of national ethics devoid of sectarian specificity and focused on a rationalized presentation of the law of karma. Like the practice of doctrinal admonition they developed with incarcerated Christians, the curriculum produced by and for Buddhist national instructors outlasted the context of its creation. The curriculum was subsequently adopted by the prison chaplaincy, and its influence can still be seen in Japanese prisons today.

One implication of this history is that the structure of the Japanese prison chaplaincy is deeply informed by Shin Buddhism. There are both pragmatic and philosophical reasons to explain why the Shin sects proved the most effective advocates for Buddhist participation in the Great Promulgation Campaign and subsequently in the prison system. First, Honganji was an important financial backer of the Meiji Restoration. The twentieth patriarch of Honganji, Kōnyo (1798–1871), enjoyed close relations with members of the imperial family, and as the movement to restore imperial rule swept the country in 1863, Kōnyo disseminated a circular to all branch temples declaring that the sect's political goal would be to "serve the sovereign."[12] When hostilities broke out between Restoration and shogunate forces, the Honganji sect provided financial support to the restorationists in the form of 8,000 *ryō* of gold donated to the imperial forces.[13] In the wake of the regime change, even as anti-Buddhist sentiment was unleashed, both the Ōtani and the Honganji branches of the Shin school were called upon to provide monetary support to the financially struggling new government.[14] The Shin sects thus had some degree of leverage with the state. Second, the Shin sects were comparatively less troubled by the government's order to separate Buddhas from Kami because Shin doctrine, ritual, and temple architecture were not heavily integrated with Kami worship.[15] When some regional authorities pressed for Shin temple closures, the Shin sects successfully lobbied for the opening of a centralized Office of Temple Affairs (Jiinryō) in 1870 to liaise with all Buddhist sects, thereby preventing local governments from forcing temple closures at will and effectively putting the brakes on the excesses of the anti-Buddhist disturbances. Finally, the financial base for the Shin Buddhist sects survived the Restoration relatively intact because it was not derived from the support of the now defunct shogunate or the aristocracy but rooted in contributions from private parishioners—ordinary people who largely continued to pay for funerary services despite the regime change. The fact that Shin sects continued to hold wealth later played a determinative role in facilitating their expansion into prison proselytization.

Philosophically, Shin political thought proved to be a valuable intellectual resource for articulating new forms of relationship between sects and state, and this tradition gave birth to a mode of dharma instruction intended for prisons. Kōnyo died at the age of seventy-three in 1871, and in his last testament, he bequeathed the ambiguous directive that the principle guiding Honganji should be the doctrine that there are two domains of law—the worldly and the transcendent (*shinzoku nitai*).[16] Shin thinkers since the Tokugawa period have traced this doctrine to the political and institutional reforms initiated by Rennyo.[17] In the modern Shin tradition, the dominant interpretation of this idea is that the human heart cannot be reduced to or satisfied by the possibilities offered by politics because there will always be a remainder or some need left unfulfilled. The key soteriological concepts of Shin Buddhism speak to this internal need: the heart of faith (*shinjin*) and the heart of peace (*anjin*). The implication is that though the political authorities rightfully demand obedience in the public realm, the inner life of humanity—the private realm—must also be structured (by the sect) and oriented toward hope. On the one hand, this principle expresses the need for a private space to entertain Buddhist commitments. On the other, it implies that the sect makes a social contribution by helping to maintain public order. The private aspirations of the masses may be channeled through the dharma away from potentially disruptive political action and toward the transcendence of suffering through faith.[18] In the early Meiji period, the two domains of law doctrine was also invoked to advance claims that the law of the state should be in harmony with a higher law (the dharma). The concept of two domains of law thus condenses within itself possibilities for conceiving of the public-private distinction around Buddhist commitments *and* the means of expressing an ideal of harmony between Buddhist law and the law of the sovereign. It provided a rich resource for Shin thinkers who sought to renegotiate their sect's relationship with the state, and I show shortly that it also became the basis for Shin prison preaching.

The argument that the state creed ought to be in harmony with the dharma was essential to Buddhist lobbying efforts surrounding the Great Promulgation Campaign. In that context, in 1871 the young Shin priest Shimaji Mokurai wrote a petition calling for the establishment of a Ministry of Doctrine that would allow Buddhist sects to participate in the state's proselytization effort on a more equal footing with Shintoists.[19] Shimaji presented Buddhism as a public benefit that the government has an interest in promoting. The gist of his argument is that Buddhism contributes to social stability by indoctrinating the populace into a civic ethic. He supports this claim with a historical argument: Buddhism has long been the dominant belief system among the Japanese people. For this reason, the anti-Buddhist movements may be expected to impede the goal of political unity. Without Buddhism, the people would flock to Christianity, thereby compromising their loyalty to the emperor and the state. Furthermore, Shimaji maintains that the Shinto evangelists have failed because morality can be taught only with reference to the doctrine of karma. The implication is that despite any sectarian differences between Buddhist sects, the core of the Buddhist teaching reflects a universal law that must be recognized by all. The basic framework underlying this proposition is none other than the Honganji sect's ideal of two domains of law.[20] Notably, Shimaji in this petition does not attempt to negotiate the public-private distinction to carve out a place for Buddhism in private life. Rather, he claims that Buddhism should be part of the state-imposed national creed. Shimaji invokes karma as a universal law to which the national ideology ought to be beholden. However, he can make this claim for an ideal union between dharma and law only at the cost of eschewing sectarian specificity. The Pure Land doctrine of Amida Buddha's universal saving grace—oft criticized as potentially antinomian and socially disruptive—is entirely absent. What remains instead is the idea that there is a minimal shared Buddhist doctrine that is rational (not superstitious) and ready-made for promoting public order.

As the anti-Buddhist movements dissipated, the state moved to harness a greater variety of sects for the Great Promulgation Campaign. In response to petitions from Shimaji and other Buddhists, the Ministry of Doctrine was established to oversee the campaign in 1872. Buddhist sects financed the opening of the campaign's central seminary, the Great Teaching Institute (Daikyōin) at Zōjōji, a Jōdo sect Buddhist temple in Tokyo.[21] All religious institutions were placed into a hierarchy under the Great Teaching Institute, and the corps of national instructors was instituted to replace the earlier Shinto evangelists, initiating the second phase of the Great Promulgation Campaign. All religious professionals (Buddhist priests and Shinto priests) were now required to pass licensing examinations on the national creed to continue to proselytize.[22] According to one estimate, there were approximately 87,558 Buddhist temples in Japan in 1873.[23] Ideally, every temple would have been incorporated into the new system. Yet the official history of the Honganji sect reports that under the Great Teaching Institute, there were 7,247 national instructors, of which 728 were Shin priests (a small fraction of the total number of Shin priests).[24]

Despite the inclusion of Buddhist priests, the revamped Great Promulgation Campaign initially promoted doctrines of a Shinto character and excluded all Buddhist influence.[25] In the winter of 1872, the Great Teaching Institute published *The Essence of Preaching for the Various Sects* (*Shoshū sekkyō yōgi*), summarizing how each Buddhist sect was expected to bring its preaching in line with the campaign's three teachings: (1) respect for the gods, love of country; (2) making clear the principles of Heaven and the Way of Man; and (3) reverence for the emperor and obedience to the will of the court.[26] The Shin sects collectively disseminated directives for their own national instructors under the heading "The Great Standard for Instruction" (*kyōyu no daikihon*). Predictably, the section titled "The Aim of Instruction" is a discourse on the two domains of law:

> As a rule, the reason that doctrines are valued is for their capacity to influence the spirit of a people. [. . .] The fate of a nation depends on its customs, and its customs depend on the moral nature of the hearts of its people.

The evil shall be made good, the heretical shall be brought to orthodoxy, and doubt shall be turned to faith. The imperial government shall rule by this, and the promulgation campaign will persuade the people of the cause. Is there not a means to unite rule and doctrine to bring about spiritual change in the realm? This is the very principle our sect venerates: our teaching is the doctrine of two domains of law.[27]

The undergirding logic is that both social order and national strength require cultivation of a virtuous public. The sect's role is presented in a functionalist way: the Shin Buddhist clergy will teach the people to venerate two domains of law and thereby encourage positive spiritual change, inculcating goodness, orthodoxy, and faith in imperial subjects. The population's growing virtues will determine the fate of the nation. It is taken for granted that the Buddhist sect must promulgate the three teachings in support of the secular authorities. However, the promotion of the secular law was only half of the sects' stated mission. In the context of preaching about two domains of law, what form of dharma will they teach to influence the spirit of the people?

Buddhist sects produced a general Buddhism curriculum (*buppō tsūron*) for their national instructors.[28] This curriculum found its way into the Great Promulgation Campaign after Buddhists petitioned the government for permission to combine the government's three teachings with their own sectarian doctrines.[29] The Great Teaching Institute conceded, granting permission to Buddhist sects to establish qualifying exams in their own fields.[30] A standard examination covering a general overview of Japanese Buddhism was established, and other examinations were provided on a sect-specific basis (for example, an exam in Shin doctrine). The primary characteristic of this general Buddhism curriculum is its emphasis on a rational system of Buddhist ethics intended to promote public order—it is precisely the model of Buddhist instruction that Shimaji advocated in his petition to establish a Ministry of Doctrine. For example, an 1875 study guide produced for aspiring Shin national instructors explains that the dharma's purpose is to support governance (*matsurigoto*).[31] The chapter on the Buddhist law of cause and effect refers specifically to legal transgressions and punishment: "Shame and criminal penalties are the harms born of evil karma."[32] The general Buddhism curriculum was tailored to suit the needs of national instructors tasked with promoting the public ethos. Sectarian identity was whitewashed, and the doctrine of karma was invoked as natural law. The purpose of this doctrinal framework was not to liberate, but to govern.

To survive, Buddhists needed to present their tradition as useful to the secular authorities. They had to offer a rational teaching, to avoid any appearance of superstition that might trigger the prejudices of ruling elites, and to articulate how their doctrine might contribute to the public good. The rise of the educative model of punishment and new ways of thinking about the management of crime presented an opportunity. This line of thinking dovetailed precisely with the aims of the Great Promulgation Campaign, which, like the prison system, was founded upon the belief that people are educable and therefore malleable. I turn now to examine how grassroots Buddhist activists put the general Buddhism curriculum to use in the Great Promulgation Campaign and in the prisons.

A Captive Audience

While the Great Promulgation Campaign was in full swing, bureaucrats developed new strategies of policing the populace and managing crime.[33] The changing nature of punishments, away from inflicting physical pain toward moral education, created a space for prison proselytization. These developments made it both possible and logical for national instructors to become involved in the prison system at its inception.

The Meiji government dispatched officials to Hong Kong and Singapore to study the British colonial prison system in 1871. The leader of this research expedition, Ohara Shigechika (1836–1902), became the architect of the Japanese prison system.[34] In 1872, Ohara published *Prison Rules with Charts* (*Kangoku soku narabi ni zushiki*), a text that would become a road map for the development of the carceral system. The text begins with the question, "What is a prison?" Daniel Botsman translates this work's opening passage as follows:

It is a means to hold criminals in custody in order to discipline them.

The purpose of a prison is to show people love and benevolence, not to do them violence.

Its purpose is to discipline people, not to cause them pain.

Punishments are applied because there is no other choice. Their purpose is to expel evil in the interests of the nation.[35]

Ohara's claim that the "purpose of a prison is to show people love and benevolence" is cited in the postwar history *One Hundred Years of Prison Chaplaincy* as the impetus for the beginning of prison ministry.[36] Ohara's educative model of punishment provides a rationale for a role for religious workers in the prisons by declaring that punishment's purpose is to mold the hearts of the incarcerated.

In line with Ohara's proposals, the Penal Labor Law (Chōeki hō), was enacted in 1872. This law represents a significant shift away from physical punishments toward punishment by deprivation of liberty. The Department of State issued Order No. 103, which included a chart for converting the shogunate's flogging and caning punishments into recommended periods of incarceration (table 2.1).

As regional authorities established prisons and started to incarcerate people, a "captive audience" was created.[37] By 1874, Osaka and six

Table 2.1   Conversion of Physical Punishments to Imprisonment, 1872

	Penal Labor (days)
Flogging (blows)	
10	10
20	20
30	30
40	40
50	50
Caning (blows)	
60	60
70	70
80	80
90	90
100	100

Source: Based on Department of State Order No. 103, adapted from Ishii et al., *Hō to chitsujo*, 144.

Table 2.2   Japanese Prison Population, 1877–1990

	Prisoners		Prisoners
1877	25,856	1889	64,008
1878	30,539	1890	69,446
1879	34,626	1891	73,574
1880	36,161	1892	76,057
1881	36,375	1893	79,175
1882	43,304	1894	81,001
1883	56,698	1895	77,551
1884	72,019	1905	56,737
1885	78,687	1906	53,003
1886	72,070	1925	43,135
1887	64,050	1930	46,437
1888	61,057	1990	46,458

Source: Adapted from Yasumaru, *Ikki, kangoku, kosumoroji,* 131.

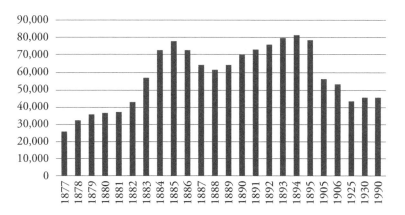

FIGURE 2.1   Japanese prison population, 1877–1990.

other domains had produced new institutions for imprisonment with hard labor (*chōekijō*), and by the end of the year, Ohara's plan to produce the first Western-style prison had been approved.[38] The production of new facilities for incarceration proceeded apace over the following years. After 1874, confinement to prison became a standard punishment.[39] The prison population in the Japanese Home Islands increased steadily from 1877, the first year reliable records were produced (table 2.2 and fig. 2.1).

In the prewar *History of Japanese Prison Chaplaincy* (*Nihon kangoku kyōkaishi*), published in 1927, the trajectory of the criminal justice system in the Meiji period is characterized as a shift from objective punishments (*kyakkan shugi*) to subjective punishments (*shukan shugi*).[40] In *Discipline and Punish*, Michel Foucault argues that the modern carceral system takes as its object not the physical body of the offender but rather his soul.[41] In an analogous transformation, the modernization of the Japanese penal system saw the authorities becoming increasingly concerned with the hearts of the incarcerated as the object of punishment changed from the physical body to the human subject understood in a nonphysical way. The shift in focus to the subjective dimension was not caused by the introduction of the general Buddhism curriculum to the prisons. Rather, the goal of molding the inmate's character was already a component of the educative model of punishment when it was imported to Japan. However, given the exclusion of Christian moral education from Japanese prisons, there was something of a moral instruction deficit in the early Japanese carceral program (as compared with its foreign models). These conditions provided a pretext for national instructors to ply their trade in the prisons. As with the appearance of the illegal Christians in Urakami, again anti-Christianity (the initial exclusion of Christian influence from Japanese prisons) created an opportunity for Buddhist activists keen on maintaining a position of moral authority in Meiji society.

The First Prison Chaplains

As the prison population increased, national instructors with the Great Promulgation Campaign began to petition regional authorities for permission to preach to the incarcerated. According to the official chaplaincy histories, the first Shin priests to proselytize to the incarcerated were Ōtani sect clerics Ugai Keitan (1832–1885) of Jōsaiji temple in Nagoya and Minowa Taigaku (1838–1879) of Gōmyōji temple in Fukui.[42] Minowa was temporarily stationed at Asakusa Honganji temple in Tokyo when he filed his petition.

In June 1872, the Ministry of Doctrine issued Order No. 3, declaring that both temple and shrine authorities would now be responsible for proselytizing with the Great Promulgation Campaign. The following month, Ugai Keitan applied for permission to preach to prisoners in Nagoya. Tokugawa Keishō (1824–1883), the governor of Aichi Prefecture (a newly established administrative region), granted his request:[43]

> In response to your petition: "Feeling moved by the advent of this campaign of sacred indoctrination and hoping to repay a small ounce of debt to my country, I request permission to teach prisoners two times per month in the stockades and the jails. By means of the three teachings combined with the Buddhist doctrine of karmic rewards and punishments, I hope to bring them to repent of their past mistakes and to change their hearts so that they may stand on new ground." Permission is hereby granted for you to expound the Way by this means.
>   July, Meiji 5 [1872], Aichi Prefecture.[44]

Unfortunately, Ugai's temple burned down during the wartime bombing of Nagoya, so most of his records do not survive.[45] However, it is known that Ugai was responsible for admonishing a group of illegal Japanese Christians exiled from Urakami to Nagoya in the summer of 1870.[46] Thus Ugai petitioned for access to the newly incarcerated after his experience trying to convert the illegal Christians to Buddhism. It is evident from his petition that he intended to sermonize within a framework derived from both the three teachings of the Great Promulgation Campaign and a generalized Buddhist concept of karmic rewards and punishments—that is, in accordance with the Buddhist curriculum for Shin national instructors. In addition to karma, Ugai's petition makes reference to three other doctrinal terms: debt to the country (*kokuon*), repentance (*zange*), and change of heart (*kaishin*). The logic of Ugai's petition holds that preaching the dharma may bring the incarcerated to repent, undergo a change of heart, and thus learn to honor obligations to the state. Teaching the law of karma is a means to influence the formation of a healthy conscience. This petition initiated Buddhist prison proselytization in Japan, and the basic elements of what would become prison chaplaincy doctrine appear to have been in place from the outset.

Ōtani sect priest Minowa Taigaku wrote the second petition for access to the incarcerated in order to proselytize.[47] Minowa petitioned the

Ministry of Doctrine for permission to preach to prisoners in an early carceral facility in Tokyo (a forerunner to Fuchū Prison):[48]

> At this time, I am serving as a mid-ranked provisional national instructor, and I work tirelessly day and night to fulfill these responsibilities because I aspire to proselytize effectively. However, although there are those who abide in the light of day, exposed to the benefits of our indoctrination, there are also those who are sequestered in darkness, unaware of our work, who remain unaffected.
>
> I have heard that the governments of Western countries imprison citizens who violate the law in jails that are staffed with instructors. These teachers kindly educate them so that they are awakened through remonstration to the error of their ways. This must be extremely moving to behold.
>
> However, in our country, I have never heard of the existence of such a law. For that reason, when our criminals are released, they once again violate the law. For many years I have been lamenting that our failure to employ the means of instruction brings us to this. I am thus most pleased, in my capacity as a national instructor in service to the court, to request permission to be allowed to offer my services in the ardent persuasion of those in the jails and penal camps. To this effect, I humbly submit my petition to the Ministry of Doctrine. I ask you to please grant permission as soon as possible.[49]

Minowa's reference to Western models of prison instruction is notable. Given the obvious motif of competition with Western powers, Minowa's rhetoric can be understood as an appeal to the regime's stated objective of civilization and enlightenment. He also provides a pragmatic rationale to support his request: the rate of recidivism is high, and this can be attributed to the lack of moral instruction in the jails. It appears that Minowa envisioned a role for Buddhist instructors in Japanese prisons analogous to that played by "instructors"—really, Christian prison chaplains—in the prisons of the West.

Minowa's petition traveled a circuitous route through the Ōtani sect to the Ministry of Doctrine to the government of Tokyo then finally to the Secretary of the Judiciary (Shihōkyō).[50] In September, likely in response to this petition, the Ministry of Doctrine ordered the Great Teaching Institute and its subsidiaries to encourage national instructors to follow Minowa's lead by entering the prisons to preach to the incarcerated on Sundays.[51] Prison proselytization thus became a component of the Great Promulgation Campaign project.

By the fall of 1872, Minowa had received permission to enter Ishikawa-jima Jail in Tokyo. It is possible to gain a sense of his sermons because Minowa produced his own *Manual for National Instructors* (*Kyōdōshoku hikkei*, date unknown) in which he discussed preaching to incarcerated people (robbers in particular).[52] He writes that the goal for the incarcerated is "to work diligently at their duties; to observe the laws; as quickly as possible, to turn back to the heart of goodness; and to become good subjects."[53] The Shin histories report that the earliest chaplaincy sermons were grounded in the three teachings of the Great Promulgation Campaign combined with the conventional Buddhist doctrine of karmic rewards and punishments and the Shin doctrine of two domains of law.[54]

Buddhist prison proselytization began when national instructors Ugai Keitan and Minowa Taigaku petitioned for permission to preach to the incarcerated in 1872. Minowa Taigaku's activities were reported in the newspaper that year, and prison proselytization began to receive considerable attention from religious groups and, particularly, the Shin sects.[55] Based on what little documentary evidence remains, it appears that the earliest prison sermons shared many of the themes that remain standard in the discourse of chaplaincy: an emphasis on indebtedness to the nation; a stated goal of encouraging repentance; and a rationalized interpretation of the doctrine of karma. Ugai and Minowa started a trend that took off at the national scale as national instructors throughout Japan began to petition for access to the incarcerated.

The End of the National Instructors and the Rise of Prison Chaplaincy: 1872–1885

Already by 1872 many Buddhists were turning against the second iteration of the Great Promulgation Campaign. While on a research trip to Europe, Shimaji Mokurai became the de facto leader of a faction in favor of abolishing the Great Teaching Institute—a monster of his own creation. Having developed his own understanding while in Europe of the necessity of religion-state separation, he prepared petitions that would solidify his reputation as a sectarian hero: these include his *Petition Criticizing the Three Teachings* (*Sanjō kyōsoku hihan kenpakusho*, 1872) and the *Petition to Separate from the Great Teaching Institute* (*Daikyōin bunri kenpakusho*, 1873).[56] In these petitions, Shimaji argues forcefully that only the separation of religion from state would enable Buddhist sects, through the free teaching of their own doctrines, to contribute to the moral improvement of the people and to prevent the Christianization of the Japanese populace. The crux of Shimaji's argument is that separation of religion from state will be of greater benefit to the nation than the Great Promulgation Campaign. His advocacy for religion-state separation was not tantamount to advocacy for unlimited religious freedom for individuals. Rather, he sought a rapprochement with the authorities in a manner favorable to the Buddhist sects—his own sect in particular.[57]

Ultimately, the powerful Shin sects abandoned the campaign in 1875, adhering to Shimaji's view that separation of religion from state would better serve the national interest. Their departure precipitated the closure of the Great Teaching Institute later that same year. These developments contributed to the trajectory for the subsequent legal separation of religion from state and the recognition of a degree of religious freedom under the Meiji Constitution of 1889. However, the fundamental issue of how to define the relationship between Buddhism and the state was not resolved with the end of the Great Promulgation Campaign. Even as Buddhist sects dropped out one by one, many members of the Buddhist clergy remained registered as national instructors until that office itself was formally abolished in 1884. Buddhist sects and individual Buddhist priests generally wanted to contribute to the nation, but they wanted to have some say over the terms of that contribution.

Between 1872 and 1881, as the Great Promulgation Campaign was fraying, prison proselytization spread at a grassroots level with no overarching government program in charge. The aforementioned official histories of the Shin prison chaplaincy recount the origins of prison chaplaincy in each major correctional facility.[58] In many reported instances, prison preaching was introduced in response to religious workers petitioning for access to prisoners. At the outset, the prisons notably did not request the assistance from religious groups; rather, individual religious workers asserted that prison ministry was their responsibility. It should come as no surprise to learn that Saigenji and Saishōji (the temples that had petitioned for access to the illegal Christians in Kanazawa, as discussed in chapter 1) were among the first to be granted access to the incarcerated to preach in 1872.[59]

Even after the Great Teaching Institute folded in 1875, national instructors continued to preach in penal institutions. In chaplaincy's early days, national instructors hailing from a wide variety of sects sought to take up such work. Various Buddhist and Shinto groups were represented and so was the popular doctrine of Sekimon Shingaku. During this period, wardens (*tengoku*) had relative autonomy, and a great variety of teachers appeared. Sources differ in their numbers, making it difficult to get an exact picture, but they offer a sense of the overall trend of expansion. Shin Buddhists were the most active in applying for permission to enter the prisons.[60] The doctrine these Buddhist priests preached to their incarcerated audiences continued to be structured by the general Buddhism curriculum devised for the Great Promulgation Campaign. By 1885, virtually all Japanese prisons featured clerics preaching in the mold set by Ugai Keitan and Minowa Taigaku (table 2.3 and fig. 2.2)

The Prison Chaplaincy Becomes Official

Government documents from the mid-1870s refer to the work of religionists in prisons as "admonition" (*kyōkai*).[61] However, the neologism "prison chaplain" (*kyōkaishi*) first enters the law in 1881 in Article 92 of Ohara Shigechika's revised *Prison Regulations* (*Kangoku soku*). Article 92 defines the responsibilities of the prison chaplains as follows: "Chaplains are to admonish prisoners through lectures explaining the Way of repentance and turning to the good [*kaika senzen no michi*]."[62] Article 93 further stipulates that prison chaplains should minister to the inmates on their days off or on Sunday afternoons.[63] The four character phrase "repent errors; turn to the good" (*kaika senzen* 悔過遷善) implies "change of heart." The original aim of the Great Promulgation Campaign had been to establish a "Great Way" for all Japanese people. In the context of the prison, there is a more limited interpretation of the Way. "The Way of repentance" is prescribed for those who have somehow fallen afoul of the law. The concept of a Way resonates with the notion that Japanese citizens are the bearers of sacred obligations to live in accord with a public ethos. Doctrinal admonition became a generalized strategy for reforming

Table 2.3 Expansion of Prison Chaplaincy, 1872–1885

	Total Facilities with Chaplains	Facilities that Added Chaplains[a]	Chaplains' Sectarian Affiliation	Start Date
1872	7	Sugamo (Tokyo)	-Shingaku	1870–1871?
		Nara	-Kegon	1870–1871?
The Great Teaching		Nagoya	-Ōtani	May 7
Institute opens.		Ishikawajima (Tokyo)	-Ōtani	September
		Kanazawa	-Honganji and Ōtani	October
		Toyotama (Tokyo)	-Shinto and Buddhist	?
		Okayama	-Shinto and Buddhist	?
1873	17	Yokohama	-Shinto and Buddhist	April
		Gifu	-Honganji	April
The Urakami Christians		Odawara (Kanagawa)	-Shinto and Buddhist	May
are released in March.		Kumamoto	-Ōtani	September
		Fukuoka	-Shinto and 6 Buddhist sects	October
		Wakayama	-Shinto	November
		Chiba	-Shingon, Jōdo, Nichiren, Honganji	?
		Niigata	-Shinto	?
		Fukushima	-Honganji	?
		Zeze (Gifu)	-Ōtani	?
1874	27	Tokushima	-Shinto and Buddhist	March
		Akita	-Shinto, Honganji, Ōtani	March
Confinement to prison		Sakuramachi (Nagasaki)	-Buddhist sects	May
becomes a standard		Aomori	-Shin	July
punishment.		Yamaguchi	-Shinto, Buddhist	?
		Tottori	-Shin	?
		Kosuge (Tokyo)	-Shinto, Confucian, Buddhist	?
		Hakodate (Hokkaido)	-?	?
		Kōfu (Yamanashi)	-7 Buddhist sects	?
		Yamura (Yamanashi)	-Buddhist sects	?

Year	No.	Location	Sect/Group	Month
1875	37	Kōchi	-Honganji	February
		Wakamatsu (?)	-Shinto and Buddhism	April
		Maebashi (Aichi)	-Honganji	July
		Tokyo	-Shinto and Buddhism	October
		Kokura (Fukuoka)	-Honganji	?
		Utsunomiya (Tochigi)	-Buddhist sects	?
		Nagano	-Buddhist sects	?
		Toyooka (Hyogo)	-Buddhist sects	?
		Hiroshima	-Honganji, Ōtani	?
		Hamada (Shimane)	-Shinto, Confucian, Buddhist	?
Honganji and Ōtani sects abandon the Great Promulgation Campaign.				
1876	44	Ōita	-Shinto	June
		Matsuyama (Ehime)	-Honganji	November
		Urawa (Saitama)	-Shinto	?
		Kyoto	-Shinto	?
		Sakai (Osaka)	-Shinto and Honganji	?
		Matsue (Shimane)	-Shinto and Sōtō	?
		Morioka (Iwate)	-Honganji	?
1877	51	Daikokuchō (?)	-Various sects (?)	December
		Kawagoe (Saitama)	-Various sects (?)	?
		Shirakawa (Fukushima)	-Honganji	?
		Osaka	-Shinto, Buddhist, Shingaku	?
		Sendai (Miyagi)	-Honganji, Ōtani	?
		Yamagata	-Shinto	?
		Yōkaichiba (Chiba)	-Jōdo	?
1878	55	Sapporo (Hokkaido)	-Sōtō	June
		Shizuoka	-Honganji	December
		Kobe (Hyogo)	-Honganji	?
		Komatsu (Ishikawa)	-Shinto, Buddhist	?

(continued)

Table 2.3 (continued)

	Total Facilities with Chaplains	Facilities that Added Chaplains[a]	Chaplains' Sectarian Affiliation	Start Date
1879	57	Yatsushiro (Kumamoto)	-Honganji	?
		Kagoshima	-Honganji, Ōtani	?
1880	62	Takada (Nara)	-Honganji	January
		Kurume (Fukuoka)	-Ōtani	January
		Takamatsu (Kagawa)	-Shinto	May
		Miyazaki	-Honganji	?
		Tanabe (Wakayama)	-Confucian	?
1881	69	Fukui	-Honganji	April
		Nakatsu (Oita)	-Honganji	July
The term kyōkaishi		Okinawa	-Ōtani	December
appears in the penal code		Tamashima (Okayama)	-Honganji	?
for the first time.		Takahashi (Okayama)	-Honganji	?
		Miyazu (Kyoto)	-Honganji	?
		Anotsu (Mie)	-Shin Takada	?

Year	No.	Place	Affiliation	Month
1882	83	Hachiōji (Tokyo)	Ōtani	January
		Shimoda (Shizuoka)	Confucian	January
		Sakata (Yamagata)	Ōtani	February
		Nemuro (Hokkaido)	Jōdō	June
		Hamamatsu (Shizuoka)	Shingon, Rinzai	September
		Iida (Nagano)	Honganji	?
		Kumagaya (Saitama)	Honganji	?
		Mito (Ibaraki)	Confucian	?
		Nakamura (Kōchi)	Rinzai	?
		Yonago (Matsue)	Sōtō	?
		Tsuchiura (Ibaraki)	Shinto and Buddhist	?
		Kabato (Hokkaido)	Sōtō	?
		Ujiyamada (Mie)	?	?
		Taira (Fukushima)		?
1883	95	Yamaguchi (Kumamoto)	Ōtani	June
		Aikawa (Niigata)	Ōtani	August
		Saga	Ōtani	September
		Shimonoseki (Yamaguchi)	Honganji	September
		Miike (Fukuoka)	Honganji	November
		Okazaki (Aichi)	Honganji	December
		Gojō (Nara)	Ōtani	December
		Ōmagari (Akita)	Honganji	December
		Toyama	Ōtani	?
		Sorachi (Hokkaido)	Shinto, Ōtani, Honganji	?
		Ueda (Nagano)	Shinshū	?
		Saigō (Shimane)	Honganji?	?
			Jōdo, Sōtō	?

(continued)

Table 2.3 (continued)

	Total Facilities with Chaplains	Facilities that Added Chaplains[a]	Chaplains' Sectarian Affiliation	Start Date
1884	106	Tsuyama (Okayama)	-Honganji	April
		Hikone (Shiga)	-Ōtani	June
The Great Promulgation Campaign officially ends.		Akashi (Kobe)	-?	July
		Miyoshi (Hiroshima)	-Ōtani	July
		Shinjō (Yamagata)	-Ōtani	September
		Saijō (Ehime)	-Nichiren	October
		Tatsuno (Kobe)	-Honganji	December
		Sasayama (Kobe)	-?	?
		Yonezawa (Yamagata)	-?	?
		Numazu (Shizuoka)	-Nichiren, Ōtani	?
		Karatsu (Saga)	-Sōtō	?
1885	109	Uwajima (Ehime)	Shingon	May
		Tsuruoka (Yamagata)	-Sōtō	June?
Prison chaplaincy is now virtually universal.		Iwakuni (Yamaguchi)	-Honganji	

Source: Adapted from Yoshida, *Nihon kindai Bukkyō shakaishi kenkyū* 5: 208–12.

The facilities are listed in the order in which they accepted chaplains.

a The names in this column represent the names of carceral institutions, but many no longer exist. Some entries are less specific than others because of ambiguity in the original source. In cases where the location is not obvious from the name of the prison (and where it has been possible to pinpoint the site with a degree of certainty), the name of the modern prefecture is added in brackets.

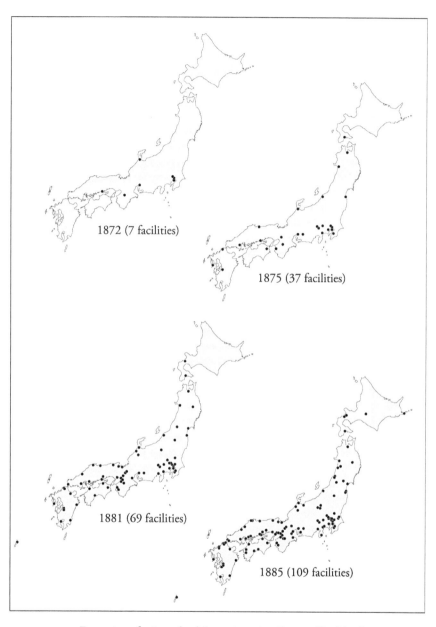

1872 (7 facilities)

1875 (37 facilities)

1881 (69 facilities)

1885 (109 facilities)

FIGURE 2.2 Expansion of prison chaplaincy, 1872–1885. Prepared by Matthew Stavros.

people convicted of all manner of crimes by encouraging repentance and change of heart. In theory, admonition could bring the hearts of transgressors into harmony with the values of the national community. This aim aligns perfectly with the logic of Ohara's modern penal institution and its purpose of instilling discipline.

In 1881, there were prison chaplains in approximately sixty-nine penal institutions. From that year onwards, the prison chaplaincy expanded rapidly until it was essentially a universal component of the Japanese prison system by 1885. Despite the prison chaplains' ubiquity, until 1892 their pay was entirely the responsibility of each religious group's head office or temple (*honzan*).[64] Though some prisons covered travel expenses, many chaplains went without remuneration. Reading between the lines, it seems reasonable to imagine that, one by one, groups without financial or human resources dropped out. The relatively wealthy Shin sects, however, were able to continue investing money and personnel in prison chaplaincy.

The prison chaplaincy reached a landmark in 1889. That year saw the promulgation of the Meiji Constitution with its provision for limited religious freedom.[65] In the same year, the work of chaplains in the prisons was formally recognized in the Prison Staff Regulations (Kanshu oyobi kangoku yōjin bunshō rei) and in another revision to the Penal Regulations, which included the Regulation for the Employment of Prison Chaplains (Kyōkaishi kinmu kitei).[66] The latter enumerated for the first time the specific duties of prison chaplains. They were to teach reading, writing, and arithmetic to prisoners under sixteen, to teach ethics (*dōgi*) to all prisoners, and to perform group and individual chaplaincy sessions. With additional penal code reforms in 1892, prison chaplains were finally recognized as prison employees.[67] By this time, chaplains were present in virtually all Japanese correctional facilities, and with a few exceptions, the majority of them were Shin priests.

Conclusions

Although the central authorities had no intention to do so, the criminal justice reforms of the 1870s created a captive audience for the newly instituted national instructors. Prison proselytization developed in the context of the Great Promulgation Campaign as religious workers sought ways to contribute to the nation. Shin Buddhists were eager to find their place in Meiji society, and the ideal of two domains of law working in harmony provided them with a powerful rationale for thinking about preaching dharma as a contribution to public order. Pushing back against the Meiji state's Shinto-centrism, Shin sects produced a general Buddhism curriculum for their own national instructors. This Buddhist brand of civil religion was based on an interpretation of the doctrine of karma as a natural law undergirding the law of the state. Prison proselytization began when Shin Buddhist national instructors Ugai Keitan and Minowa Taigaku received permission to preach these doctrines to the incarcerated. Even after the Shin sects dropped out of the Great Promulgation Campaign in 1875, local religious activists (many of them Shin priests) continued to press for access to inmates, and prison proselytization took off at a grassroots level nationwide. By 1884, even though the Great Promulgation Campaign collapsed, doctrinal admonition had become integrated into virtually all prisons in Japan, with Shin Buddhist clergy responsible for the lion's share of the work. The general Buddhism curriculum produced for national instructors became the foundation for prison chaplaincy doctrine.

As an accident of history, Japanese prisons became a testing ground for innovative, self-consciously "modern" modes of religious practice. Prison was one venue through which religious workers demonstrated their capacity to contribute to the public good by propagating their own doctrines. Despite the fact that the Meiji government did not import prison chaplaincy together with prison institutions, Japanese religious activists entered the prisons of their own accord to produce something that in retrospect has come to be seen as prison chaplaincy anyway. This enduring institution is one overlooked legacy of the Meiji Restoration's lasting impact on religious life in Japan. Even in the twenty-first century, the idea that religions should contribute to good citizenship and social harmony continues to structure religious work both within and beyond prison walls.

CHAPTER 3

The Ideal of Harmony between Dharma and Law

A Buddhist Vision of Social Mission: Harmony between Sect and State

By 1885, the Great Promulgation Campaign had collapsed along with the Tokugawa ban on Christianity and the temple certification system. The anti-Buddhist movements were a memory, and political authorities and public intellectuals largely accepted that separation of religion from state and some degree of religious freedom were necessary conditions for a modern society. It was a sign of the times when, in 1884, it became legal for individuals to conduct their own funerals without the services of a Buddhist priest.[1] It was no longer a crime for a Japanese person to convert to Christianity and abandon a hereditary family grave at the local Buddhist temple. This legal change signaled a deeper transformation, as the basic unit of religious belonging shifted from the family to the individual.

When the Meiji Constitution was promulgated in 1889, it included a provision for limited religious freedom. Article 28 reads: "Japanese subjects shall, within limits not prejudicial to peace and order, and not antagonistic to their duties as subjects, enjoy freedom of religious belief."[2] As in all secular regimes, the authorities sought to ensure that religious commitments were relegated to an apolitical private realm and thus subordinated to the state's priorities. One year later, the government issued the Imperial Rescript on Education (Kyōiku ni kan suru chokugo), announcing the dominant expression of the public ethic in terms of the national polity (*kokutai*)—an idealized notion of the ethnic state unified under the divinely descended imperial line.[3]

From 1889 until 1945, the legal framework governing religion divided the social world into public-private realms in such a way that shrine Shinto and imperial mythology were officially deemed secular and promoted in the public sphere through state rituals and public education. Under this system, some major Shinto shrines came under state management (for example, the Ise Shrine, dedicated to Amaterasu, the Sun Goddess and divine ancestor of the imperial house). These state-backed institutions were associated with the government's legitimating ideology, rooted in the imperial mythos and its concomitant royalist interpretation of Japanese heritage and the civic duties of subjects. To this day, scholars continue to debate the nature of this arrangement under the rubric of State Shinto, but there is no doubt that imperial myths, rituals, and symbols of indigeneity drawn from the Shinto tradition came to the forefront to define the secular, public ethos, while religions were required to withdraw into private life.[4] Religious organizations were expected to work for the benefit of the nation-state within the dominant ideological framework, but Buddhist temples, newly organized sectarian Shinto groups (a category that included legally approved new religious movements like Kurozumikyō, for example), and recently legalized Christian churches were now forced to compete for followers. Without guaranteed support from the government or parishioners, Buddhist sects were pressed to articulate a vision of social mission.

In this time of religious transformation, Japan's carceral system reached maturity. To prisons operating nationwide, the defunct Great Promulgation Campaign bequeathed a workforce of prison chaplains charged with inmate education. Correctional officials and prison chaplains worked to develop a model of correctional rehabilitation focused on rectifying individual moral failings. The majority of prison chaplains were Shin Buddhist priests, and their convenient placement inside institutions of governance provided an opportunity for the Shin sects to campaign for closer relations with the secular authorities.

Both the constitutional framework governing religion and the structure of corrections were informed by an international context in which Christianity was politically dominant. This chapter situates the development of Buddhist prison chaplaincy in the larger context of Buddhist-Christian competition in the 1890s to show that their rivalry catalyzed the production of an enormous amount of Buddhist doctrines and practices intended to serve the purposes of the Japanese correctional system. I argue that, in order to maintain the upper hand over newcomer Christian competitors, the Shin sects invested in the prison chaplaincy as part of a broader strategy to position themselves as guardians of the public good. The enduring chaplaincy orthodoxy still bears the influence of the late nineteenth-century Shin political commitments that inspired the formalization of chaplaincy theory and practice.

The Department of State issued Order No. 19 in 1884, officially bringing a close to the national instructor system (the Great Promulgation Campaign) and simultaneously requiring both Shinto and Buddhist sects to produce their own constitutions or charters.[5] This shift catalyzed a wave of sectarian constitution writing as sects were pressed to formally define their institutional structure, doctrinal core, and public contributions outside the context of the Tokugawa temple parishioner system and beyond the framework of the failed Great Promulgation Campaign.[6] Shin Buddhist thinking about prison chaplaincy developed in line with a vision of social mission. The 1886 Honganji sect charter defines this mission according to the ideal of complementarity between two domains of law. This principle was the core political platform of the most influential Japanese Buddhist sects during the Meiji period. The ideal was shared by the Ōtani sect, who were obliged to follow Honganji leadership in negotiations with the state at the time.[7] The doctrine of complementarity offers an interpretive key to understand the relationship between the sects' political activities and the undergirding structure of prison chaplaincy doctrines. Reading this history through the lens of complementarity situates doctrinal production in the context of political negotiations about the place of Buddhism in society.

The charter's central principle of two complementary laws (the dharma and the law of the state) advocates for normative parameters around religion: *the right kind of religion can harmonize private interests with the public good.* Article 2 of the Honganji charter reads: "The essential doctrine of this sect is as follows. The ultimate law is to be mindful that it is through the blessing of the Buddha's great mercy that we hear and trust in the name of the Buddha. The provisional law is to respect the sovereign who governs dealings in the Way of humanity. We make this the excellent principle of our sect: these two domains of law complement one another (*nitai sōshi*). We oversee the repayment of the ruler's benevolence precisely by abiding in the heart of peace that arises through other-power."[8]

In the charter's language, the key soteriological concept "the heart of peace" (*anjin*) is linked to the repayment of the ruler's benevolence, marrying a concept of salvation to a notion of sovereignty. The charter's recognition of two domains of law corresponds to the public-private distinction as it was being negotiated around a concept of religion in the 1880s. The charter does not embrace unrestricted religious freedom. Rather, it calls for a division of roles between the Shin sect and the state, and it presents cooperation between the Buddhist authorities and the government as beneficial to public order. The sect's declared aim is to structure the relationship between the intimate realm of private beliefs and the encompassing realm of public responsibilities so that private interests are aligned with the public good.[9] According to this ideal, the nation-state has a vested interest in promoting the dharma over and against other religions (specifically Christianity) that may disrupt the idealized harmony between sect and state and its concomitant unity of private values with public duties. The charter asserts Honganji's commitment to the public ethic promoted by the state while simultaneously reserving the private domain as the sect's exclusive purview.

This charter set forth certain possibilities for religious thought and action while restricting others. On the one hand, the sect charter's framing of the relation between dharma and state undergirds the thinking about the role of the chaplain in managing crime. The chaplain, as a representative of both sect and state, works to harmonize the private realm of the conscience with the public good as defined by the political authorities. This orientation ensured that admonishing inmates based on Buddhist doctrine became the mainstream of chaplaincy practice and the primary theme in their publications. On the other hand, the sect charter also implies that the private dimension cannot be entirely reduced to the political. The interior realm is the locus of suffering, but also that of moral transformation and salvation. In the soteriological language of Shin (and Japanese religious discourse broadly) this is the realm of the heart—the object of the religious worker's concern. The focus on interiority creates a space for chaplains to tend to problems of suffering and existential concerns. This work was subordinated to the primary responsibility of doctrinal admonition, but the existential counseling dimension of prison chaplaincy practice became increasingly important over time.

As this chapter shows, Shin sects achieved a monopoly over prison chaplaincy by the turn of the twentieth century by forcing early Protestant social welfare activists out of the prison service. With the only serious competition eliminated, the result was that the Japanese prison chaplaincy would be molded in the image of the Shin sects and their ideal of sect-state collaboration. The point is not that the prison was shaped around the priorities of Shin Buddhists. Rather, the Shin sects' political orientation underwrote their efforts to build a prison chaplaincy to serve the carceral system's aims. The Shin sects drew on the newly established constitutional framework that delimited the sphere of religion to the private realm and then capitalized on the fact that the subjective orientation of correctional rehabilitation invites a focus on the hearts of the incarcerated. The prison door was open to religion.

Defining Prison Chaplaincy, Building Prison Chapels

Beginning in 1892, the Shin sects sponsored a series of prison chaplains' conferences with the aim of shaping the chaplaincy in their own image. The records of these conferences show the evolution of a national network of chaplains and the production of a Shin Buddhist chaplaincy curriculum. From April 17, 1892, Honganji sect sponsored a week-long chaplaincy conference at the Tsukiji Honganji Betsu-in temple in Tokyo.[10] The conference culminated in the decision to open a regional Prison Chaplaincy Office (Tokyo Kyōkai Tsūshinsho) at the temple. Later that year, this office began publishing the vocational journal *Prison Chaplaincy* (*Kangoku kyōkai*). Subsequent conferences in Kyoto and Kyushu also concluded with the opening of regional prison chaplaincy offices. The Shin Buddhist priests who had gained access to the carceral system to proselytize through the preceding decade outlasted the Great Promulgation Campaign and continued their work in the prisons after its end. In the wake of the Meiji

Constitution's imposition of a new degree of religious freedom and the state's adoption of the chaplaincy as part of the prison service, this disconnected cohort of former national instructors started to stitch together a nationwide network for the new vocation of prison chaplaincy.

At a conference held in Kyoto the same year, Shin chaplains standardized chaplaincy sessions based on the routines of prison facilities.[11] They divided sessions into two general categories: group chaplaincy (dharma talks) and individual chaplaincy (akin to counseling sessions).[12] These chaplaincy sessions were already integrated into the prison facilities' daily schedules. The Kyoto conference also saw chaplains sharing their methods for observing the inner lives of inmates. They produced a list of metrics: "How does the inmate conceive of Kami, Buddhas, and ancestors? How is the depth of an inmate's religion or faith? How is the inmate's attitude of love and respect toward his parents, wife, and children?"[13] Many questions focused on the internal, psychological dimension, while others delved into the realm of private life, the home, and the family. These records suggest that chaplains were developing a clinical gaze to diagnose what they saw as religious problems underlying criminal conduct. At a subsequent conference held in Kyushu in 1893, Shin chaplains produced basic guidelines for the two main types of chaplaincy sessions.[14] The standard group chaplaincy session was an opportunity to preach the law of cause and effect; individual sessions (in the cell, in the infirmary, and on death row) would focus on issues related to "religious peace of mind" (*shūkyōteki anshin*). Over time, the individual sessions would become the place for consultations about postrelease plans and also for existential counseling. However, these topics were not yet a major issue in the earliest chaplaincy publications of the 1890s. (See figs. 3.1, 3.2, 3.3, and 3.4.)

Shin sects further integrated themselves into the prison system by donating chapels and Buddhist altars (*butsudan*) to prisons nationwide. The Kyushu conference concluded with the decision to issue a formal request to the warden of each prison facility for a specialized "chapel of doctrinal admonition" (*kyōkaidō* 教誨堂).[15] The request's invasiveness indicates how deeply involved in the prison system Shin priests had become. The chaplains agreed that requests for chapels should be informed by the following principles: "The prison chapel is a sacred space, the sanctity of which should not be disturbed. The chapel should be treated with dignity and should be designated solely for chaplaincy. The Buddha images

FIGURE 3.1   Inmates assembled in the chapel for a chaplain's lecture. Drawing, 1895. Source: Sano Shō, ed. *Dai Nihon keigoku enkaku ryakushi*. Courtesy of the Japanese Correctional Association Library.

FIGURE 3.2   Prison chaplains preparing for work. Drawing, 1895. Source: Sano Shō, ed. *Dai Nihon keigoku enkaku ryakushi*. Courtesy of the Japanese Correctional Association Library.

FIGURE 3.3 Chaplains perform rites before a prison altar. Drawing, 1895. Source: Sano Shō, ed. *Dai Nihon keigoku enkaku ryakushi.* Courtesy of the Japanese Correctional Association Library.

FIGURE 3.4 A chaplain visits a group cell. Drawing, 1895. Source: Sano Shō, ed. *Dai Nihon keigoku enkaku ryakushi.* Courtesy of the Japanese Correctional Association Library.

enshrined in the chapels must be treated with appropriate reverence. When chaplaincy sessions are conducted, beginning with the warden, all prison staff in attendance must bow in reverence to the Buddha image."[16]

By the end of the Meiji period (1912), Buddhist sects (predominantly Shin) had financed the construction of chapel buildings at fifteen different penal institutions. By 1927, they had provided 115 penal institutions with an assortment of Buddhist paraphernalia, including Buddha images (typically Amida figures), paintings, altars, sutras, sutra boxes, and stands for ritual offerings.[17] Thus, by the late Meiji period, most prisons in Japan featured either a free-standing chapel or at least an altar space designated for chaplaincy, typically set up in a corner of the workshop or the cafeteria.

The donations were supported by doctrinal ideas about the effectiveness of Buddhist ritual in the cultivation of the heart. Ōtani sect chaplain Fujioka Ryōkū (1847?–1924) published a pamphlet entitled *Draft Outline of Prison Chaplaincy Studies* (*Kangoku kyōkaigaku teiyō sōan*) in May 1892. In this petition, Fujioka argues for the construction of Buddhist sacred spaces inside the prison system. He claims to have had discussions with prison staff claiming that since a Buddha image had been installed in the prison chapel, the number of dangerous incidents had declined. Fujioka attributes this improved orderliness to the karmic connection produced by venerating the Buddha.[18] He argues that the key to success is to maintain the prison chapel's sanctity by ensuring guards follow the chaplains' lead in treating the enshrined Buddha image with appropriate reverence: if guards fail to remove their hats before the Buddha, then what will the inmates think?[19] In the case of the Urakami Christians discussed in chapter 1, Buddhist remonstrators sought to force the "heretics" to bow before Buddha images both to demonstrate and to actualize their "conversion." Fujioka connects the same traditional focus on inculcating bodily attitudes of reverence toward Buddha images to the specific ends of the carceral program as a means of inculcating the desired moral feelings and catalyzing reform. As if this were not enough, Fujioka adds that even the French legal scholar Gustave Boissonade (1825–1910), then in the employ of the Meiji government, stated at a public lecture that "the Kami and Buddhas of Japan should not be neglected" in the project of inculcating virtues in the populace.[20] By this logic, the Buddha image is associated with national character, and Buddhist ritual has the power to change peoples' hearts for the better. Given that the mission of the prison is to promote reform, it is only natural that Buddhists participate in the effort.

The Shin sects matched their rhetoric about the power of Buddhist symbols and rites with strategic donations to the prisons, and by the 1890s, Shin Buddhist architecture and iconography became a fixture of Japanese prisons. Few examples of Meiji-era prison chapel architecture remain, but Hokkaido's Abashiri Prison, the northernmost prison in Japan, has been converted to a museum, and its chapel, built by prisoners in 1912, still stands.[21] Its exterior resembles a Buddhist temple, and the interior was used as a lecture hall for chaplaincy sessions (figs. 3.5 and 3.6). As of 2020, most major correctional facilities in Japan feature designated chapels (*kyōkaishitsu*, literally "chaplaincy rooms").

In sum, Shin Buddhists asserted control over prison chaplaincy by organizing a national network, standardizing their doctrines and practices, and making unsolicited donations to prisons. By the 1890s, not only were most prisons staffed by Shin chaplains (who held 85 percent of chaplaincy posts by 1894), prisons also featured Buddhist sacred spaces that enshrined Shin Buddhist images of Amida.[22] Regular chaplaincy sessions saw inmates throughout Japan gathered in prison chapels to engage in ritual veneration of these Buddha images and to listen to dharma talks about the moral law of cause and effect.

The Shin Prison Chaplaincy Journal and the Buddhist Social Pathologists

The first volume of the vocational journal *Prison Chaplaincy* published in July 1892 represents the beginnings of the professionalized discourse of the Buddhist prison chaplaincy. The first volume begins with a declaration of the publication's aims, stating that the intention is to "promote the goal of correctional reform."[23] This journal initiated the discourse of prison chaplaincy, a modernist genre of Buddhist doctrine characterized by the blending of traditional ideas about karma and self-cultivation with the correctional paradigm. The result is an early form of Japanese Buddhist social work connected to the administrative state.

FIGURE 3.5   Abashiri Prison chapel interior. The chapel was built in 1912. Courtesy of the Abashiri Prison Museum.

FIGURE 3.6   Abashiri Prison chapel exterior. Courtesy of the Abashiri Prison Museum.

The journal's political orientation is fundamentally statist. Its essays focus on the task of rectifying the hearts of offenders through doctrinal admonition. From the dharma talks and methodological works included in the journal, it is clear that Shin chaplaincy was conceived within the limits of a dogmatic framework wedded to state priorities. The journal's prevailing perspectives on the causes of crime and the role of Buddhism in correctional rehabilitation fundamentally rest on the political ideal of harmony between sect and state as expressed in the 1886 Honganji charter. There is nothing in the journals to suggest that Shin sects viewed participation in prison chaplaincy primarily as a means of gaining prospective converts. Rather, the journal's content supports the conclusion that Buddhist investment in prison chaplaincy was not motivated by concerns for the incarcerated so much as by a desire to prove the sects' utility to the state.

The inaugural volume's first article is a prison sermon by Honganji sect luminary Shimaji Mokurai. In this dharma talk, titled "Admonishing Prisoners," Shimaji offers an interpretation of the existential meaning of crime and rehabilitation.[24] He exhorts inmates directly, telling them that they have lost touch with human nature because of their selfish desires (*shiyoku*). He asserts that the essence of the human is a "wondrous intelligence" (*myōchi*) and that this intelligence separates us from animals. Shimaji maintains that selfish desires disrupt the harmony of an individual's heart, dull the intellect, and blind a person to the demands of morality. In this view, people commit crimes because they have been overcome by desire. Each inmate has succumbed to his baser instincts and fallen to the level of beasts because of personal weakness. Shimaji's presentation relies on the Buddhist doctrine of a graduated schema of reincarnation, wherein animals and hell dwellers are consigned to a lower place than humans and divine beings. His central point is that a human life is subject to special moral responsibilities because of our intellectual capacity to perceive morality and to imagine a metaphysical foundation underlying our moral intuitions.

Shimaji moves from the causes of crime to a proposed solution. A criminal offence leads inevitably to arrest and suffering in prison. However, doctrinal admonition may lead inmates to repent.[25] If an inmate understands that he has violated the moral order, then there is a possibility of redemption. He may undergo a change of heart and reform to live in accord with both the dharma and the law of the state. If all goes well, his internal harmony will be restored, and his conscience properly tuned to both the social order and the laws of karma. Finally, the safely reformed inmate may be released to "return to the fold as a law-abiding citizen" (*ryōmin ni tachi-modoru*). Shimaji adopts some language applied in the admonition of the illegal Christians in the 1870s as recorded by Matsumoto Hakka.

Shimaji links religious transformation to the goal of correctional reform. Like most of the chaplaincy discourse that follows, his sermon is an exercise in theodicy—an interpretation of crime as a form of existential evil. Shimaji assumes that the social order is in sync with a cosmic moral order and that the individual has fallen out of harmony with moral law. The argument relies on a logic that is generalizable to much of the prison chaplaincy's official discourse:

Internal disharmony→ Crime→ Arrest→
Doctrinal admonition→ Change of heart→
Reform, release, and return to society.

Shimaji compares the crime and rehabilitation process to the rebirth cycle of samsara. To commit a crime is to fall from the human realm to an animal realm—he writes that inmates have a "human face with the heart of a beast."[26] The grand analogy disguises a common prejudice: the implication is that people in prison are subhuman. They may be redeemed, however, through admonition and repentance. In this schema, the prison chaplain is implicitly associated with the bodhisattva figure who helps sentient beings to escape from suffering.[27] Conversion is not only a matter of religious salvation but also a strategy for correctional rehabilitation and a means of reclaiming "humanity."

Shimaji's attitude toward inmates is condescending. The incarcerated are not the subject of his sympathy. Rather, he treats inmates as belonging categorically to the class of the insufficiently pious and weak-willed. He writes as if all incarcerated people have fallen into dire straits because they suffer from a lack of faith or resolve. No evidence is presented to support this premise. Instead, Shimaji prescribes doctrinal instruction according to a predetermined diagnosis: crime is the result of character defects (rather than mitigating circumstances, structural factors, mental illness, etc.). He assumes that exposure to the dharma prevents criminal conduct by mitigating the selfish desires at the root of personality flaws. Thus, Shimaji's logic holds that teaching dharma corrects individual moral failings and thereby offers a solution to the source of crime at the level of the individual offender. It is worth noting that Shimaji takes for granted that this reform strategy is effective. It is not a hypothesis to be tested, but the core dogma of chaplaincy theory. In the final analysis, Shimaji's understanding of crime and reform is delimited by foregone conclusions: the law of the nation is just, and the role of the dharma is to maintain the moral order. This understanding is grounded in the Honganji charter, which constructs the sect's role as guardians of the status quo.

Other works in the journal rely on the same procedure for deriving religious significance from crime and rehabilitation. Another 1892 edition includes a sermon delivered by Ōta Kenju, chaplain at Tokyo Ichigaya Prison (and one of the speakers at the chaplains' conference discussed in chapter 2). Ōta's sermon encapsulates the journal's prevailing understanding of sect-state relations. His sermon, "The Human World is a World of Rewards and Punishments," asserts a theory of human subjectivity defined by a metaphysical view of morality.[28] Ōta's primary concern in this text is to encourage inmates to think of the relationship between the law of the state and the law of karma as complementary. He begins with the assertion that the prison is a microcosm of the human world. Both prison and society are characterized by rewards and punishments meted out in response to good and evil deeds. These are essential components of the human condition. Since ancient times, the law of karma has been attributed to a divine origin, and the law of the state has been attributed to a human origin. However, Ōta introduces this binary only to deny the distinction: the law of the state is built on the foundations of the moral law of karma.

Ōta then leverages this argument to make a claim on the consciences of his audience. He shifts from a description of the nature of law to an argument about the nature of the human person. He points to the natural and universal human desire for happiness. He suggests that only certain strategies for living can reasonably be expected to lead to happiness. Only those who live in accordance with the law of karma and the law of the state can expect their lot in life to improve. Finally, he links the pursuit of happiness to the cultivation of one's inner qualities. Intentions must be formulated skillfully and in harmony with the two domains of law that govern our fates. He argues that bearing evil in one's heart will inevitably turn one's fortunes away from happiness because karma is an "immutable, unavoidable, and implacable natural law." The underlying logic presupposes a relationship between intentions and happiness. Intentional action drives the production of good or evil karma: bad intentions produce bad results. Thus, Ōta argues that if we want to be happy, then we must understand that the moral law requires us to cultivate the skillful intentions that will guide us toward rewards and away from punishments.

Based on the tone of the passage, it seems that Ōta's concern is to encourage inmates not to bear ill will against the state for their incarceration. By inviting inmates to see their imprisonment as the result of their own willful violation of immutable karmic laws, he implies that bearing a grudge against the human authorities will be counterproductive. An attitude of rebellion against the law of the state is completely unreasonable, because it amounts to rejecting the universal law upon which the human law rests. In this vision, karma and punishment are woven together. The result is that Ōta can assign an existential meaning to punishment. This interpretation situates the individual in a cosmological schema and invites the inmate to bring his heart into harmony with this grand scheme of things. Ōta not only provides a justification of the powers that be. He also argues that the conscience should be formulated such that the individual views the state's power to mete out punishments as a necessary component of the natural order. He suggests that the individual is always subject to the law of karma. A person's actions are always being monitored and judged. Ōta invites inmates to internalize the external gaze of the prison guards (the state) into a self-monitoring function of conscience.

Ōta's essay reveals the contours and limitations to Meiji-period Shin chaplaincy discourse. The doctrinal system, molded to the correctional program, is obviously not designed to consider whether or not the law of the state is just. In the prison context, the chaplain is an agent of both sect and state, and so Ōta takes for granted that the cosmos is on the side of the state. For this reason, he posits that punishments imposed by secular law are a function of the law of karma. This dogmatic view entails the corollary assumption that the cause (singular) of crime is necessarily seen as arising from disharmony in an individual's heart rather than from a confluence of limited agency and mitigating factors arising from deeper problems inherent in society. Chaplaincy discourse is depoliticized in that it presents the state's power to punish as natural and inevitable. Moreover, Shin chaplaincy discourse assumes that both religious instruction and the broader correctional program are efficacious means of reform.

In the 1890s, Buddhist sects tailored their services to a correctional system built on notions of repentance and reform for the same reasons they tailored their services to the Great Promulgation Campaign's national creed in the 1870s. They wanted to prove that they could contribute to society by facilitating governance. The larger sectarian orthodoxy defined by the Honganji charter authorized the production of Buddhist doctrines to suit the prisons. The sect and the chaplain retain authority over the private (the individual offender's heart), but they do not question the sovereign state's righteousness. The purpose of the prison chaplaincy was to demonstrate Buddhism's capacity to defend the public good.

Writing in a twenty-first century context in which chaplaincies around the world are typically understood in relation to notions of spiritual health and individual well-being, what is so remarkable about Meiji-era Shin chaplaincy discourse is that it exhibits virtually no concern for incarcerated people as human beings. Studies of nineteenth-century prison chaplains in Western societies highlight their work for correctional reform, and this history indicates that a case can be made for a genealogical connection between such reform-minded prison chaplains and contemporary forms of spiritual care.[29] Christian chaplains in the United States and Europe both admonished offenders for their perceived moral failings *and also* expressed concern about the suffering of the incarcerated. (In fact, Christian prison reformers played an important role in nineteenth-century Japan, too, and this history is explored in the next section.) By contrast, the Shin chaplains' journal is focused exclusively on social order, not prison reform, nor the problem of suffering, nor anything else resembling spiritual care. The mainstay of the Shin prison chaplain's job was to admonish offenders to "get themselves together," not to comfort them.

Though chaplaincies are discussed today under the rubric of spiritual care, Meiji-era Buddhist prison chaplaincy discourse appears to have more in common with another statist form of social welfare thought. The chaplaincy journals announce the birth of a certain kind of Buddhist social work vocation. Comparison with other fields of nineteenth- and early twentieth-century social work suggests that Japanese prison chaplains were by no means unique in their perspective on the causes of crime. In a classic essay from 1943, sociologist C. Wright Mills analyzes the values of American social welfare academics and social workers and finds that their assumptions about the causes of private troubles tend to reproduce the prejudices of their middle-class milieu. He maintains that they see poverty as stemming from a character flaw rather than factors inherent in social structure.[30] The title of the essay— "The Professional Ideology of Social Pathologists"—and its conclusion could just as well apply to an analysis of Japanese prison chaplaincy. Mills later defined the sociological imagination as the capacity to perceive connections between private troubles and public issues.[31] This realm of imagination is precisely what is excluded from the official publications the late nineteenth- and early twentieth-century social pathologists, Japanese prison chaplains included. The key difference between early American social work professionals and the Japanese prison chaplaincy is that the Buddhist sects leveraged the resources of their own tradition—ideas about karma and the ideal relation between sect and state in particular—to attach themselves to the administrative state. In the process, Shin sects produced something akin to "the professional ideology of Buddhist social pathologists." They did not create a nineteenth-century form of Buddhist spiritual care work.

As a final example, the scholar Murakami Senshō (1851–1929) published a methodological essay for chaplains titled "The Role and Objectives of the Prison Chaplaincy and the Preparations for Chaplains."[32] Murakami's lecture differs from the previous examples in that it is intended only for an audience of chaplains and not for inmates. This essay explains the division of labor between prison guards and chaplains by drawing on metaphors of family life. Murakami invites his audience to imagine that the prison is a household, the prison staff are father figures, and the inmates are children. Chaplains themselves should "imagine the feelings of a mother raising a child."[33] Murakami asks an audience of male chaplains to embody the virtue of compassion (*jimo*) stereotypically associated with the maternal image. The implication is that the chaplain's role is not to punish but to offer succor. This line of thought suggests that prison chaplains were engaged in practices of attentive care, but Murakami is silent on the content of that work. The metaphor based on a division of gender roles draws from a tradition in which the sovereign is rhetorically equated with the male while the dharma is aligned with the female.[34] The female role of the chaplain corresponds to the private realm of the heart, the home, and religious faith, and the male role of the prison warden corresponds to the public realm, the law of the sovereign, and the duties of imperial subjects. The male and female, public and private, chaplains and prison staff must work in harmony to raise the children—the inmates—into law-abiding citizens. Murakami's vision rests on an ideal of marriage between sect and state. Here, too, the Honganji charter's principle of complementarity between two domains of law informs the basic structure of chaplaincy methodology.

The rest of Murakami's essay is devoted to explaining that the purpose of prison chaplaincy is not sectarian advocacy. Murakami maintains that the chaplain is responsible to teach "general Buddhist doctrine" and "conventional theories of public morality" as opposed to a sectarian doctrine. He emphasizes that the doctrine he has in mind is the principle of karma, which he sees as a rational ethic shared by all Buddhist groups and a doctrine that is compatible with civic morals. As his essay makes clear, chaplains were not being dispatched to the prisons to seek converts. They were sent there to support order and, in the process, to demonstrate Buddhism's contributions to governance. The fact that chaplaincy discourse focuses on the perceived needs of governance rather than the needs of the incarcerated reflects the underlying reality that the Shin sects did not care to reinforce their numbers by drawing converts from the prisoners. What was at stake for them in the prisons was not the number of believers, nor the well-being of the inmates, but the relationship between their brand of Buddhism and the state.

The Meiji constitutional framework governing religion made Buddhist, Christian, and sectarian Shinto groups alike responsible for contributing to the public good by promoting private virtues. It also created conditions that encouraged these groups to compete with one another for prestige, finances, and believers. In the case of prison chaplaincy, it appears that the Shin sects invested in the effort primarily to gain the prestige and moral authority that came through close ties with the government. The Japanese correctional system's focus on molding the hearts of the incarcerated created an opportunity for imperiled Buddhist sects to reclaim some degree of moral authority by inserting themselves into the carceral project. To that end, Shin Buddhists formalized a doctrinal system for their prison chaplaincy based on the ideal of harmony between the dharma and the law of the nation-state. The Shin sects promoted the idea that teaching dharma can be a strategy to fight crime because doing so appeared to be in their own interest. This form of outreach provided rhetorical legitimations for the state's power to punish, but it also bolstered the sects' standing in the new context of religious competition. In this sense, the chaplain embodies the Shin sects' social mission as defined in the 1886 charter: creating harmony between the two domains of law.

Two implications of this arrangement are now clear. First, as we saw with the Great Promulgation Campaign, the price for participation in the state's ideological projects was that Buddhists had to teach a curriculum they had only a limited hand in developing. Though Buddhist prison chaplains might have imagined an equivalence between the two domains of law, in practice, they encountered a clear hierarchy in which the dharma was subordinated to the priorities of the state. Second, from the textual record it would appear that Shin investment in prison outreach was motivated primarily by the desire to secure the sects' standing through contributions to the nation-state. The early Buddhist prison chaplains do not appear to have been particularly invested in the welfare of incarcerated people, and it does not appear that they cared much about gaining converts from among the prison population either. The lack of concern for inmates that characterizes their professional discourse means that early Shin Buddhist prison chaplaincy does not fit easily into the framework of spiritual care often invoked to explain the work of chaplains in other times and places. Shin prison chaplains had more in common with the social workers C. Wright Mills described as "social pathologists" because their expressed concerns were most often framed with reference to the perceived needs of society (and not those of their individual clients). The mainstay of Shin prison chaplaincy discourse was not focused on the personal problem of suffering but on the social problem of crime. In what follows, I show that the Shin sects' position regarding chaplaincy—the idea that they could help society to get tough on crime—played a part in a larger debate about the role of religions in society.

Christians in the Prison Service

Shin advocacy for prison chaplaincy offered the sects a chance to position themselves as guardians of the public good. As we have seen, the fundamental premise of Shin prison chaplaincy was that a universal moral

law undergirds the law of the state. The prison chaplain was inserted between these two domains of law as an agent of both sect and state. According to the dogmatic line of thought, all Japanese subjects should rightfully
owe allegiance to both the law of the sovereign and the trans-sectarian
principles of the dharma. Shin sects championed the ideal of complementarity between dharma and law as part of an attempt to avoid competing
on an even playing field with newcomer Christian missionaries.

Following the passage of the Meiji Constitution, Christianity's social
status changed dramatically. Christian missions gained an increasing
degree of legal and public recognition, in large part because of pressure
from foreign powers. Throughout the 1890s, though Christianity was still
viewed with suspicion, the prestige of the newcomer religion was enhanced through its connection with Western culture, the establishment
of Christian educational institutions, and the efforts of Christian social
welfare activists drawn from the ranks of converted Japanese Protestants.[35]
Japanese Protestants were particularly active in proselytization efforts in
Japan's northern territory, Hokkaido. Some notable Japanese Christian
converts served in the correctional service, and they are remembered for
their efforts to reform the brutal frontier prisons.[36] Arima Shirosuke
(1864–1934) and Tomeoka Kōsuke (1864–1934) played a particularly significant role in the development of prison chaplaincy. From the perspective of a genealogical investigation of Japanese prison chaplaincy, the most
significant impact of their careers was to galvanize Shin Buddhist opposition to Christian prison chaplains. Arima and Tomeoka unwittingly
set in motion a chain of events that resulted in half a century of Shin
Buddhist monopoly over prison religion in Japan.

In the Meiji period, prisoners from various regions of Japan were exiled
to Hokkaido to perform penal labor breaking down the brush and building roads into the frontier. Arima Shirosuke served in the Hokkaido prison
service from 1886, and he was appointed the first warden of the newly
opened Abashiri Prison in the far reaches of the territory in 1891.[37] Arima
was responsible to deploy prisoners to build a road between the settlement
of Asahikawa, in central Hokkaido, and the remote Abashiri.[38] However,
work conditions were inhumane, and within the year, out of a total of 1,264
inmates under his charge, more than 150 died, and many more suffered illness and injuries.[39] Arima was horrified, and he dedicated himself to im-
proving prison hygiene and labor conditions so as to prevent more deaths.

By this time, the government had started to appoint chaplains to all prisons, and it so happened that eleven Protestant missionaries were on rotating assignments through the Hokkaido frontier prisons. Ten of these men had connections to the private Dōshisha English School (forerunner of Dōshisa University).[40] The American-trained Protestant convert and educator Niijima Jō (1843–1890) established this Christian educational institution in 1875, and the school became an incubator for Japanese Protestant social activism. In line with Dōshisha's relatively progressive values, the Protestants in the prison service were indeed committed to reform. Tomeoka Kōsuke was one of the Dōshisha graduates stationed in Hokkaido.

From 1892 until the end of 1895, Christian prison chaplains in Hokkaido, including Tomeoka and Hara Taneaki (1853–1942), published a journal titled *Prison Chaplaincy Series* (*Kyōkai sōsho*).[41] This publication was aimed at an audience of inmates, and the goal of the journal was to promote the education and rehabilitation of the incarcerated. Notably, one of the journal's primary themes was the topic of "compassion" (*dōjō*) for prisoners, and as the term suggests, the Protestant chaplains were invested in the moral reform of both prisoners and the prison system itself. Compared with the Shin chaplaincy journals discussed in the previous section, the Christian chaplains' journal did not circulate widely beyond Hokkaido because the Protestants were not connected to the developing network of Buddhist prison chaplains who controlled the majority of posts.

Though he was originally suspicious of Christianity, warden Arima admired the efforts of the Christian chaplains, and this admiration attracted him to their faith. Arima became intimate friends with a Christian chaplain by the name of Ōtsuka Hiroshi in particular, and Ōtsuka introduced Arima to the study of the Bible through a lengthy correspondence.[42] After nine years in Hokkaido, Arima was highly respected in the prison service for his effective management of Abashiri. He was promoted to warden of Saitama Prison in 1895.[43] Though he departed Hokkaido, he remained in contact with his Christian friends, and in May 1898, he asked Tomeoka Kōsuke (who had also relocated to the capital) to baptize him at Reinanzaka Church in Tokyo.[44] One month later, Arima was promoted yet again. From September he became warden of Sugamo Prison, Japan's flagship penal institution. Arima immediately invited Tomeoka to serve as prison chaplain.

The Sugamo Prison Chaplain Incident

When Arima was appointed warden of Sugamo Prison, there were four Ōtani sect prison chaplains on the staff: Tōgō Ryōchō, Mano Senmon, Nakazawa Ryōyū, and Miyama Genju.[45] On the first Sunday of September 1898, Arima paid a visit to the ranking Ōtani sect official Ōgusa Keijitsu at the Asakusa Honganji temple. He informed Ōgusa that he would be changing the structure of the prison chaplaincy to emphasize moral instruction rather than religious chaplaincy.[46] To that end, he indicated that he would retain only one Buddhist chaplain and asked for the sect to choose either Tōgō or Mano to serve as its representative.[47] Arima added that, in order to respect the constitutional requirement for religious freedom, one Christian chaplain would also be added to the staff. The next day, Arima met with the chaplains and informed them that only one would be retained and that he had already informed their superior Ōgusa of his decision.[48] The Shin chaplains were stunned.

The chaplains immediately went to confer with Ōgusa. They decided that all four would resign the very next day and that they would raise the issue with the sect.[49] The following day, the four chaplains each headed to separate workshops within the prison to perform a dramatic farewell before the assembled inmates.[50] Tōgō announced the departure of the Buddhist chaplains by declaring that the donated Buddha images installed in both the north and the south prison chapels would be leaving with the Buddhist priests. He closed by reminding the inmates: "[Do] not forget your debts to the sovereign, to your parents, and to the Buddha."[51] Mano addressed another crowd and declared that he felt like a parent forced to abandon a sickly child.[52] Nakazawa bid farewell with a discourse on the Confucian virtues of filial piety and loyalty.[53] Miyama was the most blunt: "Just because the new chaplain is a Christian [. . .] you must not go breaking the rules!"[54] After announcing their departure to the inmates, the four chaplains informed the warden of their resignation. They wrote to the sect requesting advice about how to proceed.[55]

The weight of opinion within the sect held that Arima himself must be a Christian like his new appointee Tomeoka. (In fact, Arima had been baptized not six months before.) The dominant view of the Shin faction was that Arima was using his public station to advance his own private interests.[56] In retaliation, the sect mobilized its lobbyist Ishikawa Shundai to reach out to politicians and the media. (We encountered Ishikawa already in chapter 1. After the Restoration, he served together with Matsumoto Hakka in the campaign to admonish the illegal Christian detainees in Kanazawa; he was a fervent opponent of Christianity.) Ishikawa first wrote to Home Minister Itagaki Taisuke (1837–1919) in a letter dated September 19, 1898.[57] He complained that the introduction of Christianity into the prison system would "confuse relations between the public and the private."[58]

Ishikawa believed that Buddhism should rightfully be left in charge of the private realm because Buddhism is a force for harmony. In this light, he depicted Christianity as socially disruptive. Arima's stated rationale for altering the chaplaincy system was that he was promoting ethical instruction (as opposed to religious instruction), but Ishikawa viewed this as a lie. He saw Arima and Tomeoka as Christian agents attempting to infiltrate and convert the prison system. A skillful propagandist, Ishikawa painted a slippery slope scenario: if Christianity is able to infiltrate the public office of the prison chaplaincy, then in the future, it may be able to extend its reach into the government; to allow Christianity to gain a strong foothold in the prisons was thus to risk creating a conflict between religion and state.

Ishikawa followed this letter with two highly publicized open letters to Prime Minister Ōkuma Shigenobu (1838–1922).[59] In these letters, Ishikawa railed against Christianity's supposedly subversive nature, declaring it to be incompatible with the civic ethic of the Imperial Rescript on Education and contrary to the spirit of loyalty to the emperor.[60] The home minister grew so frustrated with Ishikawa that he wrote to the chief abbot of the Ōtani sect to insist that Ishikawa be disciplined.[61] However, it was too late—the Buddhist press (*Meikyō shinshi* and *Seikyō jihō*) picked up the story, and the issue became a political cause.[62]

Two related political issues were read into the Sugamo Prison Chaplain Incident: immigration and religious freedom.[63] In 1897, the Japanese government was negotiating treaties with foreign powers in which the issue of foreign residency was under discussion. This issue impacted the prison system because prisons would also need to be equipped to house foreign inmates, who, presumably, would be Christians. At the same time, there was a move within the government to craft a unified legal framework for governing religion. Buddhist sects were adamantly opposed to the idea that newcomer Christians could be placed on the same footing as the "established religions."[64] Contentious political debates about immigration and religious freedom formed a backdrop against which the Sugamo Prison Chaplain Incident ignited a scandal.

In 1901, the debate reached the Diet. A member of the lower house, Kōmuchi Tomotsune (1848–1905), proposed a bill to resolve the prison chaplaincy incident in favor of the Shin sects.[65] The debate was fierce, but the Buddhist temples were important political backers for some members of the Liberal Party (Jiyūtō), and more than twenty members threatened to drop out of the party if the government would not see fit to support the Buddhists.[66] (The Buddhist temples could leverage the fact that most Japanese—and thus most voters—were officially Buddhists themselves—an appeal to populism.) A motion was made to send the bill to a subcommittee for further discussion, but it failed, gaining only 89 votes in favor, compared with 104 votes against. The refusal to send the bill to committee meant that the Diet had to decide the issue then and there. The atmosphere on the floor descended into a shouting match before a final vote was taken. Out of 193 in attendance, 102 voted in favor of Kōmuchi's proposal and 91 voted against. This vote handed the Shin Buddhists control of the prison chaplaincy.[67]

In the political realignment that followed, both Home Minister Itagaki and Prime Minister Ōkuma were forced to resign, and Yamagata Aritomo (1838–1922) formed his second cabinet. The incoming Home Minister Saigō Tsugumichi (1843–1902) ordered Arima to be transferred from Sugamo Prison to Ichigaya Prison (also in Tokyo), where he would take over as warden. The following year, Tomeoka was appointed professor at the newly opened Police and Prison Academy (Keisatsu Kangoku Gakkō), and he too left Sugamo Prison.[68] With the departure of Tomeoka, Christian prison chaplaincy came to end and did not resume until the postwar period. With the activist Protestant chaplains expelled, organized support for prison reform among the chaplaincy was effectively nipped in the bud. The prison chaplaincy took another path.

At the turn of the twentieth century, prison chaplains—virtually all of whom were now Shin priests—were officially appointed to the civil service.[69] Like some members of the shrine Shinto priesthood, 180 Shin priests were paid salaries funded by the government from 1903, and even as the number of chaplains gradually increased, they continued to receive state funding until 1945.[70] For the most part, these civil service appointments were rotating, with typical Shin prison chaplains serving periods of three to five years before moving on to other posts; however, some dedicated chaplains made a career of the work.[71] In the wake of the Sugamo Prison Chaplain Incident, the Shin model of doctrinal admonition became the universal standard for prison chaplaincy in Japan for the next half century.

Conclusions

The ideal of complementarity between sect and state is the key to understand the Shin Buddhists' political platform at the turn of the century as well as the chaplaincy doctrine they developed. Politically, this principle amounts to a hedge against an excess of religious freedom. The Sugamo Prison Chaplain Incident galvanized Shin thinking about the role of temples as defenders of society. The political struggle over prison chaplaincy that broke out in 1898 was a battle over where to draw the line between public obligations and private religious commitments. The Ōtani sect, led by Ishikawa Shundai, regarded the encroachment of Christians into the prison service as a threat to Buddhism. Ishikawa argued that Buddhist sects were rightfully in control of the private realm and that Christians could not be entrusted with this task because Christianity could disrupt relations between the public and the private. The argument that prison chaplaincy should be the exclusive responsibility of the Shin sects accomplished two things. First, Shin partisans emphasized that their sects contribute to the maintenance of the social order by reforming offenders. Second, they staked a claim on the correctional system and promoted the legitimacy of their religious mission by wedding it to the state. The Sugamo Prison Chaplain Incident culminated in the government's decision to hand the Shin sects a monopoly over prison religion that lasted until the end of World War II. For this reason, prison chaplaincy in Japan developed in the image of the Shin Buddhist sects.

Late nineteenth-century Shin political commitments structured the dominant tradition of Japanese prison chaplaincy from its outset and shaped the development of chaplaincy theory and practice. The ideal of complementarity between two domains of law defined prison chaplaincy as a matter of harmonizing the private realm of beliefs, aspirations, and conscience with the requirements of public duties. Shin prison chaplaincy binds the normative understanding of religion (as a means of inculcating private virtues for the public benefit) to the correctional program. Doctrinal admonition became one means to rectify the disordered hearts of offenders. Shin sects saw crime as a spiritual problem that their brand of Buddhism could ameliorate.

By looking for the causes of crime solely in the hearts of incarcerated people, the Shin chaplains ended up creating a doctrinal system that turns a blind eye to social problems with a bearing on crime. One result of this arrangement was early Shin chaplaincy discourse's unsympathetic perspective on incarcerated people. Shin chaplains left extensive records in their vocational journal detailing the content of sermons in the mold of doctrinal admonition. By contrast, although chaplains clearly also engaged in practices akin to counseling from as early as the 1890s, the same vocational journals provide scant evidence of the actual content of this work. This gap exists precisely because the dominant focus of Japanese prison chaplaincy was on fighting crime rather than relieving suffering—doctrinal admonition rather than something more like "spiritual care." It should come as no surprise that in the prison memoirs that started to appear in the 1910s, the formerly incarcerated authors paint a dismal picture of chaplains as condescending and out of touch.[72]

In the Meiji period, the Shin sects were extremely effective advocates for their own interests. They engaged in coordinated political activism to drive Christians out of the prison service. They mobilized so powerfully to claim authority over the private beliefs of the incarcerated that they toppled a prime minister. This history leads us to ask: were they also champions for the incarcerated? It would be more accurate to say that Ishikawa Shundai and his backers treated the incarcerated as a political football in efforts to effectively lobby to limit the religious freedom of people in prison. It seems ironic, but the long-term result of vigorous Shin political activism surrounding prison chaplaincy was to enshrine an understanding of crime that is completely depoliticized and a doctrine that is whitewashed of sectarian specificity and liberatory potential. Be that as it may, from the turn of the twentieth century until the end of World War II, incarcerated people serving sentences in the Japanese correctional system were required to attend meetings in prison chapels where Shin Buddhist chaplains would exhort them to obey the law of the state and the law of karma.[73]

CHAPTER 4

Thought Crimes and the Opium of the Masses

Religious and Political Conversions

In 1925, the passage of the Peace Preservation Law (Chian iji hō) strengthened the state security apparatus in an effort to stamp out a new kind of ideological crime. The criminal code allowed for the classification of Marxists, leftists, some members of new religions, and a variety of other political enemies as "thought criminals" (*shisōhan*).[1] In the wake of these reforms, Shin prison chaplains became intimately involved in the "ideological conversion" (*tenkō* 転向) of political prisoners. The term *tenkō* (literally "change in direction") refers to a wave of conversions from the left to the imperialist right that occurred chiefly between 1933 and 1945. *Tenkō* has also been interpreted as a broader cultural turn that took place at the time as many Japanese intellectuals and much of public discourse shifted rightward.

The most comprehensive study of the forced ideological conversions is a three-volume set titled *Tenkō* published between 1959 and 1962 by Tsurumi Shunsuke (1922–2015) and the Science of Thought Research Group (Shisō no Kagaku Kenkyūkai). Tsurumi offers a relatively loose definition of *tenkō*: "A change in thought that occurs due to compulsion by authority."[2] The Science of Thought Research Group's aim was to understand the connection between the private experience of ideological conversion and the structural conditions (legal, social, ethical) that led to the change. They held *tenkō* to be both a generalizable phenomenon (with analogues in Maoist China, Stalinist Russia, and Orwell's dystopian novel *Nineteen Eighty-Four*) and a product of Japan's particular historical conditions (as a recently developed country harboring both imported liberal thought and a feudal emperor system). In English, Patricia Steinhoff has published a detailed sociological study of *tenkō* as a method for handling the problem of social integration, and Max Ward has more recently analyzed the forced conversion of thought criminals as a representative form of ideological control in imperial Japan.[3]

In this chapter, I reconsider the relationship between *tenkō* and religion in imperial Japan. Forced conversion programs relied on Shin Buddhist prison chaplains to administer the reeducation of political prisoners. I argue that the chaplaincy's role in overseeing forced conversions during this period was emblematic of Shin Buddhist work for the public benefit. In accord with the sect's vision of harmony between dharma and law, chaplains used Buddhist instruction to align the private beliefs of thought criminals with the public ethos promoted by the state. According to one directional metaphor for *tenkō*, the key shift is politically from left to right, and this is certainly accurate. However, this study shows that a different directional metaphor more accurately accounts for the intellectual shift detailed in the administrative records of the chaplaincy and the *tenkō* statements chaplains elicited from prisoners. Chaplains understood *tenkō* as a change of heart, a matter of religious conversion. By this logic, *tenkō* was a turn inwards, away from political engagement in the public sphere and toward the private realm of family, home life, and religious experience. Correctional bureaucrats and Shin chaplains sought to discourage political activism by supplanting it with introspection, and they understood this turn as an effect of religion. Moreover, the work of *tenkō* was never complete. After thought criminals were reformed and paroled, they were subjected to continuous monitoring to ensure the "purity" of their conversions. Shin Buddhist prison chaplains coordinated with the correctional system and civic institutions (including religions) to build a network of ideological surveillance: a modern probation system reliant upon volunteer labor. In effect, the persecution of thought criminals produced a facsimile of the Tokugawa-period temple certification system. From the 1920s, Shin chaplains continued their sect's mission of promoting complementarity between the dharma and the law of the state: they contributed to public order by converting politically disruptive (criminalized) beliefs into socially acceptable religious aspirations contained to an apolitical private realm. *Tenkō* programs during the imperial period were one face of Shin Buddhism's efforts for the public benefit.

Religious Work for the Public Benefit in Imperial Japan

In what follows, I situate the development of *tenkō* programs in relation to Shin Buddhism in the imperial period, highlighting institutional and discursive trends. I emphasize that chaplains' activities inside prisons were connected to religious work for the public benefit in broader society. At the level of national policy, the imperial government relied on religions to collaborate with the state to facilitate governance through public-private partnerships.

The Russo-Japanese War marked a turning point for Japanese religions, as both government and public expectations called for religious organizations to make contributions to the empire. The Shin sects aimed to meet these demands chiefly through proselytization (*shakai kyōka*) and social work (*shakai jigyō*). The posting of 105 Honganji priests to serve as military chaplains (*jūgun fukyōshi*) in the war was one manifestation of sectarian work for the public good. These chaplains were responsible to offer sermons to encourage the soldiers, to comfort the sick and wounded, to perform rites for the dead, and in some instances to minister to bereaved families. Honganji also held a blood drive, established an orphanage for the children of the war dead near its head temple in Kyoto, and, through its nonprofit, the Japanese Buddhist Mercy Foundation (Dai Nihon Bukkyō Jizenkai Zaidan), applied for 5 million yen in government bonds. Throughout the war, leaders of both major sects of Shin Buddhism continually reasserted that the ideal of harmony between two domains of law requires Buddhists to support the national cause.[4]

The expectations for religious groups changed with the times. In the wake of the Russian Revolution and World War I, Japan entered a period of economic instability. During the Taishō era (1912–1926), labor movements achieved broad support among the public, and socialism and other imported liberal ideas began to have an impact on popular thought.[5] The 1923 Great Kantō Earthquake was followed by a wave of public disturbances, and the government responded to the unrest by issuing the Promulgation on Promoting the National Spirit (Kokumin seishin sakkō ni kan suru mikotonori). This promulgation signaled the beginning of a campaign to mobilize thought—a strategy to influence popular consciousness led by the Ministry of Education (Monbushō) and the Home Ministry (Naimushō). The goal of the campaign was to combat the "worsening of thought" (*shisō no akka*)—the spread of socialism and other forms of liberalism—with "positive intellectual guidance" (*shisō zendō*).[6] The promulgation emphasized the need for citizens to cultivate traditional values seen as rooted in the national polity. These include the virtues of loyalty, diligence, and thrift—all values required of a working population facing austerity in light of an economic downturn.

One year after the promulgation was issued, leaders from Buddhist, Shinto, and Christian sects were summoned to the prime minister's residence where they were asked to participate in the drive to support the national spirit.[7] Prefectures throughout Japan saw the creation of social welfare organizations (*shakai jigyō dantai*) and moral suasion groups (*kyōka dantai*).[8] These civic groups coordinated with prefectural bureaucrats to provide both poverty relief work and intellectual guidance. In general, practical efforts at relieving the suffering of the poor were intertwined with promotion of the conservative ideology of the family state united under the emperor.[9]

The civic groups that flourished in the 1920s shared a common politics. They adopted a stance on social problems premised on turning away from the pursuit of the kinds of systematic relief that would require changes to the social structure. They emphasized instead the importance of personal virtues like kindness (*shinsetsu*) and love (*aijō*) as methods of relieving the suffering brought on by economic hardship.[10] Coordinating with the state's moral suasion campaign, many religious groups promoted meliorist doctrines, teaching that the solution to social problems was for individuals to engage in self-cultivation (*shūyō*). Religions were expected to work for the public benefit by encouraging private virtues, and this work was seen to contribute to the ideological struggle against leftist and reformist tendencies.

As the number of moral suasion groups and social welfare organizations increased, chaplains became the link between prisons and the outside world. They coordinated with the network of civic groups to facilitate the social reintegration of offenders. The Japanese probation system (*hogo jigyō*) traces its origins to ad hoc work done by prison chaplains in the 1890s. Since that time, chaplains had been responsible to help wardens with decisions about early release and with strategies for promoting social reintegration.[11] Some dedicated prison chaplains operated halfway houses (*kankain*)—in some cases out of their own homes or temples.

By the 1910s, prison chaplains were involved in nonprofit probation groups (*hogokai*). General amnesties marking the death of Emperor Meiji (1912) and the enthronement of the Taishō emperor (1915) granted early release for nearly 70,000 parolees. To handle this influx, in 1914, Count Mitsui Hachirōjirō (1849–1919) donated 750,000 yen to establish the Hoseikai Foundation to oversee the developing network of civic groups working in the probation field. By 1917, there were more than 750 probation groups active in Japan, and many had connections to religious organizations.[12]

Until 1936, the government employed not a single probation officer. The nascent probation system was run entirely by private nonprofit groups. Prison chaplains worked as liaisons between prisons and the outside network of nonprofits to arrange parolee placements.[13] It was only after "thought crime" became the high-profile issue in the correctional field that the Japanese probation system was centralized and the office of probation officer established. Thus, the success of *tenkō* programs catalyzed the development of the probation system.

Shin Modernism: Spiritual Seekers and Repentance Narratives

While chaplains were working to build a volunteer probation system, a form of religious individualism was taking root among the Shin clergy. The ideal of the individual as a "religious seeker" became enormously influential in Shin Buddhist discourse.[14] This trend in popular religious thought created space for an existential perspective (*jitsuzon no tachiba*) that became essential to the administration of reform programs for thought criminals.[15]

No figure better represents the trend toward religious individualism in prewar Shin Buddhism than the Ōtani cleric Chikazumi Jōkan (1870–1941). Chikazumi was a popular writer and lecturer who enjoyed wide readership from the first decade of the twentieth century.[16] He was also a graduate of the prestigious University of Tokyo, and he is known today for financing, building, and managing the Seekers' Hall (Kyūdō Kaikan) near the university campus from 1915.[17] He was at the center of Shin Buddhism's intellectual and social circles in the metropolis. Chikazumi also served as a prison chaplain.[18] Perhaps because of a shared milieu, two of Chikazumi's favored concepts became mainstays of chaplaincy discourse from the 1920s. The first is the notion of an inner psychological transformation brought about by repentance. Chikazumi's *Records of Repentance* (*Zangeroku*, 1905) offers psychologized interpretations of this classical trope, wherein the traditional Buddhist notion of repentance is combined with a Shin modernist account of interiority to highlight personal struggles of spiritual transformation. In this sense, Chikazumi wrote that "religion is experience" (*jikken*).[19] In the same vein, Chikazumi popularized a neologism for the individual "religious seeker" (*kyūdōsha*)—literally "one seeking the path."[20] These terms are a pair: the initial step of repentance is the mark of one who seeks the path and thus the beginning of a religious awakening. These ideas contributed to the formation of modern Shin conversion (repentance) narratives.[21]

The official history of the prison chaplaincy introduces Chikazumi only briefly and primarily to report the circumstances of his resignation. He was the first high-profile chaplain to refuse to participate in an execution, saying he "could not be a willing party to the murder of a reformed man."[22] Nonetheless, Chikazumi's emphasis on the value of the individual was likely a basis for his crisis of conscience. Although Chikazumi broke ranks, the concept of repentance and the idea of the individual as a spiritual seeker circulated widely in the civil service prison chaplaincy. The popularity of these ideas in Shin circles primed chaplains to receive incarcerated thought criminals as religious seekers.

Marxism, Law, and Religion

Marxist thought and translations of Bolshevist texts began circulating widely in Japanese in the aftermath of the 1917 Russian Revolution. Riding the wave of liberalism that took off during the Taishō period, the Japan Communist Party was first formed in 1922 as a branch of the Communist International and with a membership base drawn primarily from intellectuals and university students. After an initial suppression leading to their dissolution, the party's second incarnation formed in 1925. The party was still dominated by intellectuals, but they aspired to incorporate more laborers into their ranks and to draw in members of the socialist left.[23]

As a response to the rise in "dangerous thought," the 1925 Peace Preservation Law passed shortly before the act granting full manhood suffrage and the dawn of the Shōwa era (1926–1989). The state permitted the democratic process (for men) only after preventing the possibility of leftist parties like the Communists from coming to power through the vote. The Peace Preservation Law made it a crime punishable by up to ten years' incarceration for any person to advocate or organize for the purposes of changing the national polity (*kokutai*) or political system (*seitai*) or for the aim of rejecting the private property system.[24] The law authorized the Special Higher Police (Tokubetsu Kōtō Keisatsu, the political police agency founded in 1900) to target ideological enemies of the government.[25] This agency conducted two mass arrests targeting communists on March 15, 1928, and April 16, 1929; 8,368 persons were rounded up, with 964 eventually charged as "thought criminals" under the Peace Preservation Law. Arrests continued over the following years as more and more individuals (leftists, independents, and members of new religions) were charged either as thought criminals or for *lèse-majesté* (table 4.1).

The Special Higher Police continued the campaign against thought criminals until 1945, and this political suppression has been the subject of considerable scholarship.[26] For my present purposes, the most important fact is that from 1925, for the first time in the history of the Japanese prison system, a huge influx of middle-class, highly educated, and politically engaged youths faced imprisonment. Rather than simply forcing these youths to serve the full decade called for by the Peace Preservation

Table 4.1   Arrests of Thought Criminals under the Peace Preservation Law,
            1928–1943

	Leftists	Independent	Religious Groups	Total
1928	3,426	0	0	3,426
1929	4,942	0	0	4,942
1930	6,124	0	0	6,124
1931	10,422	0	0	10,422
1932	13,938	0	0	13,938
1933	14,622	0	0	14,622
1934	3,994	0	0	3,994
1935	1,718	0	67	1,785
1936	1,207	0	860	2,067
1937	1,292	7	13	1,313 [*sic*]
1938	789	0	193	982
1939	389	8	325	722
1940	713	71	33	817
1941	849	256	107	1,212
1942	332	203	163	698
1943	87	53	19	159

Source: Adapted from Okudaira, ed. *Chian iji hō*, 646–49. This chart is based on a government document dated April 30, 1943. Not all those arrested were charged.

Law, the prosecutor's offices and the correctional system opted to press them to renounce their forbidden beliefs—to convert (*tenkō*) into loyal subjects of the emperor in exchange for parole.

Buddhist, Christian, and Shinto groups were eager to support the government campaign against Marxists. The Conference of Japanese Religions to Commemorate the Enthronement of the Shōwa emperor (Gotaiten Kinen Nihon Shūkyō Taikai) was held on June 5–6, 1928, and more than 1,100 persons attended, including scholars and members of civic groups affiliated with the three major religions. The conference culminated in a joint statement of shared goals, one of which was the extermination of Marxism—a threat to the national polity.[27] The appearance of a common enemy of all religions appears to have provided an impetus for interreligious cooperation.

Religions had reason to be wary of the Marxists. Government persecution of thought criminals happened to coincide with high-profile public debates between Marxists and religionists that took place between 1930 and 1934.[28] A series of articles introduced the debate in the *Chūgai nippō* journal under the title *Marxism and Religion (Marukishizumu to shūkyō)*.[29] These initial debates offered a wide range of perspectives. The philosopher Miki Kiyoshi (1897–1945), for example, thought the essence of religion could be found in the universal hope for happiness. He regarded religion not as a repressive mechanism of ideological control, but as "an ally of the weak, the poor, and the oppressed" proletariat.[30] Others were more critical. Journalist, social critic, and future Diet member Kamichika Ichiko (1888–1981) offered withering criticism of religions' work in the government's thought mobilization campaign. She writes: "Religious workers themselves are to blame for making religion into the slave and tool of the ruling class because they eagerly participate in the government's campaign of moral suasion."[31] Kamichika maintains that the Japanese proletariat toil away in conditions akin to slavery while the wealth produced through their labor is stolen from them. Religions should be helping to awaken the workers to the material conditions of their exploitation, but in the case of Japan: "Whenever religions become involved in political activity, they end up working for the ruling classes, using their traditional powers of proselytization to preserve the vested interests of the rulers. They help to make the proletariat powerless and nonresistant—this is precisely why we call religion an opiate."[32]

She reserves particularly harsh criticism for Shin Buddhism, claiming that the Shin sects became the wealthiest by appealing to the masses only then to turn against the people by serving in suppressive (anti-leftist) campaigns of moral suasion. She concludes that the proletariat should hate nothing more than Shin preachers and prison chaplains exhorting them to work hard in the factories and prison workshops of their exploitation.[33]

Following these debates, two organized secularist movements, the Anti-Religion Struggle Conference (Han Shūkyō Tōsō Dōmeikai—later known as Nihon Sentōteki Mushinronsha Dōmei) and the Anti-Religion Movement (Han Shūkyō Undō) rose to prominence by proclaiming that traditional religious institutions were "the opium of the masses." The former published its own polemic in *Under the Flag of the Anti-Religion Struggle (Han shūkyō tōsō no hata no shita ni*, 1931), with a declared aim of freeing laborers and farmers from the ideological fetters of religion so that they may join the revolutionary struggle.[34] On May 23, 1931, the Anti-

Religion Struggle Conference held a meeting in Ueno, and the press reported that the attendees amounted to more than 1,200 people inside the auditorium, with 1,500 more outside.[35] This high-profile event brought police scrutiny upon the secularist movements, and by 1934, they were suppressed into nonexistence. Nonetheless, the importation to Japan of Marxist critiques of religion engendered a strong backlash among religious thinkers, many of whom regarded the rise in secularism as a threat to both religion and society.[36] As the conflict between religion and Marxist movements played out in the press, the police and the correctional system wrestled with the problem of thought crime.

Administering Tenkō: From Marxism to Religion

The Ministry of Justice (Shihōshō) held a conference for correctional workers in October 1931 to establish methods for eliciting *tenkō* from the growing number of incarcerated thought criminals. The record of this conference indicates that the correctional field approached *tenkō* primarily as a problem of moral education.[37] They hoped that thought criminals would "grow up"—that they would turn their critical attention inward and devote themselves to "self-cultivation" rather than social change. The Minister of Justice Watanabe Chifuyu (1876–1940) informed the audience of correctional officers that the problem with thought criminals is fundamentally a matter of personality development. These "inexperienced youths" have fallen prey to "reformist thought," he explained, and so they do not realize that "each country has its own particular national circumstances." He proposed that the correctional strategy would be to encourage thought criminals to engage in critical self-reflection (*hansei*) so that they might "comprehend the intellectual life of their ancestors and awaken to the soul of our country." The head of the Corrections Office followed, instructing his audience that the primary responsibility for re-education would lie with the prison chaplaincy.[38]

The conference produced basic principles to guide chaplains in their efforts to elicit *tenkō* from incarcerated thought criminals. It was determined that the leftist thought criminals were motivated by a sense of social justice (*seigi shin*) and that this motivation in itself should be recognized as valid and not scorned. The problem was rather the young idealists' lack of knowledge (*ninshiki busoku*). The strategy for *tenkō*, in essence, relied on educating thought criminals to turn away from public issues and to focus on private troubles: "*Tenkō* is to shift perspective away from social evils to the understanding that these are a product of human evil. Fanning the flames of class consciousness will result only in struggle for the sake of struggle. It destroys the peace and abandons the purity of its own motivations."[39]

The strategy for the forced conversion of political prisoners relied on religion—Shin Buddhism specifically—as a means to defuse potentially disruptive political activism by turning it into reflective introspection about the moral failings of the self. The ideal of self-cultivation was promoted as a substitute for political engagement. The invocation of "human evil" over and against "social evil" borrows the language of universality to imply that the social order is natural and therefore just. Injustices in society are not products of social policy or political decisions. They are rooted in a corrupt human nature. For the people in charge of administering forced conversions, *tenkō* was understood to be a matter of substituting an introspective exercise in theodicy for criticism of the economic and political hierarchy.

To bring about this change, prison chaplains conducted both group sessions and individual counseling sessions.[40] In group sessions, thought criminals were taken to the prison chapel where they were made to clasp hands before images of Amida Buddha and listen to the chaplains' dharma talks. In individual sessions, chaplains would talk with inmates about their intellectual journey and encourage them to consider the impact of their actions upon their families and their community. In addition to providing private counseling, chaplains also assigned readings to inmates. For this purpose, the Honganji sect donated books to prisons throughout Japan. Assigned readings were arranged according to a list of prescribed topics covering areas like the Japanese spirit (works by Watsuji Tetsurō, Inoue Tetsujirō), religion (specifically Buddhism; Kaneko Daiei, Shimaji Daitō, Tomomatsu Entai, Chikazumi Jōkan), self-cultivation, anti-Marxist economics, and *tenkō* statements written by former Marxists—for example, reformed thought criminal Kobayashi Morito's (1902–1984) memoir, published under the pseudonym Ono Yōichi and titled *Until I Escaped the Communist Party* (*Kyōsantō o dassuru made*).[41]

Incarcerated thought criminals were separated from each other and forced to spend much of their time in solitary confinement, where they were made to read from this limited selection of works over and over again to internalize the contents.[42]

As these programs became routinized, chaplains developed their own understanding of the thought criminals, borrowing Chikazumi Jōkan's term to refer to them as misguided "religious seekers" (*kyūdōsha*). An unnamed university professor provided them with ammunition for their cause by promoting the idea that the thought criminals were actually motivated in their activities by their confused religiosity (*shūkyōshin*). He argued that these youths saw the contradictions in the world of social affairs as cause for indignation. At heart, they were wrestling with existential doubts, and out of naivete, they became convinced that Marxism was a path to resolve injustices. The professor said that "the question of how best to live is precisely the problem of religion. It is the seed of religiosity, and it leads the heart to seek the path [*kyūdōshin*]." He envisioned a solution: "Introduce them to the world of religion so that they may shift their concerns from social evil to the evil of the self and see the true nature of humanity. Through faith, we can make them establish a new view of life—one that may become the basis for correctional rehabilitation."[43]

The professor and his audience shared an understanding that the inward turn—to shift attention from social relations to the "true nature of humanity"—was a step toward maturity and deeper insight into the world. Faith was imagined as a source of knowledge and virtue. The reflexive turn was seen as the basis for a thought criminal's reform.[44] On the one hand, rehabilitation meant being reformed into a conservative citizen: loyal to the emperor and supportive of the government. On the other hand, the political shift was premised on the idea that chaplains could, through religious instruction, make thought criminals direct their focus internally to the private realm, "the evil of the self" and "the world of religion."

The prison chaplaincy and the professor appear to have shared the assumption that social criticism and self-criticism were somehow mutually exclusive activities. This apparent oversight was in fact consistent with the Shin sects' prevailing understanding of the public-private division based on the ideal of complementarity between the two domains of law. The sovereign dominates the political sphere while religion (Buddhism) promotes morality in the private realm of the heart, thereby contributing to social harmony. In line with this social mission, Shin prison chaplains were responsible for harmonizing the private beliefs of thought criminals with the public good as defined by the political authorities. Chaplains were responsible for turning the politically engaged youth away from social issues and toward private ones. The administrators of the *tenkō* program premised the project on an understanding of religion as a force for social harmony—a mechanism for mitigating against crime, quelling dissent, and upholding the status quo.

Tenkō Statements: Anxiety, Repentance, Conversion, Purification

Matsumoto Hakka, Ishikawa Shundai, and other Buddhist remonstrators pressed illegal Christians to sign certificates of conversion in the 1870s. Most of the Urakami Christians had limited literacy, and remonstrators had no interest in their internal experience of conversion. In the 1890s, the mainstream of Shin chaplaincy discourse took the form of a harangue: Shimaji Mokurai admonished ordinary inmates, telling them that they were beasts. He did not ask them how they felt. In the 1930s, the adoption of the *tenkō* method for dealing with thought crime initiated a sea change in chaplaincy discourse and practice. Suddenly, chaplains had on their hands a wave of highly literate people, many straight out of college. In the context of the *tenkō* program and under the influence of Buddhist modernist literature, suddenly prison chaplains became invested in keeping records of their forays into existential counseling. Chaplains required thought criminals to write their own detailed *tenkō* statements. The *tenkō* statements that chaplains preferred (the ones they circulated among the inmates and wrote about in their vocational journals) fit the mold of the repentance narratives prevalent in the popular religious literature of the day.

The highest-profile *tenkō* was a joint statement issued in 1933 by Communist Party leaders Sano Manabu (1892–1953) and Nabeyama Sadachika (1901–1979) while they were serving life sentences. In this statement, both Sano and Nabeyama renounced the Communist Party and globalism, affirmed Japanese cultural uniqueness (symbolized by the imperial institution), declared support for the Japanese military, and committed themselves to a form of "national socialism" (*ikkoku shakai shugi*).[45] This statement was reprinted in the press and circulated to all incarcerated thought criminals. It opened the floodgates for mass *tenkō*, and by the end of July 1933 (little over a month after the Sano-Nabeyama statement was released), 548 other inmates had agreed to *tenkō*, and the number rose steadily over the following years. In Steinhoff's assessment, by 1935, the Communist movement had been totally destroyed and, with it, the opposition to the mounting war effort.[46]

In the *tenkō* statement itself, Sano and Nabeyama avoid discussing religious issues directly. However, in an essay written in Kosuge Prison (the forerunner to Tokyo Jail) in April 1942, Sano reflects on the change in his thinking. Under the direction of prison chaplains, he spent years "purifying his heart" by rereading Chinese and Japanese classics and Buddhist and Shinto texts. Sano frames his *tenkō* as an act of repentance:

> I realized that the basis for everything has to arise from repentance for the original evil karma of humanity. Only through repentance can one abandon the false pretense of knowledge to be purified through one's own tears. I awakened to the fact that a new start is possible only by returning to the border of the absolute life force in which good and evil are undifferentiated. I realized that repentance was a necessity and that it requires the intervention of a higher power. I knew I had to abandon the arrogant self-love eating away at my own heart because it is the root of all human evil. By humbling myself, I could be reborn as a pure Japanese. I was overjoyed to have achieved my own reform.[47]

This conversion statement from the former intellectual leader of the Japanese Communist Party corresponds to conventions established in Chikazumi Jōkan's *Records of Repentance*. Sano presents himself as a misguided religious seeker who struggled to find himself. After an arduous journey, he realized the error of his ways and the truth of Shin Buddhist doctrine. He implies that he matured—abandoning the false pretense of knowledge and humbling himself. The key step in this process is presented as a turn away from politics (which was still the focus of the initial *tenkō* statement of 1933) toward the internal realm of subjective religious experience (a more subtle and purified level of conversion). He realized, "the arrogant self-love eating away at my own heart [. . .] is the root of all human evil." He invokes the intervention of a higher power. Before he reached this point of surrender, he was tortured, locked in a cell, starved to the point of malnourishment, socially isolated, and subjected to years of reprogramming. Through repentance, he relinquished rationalism, humanism, and universalism to arrive at a total and "pure" ethnocentrism.

In 1923, the Prison Chaplaincy Training and Research Institute (Keimu Kyōkai Jigyō Kenkyūsho) opened at Tsukiji Honganji in Tokyo with backing from both major Shin sects. Its mission was to prepare chaplains to work in the correctional system and to refine their methods. In line with these goals, the institute ran training sessions and published the vocational journal *Chaplaincy Studies* (*Kyōkai kenkyū*) from 1925 (followed in 1927 by the two-volume *History of Japanese Prison Chaplaincy*). From 1931 on, *tenkō* became a frequent topic in *Chaplaincy Studies,* which was rebranded as *Chaplaincy and Probation* (*Kyōkai to hogo*) after 1939. The journals ran essays with titles like "The Case of One Thought Criminal's *Tenkō*" (June 1931), "Mahayana Buddhism and the Logic of *Tenkō*" (September 1933), "The *Tenkō* Diary of a Chinese Communist Party Member" (January 1937), "The *Tannishō* of a *Tenkōsha*" (February 1941), and "*Tenkō* and Its Purification" (September 1942).[48] Throughout this literature, the constant refrain is that thought criminals are religious seekers and, in the words of one chaplain, that "repentance is the absolute condition for *tenkō.*"[49] A 1933 essay titled "From Communism to Religion" by chaplain Futaba Hōshun presents a general schematic for the process of *tenkō.* He describes it as a religious conversion that can arise only after a period of intense anxiety (*hanmon*).[50] Futaba cites one political conversion testimonial from an inmate who describes losing faith in Marxism (*shinnen o ushinatta*) and falling into loneliness and despair after reading Sano and Nabeyama's statement. The chaplain writes that because most inmates are young, educated, truth-seekers, when their faith in Marxism collapses, they will seek another truth to replace it. It is at this point they become repentant and receptive to the Buddhist teaching. In much of the discourse, the process of conversion is described in the language of purification.

One of the most important sources for understanding *tenkō* is *The Diaries of Tenkōsha* (*Tenkōsha no shuki,* 1933). With the help of prison chaplain Fujii Eshō (1878–1952, head of the Prison Chaplaincy Training and Research Institute) and reformed former thought criminal Kobayashi

Morito, the Daidōsha publishing house compiled this collection of ten conversion statements for circulation among inmates. The preface asserts that "life without religion is corrupt." It claims that there are two types of *tenkō*: horizontal and vertical. The text maintains that horizontal conversion is merely a superficial change in political orientation. Far better is the vertical *tenkō*—a fundamental change grounded in the experience of religious conversion. According to this schematic, Sano Manabu made progress in his *tenkō* from the political conversion of 1933 toward the religious conversion of 1942. In line with this vision, the preface presents the *tenkō* diaries as "accounts of religious experiences" (*shūkyō taikenki*).[51]

One of the collection's most moving stories is that of Kojima Yuki, a woman from Akita Prefecture who became involved in the student movement while studying in Tokyo.[52] Kojima's family traced its ancestry to the samurai class, but her father died young and her family fell into poverty. Despite this, she enjoyed a happy childhood and close relationships with her mother and brother. She excelled in her studies and was able to travel to Tokyo to pursue her education. Initially, her aspiration in life was to become a "good wife and wise mother" (*ryōsai kenbo*)—the ideal promoted in public education for women. However, while studying at a women's college, she developed an interest in socialism and then Marxism by reading newspapers and novels.

She recalled being particularly moved by a story about a young mother with a baby who sank into poverty after the death of her husband—a reflection of her own childhood circumstances. In the story, the destitute woman is forced to turn to a life of petty crime in order to feed her starving child. The story inspired Kojima to consider the limitations to the "good wife and wise mother" paradigm that had been the basis of her education. Kojima became convinced that the goal of becoming a good wife and wise mother was beyond reach for many people who were struggling to get enough "bread" to eat each day. In her own words, she realized: "Up until that point, I had been thinking only of myself. I hadn't been thinking about society at all."[53]

She began studying the translated works of Karl Marx, Friedrich Engels, and Rosa Luxemburg. Her interest in activism deepened, and she developed political ambitions: "By myself, I would have little power, but if I joined my own strength to a powerful organization, [then] I would become powerful too, and I would be able to accomplish great things."[54] Within a short time, she became a full member of the Communist Party.

She threw herself into the movement, devoting day and night to political work: "My whole existence was entirely for the party."[55]

In the crackdowns enacted under the Peace Preservation Law, Kojima was arrested by the Special Higher Police and locked in a cell at Ichigaya Prison in Tokyo. She describes in detail how she collapsed under interrogation, spilling Party secrets despite her resolve: "It turned out I was just a weak woman after all."[56] At first, she was wracked by feelings of guilt for "betraying the party." However, after some days in a dank cell wearing filthy clothes, a package from her mother arrived. She opened it to find clean clothes. Without thinking, she cried out, "Oh, mother!" She was overcome by the sense that by pursuing her career in politics, she had abandoned her family. Her feelings of guilt began to focus increasingly on the relationship with her mother, whose letters became her only lifeline to the outside world.

In time, the chaplain came to her offering the teaching of Amida Buddha. He provided reading materials and instruction in the doctrine of the Shin sect. In her own words, Kojima arrived at a new understanding: "I came to know the enormous unlimited love of Amida Buddha through the love that moved my heart, the love of my mother. I came to see the figure of the Buddha through my mother's love. [. . .] Isn't that what absolute, eternal love is? The compassion of the Buddha [*hotoke no jihi*] is the love of a mother made complete and universal."[57]

Just as she had done with Marxist literature before, Kojima read Buddhist works extensively, including the *Lamentation of Divergences* (*Tannishō*, a thirteenth-century Shin Buddhist doctrinal work that became popular in the modern period) and the writings of the Shin modernist thinker Kiyozawa Manshi. She felt she was finally able to achieve a degree of calm, finding in the Buddhist teaching "a quiet world of peace." This inner quietude was accompanied by a political reorientation: "My concerns about bread [for the poor] were completely resolved. I read [Kiyozawa] and felt that fighting over material goods is utter foolishness. I finally understood: no matter how poor a person is, if they live meekly and peacefully [*sunao ni, anshin shi*], there can be no difficulties."[58]

Kojima Yuki was released from Ichigaya Prison sometime before 1934, and she resolved to live quietly, with no more involvement in politics, as an "ordinary woman." The treatment she received in prison turned her away from engagement in the public sphere. Her aspirations for power and political greatness destroyed, she retreated into herself and into the private realm of the home, symbolized by the maternal image. This reorientation entailed denying the reality of the material problem that had inspired her initial interest in politics. Living meekly and peacefully is not a solution to the problem of starving children—but she no longer recognized this problem as something that she might have the power to change. Chaplains circulated Kojima's story to prisoners to motivate other thought criminals to repent and convert. Her tale is representative of the *tenkō* program. The correctional system relied on a combination of social isolation and religious instruction as a strategy for replacing political activism with personal soteriological aspirations.

The discourse on repentance was embedded in the correctional system and applied ubiquitously. In all cases of *tenkō*, inmates had to convince chaplains of the sincerity of their conversion. The imprisoned Buddhist leftist writer Hayashida Shigeo (1907–1991) refused to *tenkō*, and he looked at political conversions with cynicism: "If you could win favor with the chaplain, you would get better treatment in prison, and you might even get an early release. More than anything else, *tenkō* was a matter of securing worldly benefits [*genze riyaku*]."[59] Nonetheless, prison chaplains themselves discussed the necessity of undergoing their own religious struggle in order to be able to tackle thought criminals. Even one of the prominent prosecutors responsible for thought criminals, Osabe Kingo (1901–1991), thought it was necessary to confront the political indiscretions of his youth. He ended a 450-page report on thought crime by confessing to having once been a leftist individualist himself! "This report is a record of my repentance [*zangeroku*]."[60] In 1963, the former thought prosecutor was rewarded for his efforts with an appointment to the supreme court.

The 1936 Thought Criminals Protection and Surveillance Law

In many cases, signing a statement of *tenkō* was sufficient to earn parole. The number of parolees increased dramatically with the wave of *tenkō* that followed the 1933 Sano-Nabeyama statement. By 1942, the number of "converts" (*tenkōsha*) out on parole and under surveillance was 2,888 (2,710 of these were male).[61]

The success of the *tenkō* program led to the centralization of Japan's probation system with the passage of the 1936 Thought Criminals Protection and Surveillance Law (Shisō han hogo kansatsu hō).[62] This law expanded an existing system for monitoring juvenile offenders (in place since 1923) by providing for the protective custody of adults.[63] It established a central probation department in the Ministry of Justice and opened twenty-two probation offices (*hogokansatsusho*) throughout Japan to coordinate with local civic groups, temples, shrines, churches, hospitals, and other appropriate authorities to build a network of supervision intended to prevent paroled thought criminals from "reoffending."

The law created a new class of civil servants by appointing thirty-eight full-time probation officers (*hogoshi*). Twenty-three of these probation officers were drawn directly from the prison chaplaincy, and all of them had experience working with thought criminals.[64] The new Probation Department harnessed the Hoseikai Foundation and its existing network of probation groups, thus inheriting an enormous workforce of volunteer probation officers.[65] One of the most important civic groups specializing in the reintegration of thought criminals was the Teikoku Kōshinkai (founded in 1926), under the leadership of chaplain Fujii Eshō and his protégé Kobayashi Morito, the former thought criminal.[66]

By 1941, there were 971 probation districts and over 35,000 volunteer probation officers.[67] As the number of volunteers dwarfed the number of *tenkōsha*, their work expanded to include the monitoring of all parolees (not just thought criminals). The increasingly robust probation system relied on private sector volunteers to conduct home visits with parolees and to provide neighborhood surveillance, and it also maintained a network of nonprofits including halfway houses (many run by religious organizations). Perhaps the most lasting impact the *tenkō* program had on the correctional field came because the persecution of thought criminals provided the impetus for creating a national probation system for all adult offenders.

There is no exact statistic for the number of clergy among the volunteer probation officers. Nonetheless, Shin Buddhists played a formative role in generating the Japanese probation system. The initial volunteer work was done by Shin Buddhist prison chaplains beginning in the 1890s. Shin chaplains organized many of the earliest "probation groups," and they remained responsible for coordinating with this network of civic groups to arrange placements for parolees until the postwar period.[68] Shin prison chaplains not only stood between sects and the state, public and private realms—they became the gateway between the prison and outside society. Inmates were funneled through chaplains from state custody into private custody (with governmental oversight).

Conclusions

The 1936 Thought Criminals Protection and Surveillance Law harnessed temples and other religious and civic institutions into a network of surveillance. The link between private groups and the state's probation offices effectively reproduced some of the population monitoring functions last seen under the Tokugawa temple certification system. In both cases, the political authorities turned to religious authorities for help maintaining the social order primarily because of a perceived ideological threat posed by imported ideas. In the Tokugawa period, temples were a firewall against Christianity, and in the 1930s, chaplains/volunteer probation officers became bulwarks against Marxism. In both cases, once established, the networks of surveillance proved to have a range of utilities for maintaining rule. The temple certification system allowed the shogun to conduct a census; the connection between nonprofit probation groups and state-run probation offices provided a means to prevent all forms of recidivism (not just thought crimes).

One key difference is that by the twentieth century, Shin prison chaplains were influenced by religious individualism and modernist religious literature. They became deeply invested in the inner workings of inmate psychology. They hoped to document and examine inmates' inner experiences of repentance and religious transformation as evidence for the truth of doctrinal claims. It is perhaps not surprising that a tectonic shift in the nature of chaplaincy discourse (from a one-directional pattern of admonition to a counseling practice based on conversation) coincided with the sudden influx of middle-class, educated, political prisoners who could share with the chaplains not only a class background but also a passion for reading literature ranging from modern novels (like the works of Kurata Hyakuzō) to philosophical treatises (including those of Kiyozawa

Manshi). Here, finally, the prison chaplaincy's tradition of existential counseling begins to enter the archival record in a flood of writings about *tenkō* as religious experience. The *tenkō* campaign heightened the chaplains' focus on the prisoners' psychological interiority, and this emphasis reflected the larger trend of rethinking (and writing about) subjectivity that characterized the mainstream of modernist religious discourse in early twentieth-century Japan. The result was that Japanese prisons—like prisons elsewhere in the world—became an incubator for prison conversion stories.[69] The institutional focus on reforming subjectivity combined with routinized directed writing exercises on the theme of repentance perhaps inevitably yielded a voluminous body of works on the theme of spiritual transformation.

However, even the subjective transformation of chaplaincy discourse rests on a deeper continuity in the political orientation of the admonishers. It is clear that the tradition of rectifying inmates' errant hearts based on doctrinal instruction was prioritized over the work of mitigating suffering (at least in the literature). The essential continuity between the campaign against the illegal Christians of Urakami in the early 1870s and the campaign against Marxist thought criminals in the 1930s was that many Shin Buddhist priests regarded it as their sacred duty to contribute to social order by harmonizing religious commitments with the public good defined by the authorities. In both cases, the admonishers were fighting against state-designated heresies.

Thus, *tenkō* statements see the modern emphasis on the individual religious experience of conversion wedded to the long-standing political ideal of complementarity between dharma and law. The representative statements of Sano Manabu and Kojima Yuki imply that the turn toward religion is a turn away from politics. Attention was redirected to the interior of the self and away from social structure. At this basic level, the *tenkō* statements adopt a perspective (or a lack of perspective) on social issues that is a mirror image of the depoliticized logic of the mainstream chaplaincy discourse the Shin sects created in the 1890s. Chaplaincy theory holds that the source of evil (crime) is always to be found in individual hearts, and the chaplains preferred *tenkō* statements that conformed to this view. Chaplains encouraged the incarcerated thought criminals to write statements of conversion that reproduced the logic of the chaplaincy's own orthodoxy.

In the chaplaincy's vocational journals and in prisoners' *tenkō* statements, it is not simply that religion is depoliticized. Rather, religion is imagined as a mechanism for depoliticizing dissidents by redirecting their hopes for a better society toward private, soteriological goals, thereby neutralizing opposition to the sovereign authorities. The structure of both *tenkō* and the forced conversion program fundamentally rest on the ideal of complementarity between sect and state. *Tenkō* was not just a shift of allegiances from the left to the right end of the political spectrum; for the chaplains, the best *tenkō* involved turning the mind's eye away from the contradictions and tensions inherent in society and inwards against itself.

The question remains, Should the role of Shin prison chaplains in the forced conversion campaigns of the 1930s be seen as a historical aberration or as a logical consequence of the way the chaplain's duties were constructed over the preceding decades? It is possible to approach this issue by asking whether prison chaplains understood their involvement in *tenkō* campaigns as somehow qualitatively different from their work with ordinary offenders. In an essay published in the *Prison Society Journal* (*Kangoku kyōkai zasshi*) in 1918—before the *tenkō* campaigns—influential chaplain Kariya Tetsukō (1874–1960) offers a clear statement of an idea implicit in much chaplaincy discourse. He writes that nonreligious attitudes or the wrong set of religious beliefs contribute to criminal conduct.[70] This foundation paved the way for chaplains to become involved in the persecution of predominantly Marxist, atheist "thought criminals" without necessitating any major adjustments to chaplaincy theory. And what about after the war? I asked a senior chaplain, whose father, greatgrandfather, and mentor had all served before him, for his impression of what the war generation of chaplains thought when they looked back on the work with thought criminals. He emphasized continuity: "The oldtimers seemed to think it was totally normal. The whole country was moving in that direction, and they thought that they were doing their part to protect their communities and their families. They thought of what they were doing as a contribution to the public good. Times have changed now, but to them it was just normal."[71]

The role of chaplains in the forced conversion of thought criminals developed in response to a demand from the state. It so happened that the correctional field's shift toward ideological reeducation coincided with a boom in religious literature about repentance and religious experience. Shin Buddhist priests tailored their services to the prison system by drawing on the resources of their own tradition in line with the ideal of complementarity between sect and state. In this instance, the Peace Preservation Law defined the public good and designated Marxism as a heresy to be wiped out. As they had with the illegal Christians in the 1870s, Shin Buddhist priests contributed to the state-backed ideological campaign against dangerous thought. The chaplains, the Corrections Office, and the probation system aimed to create reformed subjects who would abide by the new orthodoxy defined by the Peace Preservation Law. Shin prison chaplains eagerly contributed to this effort, fulfilling their self-appointed role as defenders of society.

CHAPTER 5

War Crimes and the Discovery
of Peace

War and Peace, Crime and Religion

This chapter examines the prison chaplaincy in the aftermath of Japan's total defeat in World War II and in relation to the broader currents of postwar transformation and continuity in religion's work for the public benefit. The principles of religious freedom and separation of religion from state are enshrined in the 1947 Constitution.[1] Excepting these two ideals, no facet of legal history has had a greater impact on the course of postwar Japanese religion-state relations than the issues surrounding war crimes (*sensō hanzai*). Stated negatively, after the war, with coaxing from the Occupation authorities, Japanese religions reimagined their social role based on opposition to newly conceived crimes against peace and crimes against humanity. This statement inverts a more typical formula: postwar Japanese religious organizations and their ecumenical umbrella groups—chief among them the Japanese Association of Religious Organizations (Nihon Shūkyō Renmei, founded 1946), or JARO—have maintained a near-universal commitment to pacifism and human rights (including religious freedom).[2] This orientation respects the new constitutional foundation: Article 9 of the Postwar Constitution famously renounces war. Under the Occupation, many religious organizations expressed the newfound conviction that pacifism and reverence for human dignity were essential and universal characteristics of religion. These shared commitments became a basis for interreligious cooperation. The idea that religions should work for the public benefit was maintained even as the understanding of the public good shifted from supporting the war to keeping the peace.

I argue that postwar religious discourses about the problem of war and the problem of crime (1) interpreted both social phenomena in relation to doctrinal understandings of the problem of evil and (2) proposed the same solution to these problems: a redemptive spiritual transformation for individuals and ultimately the nation. I maintain that this platform developed as religious organizations and government administrators cooperated to retain a place for religions as defenders of the public good in postwar society. The move toward pacifism and human rights arose together with the understanding that war was not merely a crime, but an existential evil against which religions must protect society. Thus, religious organizations applied the same lens of theodicy to both war and crime, and postwar religious thinking about war developed in a way that was structurally identical to the interpretations of crime seen in nineteenth-century Shin chaplaincy publications. These twinned discourses (on war and crime) continued to rely on the idea that evil arises from the hearts of human beings—from the private realm that is of particular concern to religions. Thus, postwar religious discourses about both war and crime functioned to promote a social role for religion. As in the prewar period, a core component of religion's role continued to be the work of harmonizing private interests with the public good, elevating the morals of the populace to benefit the nation and defending the status quo.

The postwar development of the prison chaplains' role reflects in microcosm continuity and changes in the normative role for religions in society. On the one hand, the war's aftermath ushered in enormous changes. Occupation officials, academics, and sectarian authorities alike proposed that the shared essence of religions was pacifism, and this new universalist understanding of religion took hold. Religious organizations banded together to reimagine their contributions to society in relation to the goal of promoting peace in individual hearts and thereby encouraging peace in society and the world. On the other hand, there was also a remarkable continuity. The idea that religion can help to align the private commitments of individuals with the greater good of the community endured not least because the public-private divide continued to be negotiated under the Postwar Constitution around a concept of religion.

The ideal of harmony between religion and state was thus not exclusive to the prewar Honganji sect's vision of complementarity between two domains of law. To the contrary, the notion that religions could contribute to society by promoting prosocial values and engaging in social work continued to inform religion's role in the postwar period. After 1945, the expectation that religion should remain a private affair while religious organizations should offer some form of public benefit remained intact. In what follows, I first examine the high-profile case of Hanayama Shinshō, chaplain of Sugamo Prison, and his work with war criminals and then outline the less well-known origins of the National Chaplains' Union. I show that in both instances prison chaplaincy was updated for the new era of pacifism and human rights by interpreting war and crime as arising from the same form of moral evil. Hanayama and the National Chaplains' Union (and its backers) invoked the same ideal of individual spiritual transformation as a solution to the problem of evil, envisioning a kind of religious conversion that functioned as a moral rebirth. The construction of the postwar ecumenical prison chaplaincy was one manifestation of the enduring social role for religions as defenders of the public good.

War Crimes, SCAP, and Sugamo Prison Chapel

Supreme Commander for the Allied Powers General Douglas MacArthur (1880–1964) arrived at Atsugi Air Force Base on August 30, 1945, marking the beginning of the Occupation of Japan.[3] The acronym SCAP refers to both the man and the Occupation organization of which he was head. On September 14, SCAP arrested the official in charge of the Japanese prison system, Minister of Justice Iwamura Michiyo (1883–1965), on suspicion of war crimes.[4] By the end of October, SCAP had suspended the Peace Preservation Law and initiated the unconditional release of all political prisoners (including so-called thought criminals).

On October 30, the General Headquarters of the Occupation (GHQ) declared that the Japanese had twenty-four hours to hand over Sugamo

Prison.[5] As arrests continued over the following weeks, Occupation forces filled the cells with suspected war criminals (*senpan*).[6] According to the official records of the postwar prison chaplaincy, 5,472 persons were ultimately charged with war crimes, and of these 920 were eventually sentenced to die.[7]

The prisons now belonged to the Occupation, and a great inversion took place. The 1948 "Confidential SUGAMO After-Action Report" compiled by the Tenth Information and Historical Service of the US Eighth Army reveals that the Occupation authorities were ready to borrow the solemnity of Sugamo Prison's Buddhist chapel for their own ends. Military historian John G. Roos cites this report as follows:

> On the Evening of April 29th, 1946, 26 middle-aged and elderly Japanese filed into a brightly lighted chapel. The distinguished-looking gentlemen seated themselves quietly in pews facing the pulpit and the colorful Buddhist altar. A guard locked the door. This was not to be a religious service.
>
> These were the men who had guided the destiny of millions of their fellow Japanese to the "threshold of annihilation." Kingoro Hashimoto was there, the man who had commanded a regiment of artillery during the Rape of Nanking; Koichi Kido, former Lord Keeper of the Privy Seal and confidential adviser to the Emperor; Mamoru Shigemitsu, once Japan's Foreign Minister and Ambassador to the Court of St. James; Hideki Tojo, the General, Premier, and War Minister who had led his nation into war and down to defeat; 26 men, all former military and political leaders who would be charged with conspiring so Japan might rule the world.
>
> A document was read to them—the most damning ever read from a pulpit. It was the formal indictment of the major war criminals of Japan, a document signed by the representatives of 11 nations charging every man there with murder and with crimes against peace and humanity.
>
> The scene took place in the chapel of Sugamo Prison.[8]

Occupation officials read the formal indictment to twenty-six Class A war criminals in a ritual performed before a Buddhist altar. There is no small irony in the fact that Occupation forces were admonishing the former political leaders of Japan in the same kind of Buddhist chapel where prison chaplains had until recently been remonstrating with political dissidents.[9] This was in fact one of the very chapels that had been at issue during the Sugamo Prison Chaplain Incident when Shin sects mobilized to bar Protestants from the prison service in 1898. Now it served a different purpose. The new political authorities had deposed the wartime leaders and authorized a new conception of the public good. The ritual reading of the "damning" indictment signaled that support for the military was henceforward seen as illegitimate and that formerly criminalized pacifism was now to be promoted. In chapter 4, I introduced Tsurumi Shunsuke's definition of *tenkō*: "A change in thought that occurs due to compulsion by authority."[10] The Occupation enforced precisely this kind of political conversion on Japanese society at large and on religions in particular. Legal and cultural transformations were premised upon the recognition of a new evil: crimes against peace and humanity.

The Shinto Directive: Pacifism Good, Militarism Evil

Within its first few months, the Allied Occupation of Japan imposed a strict separation of religion from state. On December 12, 1945, SCAP issued SCAPIN 448, "Abolition of Governmental Sponsorship, Support, Perpetuation, Control, and Dissemination of State Shinto (*Kokka Shinto, Jinja Shinto*)."[11] This order is known as the Shinto Directive (Shintō shirei), but its stipulations had a wide-ranging impact on all Japanese religions.[12] Jolyon Thomas analyzes the binary thinking underlying the Directive as follows: the Occupation was committed to identifying and destroying State Shinto in order to establish religious freedom based on the idea that the former was inherently militarist and antidemocratic (bad), while the latter was conducive to democratization and human flourishing (good).[13] For my purposes, I want to highlight that the objectives of the Shinto Directive were also tied to *the promotion of pacifist values*. This reading situates the Shinto Directive in the same category of ethos- and era-defining government proclamations as the three teachings of the Great Promulgation Campaign (1872), the Imperial Rescript on Education (1890), and the Peace Preservation Law (1925).

William P. Woodard (1896–1973) was head of the Religious Research Unit within the Civil Information and Education Staff Section for most of the Occupation. In his landmark work *The Allied Occupation of Japan*,

1945–1952 and Japanese Religions (1972), Woodard summarizes the purpose
of the Shinto Directive as follows:

> (1) to free the Japanese people from direct or indirect compulsion to be-
> lieve or profess to believe in a religion or cult officially designated by the
> state, (2) to lift from the Japanese people the burden of compulsory finan-
> cial support of an ideology which had contributed to their war guilt, de-
> feat, suffering, privation and current deplorable condition, (3) to prevent a
> recurrence of the perversion of Shinto theory and beliefs into militaristic
> and ultranationalistic propaganda designed to delude the people and lead
> them into wars of aggression, (4) to assist them in a rededication of their
> national life to building a new Japan based upon the ideal of perpetual
> peace and democracy. An additional purpose was to strengthen the princi-
> ple of religious freedom.[14]

The Directive was intended primarily to destroy what was regarded as the
ideological source of Japanese militarism. Although the title of the Shinto
Directive seems to imply that Shinto was held uniquely responsible for
Japanese militarism, Woodard himself regards the titular focus on Shinto
as misleading. He maintains that the true object of the Occupation's concern was not merely Shinto, but rather "the Kokutai Cult [*sic*]."[15] This
cult was understood as an ultranationalistic and militaristic ideology
rooted in the myth of Japanese racial superiority and the divine status of
the emperor.

For Woodard, the *kokutai* cult was not solely the responsibility of
Shinto, and in fact, the wording of the Shinto Directive itself refers to
religions in general rather than Shinto in particular:

> The purpose of this directive is to separate religion from the state, to pre-
> vent misuse of religion for political ends, and to put all religions, faiths,
> and creeds upon exactly the same basis, entitled to precisely the same op-
> portunities and protection. It forbids affiliation with the government and
> the propagation and dissemination of militaristic and ultra-nationalistic
> ideology not only to Shinto but to the followers of all religions, faiths, sects,
> creeds, or philosophies.[16]

The architect of the Shinto Directive was the Religions Division chief,
Dr. William K. Bunce (1907–2008).[17] Woodard credits Bunce with expanding the scope of the Directive to separate all religions from the state.[18]

Thus, despite its name, the intent of the Shinto Directive was actually to prevent the Japanese state from co-opting *any religion* as a strategy for legitimating militarism and ultranationalism. Seen in this light, one primary aim of the Shinto Directive was to redefine Japanese religious life around clear moral poles: pacifism is good, and militarism is evil.

It would not be going too far to conclude that the Occupation authorities viewed the Japanese state's reliance on religions to drum up support for the war effort as a "perversion" of religion's proper social role. SCAP embraced the assumption that the natural state of religions is found in their shared pacifist essence. It is telling that the architects of the Shinto Directive do not seem to have considered it problematic that American religions supported the Allied war effort. The victor's moral judgment— the view that Japan was fighting a militarist campaign while the Allies were fighting a just war for peace—preceded and informed the Directive's attempt to realign religions with pacifism. The Shinto Directive signaled SCAP's intention to harness religious organizations to promote a certain interpretation of history and the values to go along with it. SCAP expected religions to defend society from the evils of militarism and to contribute to democratization. The irony is that the Occupation administration shared with Japan's wartime regime the understanding that a key role for religions was to contribute to the public good in ways defined by the political authorities. This arrangement had a broad influence over the postwar development of religious work for the public benefit.

The Shinto Directive sent the correctional system scrambling. Although the Shin Buddhist prison chaplaincy was not ostensibly a manifestation of State Shinto, the single-sect monopoly over this area of the civil service appeared to violate the mandated separation of all religions from the state.[19] On December 26, 1945, the Corrections Office issued an order prohibiting prisons from forcing inmates to participate in any form of religious worship.[20] Prison chapels, Buddhist altars, and Shinto altars were to be removed—but with reverence so as not to offend the religious sensibilities of believers. However, one month later, on January 28, 1946, the Corrections Office backpedaled. This time, it was decreed that Buddhist altars could be returned to the prisons to be used by inmates who might *choose* to pray.[21] It was clear that the Shinto Directive signaled the demise of the civil service prison chaplaincy. However, SCAP had no intention of barring religion from the prisons, and prison chapels did not go unoccupied for long (figs. 5.1, 5.2, 5.3, and 5.4).

FIGURE 5.1   Fuchū Prison chapel interior. The prison was completed in 1935. Source: Fuchū Keimusho, *Fuchū Keimusho rakusei kinen shashinshū*. Courtesy of the Japanese Correctional Association Library.

FIGURE 5.2   Fuchū Prison chapel exterior. Source: Fuchū Keimusho, *Fuchū Keimusho rakusei kinen shashinshū*. Courtesy of the Japanese Correctional Association Library.

FIGURE 5.3   Fuchū Prison chapel garden. Source: Fuchū Keimusho, *Fuchū Keimusho rakusei kinen shashinshū*. Courtesy of the Japanese Correctional Association Library.

FIGURE 5.4   Fuchū Prison, third-floor chapel for individual use. Source: Fuchū Keimusho, *Fuchū Keimusho rakusei kinen shashinshū*. Courtesy of the Japanese Correctional Association Library.

The Discovery of Peace: Hanayama Shinshō,
Sugamo Prison Chaplain

SCAP's most intimate involvement with the Japanese correctional system took place at Sugamo Prison. The facility was used to house suspected war criminals throughout the proceedings of the International Military Tribunal for the Far East (commonly known as the Tokyo War Crimes Trial) from 1946 to 1948.[22] Convicted war criminals remained at Sugamo to serve their sentences after the trials were concluded.

At Sugamo, SCAP policy regarding chaplaincy was governed by the idea that inmates would naturally have a religious preference. General MacArthur hoped that the Japanese would embrace Christianity, but there was no overarching Occupation policy for introducing Christianity to the Japanese prison system.[23] However, the Occupation stationed two American military chaplains at the prison (one Catholic and the other Protestant) to minister to the needs of the detainees.[24] These were the first Christian chaplains to serve in the Japanese prison system since the Sugamo Prison Chaplain Incident almost a half century earlier. Despite the aid of translators, these American Christian chaplains faced difficulties communicating with their charges. They conducted a survey of the inmate population to determine the religious preferences of the inmates, only to learn that "over 90 percent" self-identified as Buddhists.[25] The Occupation authorities at Sugamo Prison filed a request with the Corrections Office for a suitable Buddhist chaplain.[26]

According to his own account, Hanayama Shinshō, a Honganji sect Shin priest and University of Tokyo professor specializing in Japanese Buddhism, heard of the opening through a friend. Although he had no experience as a prison chaplain, Hanayama immediately volunteered. He had an advantage over most career prison chaplains in that he could speak, read, and write fluently in English, and his application was accepted without delay. The work was part-time, and he was able to continue his university lectures while visiting the prison several times a week.

Hanayama began visiting Sugamo Prison on February 28, 1946.[27] He soon learned from the American chaplains about their religious preference surveys, and he was surprised by the earnestness with which the

Americans interpreted the detainees' self-identification as Buddhists: "When asked about their religion, those who wrote Buddhist did not do so primarily because of some deep belief in the teachings of Buddhism. Rather, they absolutely could not answer that they were Christians, so it seems that they simply wrote Buddhism because that was the religion of their household. However, on the receiving end, from the perspective of religious freedom, the Americans interpreted these answers differently and with a serious attitude."[28] There was a clash between different cultural conceptions of chaplaincy. The guiding logic of "doctrinal admonition" had been that Shin Buddhism could aid in the strategies of governance by contributing to correctional reform, but the American military chaplains assumed that the Japanese inmates were in need of the services of a Buddhist religious counselor. Under the Occupation, the establishment of religious freedom was a cornerstone of SCAP policy toward religions. Hanayama was employed based on the American's commitment to the idea that inmates had religious needs that must be protected as human rights.

Hanayama provides a detailed account of his work as a chaplain in his 1949 memoir *The Discovery of Peace: A Record of Life and Death at Sugamo Prison* (*Heiwa no hakken: Sugamo no sei to shi no kiroku*).[29] In English, Melissa Curley interprets this work as an engagement with the question of war responsibility and examines how Hanayama draws on the repertoire of the Pure Land Buddhist tradition to paint a picture of the prison as a site of liberation. Curley's reading highlights Hanayama's investment in the idea of "a connection between the absolute peace that the condemned discover in death and the political peace that the living are charged with making a reality."[30]

For my purposes, I emphasize that Hanayama's memoir inaugurates the postwar vision of prison chaplaincy in two ways. First, Hanayama uses his position as a prison chaplain to reflect on the meaning of the war and religion's role in the emerging postwar order. In doing so, he asserts that his position (as a chaplain and a writer) is "religious and not political." This orientation represents continuity with the Shin prison chaplaincy tradition. He retains a focus on "matters of the heart" over problems emerging from the social structure. Second, Hanayama's presentation of prison chaplaincy relies on the emerging universalized understanding of religion as a source of peace. The undergirding logic is a concept of spiritual transformation: the notion is that religion in general and Buddhism in particular can contribute to peace within the individual heart and in society more broadly. Writing in his capacity as a chaplain, Hanayama interprets war as a problem of the heart—a mirror image of the interpretation of crime as a problem of the heart that characterizes chaplaincy discourse more broadly.

Hanayama had his own reasons for pursuing involvement at Sugamo Prison. He declares his intentions in his preface:

> It goes without saying that I am just a scholar of Japanese Buddhism and that I do not hold a political position [in support of the suspected war criminals]. To the contrary, I cannot help but to feel anger from the bottom of my heart about policies from the Meiji period onwards that have been both suppressive of Buddhism and militaristic. Thus, I do not offer my account with the intention of preserving a record of the lives of these men so poisoned by their own militarism. My position is the opposite.
>
> I believe that a record of these people should be made available so as to promote the realization of true world peace and a peaceful Japan. For this reason, I have decided to go public with my materials. [. . .] Through my contact with former military officers, government ministers, and even poor soldiers, I have come to know that even persons living such lives have managed to find through their faith a happiness that is diametrically opposed to war and conflict.
>
> Furthermore, if I did not publish this record, no one else would write such a book. I felt a responsibility toward the citizens of this country and toward history to fulfill a duty, and that is why I decided to write. I have written from the perspective of a religionist [*shūkyōsha*], [. . .] and political opinions are beyond the realm of my responsibilities, so [in writing this book] I have refrained from recording such thoughts.[31]

Despite his disavowal of any political intent, Hanayama's work is an interpretation of politics and history informed by Buddhist doctrine. The unifying theme is that political leaders were "poisoned" by their own militarist ambitions because the Japanese people since the Meiji period have turned against the dharma. The book's objective is to call for a return to the Buddhist values that he claims modern Japanese have foolishly rejected. Although Hanayama rightly assigns war responsibility to Japan's secular leaders, his thesis is rather that the war arose from the spiritual corruption of the hearts of the Japanese people. This narrative of national guilt was by no means original or unique to Hanayama. His work shares characteristics with other calls for "collective repentance" that circulated widely in the public sphere during the early postwar years.[32]

Hanayama offers case studies of his prison chaplaincy sessions with various suspected (and later convicted) Class A, B, and C war criminals in order to suggest a means of redemption. He claims that even some of the former military leaders were able to achieve a degree of moral reform through "faith." Hanayama's vision of redemption aligns with the goals of Shin prison chaplaincy: spiritual transformation arises through critical self-reflection about one's misdeeds. Like other Shin prison chaplains, Hanayama links the concept of self-reflection to the doctrine of karma. He introduces this theme in his account of his first sermon, given to a group of forty detainees charged as Class B war criminals: "After the dharma talk, one of them came to me and asked, 'I have heard that according to Christianity, the things that happen in a person's life are predetermined by destiny. What does Buddhism say about this?' I explained to him the Buddhist doctrine that one must always suffer the consequences of one's actions [*jigō jitoku*]."[33]

The term *jigō jitoku* is shorthand for the doctrine of karma. This idea grounds Hanayama's interpretation of the religious meaning of the war and the defeat. He invokes this concept in order to call for self-reflection about unskillful conduct. In his discussion of individual cases, Hanayama suggests that religious salvation can be realized through such self-reflection and through faith in the Shin doctrine of Amida's saving grace.[34] However, his primary aim is not sectarian advocacy.

Hanayama collectivizes and historicizes the process of self-reflection to produce a narrative of national guilt that amounts to a criticism of State Shinto. He presents this position clearly in an op-ed he published in the *Chūgai nippō* journal on January 1–3, 1947:

> A tradition of thought arising from one group of Shintoists and Kokugaku scholars at the end of the Edo period led this country to the great Meiji Restoration of imperial rule. However, this same tradition of thinking led us to abandon our reverence for the eternal and unchanging law of the

dharma, and it is extremely regrettable that this thinking led Japan down a path that the whole world calls militarist and imperialist.

Of course, the apathy and lack of self-reflection among the Buddhist community is also one great factor in the war, and it goes without saying that we Buddhists must first reflect within ourselves before criticizing others. It is because of a lack of effort on the part of the Buddhists that Shinto was transformed to the point that it became a form of imperialism and militarism. We must reflect [*hansei*] deeply upon this fact, and we cannot help but to feel shame.[35]

Hanayama acknowledges that Buddhists were complicit in the war to the extent that they failed to restrain the militarists. At the same time, he carefully distinguishes between Buddhism and Shinto. In so doing, he locates the cause of the war not in concrete political decisions taken by particular persons, but rather in "militarism" understood as generalized spiritual corruption. It is because Japan abandoned "reverence for the eternal and unchanging law of the dharma" in favor of a militarist ideology that the suffering of the war was unleashed. The implicit claim underlying this argument is that Buddhism is inherently pacifist—unlike Shinto, which is presented as militarist. He asserts this despite the fact that every reasonably informed Japanese person alive in 1947 (and Occupation staff working on religions, like Woodard and Bunce) knew full well that Buddhist sects had been eager cheerleaders for the war effort (along with Shintoists and Christians).[36]

By locating the cause of the war in the collective rejection of Buddhist teachings, Hanayama's mythologized account amounts to an exercise in theodicy. His story works within the established framework of Shin chaplaincy discourse: he situates the origins of evil and suffering within the hearts of the Japanese people and offers the possibility of redemption through the embrace of the dharma. In this interpretation, the way forward for the Japanese nation is collective self-reflection (*hansei*)—a secularized version of the Buddhist concept of repentance (*zange*). Hanayama's account boils down to an argument that the dharma can contribute to peace both within the individual heart and between societies. This is the meaning of his title: "The Discovery of Peace." The term peace (*heiwa*) reflects both the end of war and the transcendence of internal, subjective turmoil. The essential claim is that there is a link between the peace of nations and the peace of the individual heart. Hence, Hanayama maintains that his clients found happiness through faith and not through militarism.

This internal focus on the subjective dimension of religious experience is what Hanayama appears to have in mind when he claims that his work is religious and not political. There are two things to note about this maneuver. First, Hanayama's shift away from political issues to a focus on the incarcerated war criminals' inner experience of repentance and spiritual transformation reproduces the same operation performed by chaplains who, through the 1930s, worked to convert thought criminals to imperialist ideology. Seen in this light, Hanayama's work is a successor to and continuation of the thought criminal "conversion" literature. Second, the flight away from history and into phenomenology could also be seen as a sleight of hand to divert attention from the role of Buddhist sects in supporting the war. One need not look beyond Hanayama's own early career to get a sense of the scope of the issues being elided. As is well known, the wartime regime promoted its favored version of national ethics through the public education system, and the textbook *Essence of the National Polity* (*Kokutai no hongi*, 1937) has become synonymous with the nationalist ideology of the wartime state.[37] The textbook authors remain anonymous as the work is credited to the Ministry of Education. However, Orion Klautau has pointed out that Hanayama played a leading role in crafting an image of Japanese Buddhism closely related to the textbook's presentation of nationalist ethics.[38] Hanayama's own research focused on the semilegendary figure of Shōtoku Taishi (574–622 CE), an imperial prince credited with transmitting the dharma to Japan. Hanayama drew on this material to publish a commentary on *Essence of the National Polity* in 1942 (reprinted and expanded in 1944) where he extolled the defining characteristic of Japanese Buddhism as its "spirit of protecting the nation" and the imperial household.[39] When he published his 1949 memoir, Hanayama washed his hands of these previous efforts to depict Japanese Buddhism as a tributary to nationalism. It is conceivable that he wanted to distance himself from some of his prewar research precisely because many in Occupied Japan would have seen it as supportive of the now forbidden State Shinto ideology. Nonetheless, it is remarkable how quickly Hanayama's presentation of Buddhism's social utility could shift from a laudatory historical narrative about the dharma as a protector of the nation to a subjective and personalized story about dharma as a source of individual peace. Hanayama's changing story represents the broader shift in religions' normative role from wartime to the Occupation era—a society-wide *tenkō*.[40]

If Hanayama sought to elevate his memoir above criticism by claiming it to be of a religious nature, the strategy backfired. Religionists of various stripes rallied against him. A professor from the rival Nichiren sect's university wrote that Hanayama did well to publish a best seller, but he argued that Hanayama's writing was self-congratulatory and lacked any of the critical self-reflection it called for: "[Hanayama] should have admonished himself first!"[41] The official history of the Federation of New Religious Organizations of Japan (Shin Nihon Shūkyō Dantai Rengōkai, founded in 1951) includes a similarly scathing review.[42] Even a former employee at Sugamo Prison criticized Hanayama, depicting him as pompous, disingenuous, and self-aggrandizing.[43] Despite such criticism, Hanayama became the highest-profile prison chaplain in Japanese history, and he contributed to popularizing a Shin Buddhist narrative of collective repentance in the wake of the war.

Hanayama was not a typical prison chaplain, but his problematic assertion of a religious position that stands apart from a political one signals an important continuity in the chaplains' role and highlights some of that position's complexities. Hanayama equates religion with the private realm and separates it from the public realm of politics. This understanding reflects the prewar Shin tradition of viewing the dharma and the law of the sovereign as existing in a relationship of complementarity wherein the dharma rules the heart while the sovereign rules the state. On the one hand, this interpretation invites members of the public at large to consider how they may have been complicit in crimes perpetrated under the authority of the state. On the other hand, Hanayama's capacity to reckon seriously with history is hobbled by his decision to subjectivize and collectivize guilt. By turning inward and away from the political realm, Hanayama avoids attributing responsibility to any particular party or person while rigorously excluding from consideration social or structural factors (for example, colonialism, imperialism, economic exploitation). His religious (and not political) perspective suffers from the same lack of a sociological imagination that renders mainstream Shin chaplaincy discourse so blind to public issues beyond prison walls. Hanayama frames religion as a component of private life, not a contender in the public sphere. The chaplain's characteristic focus on the heart is already on full display in Hanayama's memoir—the first major work representing the postwar prison chaplaincy.

Hanayama's memoir also indicates an important change in direction. First and foremost, his eager cooperation with the Occupation makes clear that Hanayama readily adapted the discourse of the chaplaincy to support the newly established public authorities. Though he retained the chaplaincy's traditional focus on the heart, his most obvious innovation was to articulate an ecumenical vision of prison chaplaincy that bridged Buddhism and Christianity.

Hanayama attempted to translate his work into terms that his American counterparts could understand, and in so doing, he sought to give them a favorable impression of Buddhism and Buddhist prison chaplaincy. He was at pains to convey a message of Buddhist pacificism to the American chaplains at Sugamo.[44] He also went to great lengths to offer mutually intelligible interpretations of the Buddhist rites of prison chaplaincy. When one American prison chaplain asked him to explain why flowers are necessary for a Buddhist chaplaincy session, Hanayama offered a response that is a striking example of postwar religious universalism:

It was March ninth [of 1946]. Chaplain Scott approached me with an embarrassed look and said, "Doctor Hanayama, do you absolutely need flowers? In the Christian tradition, we can still conduct a rite without the flowers."

Some time ago I had made a request of him. "We Japanese can't get our hands on them, but perhaps the American military could procure some flowers?"

At that time, he had agreed to help me, but finding flowers proved harder than he had anticipated. In light of this difficulty, he had decided to ask me the reason for my request.

"Flowers are absolutely necessary. From a religious perspective, they are a necessity. They are not simply for decorating the table. There is a meaning attached to the flowers. [. . .] The candles represent light, the light of human life. We Buddhists would call this a symbol of the Buddha's wisdom."

"I understand. And the flowers?"

"The flowers represent mercy. God's love, the love of the Kami."

"I see. And what about the incense?"

"The incense purifies the sins of human beings, so it is a symbol of purification."

"In that case, I understand. We will find a way to get you some flowers."

In this way, we were able to make offerings to the Buddha of yellow chrysanthemums, daffodils, and seasonal flowers, and the *butsudan* was always decorated. Even if only a little, we could offer some comforts from this lively floating world to the deprived senses of the war criminals.[45]

Hanayama translates three symbolic components of the Shin Buddhist prison chaplaincy session into a language of religious universalism that produces equivalencies between Christian and Buddhist concepts. Candles represent the light of human life; flowers represent the Buddha's mercy, "God's love" or the love of the Kami; and incense purifies the sins (*tsumi*) of human beings. The invocation of life, love, and the purification of sin provides only a skeletal framework for interreligious dialogue, but the assumption of the fundamental translatability of Buddhist rituals and concepts into a language intelligible to Christianity evinces a turn toward religious universalism. This is in stark contrast to the prewar chaplaincy. Since the Sugamo Prison Chaplain Incident, Shin chaplains had rejected outright any sharing of responsibilities with Christians. However, in the postwar period, a concept of religious universalism became the guiding principle of the prison chaplaincy.

Hanayama served as chaplain at Sugamo Prison for almost three years. During that time, in addition to his dharma talks before larger audiences, he also oversaw the last rites of thirty-four men. Seven of these were Class A war criminals (including former prime minister Tōjō Hideki, 1884–1948), and the remaining twenty-seven were Class B and C war criminals.[46] In 1949, Hanayama resigned his post as Sugamo Prison chaplain in order to attend the Second Conference on Eastern and Western Philosophy at the University of Hawai'i together with D. T. Suzuki (Suzuki Daisetsu Teitarō, 1870–1966). The prison management considered asking Suzuki to take over for Hanayama as prison chaplain but in the end opted to hire Tajima Ryūjun (1892–1957), a priest of the Buzan sect of Shingon and a professor of Taisho University.[47] While he ministered to the convicted war criminals at Sugamo, Tajima became the driving force behind the publication of *Testaments of the Century* (*Seiki no isho*, 1953), a collection of excerpts from the personal letters of some 692 Japanese executed as war criminals throughout Asia.[48] Both Hanayama's memoir and Tajima's *Testaments* arose from their experiences as prison chaplains, and each work offers a different reflection on the meaning of war guilt combined with a meditation on the importance of maintaining the peace. Each work borrows the authority of the dead to present an admonition intended for the entire nation.

Keeping the Peace: JARO's Pacifism and the Postwar Spiritual Transformation

Hanayama saw religion as a prophylactic against the outbreak of war. Outside Sugamo Prison, the same logic was applied ubiquitously in society at large. The Occupation coordinated with religions to encourage the development of a robust civil society and to ensure that the social role for religious organizations would be defined in terms of contributions to keeping the peace. As the phrase implies, the role for religion was imagined in relation to both promoting the values of pacifism and maintaining social order. For religionists themselves, the understanding of their social role relied on a shared faith in religion's capacity to effect spiritual transformation—a moral rebirth for the individual and ultimately for the nation.

As part of the broader project of redefining postwar religion-state relations, the prison chaplaincy was reorganized by relying on established methods of public-private coordination. JARO was founded in 1946 to play a central role in orienting religious life around the values of pacifism and respect for human rights. The organization's story in many ways represents the generational "*tenkō*" of postwar religions. JARO had its origins in the wake of the passage of the repressive Religious Organizations Law (Shūkyō dantai hō) implemented in 1940.[49] By 1943, all legally recognized religions (Buddhist, Christian, and sectarian Shinto groups) were organized under the umbrella of the Japanese Association of Religions for Contributing to the Country during War (Zaidan Hōjin Nihon Senji

Shūkyō Hōkokukai). As the name implies, this was a pro-military ecumenical alliance, and it operated under the direct authority of the Ministry of Education.

In the aftermath of the war, SCAP abolished the repressive Religious Organizations Law. Rather than disbanding, the wartime umbrella organization had by 1946 reversed its institutional orientation from a militarist stance to a pacifist one and reemerged as JARO.[50] On June 22 of that year, JARO declared its new principles: "Through the intimate cooperation of the various Shinto, Buddhist, and Christian groups, we plan to actively develop an educational movement so as to contribute to the establishment of world peace by serving to rebuild Japan into a culture based on morality."[51] The association held a major conference on December 13, 1946, to declare their rejection of wartime militarism and to discuss the mobilization of religious resources for the benefit of a democratic and peaceful society. The group's official history, published in 1966, describes the objectives of the conference as follows: "The Preface to the UNESCO Charter states that because war begins in the hearts of human beings, we must work to preserve peace in the hearts of human beings. Until each and every Japanese citizen internalizes the abandonment of war and the absolute pacifism of the new constitution, the Japanese Association of Religious Organizations must continue our dedicated efforts [to promote the message of peace]."[52]

JARO officially renounced religionists' earlier efforts to contribute to the war by reading a statement of repentance (*zangebun*) at their conference.[53] The essence of this statement is that all religions are by nature inherently pacifist and that Japanese religions fell short of their own ethical standards by failing to stand up to the militarist regime. After this statement was read, SCAP's chief religion specialist Dr. Bunce gave a speech declaring that the most significant task facing religions was their cooperation to build peace: "Until each and every person realizes from the depth of the heart that war is evil, there can be no hope for a lasting peace."[54] As we saw with Hanayama above, religious life in the immediate postwar period was marked by the efforts of leading religionists to find a common language. JARO found a guiding principle in the assertion of a common pacifist essence shared by all religions, and SCAP actively encouraged this direction.

The religionists' shared commitment to a belief in the power of spiritual transformation, in addition to advocacy for pacifism and the new constitution, provided JARO with a unifying perspective. JARO aimed to promote pacifism through educational activities like the proselytization of moral teachings (religious doctrines). The hope was that teaching doctrines grounded in the "absolute pacifism of the new constitution" could contribute to rebuilding Japanese culture "based on morality" by transforming "each and every" person. This logic of spiritual transformation relies on the assumption that religion contributes to peace by making individual people more peaceful in their private and public lives. It resonates with the logic Hanayama employs in *The Discovery of Peace*.

Religious organizations were not the only authorities to commit to the efficacy of spiritual transformation. Under instructions from the Occupation, the Corrections Office petitioned JARO for help restructuring the prison chaplaincy. Issued on January 4, 1946, the Declaration of Postwar Corrections announced a new direction for corrections based on the recognition of human rights.[55] The provision declared a respect for inmates' religious needs—while simultaneously correlating criminal conduct with the perceived irreligiosity of the incarcerated. Article 6 reads: "The majority of prisoners are lacking in religious sentiment. One of the foundation stones for the new Japan will be the cultivation of religious sensibility. Bearing in mind the goal of recognizing and cultivating true humanity, religious chaplaincy is to be expanded, and it is to be hoped that the expansion of activities by religionists in the prisons will contribute to an atmosphere of moral rehabilitation."[56]

Prison chaplaincy was not to be eliminated. Rather, the Occupation planned to expand the role of religion in the prisons and to open prisons to a wide range of religions.[57] Like JARO (a private organization), the Corrections Office (the public authorities) committed to the idea that religion could be a source of morality and sought to incorporate religion into the carceral program to harness the power of spiritual transformation for the ends of correctional rehabilitation.

To meet the state's demand, JARO developed a new form of prison chaplaincy based on their ecumenical and pacifist educational platform. JARO's program shares with the Great Promulgation Campaign of the 1870s an emphasis on doctrinal instruction's capacity to contribute to the virtues of the populace and thereby to social stability. This resonance is clear in the *Religions Handbook* (*Shūkyō benran*, 1947), published by JARO and the Ministry of Education's Religions Research Group (Monbushō-nai Shūkyō Kenkyūkai). The handbook introduces the core doctrine for the new prison chaplaincy as follows:

> Broadly speaking, there are two ways for religion to contribute to the elim-ination of crime. The first is to elevate the moral sensibilities of the general society so as to stop crimes before they occur. The second is to reform people who have committed crimes so that they will not reoffend. Prison chap-laincy is this second method of reform.
>
> Originally, the religious heart arises from the realization of the many crimes and evils of humanity [. . .] or through the realization of one's own weakness. For this reason, teaching religion to prisoners troubled by their own serious crimes often leads to a sincere conversion. Throughout history there are many examples of those who are extremely evil, only to achieve some realization one day and transform into exemplary persons the next.[58]

The doctrine applied the logic of spiritual transformation to the problem of crime in the same way that logic had been applied to the problem of war. This line of thought also reproduces the logic of Shin chaplaincy dis-course: evil (crime, war) arises from problems of the heart, and religion is a solution to these underlying spiritual troubles. JARO retained the linkage between change of heart and correctional rehabilitation, but the understanding of spiritual transformation was universalized so that all religions could be seen to contribute to character reform and social sta-bility. The essential difference is that prison chaplaincy's postwar incar-nation is defined by the pacifist Constitution of 1947 and its separation of religion from state and its recognition of religious freedom as a uni-versal human right. In line with this legal basis, specific Shin doctrines recede into the background to become just one viable permutation of religion-based reform. At the same time, the JARO chaplaincy platform retains the principle that the law of the state is righteous and that reli-gions play a part in upholding the legal and social order. The undergird-ing continuity is the belief that religions contribute to keeping the peace by encouraging the private virtues that make for good citizenship in the nation and the world.

I do not claim that the Shin Buddhist principle of complementarity (articulated in the 1886 Honganji sect charter) somehow *caused* these postwar developments in a deterministic way. The idea that the right kind of religion could harmonize private interests with the public good was not the sole driver of historical development. Rather, my point is that even into the postwar period, the principle of complementarity between religions and state, as an interpretive lens, aptly describes the way that religion's social role was being carved out. Religious organizations and state actors continued to negotiate their relationship largely with the shared understanding that religions would be both a private affair and a public benefit. The idea that religions encourage socially beneficial spiritual transformation in individuals became the lynchpin for thinking about the role for religions in postwar society.

Building the Chaplains' Unions: Universalizing "Doctrinal Admonition"

In 1948, JARO established a committee to work with religious organizations nationwide to build a network of volunteer prison chaplains.[59] The constitutional principles of religious freedom and religion-state separation required the new chaplaincy to respect the human rights of the incarcerated by accommodating the inmate population's religious diversity. Chaplains from various sects would be invited to the prisons, they could no longer be state employees, and inmates could now choose whether to meet with prison chaplains for religious counseling or group sessions. However, even as the prison chaplaincy was privatized and diversified, the basic assumptions of chaplaincy programs remained the same.

I emphasize here that rather than rethinking the foundations of the chaplain's role, the postwar ecumenical chaplaincy adapted the prewar Shin Buddhist model of "doctrinal admonition" into a universal mode of religious discourse common to a variety of religions. The postwar model of prison chaplaincy was cast in the mold of what came before: crime continued to be understood as arising from private troubles of the individual heart. This understanding was updated so that religion (not just

Table 5.1 Survey of Inmates' Religious Preferences, 1947

	Number of Inmates	Percentage (*sic*)[a]
Shinto	2,301	2.8 (2.9)
Buddhism	59,122	75.7 (74.5)
Christianity	6,823	8.6
No Answer	11,126	12.9 (14.0)
Total Population	79,372	100

Source: SSKS, 57–58.

a Some of the percentages given in the original chart are incorrect. Correct calculations (rounded to the nearest decimal) are included in brackets where appropriate.

Buddhism) could contribute to spiritual transformation and correctional reform. A wide range of sects produced variations of doctrinal admonition. Mapping their soteriology onto the correctional program, they demonstrated the capacity of their teachings to induce within the incarcerated the desirable spiritual transformation, which was taken as tantamount to reform.

To prepare a chaplaincy based on the principle of religious freedom, the Corrections Office conducted a survey of the prison population in 1947 to determine inmates' religious preferences (table 5.1).[60] Though the Occupation ended in 1952, the work of building the postwar chaplaincy dragged on for another decade. The National Chaplains' Union traces its origins to a committee formed in 1956 to promote prison chaplaincy (fig. 5.5). In 1962, the National Chaplains' Union Foundation (Zaidan Hōjin Zenkoku Kyōkaishi Renmei) was officially approved.[61] In the documents registering this union, the founder and president is listed as Honganji abbot Ōtani Kōshō (1911–2002). This honorary appointment reflects the fact that Shin priests remained the most numerous among the chaplaincy. Many who had been in the civil service chaplaincy before the war were simply reappointed as part-time, unpaid volunteers in the postwar period.

The union registered as a type of public interest corporation (*kōeki hōjin*) out of financial necessity.[62] The legal requirement of religion-state separation meant the chaplaincy was cut off from state funding. Thus the chaplaincy's training and expenses had to be financed entirely through donations. Under Japanese law, public interest corporations are taxed very

FIGURE 5.5   The committee to promote prison chaplaincy, meeting at the Ministry of Justice in 1956. Source: Takizawa, *Nihon Shūkyō Renmei shōshi*, front matter. Courtesy of the Japanese Association of Religious Organizations.

little if at all. In the case of the National Chaplains' Union, most dona-tions came from participating religious organizations or their representa-tives. The first budget indicates that the union's annual revenue matched its expenditures at 1,755,159 yen for the 1962 fiscal year.[63] Since the union's founding, the number of chaplains has grown year by year. The postwar increase in the number of chaplains reflects the fact that chaplains are part-time volunteers and no longer full-time, salaried employees (table 5.2).

The National Chaplains' Union became the governing body of the prison chaplaincy and took responsibility for coordinating with the gov-ernment as well as appointing and training prison chaplains. The union is responsible for publishing the vocational journal *Chaplaincy* (*Kyōkai*, first published in 1963) and the standard edition of the *Chaplain's Man-ual* (*Kyōkai hikkei*, first published in 1966).[64] A number of sectarian and regional unions exist under the umbrella of the National Chaplains' Union.[65] Sectarian groups represent Buddhist, Shinto, and Christian

Table 5.2   Expansion of Prison Chaplaincy, 1964–2020

	Chaplains		Chaplains
1964	1,407	1987	1,640
1967	1,477	1991	1,645
1970	1,492	1995	1,699
1974	1,556	1999	1,747
1977	1,581	2003	1,766
1980	1,565	2005	1,802
1983	1,587	2020	1,820

Sources: Zaidan Hōjin Zenkoku Kyōkaishi Renmei, *Ayumi tsuzukeru shūkyō kyōkai*, 73.

The statistic for 2020 is from National Chaplains' Union (website), http://kyoukaishi.server-shared.com/serviceindex1.html, accessed April 25, 2020.

religious organizations. Among the largest Buddhist chaplains' unions are the Honganji Sect Chaplains' Union (founded in 1958), the Ōtani Sect Chaplains' Union (1965), and the Shingon Chaplains' Union (1963); representing Shinto shrines, there is the National Association of Shinto Shrines (Jinja Honchō) Chaplains' Research Group (1947); the largest chaplains' group representing the sector of new religions is the Tenrikyō Chaplains' Union (1953); and the largest chaplains' group representing Christianity is the Chaplains' Union of the United Church of Christ in Japan (1968).

The development of the ecumenical chaplains' union (still dominated by Shin priests) universalized the discourse of "doctrinal admonition" primarily by setting the model for chaplaincy publications. Nearly every sect with its own chaplains' union eventually published a chaplain's manual.[66] A survey of the sectarian manuals reveals that they broadly adhere to the structure and form of the standard edition of the *Chaplain's Manual* published by the National Chaplains' Union. These manuals include an overview of the correctional system, a history of prison chaplaincy in Japan, a summary of regulations relating to chaplaincy, and a section on chaplaincy doctrine and practice.

Although the newfound degree of religious freedom might seem to suggest that religions could reinvent prison chaplaincy on new foundations, there was no such fundamental change to the doctrine. The chaplains' unions molded their official discourse to the goals of the correctional system, following the Shin Buddhist model of doctrinal admonition, which had been dominant in Japanese prisons from the turn of the twentieth century until 1945. In each of these manuals, crime is interpreted as a form of moral evil arising from disharmony in human hearts. The manuals establish official chaplaincy goals that either explicitly or implicitly rely on the idea that religion encourages redemptive spiritual transformation and thereby contributes to correctional rehabilitation. These vocational guides indicate that even in the postwar period the mainstream of Japanese prison chaplaincy focused on moral edification (as opposed to the existential counseling practices associated with spiritual care chaplaincies).

In an era defined by widespread calls for religious freedom, the prison chaplaincy's most notable characteristic was the degree of its subordination to the priorities of the state and the prison system. This orientation extended even to the point of excluding core sectarian teachings. The doctrinal section of the Shin sects' joint postwar history of prison chaplaincy makes this point eminently clear: "Because the theory of the salvation of the evil person does not deny evil but rather appears to affirm it, it may become an obstacle to human development and social order. For this reason, in the context of corrections, we cannot expound the Shin doctrine of the salvation of the evil person."[67] Shinran's cardinal doctrine of "the salvation of the evil person" (*akunin shōki*) is central to Shin theology. The idea holds that salvation is available to all who have faith in Amida Buddha. Salvation cannot be attained through good works ("self-power," or *jiriki*) but must be sought through faith in Amida's saving grace ("other-power," or *tariki*). The logic is that people who realize their own limitations (the evils of the self) will be more receptive to Shin doctrine than those deluded by a misplaced faith in their own goodness. However, in the context of the prison, because this teaching could be seen to imply an antinomian perspective on prosocial values, it was to be excluded from prison chaplaincy discourse.

Leaving this core doctrine aside, Shin chaplains opted instead to continue their traditional focus on the law of karma because of its capacity to emphasize the necessity for law-abiding conduct.[68] That is, despite their broader sectarian orthodoxy, Shin prison chaplains were obliged to preach about the necessity of good works (self-power) to support the educative model of corrections. Rather than teaching Shin doctrine, they would be expected to rely on the same rationalized version of the doctrine of karma that their forebears devised in the 1890s to prove that their tradition could support the civic ethic promoted by the state.

Postwar chaplaincy theory continued to rely on the theme of theodicy. As a genre, chaplains' manuals invariably offer religious interpretations of crime's existential meaning and of a rehabilitation process focused on purification of the heart. The *Jōdo Shinshū Ōtani Sect Chaplain's Manual* raises the central questions that all chaplains' manuals seek to address and performs the genre-defining exercise. It aims to derive a religious meaning from crime by tying moral evil to an interpretation of the human:

> Day in and day out, we hear of all sorts of crimes and the tragedies brought about through crimes. Sometimes we cannot avoid experiencing these realities ourselves. What meaning do crime and evil hold for our lives? How can we best move forward [given such phenomena]? Whether crimes are perpetrated by individuals, groups, communities, or even nations, when we have encountered them they have come to be opportunities to rethink the root of what it means to be human. If we think about it, crime and evil, rather than being simply one type of human activity, are deeply connected to the essence of what it means to be human.[69]

The questions asked here reflect two important characteristics of chaplaincy discourse. The first question implies the general structure of a theodicy: "what meaning do crime and evil hold for our lives?" The second question is pragmatic: "how can we move forward?" This excerpt answers both questions by pointing to the internal dimension of the human being—"crime and evil [. . .] are deeply connected to the essence of what it means to be human." This introspective turn is at the heart of both prewar and postwar prison chaplaincy discourse. Crime is equivalent to evil, and evil is understood as a component of individual subjectivity. Rather than being seen as a reflection of social or structural issues, criminal behavior is interpreted as a spiritual problem requiring an individual religious solution. It is here that the logic of spiritual transformation applies to the problem of crime.

In the Buddhist chaplaincy manuals, the story is invariably that committing crime is bad karma, and correctional rehabilitation purifies the heart. The *Kōyasan Shingon Sect Chaplain's Manual* exemplifies the approach of the Buddhist sects.[70] It provides a detailed annual calendar of topics for chaplaincy sessions. This curriculum gives a sense of how Shingon chaplaincy might run over the course of a year.[71] For seven of the twelve months, the topic title includes the character for "heart," indicating that the Shingon chaplains, like the Shin chaplains, retain a focus on the hearts of the incarcerated. For example, September's topic is "the health of the heart":

> Human beings suffer from the blind passions of greed, hatred, and igno-
> rance. These do not only injure the hearts of the individual, they also bring
> various forms of suffering upon others by motivating the individual to act
> in harmful ways. In order to protect the health of the heart, the individual
> must cultivate the heart of repentance, the heart of gratitude, and the heart
> of repaying debts. These provide sustenance to the heart. Inmates should
> be instructed to live a lifestyle that is healthy for the heart and the body.[72]

Though the doctrinal framework of Shingon differs significantly from that of the Pure Land sects, the *Kōyasan Shingonshū Chaplain's Manual* makes clear that Shingon chaplaincy fits within the structure of the prison. It does so by providing a doctrinal framework for shaping the private, internal lives of inmates in accordance with the objectives of the institution. In other words, the manual shows that Shingon can do the same work as Shin in the prison chapel.

The Shingon model of prison chaplaincy interprets incarceration and correctional rehabilitation in line with the sect's teaching of the three mysteries—strategies for purifying karma through the cultivation of skillful thoughts, words, and deeds (*shinkui no sanmitsu shugyō*).[73] The October session focuses on the heart and the *gasshō* mudra (a ritual gesture with hands pressed together in front of the chest), and its description reflects the underlying doctrinal principle: "inmates should be instructed to harmonize their bodies and their hearts, as physical form affects the heart and the heart, too, affects the physical form."[74] The doctrinal idea is coupled with the general instruction to obey the prison rules. This is the focus of the March session, which is aptly titled "following the rules": "Rules are meaningful because they play an important role in ensuring order and because they provide a rhythm to life. A life with a rhythm can be a life with hope and ease. Inmates should be instructed to acclimatize themselves to a life bound by rules."[75] The rhythm of the prison institution appears to be implicitly compared to the rhythm of life in a monastery, and the doctrinal framework of karma is applied to this picture so as to suggest that the institution's rules be internalized as a means of purifying the heart. Finally, the Shingon curriculum adds an exhortation to take joy in labor (*hataraku yorokobi*).[76]

These sermons reinforce the program of prison labor by providing a soteriological framework to explain *how* that labor is rehabilitative: working in the prison printshop or woodworking shop can purify the heart, and it should be a source of joy. In the Shingon chaplain's manual, the sect's soteriology is molded to the prison program. As in the Shin model of prison chaplaincy, the Shingon model, as presented in the *Kōyasan Shingonshū Chaplain's Manual*, maintains that the individual heart should be harmonized with the encompassing social order represented by the prison authorities.

The chaplains' manuals of other sects perform structurally identical operations, linking sectarian teachings to the correctional program by interpreting crime in the doctrinal register of theodicy. For shrine Shinto, committing crime is interpreted as spiritual pollution (*kegare*), and correction is implicitly purification of the heart.[77] For the new religious movement Tenrikyō, the crime and rehabilitation process is interpreted as extinguishing the store of one's past evil karma.[78] Christian chaplaincy sessions often take the form of a Bible reading, but a session I attended in 2012 was clearly focused on emphasizing the capacity of faith and Christian fellowship to ensure good behavior: "When you get out of here, join a church so that you don't come back."[79] Despite some doctrinal differences, the chaplaincy theories of each sect share the conviction that violating the law of the state is an ethical transgression. This is coupled with the assertion that internalizing the sect's doctrine can encourage the offender to undergo a spiritual transformation—which carries the social benefit of ensuring law-abiding behavior.

In sum, postwar chaplaincy discourse conforms to the parameters of the Shin model of doctrinal admonition that dominated chaplaincy for a half century prior to 1945. The result is that the diverse range of chaplains' manuals set out official doctrines that continue the Shin tradition of complementarity between the dharma and the law of the state. We might say that the principle has been updated to the ideal of *harmony* between religions and state. The variety of the postwar chaplaincy doctrines were shaped by the course of political events beyond prison walls, but at the same time, the basic assumption remained: the right kind of religion contributes to good citizenship.

Remarkably, what is generally excluded from the mainstream of Japanese prison chaplaincy discourse is precisely what is most often taken as the *essence* of chaplaincy practice in Western societies. For example, most varieties of American chaplaincy appear to fit the mold established by the culturally dominant tradition of Protestant "ministries of presence," characterized by a focus on spiritual care wherein the chaplain's responsibilities are most often framed in relation to relieving the client's suffering.[80] European varieties of chaplaincy appear to share this orientation. In the case of the Japanese prison chaplaincy, where is the discourse about relieving a client's pain (spiritual or otherwise) and the therapeutic focus on personal suffering? The mainstream vocational discourse of the Japanese prison chaplaincy foregoes extended reflections on the need to comfort the incarcerated. Instead, it emphasizes the chaplain's capacity to serve the purposes of the state by effectively encouraging reform. In this literature, the balance of the chaplain's responsibilities is weighted so heavily toward supporting governance that one cannot really see these texts as participating in contemporary global discourses about spiritual care.

Even under the Postwar Constitution, religion's role in prisons is defined in relation to harmonizing the private realm of the heart with the law. The doctrinal section in the 2017 edition of the National Chaplains' Union's manual concludes: "the purpose of prison chaplaincy [. . .] is to promote faith (*shinkōshin*) among the incarcerated."[81] This objective is linked to correctional reform. This continuity reflects the genealogy of the contemporary prison chaplaincy. The fundamental orientation of the new *Chaplain's Manual* is essentially the same as the doctrine in the National Chaplains' Union's 1993 manual—and in the original 1966 manual, and in the 1920s vocational journals, and in the 1890s vocational journals before that. Prison chaplaincy in Japan is in this sense an anachronistic tradition. The official discourse continues to be premised on an understanding of doctrinal admonition as a way to promote virtue. There are changes over time as the political issues of the day shift and different groups become the targets of remonstration. However, the basic operation remains the same: crime comes from disharmony in the heart, and religion is a solution to that problem. Religious teachings that appear to fall beyond the scope of this functionalist framework are excluded from the chaplaincy's official publications. Chaplaincy literature encapsulates the dominant theme of the broader history of religion-state relations in Japan: religions are expected to encourage people to be good citizens for the benefit of society.

Conclusions

In the postwar period, the ideal of religious work for the public benefit proved extremely malleable and thus enduring. The politics were flexible enough to permit the conception of the public good to change overnight (Forget the war effort, support the peace!). This is because religions did not have much power to define the public good (especially vis-à-vis the wartime regime and the Occupation), and they needed to adapt. Just as the Shinto Directive construed the militarist politics of wartime Japanese religions as evil and pacifism as the new good, it also promoted the idea that religion is essentially a force for good (peace). The wartime militarism of Japanese religions thus appeared as a perversion rather than a logical consequence of how their social role had been constructed to support governance over the preceding decades. To the extent that the Shinto Directive reoriented the values of postwar Japanese religions, it did so by obscuring both history and continuity. The postwar settlement established by the Shinto Directive and enshrined in the 1947 Constitution separated religion from state and imposed the American-style value of religious freedom. It also wed religion to pacifism, thereby maintaining the ideal that religions could and should benefit society by orienting the private realm of the heart toward prosocial values. Even in postwar Japan, religions were expected to contribute to "keeping the peace."

In the prison system, the notion that religious instruction could promote correctional reform survived with some accommodations to the new formulation of religious freedom and religion-state separation. The most significant change facing the postwar prison chaplaincy was that

SCAP opted to end the Shin monopoly and to open the prisons to other religions. The chief continuity was that chaplaincy discourse continued to look to individual hearts for the source of evil and to propose religious instruction as the solution to that problem. Influenced by the Occupation's policies, Sugamo Prison chaplain Hanayama Shinshō and JARO expanded this line of thinking into a theodicy to derive religious meaning from the war. Hanayama's call for collective repentance and JARO's platform of ecumenical and pacifist religious education were both fundamentally rooted in doctrinal thinking about the problem of evil. Thus, in the framework for mainstream postwar religious thinking, war and crime both appear as variations of the same theme. On the surface, the chaplaincy was renovated, but the undergirding structure was retained: JARO universalized the Shin model of chaplaincy discourse among Japanese religions. A new chaplaincy developed for the postwar era of religious universalism defined by pacifism and human rights. The role of religion (conceived as a force for good) in combatting crime and war (the forces of evil) continued to be understood in relation to the private realm of the heart. So it was that the torch was passed from the generation of prewar Shin Buddhist chaplains employed in the civil service to a postwar ecumenical corps of volunteers appointed by the National Chaplains' Union to continue the tradition of religion's work for the public good behind bars.

CHAPTER 6

The Spirit of Public Service and the Social Role for Religions

From Civil Servants to Volunteers

This chapter takes up continuity and change in the prison chaplaincy from the 1960s to the end of the twentieth century. Since its origins in 1956, the National Chaplains' Union has been the central network for clergy nominated to serve as unsalaried chaplains in Japan's prison system. The chief continuity with the prewar period was that the structure of prison chaplaincy remained wedded to the government's priorities even though the Postwar Constitution separated religion from state and permitted greater religious freedom. The chaplaincy's vocational discourse maintained its focus on doctrinal admonition, emphasizing the role of religious instruction in the rehabilitation of incarcerated people and the smooth operations of the prison system.

In the postwar period, the tradition of doctrinal admonition was handed down from the prewar civil service prison chaplaincy staffed by Shin Buddhist priests to a religiously diverse corps of volunteers in a way that preserved an anachronistic understanding of religion's social role and passed on burdensome responsibilities without compensation. This chapter situates this passing of the chaplaincy baton in the larger context of late twentieth-century debates about the relation between religious organizations and the public good. It identifies the tradition of "public service" (*hōshi*) work as the key to understand the shift to the volunteer model of chaplaincy. The concept of "public service" underpins the unpaid social work performed by many religious professionals and other persons of public standing expected to contribute to the community by coordinating with state agencies to facilitate governance. The vocational and managerial discourses surrounding the postwar chaplaincy continued to rely on functionalist assumptions about religion as an effective strategy of reform and as a mechanism for ensuring inmate docility. However, the introduction of concerns about inmates' religious freedom and human rights, principles introduced by the Postwar Constitution, also provided chaplains with possibilities for rethinking their relationships with clients and shifting their focus from the problem of crime to the problem of suffering.

Although there was continuity in the normative role for religion in prisons, the new constitution also catalyzed changes in postwar religious life that impacted the chaplaincy. The most significant change was that the postwar system permitted a new level of diversity in religion-based rehabilitation programs. This shift introduced an array of different religious practices as well as sectarian motivations into an arena previously monopolized by Shin Buddhists. In the chapter's final section, I introduce case studies of late twentieth-century chaplaincy focused on Tenrikyō, shrine Shinto, Christianity, and Shin Buddhism to suggest the scope of diversification and its limits.

Religions and the Ambiguous Public Good in Late Twentieth-Century Japan

The late twentieth-century history of prison chaplaincy in Japan was characterized by tensions between the relatively stable tradition of doctrinal admonition behind bars and broader cultural changes in religious life. The crux of the issue lies in the question of how religion's contributions to the public benefit should be conceived in the late twentieth century. There was not a consensus about this issue in society at large, but mainstream religious organizations and government agencies tended to agree that one desirable role for religions was contributing to social work. Beyond this general understanding, though, the nature of the public good (and religion's relationship to it) was up for debate. Should chaplains serve the state (as in the prewar regime) or incarcerated people (as implied by the postwar era's updated language of human rights and religious freedom)? If both, then how? For the chaplaincy, the prevailing balance remained tilted toward the side of statism, but this orientation was tempered with a deep concern for human rights and religious freedom. The result was that the individuals appointed to the chaplaincy were expected to teach *something* that could effectively contribute to correctional reform and order in the prisons, but there was ambiguity about what that teaching should be. In what follows, I consider the chaplains' competing responsibilities as a refraction of ambiguity about religion's relation to the public good in the late twentieth century.

The 1997 issue of the vocational journal *Chaplaincy* includes a panel discussion that provides an expedient means for situating the moral ambiguity surrounding chaplaincy in the larger social context.[1] At the chaplains' conference that year, guest speakers addressed the problem of religion's social contributions by looking to the area of education. The panelists present a study in contrasts. Representing the National Association of Shinto Shrines (NASS; Jinja Honchō) was chief priest of Tsubaki Grand Shrine Yamamoto Yukitaka.[2] Yamamoto lamented what he perceived as a lack of religious education in postwar Japan due to the constitutional separation of religion from the state. He viewed the postwar settlement as damaging to the "national spirit" (*kokumin no seishin*) and asserted that a lack of religious instruction in schools may be driving the rising rates of youth crime. Decrying the Tokyo Trials as unjust and their historical perspective as masochistic, Yamamoto complained that Japan had taken a wrong turn by abandoning the Imperial Rescript on Education, the Meiji-era text on the national ethos that defined the prewar era. In his view, all of these changes amounted to a lamentable loss of patriotism (*aikokushin*). According to this perspective, the job of prison chaplains (and perhaps religionists in general) ought to be to teach a nationalist ethics in line with the prewar tradition.

The next panelist was the head of the social welfare department of the Japanese Buddhist Federation (Zen Nihon Bukkyōkai, founded in 1954) Nōsu Yūkō, a Honganji priest.[3] Nōsu described the impact of the postwar settlement on his own sect to make the case that the prewar system offered no religious freedom whatsoever. He pointed out that the

1936 version of the Honganji sect's scriptures ("our Bible") begins with the declaration that the dharma and the law of the sovereign should be "as two wheels on a cart." The prewar scriptures start by affirming that the sect's role is to support the sovereign. The next document included in this "Bible" is the Imperial Rescript on Education. This is precisely the ethical teaching that Yamamoto hoped to see return to the fore in public life, but in Nōsu's estimation, "None of this has anything to do with Buddhism." By contrast, the postwar version of the Honganji sect's scriptures excludes modern government-authored proclamations about national values.

Nōsu also noted that a similar transformation is apparent in changes to his sect's charter. The prewar sect regulations state that the Honganji organization's goal is "public service to the nation and society" and of course to the emperor. The postwar version, by contrast, makes no mention of the emperor and transcends the national frame, declaring instead that the mission of the sect is "to contribute to the eternal welfare of humankind." Gesturing to the scope of the change, Nōsu said, "it is hard to believe this is even the same sect." The reason for the transformation, he explained, is that the changing legal framework governing religions now admits a greater degree of religious freedom. In the prewar era, the sect's mission was bound to the government's national ethic, and clerics were required to teach the public ethos. In the postwar era, the government is constitutionally prohibited from mandating specific doctrines on religious organizations.

Whereas Yamamoto lamented the postwar settlement as insufficiently patriotic and a contributing factor to the perceived rise in anomie among the youth, Nōsu chose to highlight how changes in religion-state relations enhanced religious freedom to the benefit of his Buddhist tradition. At the same time, Nōsu also noted that the religious freedom of *individuals* threatened the financial basis of temple Buddhism by weakening family ties to community temples.[4] Though Nōsu was able to articulate clearly how the postwar version of religious freedom served the interests of religious organizations by enabling them to determine their own doctrines without state interference, he did not offer a clear perspective about how, under the postwar settlement, religious groups could in turn contribute to the public good. His nuanced and relatively liberal position appears vague on the key question of religion's social contributions.

Clearly, the panelists disagreed about what the public good is and what religious organizations ought to do in its name. The problem of religious education is particularly thorny, because, like Yamamoto of NASS and Nōsu of Honganji, religious organizations and even individual clerics are often at loggerheads about matters of doctrine and ideal sect-state relations. However, despite the disagreement between them, Yamamoto and Nōsu were invited to address a room full of prison chaplains, representing a wide range of religious organizations, appointed to perform a public service. The debate is framed by the idea that religious organizations and chaplains should do something relating to education for the public good—but what should it be? As might be expected, no consensus emerged from the conversation.

The history of the prison chaplaincy rests on a legally encoded connection between religions and the public benefit. Religious organizations, along with private schools, medical corporations, social welfare corporations, and foundations, have belonged to the class of public interest corporations since it was established by Articles 33 and 34 of the Meiji-era Civil Code (Minpō) of 1898.[5] This classification remained in effect through the twentieth century, and religious groups were always expected to offer some form of public benefit even as the conception of the public good shifted. The 1889 Constitution placed sovereignty in the hands of the mythic imperial line, and thus religions' contributions to the public good were typically conceived as work for the emperor. The 1947 Constitution placed sovereignty in the hands of the citizens. The Allied Occupation of Japan envisioned a role for religions in line with the American tradition of civil society, wherein religious groups might contribute to the public good by serving as a check on state power and as a catalyst to democratization.

In 1951, the Diet passed the Religious Corporations Law (Shūkyō hōjin hō), setting a high bar for administrative intervention in religious affairs and granting religious groups great license to operate without state interference.[6] This postwar framework allowed a relatively greater degree of religious freedom than the prewar years as more groups had access to the protections and benefits afforded by legal status as a religious corporation. The general assumption guiding this law was that *the proliferation of religious organizations would itself contribute to the public benefit.*[7] The Religious Corporations Law was part of the Occupation's broader project of encouraging the growth of civil society in Japan by severing ties between state agencies and popular associations.[8]

However, the expectations undergirding this legal framework ran counter to Japan's own history of religion-state relations. Historically, established Buddhist, Shinto, and Christian groups had competed with one another for the prestige associated with closer ties to state agencies, rarely attempting (with the exception of some notable Christians) to restrain the state on matters not directly related to private sectarian interests.[9] The combination of the Occupation's aspirations for religions and Japan's own tradition of religions' support for statism created a conundrum. The postwar framework for religion-state relations officially renounces the prewar statist orientation, but in doing so, it left the precise nature of Japanese religions' expected contributions to the public good relatively undefined in either law or vernacular discourse.[10] If not the emperor or their own narrow sectarian interests, then whom or what should religions serve? And how?

Through the latter half of the twentieth century, religious organizations enjoyed relatively lax oversight from the state, an array of tax benefits, and generally favorable public opinion until the first decade of the Heisei era (1989–2019). The situation changed after the small religious group Aum Shinrikyō (founded in 1984) was involved in a series of crimes culminating in a sarin gas attack on the Tokyo subway system in March 1995.[11] The Aum incidents catalyzed profound changes in both the legal framework governing religions and popular perceptions of religious organizations and their adherents. Public opinion of religion declined sharply, as did participation in religious organizations.[12] In the winter of 1995, the ruling coalition for the first time revised the Religious Corporations Law to increase the scope of state oversight for religions' financial dealings and membership lists.[13] These changes backpedaled on the assumption that religious organizations would necessarily and naturally contribute to the public benefit and introduced the idea that *the public would benefit from state monitoring of religions along the lines of consumer protection*.[14] The revised Religious Corporations Law to some degree marked a return to stricter scrutiny of religions, and many began to question whether religions actually contribute to the public good at all.[15] It was in the aftermath of the Aum affair that the National Chaplains'

Union hosted a panel on the relationship between religions and education in connection to the broader theme of religions' contributions to the public good.

The secretary general of the ruling Liberal Democratic Party, Katō Kōichi, admitted that the revised Religious Corporations Law amounted to an attempt to limit the influence of religions over public policy: "It's okay for religious organizations to be interested in politics, especially issues like *human rights, peace, and social welfare*, but when they try to get into the core of public power, it's another story."[16] As is well known, the law targeted not just Aum, but also the powerful new religious movement Sōka Gakkai and its affiliated political party, the Kōmeitō. In some ways, the political activism of the Sōka Gakkai membership might be taken as exemplifying the Occupation's vision for religions to participate vigorously in the public sphere in ways that could check state power.[17] However, if the 1951 Religious Corporations Law represents the Occupation's aspirations for religions to serve the public good as politically engaged actors in civil society, then the 1995 revisions to the law appear to amount to a repudiation of these assumptions about religion's social role.[18] When Katō acknowledged that religions should maintain their "interest" in social welfare, he was in fact recognizing a tradition with a longer history than religion's postwar investments in peace and human rights. From the first decades of the twentieth century, the state insisted that groups aspiring to the status of legally recognized religious organization demonstrate their capacity to contribute to social welfare on terms more or less dictated by the government authorities.[19] In the long arc of religion-state relations in twentieth-century Japan, the normative expectation for religions to work for the public benefit in the area of social work has been an important continuity.

Ambiguity about the relationship between religions and the public good in late twentieth-century Japan impacted the prison chaplaincy because chaplains were sandwiched between the old settlement of that relationship (represented by Yamamoto's view of religions as a means to promote nationalist ethics) and the new (Nōsu's vision of religious freedom, with its incumbent fuzziness about the question of religion's social contributions). As the chaplains' conference panel on education suggests, prison chaplains were expected to offer a teaching that could benefit society. But in the context of a religiously diverse volunteer chaplaincy, what should chaplains teach without falling back on prewar ideas about national essence and national spirit?

The social role for religions and the nature of the public good remain topics of debate in contemporary Japan, and there is no central authority capable of enforcing a hegemonic vision on these areas of public life. Nonetheless, the case of the prison chaplaincy shows that expectations for religions to contribute to the public benefit authorized and even required clerics to undertake certain actions in the name of the public good. The next two sections explore how this arrangement worked in practice. I consider first the late twentieth-century history of the National Chaplains' Union to show that the chaplaincy baton was passed down in the name of the public service ideal. Second, I turn to the details of administration, professional protocols, and vocational training materials to discern specific ideas about how religions ought to yield a public benefit. What is remarkable is that the expectations and arrangements surrounding religion's work in prisons consistently run counter to the Occupation's ideal of religions as civil society groups that should operate outside the sphere of political authority. Instead, there is at work an undergirding functionalist logic that, in true Durkheimian fashion, understands religions as a kind of social glue to ensure the stability of society. The guiding assumption behind prison chaplaincy has always been that religions are meant to contribute to the public good by facilitating governance.

The Ideal of Public Service vs. Separation of Religions from State

The role of religion in prisons remained relatively constant throughout the twentieth century even as the religion-state relationship beyond the prison walls transformed. This tension can be indexed to the way prison chaplaincy developed under the postwar framework that required religion-state separation but also continued to embrace public-private partnerships between government agencies and religious organizations particularly in the field of social welfare. In line with the prewar tradition, state and local bureaucracies coordinated with religious groups or their members to provide social services, including nursery schools, orphanages, elder care

facilities, volunteer probation officers, and prison chaplains.[20] Under the
Postwar Constitution, sects could no longer be legally required to teach a
nationalist doctrine, and the state could no longer employ religious workers
to serve as prison chaplains nor fund religious instruction in the prisons.
Nonetheless, a wide range of religious organizations including Buddhist
temples, Shinto shrines, Christian churches, and new religions like Tenrikyō
remained committed to the ideal of public service. The postwar chaplaincy developed under this rubric as one face of religious work for the
public good.

The first edition of the postwar vocational journal *Chaplaincy* appeared in 1963 bearing the proceedings of the Ninth National Chaplains' Conference and commemorating the National Chaplains' Union's
official approval as a foundation (a type of public interest corporation) in
November of the previous year. The guest of honor was Nobuhito, Prince
Takamatsu (1905–1987), and Diet members, from both the Upper House
and the Lower House, inaugurated the meeting with congratulatory remarks. The head of the Upper House, Shigemune Yūzō (1894–1976), proclaimed that the work of proselytizing to the incarcerated and pursuing
their salvation and reform would be critical to preserving social order and
advancing the public welfare. Shigemune described the prison chaplaincy
as a form of service to society (*shakai hōshi*) rooted in the spirit of faith
and love.[21]

Subsequent editions of *Chaplaincy* similarly included the opening remarks from that year's annual conference. In nearly every year between
1963 and 2007, the transcribed opening remarks follow along the same
lines, with a range of public figures voicing their ongoing support for the
National Chaplains' Union. Regular conference attendees included representatives of government, religions, and the business sector. Head of the
Honganji sect Ōtani Kōshō (1911–2002) served as honorary president of
the National Chaplains' Union from 1962 until he retired in 1996, and
he appeared annually to inaugurate the chaplains' meetings with words
of encouragement.[22] His successor Ōtani Kōshin (b. 1945) filled this role
thereafter and was still president of the National Chaplains' Union as of
2016. Representatives from the Ministry of Justice and the Corrections
Office regularly attended and similarly offered thanks on behalf of the
state. Leaders of JARO offered words of gratitude on behalf of religions,
and representatives of the powerful economic lobbying group the Fed-

eration of Economic Organizations (Keidanren, founded in 1946) sometimes made an appearance on behalf of the business sector to acknowledge the chaplains' work. Each year, some chaplains were selected to receive
commendations from the Ministry of Justice.

Year after year, these ceremonies provided an occasion for public and
private authorities to honor the chaplains. The cumulative message was
always that chaplains perform a much-needed public service and deserve
recognition from society for their "dedicated work for the public good."
Despite the chaplains being honored in this way, one primary implication of the term "public service" is that the work is unpaid. In the first
edition of *Chaplaincy*, the closing pages include a transcript of a conversation in the Diet about chaplaincy funding. The Minister of Justice
Nakagaki Kunio (1911–1987) declared that chaplains' work is an important public service, but impossible to fund under the constitution. He
noted that the government was thinking about how best to cover their
train fare and other travel expenses.[23] Ultimately, these minimal reim-
bursements became the standard arrangement.

Contemporary chaplains sometimes refer to what they do as "volunteering" (using the *katakana* pronunciation *borantia*), but the more
precise term is *hōshi* (奉仕), or "public service." This concept has a long
history that predates contemporary forms of volunteering, and the historical meaning of this compound is "to offer up one's services to one's
lord." The word was used to describe obligatory works performed as
thanks to the benevolent rulers. In a study of volunteering in Japan,
Nichole Georgeou writes:

> [*Hōshi*] embodies a strong sense of obligation and is characterized by no-
> tions of service and sacrifice, particularly dedicated service to the greater
> good of the Emperor and state. The cultural context from which *hōshi*
> emerged included: the hierarchical organization of society, a social system
> of interdependent social relationships associated with personal obligations
> to family, village and state, and *on*[,] the moral system upon which Japa-
> nese society was based where kindness and goodwill were used to create a
> sense of indebtedness.[24]

This concept differs from volunteering in some key respects. First, where
volunteering tends to imply individual agency and the ideal of participation

in the voluntary associations of civil society, *hōshi* evokes connections to kinship groups, neighborhood groups, or religious organizations that function like extended family networks rather than voluntary associations. Second, where the term volunteering highlights volition and time and effort "beyond the call of duty," *hōshi* entails obligation and *is* itself a call of duty. The "spirit of public service," then, is not solely a matter of private and personal motivations to do good works for the community (though it can be that as well); it also gestures to the long-standing tradition according to which private interests must be subordinated to the public good. The catch, of course, is that what constitutes the public good is never conceived in an entirely democratic way; superiors can leverage a notion of public service over their subordinates to get people to take on work "in the name of the organization."

When Japanese prison chaplains describe their work as "volunteering," they have in mind the fact that the position is unpaid work for the public good. Although I adhere to the convention of referring to the postwar prison chaplains as volunteers to distinguish them from their civil service predecessors, it is more precise (though long-winded) to say that the clerics who make up the postwar Japanese prison chaplaincy have been *appointed* to provide a public service without expectation of remuneration. One senior chaplain expressed his own experience as follows: "I know there are various opinions about this issue, but in my case, it was the sect that appointed me to the chaplaincy. [. . .] We are not civil servants, so it is not like we have a duty to listen to what the state tells us to do. The group to which I will belong for my whole life and which I could never leave is the sect. The sect is stable, and they are the ones who have asked me to do this [work]. So we might say that the Ministry of Justice and the sect gave birth to the prison chaplaincy."[25]

The prison chaplaincy is one of the many appointed public service positions that are characteristic of social work in Japan. In the prewar period, district commissioners (*hōmen iin*) were appointed as unpaid social workers to conduct social surveys and to try to improve the morals and living standards of their poorer neighbors.[26] In the postwar era, there were a wide range of bureaucracy-appointed (*gyōsei ishoku*) positions overseen by state agencies or municipalities.[27] A prime example is the welfare commissioner (*minsei iin*) system that relies on "voluntary" labor of persons selected to provide social services such as elder care.[28] As Sheldon Garon notes, "The impact of millions of volunteers on the provision of social services cannot be underestimated. [. . .] Japanese volunteers and welfare commissioners continue to perform many of the tasks done by paid social workers elsewhere."[29] The result is that the Japanese state can avoid increasing welfare expenditures by relying on labor provided by a pool of private "volunteers" appointed to provide public service without pay.

Prison chaplains are one of the three broad categories of *appointed* volunteers whose labor was (and still is) integral to the correctional rehabilitation system. The other two are volunteer prison visitors (*tokushi mensetsu iin*) and volunteer probation officers (VPOs; *hogoshi*).[30] Volunteer prison visitors are a diverse group whose numbers include educators, lawyers, clergy, therapists, teachers of the arts (tea, ikebana, dance, music), retirees, housewives, and others nominated to visit inmates in service to the goals of correctional education. As of 2020, the website of the volunteer prison visitors' union reports that there are nearly 1,800 members nationwide.[31] The volunteers' primary goal, unlike that of prison chaplains, is unconnected to the religious education of the incarcerated. Rather, they are often in charge of club activities in the prisons (for example, a class in *rakugo*, Japanese comic monologue). VPOs are unpaid appointees who are responsible to coordinate with full-time probation officers (civil servants) throughout Japan to monitor those released from prison and to facilitate their social reintegration at the neighborhood level.[32] It is not uncommon for religious professionals to be nominated as VPOs, and many sects maintain unions for VPOs alongside their chaplains' unions. In 1999, out of a total 48,815 VPOs, the largest group were housewives (6,908), followed by people working in agriculture (6,543), then retirees (5,875), and then religious professionals (5,373).[33] In some cases, clergy have been appointed to serve as both prison chaplains and VPOs. All three of these appointed civilian positions surrounding the correctional system are forms of unpaid public service work, or *hōshi*.

Between 1956, when the National Chaplains' Union was founded, and 2016, four to six generations of chaplains had worked at most prisons, and two men had served in the role of honorary president. As of 2006, five chaplains had served terms as chair of the union's board.[34] Compared with the prewar civil service chaplaincy, the postwar volunteer chaplaincy is characterized by much longer terms. In the prewar era, it was typical for salaried Shin Buddhist chaplains to serve for three to five years in the civil service (though some exceptional people made a career of it).[35] Most of these prison chaplains were younger Buddhist priests awaiting reassignment to more prestigious posts, and it is likely that many would have left the chaplaincy when they returned home to inherit the stewardship of their family temples after their fathers retired or passed away.

Under the postwar public service model, it became relatively common for chaplains to serve for a lifetime. For example, to commemorate its twenty-fifth anniversary in 1982, the National Chaplains' Union published the names (and ages) of 230 individuals who had served over twenty-five years.[36] Many on the list had been appointed during the Occupation era, and many were in their seventies. In the union's fiftieth anniversary publication from 2006, the former chairman Watanabe Fusō recalled that he had been appointed to serve as death row chaplain at Tokyo Jail (the institutional successor to both Kosuge Prison and Sugamo Prison) in 1959.[37] He continued to serve until his death in 2012.[38] My own acquaintance, Hirano Shunkō, was appointed to serve as death row chaplain at Tokyo Jail based on Watanabe's recommendation in 1981, and as of 2020, Hirano is still active. According to a Tokyo Jail chaplains roster published in 1974, of 16 individuals who had served there in the postwar era, 10 were still on duty (including Watanabe); and these 10 represented a range of religions: Catholicism (2), Protestant churches (3), the Nichiren sect (2), and the Shin sects (3).[39] At this particular institution, the lineage of Shin Buddhist chaplains since 1945 runs as follows: Suwa Jikyō (appointed in 1948), Shinoda Tatsuo (1953), Watanabe Fusō (1959), and Hirano Shunkō (1981). Hirano is thus the fourth-generation Shin chaplain to serve at Tokyo Jail as part of the postwar volunteer chaplaincy based on the ideal of public service.

Since the abolition of the civil service prison chaplaincy under the 1947 Constitution's separation of religions from state, sectarian organizations or their representatives have coordinated with the correctional system to nominate clergy members to work as prison chaplains without pay. The postwar restructuring of the prison chaplaincy replaced a branch of the civil service with a corps of volunteers who operated on the same basis as bureaucratically appointed district commissioners (prewar), welfare commissioners (postwar), volunteer probation officers, and volunteer prison visitors. Between 1956 and 2007, the state managed to extract a half century of labor from chaplains in the prisons without paying wages. Seen in this light, the constitutional principle of religion-state separation appears to have proved flexible enough to permit the state's continued reliance on religious workers' labor while simultaneously allowing the state's avoidance of remuneration. The annual ceremonies honoring the chaplains doubtless function to convey the message that the work is an honor and thus reward enough. Many chaplains doubtless agreed—but the work was certainly not lucrative.

In the late twentieth century, even as religions' relationship to the public good came under increasing suspicion, public and private authorities continued to recognize religions' public service work to be an important form of social contribution. If the 1951 Religious Corporations Law was rooted in the Occupation's view of religions as civil society groups that should operate separately from the state, then the reality of the tradition of public service ran counter to this ideal. Religions' public service work has been deeply connected to the state. Moreover, appointment to the prison chaplaincy had an obligatory character, suggesting that the National Chaplains' Union was not so much a private voluntary association as a semigovernmental body that harnessed sectarian organizations' leverage over their clergy to obtain human resources for government projects. The tradition of religious public service work represents a de facto entanglement of religions with the government in a way that appears to test the limits of the de jure requirement for religion-state separation. The fact that religions' public service work has always been recognized as a social contribution—even in an era when religions' prosocial credentials have come into doubt—appears to correlate with the intimate connections between religions and state in the area of social work.

Religious Freedom for Prisoners vs. Religious Functionalism for the Management

Under the 1947 Constitution, the legal rationale for the provision of chaplaincy services is based on a concern with inmates' constitutionally guaranteed rights to religious freedom. However, in vocational literature and managerial discourses about chaplaincy, there is also a ubiquitous functionalist logic that underwrites chaplaincy activities by drawing connections between religious education and the goals of correctional reform and institutional order. The language of human rights that characterizes postwar chaplaincy discourse coexists with an enduring statist understanding of religion's work for the public good in the prisons. As a result, compared with their prewar forebears, the postwar volunteer chaplains saw a greater ambiguity in the balance of the chaplain's responsibilities to the state on the one hand and to their incarcerated clients on the other.

It seems appropriate to begin with the operative definition of chaplaincy. As recently as 1993, the *Chaplain's Manual* of the National Chaplains' Union defined prison chaplaincy with reference to the agenda of the state:

> The term prison chaplaincy refers to the totality of psychological, ethical, and religious instruction activities carried out for the incarcerated in prisons and juvenile institutions. In short, these prison chaplaincy activities appeal to the metaphysical spirit that is the foundation of the human to provide reeducation for a legally prescribed period and thereby to encourage an inmate's return to society.[40]

The definition focuses on the purpose and effects of prison chaplaincy. The objective is to harness the "metaphysical spirit" and "the foundation of the human" for the aims of correctional reform. It bears noting what is absent from this definition. First, it does not mention anything resembling spiritual care, and it makes no reference to medical language or the problem of suffering (all features that appear frequently in the discourse of spiritual care chaplaincies in, for example, the West). Second, although the manual elsewhere discusses religious freedom and religion-state separation as important concerns, these terms actually do not appear in the definition of chaplaincy itself.[41] Here, the role of religion in prison is defined in a fundamentally didactic way as "instruction activities [. . .] to provide reeducation" for prisoners. This definition appears in the nonsectarian vocational manual that the National Chaplains' Union issues to all persons assigned to the chaplaincy. It relies on the same logic of spiritual transformation as a solution to crime that characterized chaplaincy discourse in the immediate postwar period, described in chapter 5. The official understanding of the chaplain's role thus appears to have shifted little between the 1960s and the new millennium. For the prison chaplaincy, the late twentieth century was not nearly as dynamic as the late nineteenth century.

The fact that prison chaplains' prescribed role relies on a functionalist interpretation of religion reflects a deeper logic that informs the legal framework governing religions in Japan. In 1977, the Supreme Court ruled that the city of Tsu, in Mie Prefecture, did not violate the constitutional separation of religion from state in using government money to hire a Shinto priest to conduct a grounds pacification rite (*jichinsai*). The precise details of the *Tsu City Shinto Groundbreaking Ceremony Case* (hereafter, *Tsu*) are less relevant than the verdict. The Supreme Court held that the complete separation of religion from state was not viable because:

> Religion involves more than private, personal belief; it is accompanied by a broad array of external social aspects and thus comes into contact with many sectors of social life, including education, social welfare, culture, and folk customs. As a natural result of this contact, the State cannot avoid association with religion as it regulates social life or implements policies to subsidize and support education, social welfare, or culture. Thus, complete separation between religion and State is virtually impossible in an actual system of government. [. . .] From this perspective, the principle of religion-State separation [. . .] demands that the State be religiously neutral but does not prohibit all connection of the State with religion. Rather, it should be interpreted as prohibiting conduct that brings about State connection with religion only if that connection exceeds a reasonable standard determined by consideration of the conduct's purpose and effects in the totality of the circumstances.[42]

The legal precedent derived from this verdict is known as the "purpose and effects standard" (*mokuteki kōka kijun*), and it represents a means for determining whether a particular instance of state involvement with religion is constitutional.[43] This standard holds that the government may support certain religious activities so long as the *purpose* of such support is secular and the *effects* of the same do not amount to the promotion of one religion above others or the suppression of any particular religion.[44]

The verdict in this landmark case includes a consideration of various examples of involvement between religions and the state that are deemed to meet the requirements of the purpose and effects standard. In this discussion, the court touches directly upon prison chaplaincy, declaring that chaplains' involvement in the prison system must be constitutional because the state's responsibility to ensure the religious freedom of its citizens must be balanced against the constitutional requirement for religion-state separation: "to prohibit all prison chaplaincy activities of a religious nature would severely restrict inmates' freedom of worship."[45] Thus, prison chaplaincy activities are deemed constitutional along the lines that the state's *purpose* for providing them is to uphold the religious freedom of incarcerated individuals. Hence, according to the purpose and effects standard, the provision of prison chaplaincy is constitutional because it serves primarily to protect religious freedom (even if it results secondarily in some degree of entanglement between religion and state). The verdict also clarifies that connections between the state and religious organizations in the fields of social welfare are unavoidable.

The purpose and effects standard relies on a functionalist approach to governing religion according to which state authorities have the responsibility to make judgments about the social and legal effects that their decisions will have on religions. The court considers prison chaplaincy only for the purpose of upholding its constitutionality. Its discussion focuses on the impact that the law may have on religion. In this legal framing, religion is constructed as if it were a measurable and manageable social force with powers that can be attenuated or amplified based on state actions: religion leaves a trace, and it can be curtailed or set free.

What is most interesting is that the functionalist logic surrounding the administration of religion actually extends deeper than the court's considerations suggest. The purpose and effects standard is applied to judge not only state actions or laws that may impact religion. The managerial discourse of the prisons relies on the same logic of purpose and effects to judge also the *application* of religion in the carceral system. *The focus of the administrative discourse is on the impact that religion may have on the correctional system and on the public good.* We have already seen this logic at work in the official definition of chaplaincy cited above, wherein chaplaincy's purpose is described as "encourag[ing] an inmate's return to society." In vocational discourse, the definitional purpose and effects of prison chaplaincy in situ are fundamentally didactic—and thus distinct from those supplied in the *Tsu* verdict's assessment of the constitutional-

ity of chaplaincy activities (where the purpose of protecting religious freedom appears paramount). Scaling down from the level of law to the administration of chaplaincy further highlights the widespread application
of a functionalist logic guiding the provision of chaplaincy services.
There is more to the story than a concern with the religious freedom of
prisoners.

The extent to which functionalist assumptions shape the role of the
prison chaplain was brought to my attention at the very first meeting of
the *Chaplain's Manual* revision committee that I attended in 2014. In the
introduction, I mentioned briefly that the chair of this meeting circulated
a clipping featuring an interview with the former head of the Corrections
Office, Nakao Bunsaku, to introduce the basic principles of the prison
chaplaincy. In this interview (published in 1987), Nakao offered his perspective on the multilayered purposes of the prison chaplaincy. Nakao's
functionalist interpretation of religion as a strategy of reform makes sense
in the larger context of managerial discourses about religion's purposes
and effects behind bars:

> The question has been asked, is the purpose of chaplaincy to make a be-
> liever out of someone or to prevent crime? [. . .] I think the point [that the
> purpose of chaplaincy is to make believers] is exceedingly clear.
>   It goes without saying that the field of corrections emphasizes the aim
> and role [that chaplaincy plays] in the prevention of crime, but even hav-
> ing said that religion contributes to the prevention of crime, we cannot ig-
> nore the desires of inmates and force them to receive chaplaincy on the
> grounds that it would be useful to our purposes. This would be unconsti-
> tutional. Thus, we cannot link the purpose of chaplaincy straight to the
> goal of crime prevention. [. . .] [From the perspective of corrections,] the
> purpose of conducting chaplaincy in cases when the individual desires it
> is that, to the extent that a person is living in faith, the result is the reality
> of crime prevention. This is through and through an effect of faith.[46]

The chain of logic here follows a sequence that goes from religious freedom to public benefit. First, the official rationale for permitting chaplaincy in prisons must be legally rooted in the constitutional requirement
to protect inmates' religious freedom. This is a matter of law, and it is
not up for debate. Thus, the declared purpose of chaplaincy has to be "to

make believers." However, this goal is then supplemented by a secondary managerial objective. Allowing chaplaincy in the prisons may have the added benefit of contributing to correctional reform—a bonus presented as a secondary "effect of faith." I emphasize that Nakao's view was introduced at the meeting of the *Chaplain's Manual* revision committee with untempered approval—these guiding assumptions remain in effect in the twenty-first century.

In sum, the logic of purpose and effects surrounding chaplaincy in prisons cuts two ways. On the one hand, the legal rationale for the provision of chaplaincy is to protect the religious freedom of prisoners. On the other hand, the management expect the teaching of religion behind bars to have additional benefits for running the prison system. The implicit values undergirding this arrangement are clear enough though not necessarily without tension. In the first case, religious freedom is understood to be a good in and of itself under the rubrics of constitutional law and human rights. And in the second case, promoting religion in prisons is said to be desirable because it encourages good behavior and thus contributes to correctional reform (and thereby to the public interest). One might distill this into a formula as follows: religion *must* be free, and it *should* also offer a prosocial teaching for the public benefit. The tension lies in the questions of balance and authority: How much freedom of religion can be tolerated in prisons before the public good is at risk? Who gets to decide?

Given Nakao's comments, it is clear that the rationale for the provision of prison chaplaincy within the correctional system is at least two-tiered. Returning to the same *Chaplain's Manual*, we can find reference to a third level of the management's functionalist agenda for religions. The draft of the Criminal Institutions Bill (Keiji shisetsu hōan) of 1987 (included in the manual) suggests that the designated role of chaplains goes beyond ensuring the religious freedom of inmates and the function of supporting crime prevention to include other benefits to the operations of the prison facility: "Article 120. The wardens of correctional facilities will take appropriate measures to contribute to the emotional stability [*shinjō no antei*] of death row inmates by seeking the cooperation and support of private volunteers [*tokushika*] to carry out counseling, encouragement and lectures as necessary."[47]

Though this clause does not mention prison chaplains by name, the reference to "private volunteers" denotes prison chaplains. According to legal scholar Ishizuka Shin'ichi, Japanese legal discourse uses the phrase "emotional stability" only with reference to the management of death row inmates.[48] The implication is that prison chaplains play a role in managing the emotional state of persons on death row and thereby facilitate prison operations. It is possible to detect here a resonance with spiritual care chaplaincies in that the term "emotional stability" casts the chaplains' responsibilities in terms of a medicalized or psychologized understanding of the problem of suffering. At the same time, the reference to "stability" implies that, from the perspective of the management, the therapeutic care that chaplains may provide to those on death row is expected to have the added benefit of maintaining order in the prison. This managerial discourse sees the chaplain's engagement with inmates' suffering as a service to the administrative purpose of smooth prison operations.

From the functionalist perspective of the correctional bureaucracy, prison chaplains have three proper roles: to ensure that inmates' constitutionally guaranteed religious freedom is protected; to contribute to the objective of crime prevention; and to promote the emotional stability of all inmates and particularly death row inmates so as to maintain order. These normative roles define religion's expected contributions to the public good in the context of the prison. The first goal clearly bears the influence of the postwar settlement, and it defines chaplains' responsibilities to inmates. The other two are entirely consistent with the prewar chaplaincy, and they define the chaplains' responsibilities to the state. In all three registers, the prison chaplain's responsibilities are defined with reference to the inner life of inmates.

From this point, it is possible to see the chief continuity in the prison chaplaincy from the nineteenth century to the twenty-first century. Chaplains' duties correspond to the private realm of the heart as defined in the Shin doctrine of complementarity between two domains of law (the dharma and the secular law). This tradition runs like a thread through the history of the prison chaplaincy because the role of the prison chaplain has always been defined as a matter of harmonizing the private realm of the heart with the priorities of the public authorities. This traditional role remained intact through the late twentieth century. The language was simply updated to describe the chaplain's task as a matter of appealing to "the metaphysical spirit [. . .] to encourage an inmate's return to society." The functionalist logic of corrections accepts that religion can play a part in the management of the prison population because it accepts that religion has social effects that further the ends of the prisons. These assumptions were by no means a postwar innovation. They are entirely continuous with the role for chaplains under the prewar civil service system. How, then, did the postwar era's introduction of concerns about the religious freedom of the incarcerated alter the position of the chaplain? How does the restructured postwar chaplaincy system based on human rights and religion-state separation map on to the enduring functionalist logic that holds religion to be an effective strategy for correctional reform?

The answer to these questions involves two key differences between the structure of the postwar chaplaincy and that of its civil service predecessor. These differences relate to the status of inmates (as citizens and bearers of human rights as opposed to subjects of the emperor) and the status of chaplains (as volunteers rather than government employees). From 1956 until the time of this writing, volunteer prison chaplains appointed by the National Chaplains' Union have served as proxy agents of the public authorities and have been charged with instructing inmates in group sessions and ministering to their private religious concerns in individual counseling sessions. When I interviewed the former president of the National Chaplains' Union Hirano Shunkō in 2014, he explained the postwar division of roles between the civil servants who staff the prisons and volunteer prison chaplains with reference to the rights of inmates as follows:

In Japan, the relationship between religions and politics is strange. Religionists [*shūkyōka*] cannot be state employees, and state employees cannot discuss religion. [The job of the death row chaplain] is defined as providing support to the hearts of the people on death row. That role is the role of a religionist, and chaplains are private volunteers. The government cannot pay religionists for this kind of work.

However, inmates can make requests for a Buddhist or a Christian chaplain, and the prison is permitted to meet these requests. The whole system works on requests from the inmates. This is the law. The country has to acknowledge that there are problems of the heart [*kokoro no mondai*], but the government cannot present a Buddhist or a Christian perspective. Private prison chaplains exist to answer to this need.[49]

In Hirano's framing, the guarantee of religious freedom ensures that the state is legally obligated to recognize that inmates have religious needs and to do something to answer to these "problems of the heart." However, the separation of religion from state effectively bars state employees from engaging with religious concerns while also preventing the state from offering remuneration to prison chaplains. Thus, "private prison chaplains" are brought in to the prison system to minister to the perceived religious needs that the state holds itself obligated to respect but not address. Hirano's nuanced framing of death row chaplaincy creates a space for the chaplain to face the problem of suffering and deal with an inmate's existential concerns. Chaplains have recourse to their responsibilities to the incarcerated, understood as bearers of rights including religious freedom, to step outside the didactic role they have been assigned as agents of doctrinal admonition.

The fundamental tension built into the chaplain's role (to serve the state or to serve the inmates) reflects the general ambiguity about the public good and religion's relationship to it in contemporary Japan. Chaplains' training materials invoke the language of human rights discourse and refer to an irreducible religious dimension (making a gesture toward the problem of suffering). At the same time, they also consistently adhere to a didactic formula that assumes religions should offer moral instruction for correctional rehabilitation (reverting to a statist perspective on the problem of crime). In the late twentieth century, the prison chaplaincy operated under the rationale of human rights, and yet the role for chaplains continued to be officially defined in line with a tradition that held the job of religion to be a matter of harmonizing private interests with the state's definition of the public good. Nonetheless, the centrality of human rights in postwar religious, correctional, and legal thinking provided a language and an ethical ideal for chaplains to leverage their status as "volunteer religionists." As private volunteers, postwar chaplains could stand on the side of the prisoner clients in ways that would have been difficult for their civil service predecessors.

A remarkable story published in the inaugural issue of *Chaplaincy* illustrates this point. The journal ends with a record of a conversation about chaplaincy conducted at the Lower House of the Diet. In response to a question from a member of the opposition, a Ministry of Justice bureaucrat shares a story about a certain unnamed chaplain at Fukuoka Jail who has been serving since 1952. The warden decided to prevent the chaplain from meeting with two death row inmates. The prison, however, did not relieve the chaplain of his duties as the authorities held the man "in high regard for his excellent character." The warden had come to his decision by weighing the requirement to protect the religious freedom of the death row inmates against the institutional prerogative to maintain the emotional stability of the incarcerated. It was the warden's expectation that chaplains should encourage death row inmates to reflect on the severity of their crimes so that they may "die peacefully." However, this particular chaplain had become convinced that the two inmates under his charge were wrongfully convicted. He had become politically active in an effort to save their lives and had lobbied for a retrial. On the grounds that such conduct is inappropriate, the prison ultimately refused the chaplain access to the two inmates in question.[50]

Though it goes unstated, the implicit problem raised by this story is whether or not the warden's actions were constitutional. By prioritizing the managerial objective of "emotional stability," did the prison violate the inmate's rights to religious freedom by denying them access to a chaplain of their choosing? The publication leaves this problem hanging. There is no further discussion recorded. Nonetheless, in the course of fieldwork, I heard from multiple sources that in subsequent generations, similar cases of chaplains questioning the death penalty system or advocating for inmates generally met with similar results: the loss of access privileges.

As this story suggests, in the late twentieth century, chaplains have sometimes resisted the prison authorities' attempts to harness religion for the ends of corrections by positioning themselves on the side of inmates. The record of the 1962 chaplains' conference also includes notes on a breakout session about the death penalty. A chaplain named Kimura from Fukuoka Jail (possibly the subject of the conversation at the Diet) asked a pointed question: What is the purpose of death row chaplaincy? Is it simply to subdue (*fukujū*) the inmate so the individual will die without putting up a fight? His colleague, a Tokyo Jail chaplain named Shimura, voiced the opinion that if a chaplain thinks a death row inmate has successfully reformed, then this fact ought to be able to influence trials.[51] These chaplains may not have had the power to restructure the correctional system around their values, but they show that there were certainly those who felt compelled to challenge the state about questions of the public good when they thought that inmates' human rights and religious freedom were threatened. No doubt the chaplains' status as volunteers made it easier for them to voice their opposition to the correctional program. After all, even if they were "fired," they were not drawing a salary anyway and so would face no financial harm.

Our inquiry returns now to the fundamental question facing chaplains: who should they serve—the state or the incarcerated? This survey of the layered functionalist logics surrounding chaplaincy suggests that for those appointed to the job, there was no easy answer, and there were often conflicting prerogatives. The logical conclusion seems to be that it was in fact the ambiguity about the public good in the late twentieth century that enabled postwar volunteer prison chaplains to enjoy a greater degree of personal freedom to decide what to make of their work than did their civil service predecessors (for whom clear-cut answers tended to prioritize service to the emperor and the state).

The Baseline of Doctrinal Admonition vs. the Diversification of the Chaplaincy

We have seen so far that the institutional arrangement for appointing chaplains relied on the principle of public service and that the framework governing the role of chaplains behind bars was a functionalist arrangement that burdened them with sometimes conflicting responsibilities to both their incarcerated clients and to the state. Next, the argument turns to consider the religious dimensions of chaplaincy.

The National Chaplains' Union, sectarian organizations, and individual members of the clergy invested the work with religious significance. A review of chaplaincy training materials shows that there is a shared baseline for understanding the meaning of the work in a doctrinal or theological register. This core changed so little over the late twentieth century that one can select almost at random from chaplaincy publications and find the essential themes. Crime is in part a product of anomie in society. Religion can contribute to the public benefit by teaching prosocial values to inmates and thereby fighting anomie. Prison chaplains offer religious instruction to the incarcerated to promote reform and prevent recidivism. These ideas form the backbone of chaplaincy discourse, and they present a vision of religious mission in keeping with the long-standing tradition of doctrinal admonition. The Postwar Constitution, however, permitted a variety of different religious perspectives, practices, and motivations to enter the prisons. The chief architectural symbol of this diversification was the introduction to the prisons of multiple chapels and altars (Buddhist, Shinto, and Christian).[52] In this final section, I consider the stable core of chaplaincy theory against the diversification of the chaplaincy (figs. 6.1, 6.2, 6.3, and 6.4).

Prison chaplaincy publications provide ample evidence of continuity. Invited speakers at chaplaincy conferences consistently claimed that youth crime was getting worse year after year, doing so to an extent that the statements appear to reflect something other than statistics. There is in fact something significant to the refrain. Assertions about worsening crime typically set the stage for claims about the importance of prison chaplaincy as a form of religious public benefit work. Some of the more grandiose internal publications describe the work's significance with a mythic narrative about the course of history and religion's role in it. The introduction to the Shin sect's official postwar history *One Hundred Years of Prison Chaplaincy* conforms to this pattern:

> Thanks to the remarkable advances in science and technology, human beings are enjoying a shining era of prosperity. However, even in this colorful time, human freedom is being stolen, and the heart of the human is being lost. Humanity is now facing a serious crisis.
>
> Crimes are becoming more violent. The number of juvenile offenders is on the rise. The types of crime are diversifying, and crime is proliferating. It may be that the increase in crime is due to the influence of deepening confusion and anxiety in contemporary society. Our hearts no longer have anything to rely upon, and crime may be an effect of a loss of humanity.

One of modernity's great thinkers, [Arnold] Toynbee maintains that "religion provides meaning and value to life, offering a way of salvation in these confused modern times." To restore the original hearts of humanity, to deliver humanity from suffering—at no time have human beings needed religion more than they do in the present. When we consider this modern context, it is clear that the role of religious chaplaincy as one part of correctional education is becoming ever more important.[53]

Though this official history was published by the Shin sects, it opens with an ecumenical theme. This passage is a lament of the perceived harms of secularization—deepening confusion and anxiety. The general idea is that a rise in the crime rate may be attributable to a decline in the influence of religion (not Buddhism specifically) in society. This assertion is not a social scientific argument, but rather a core statement of chaplaincy doctrine: religion is a solution to crime and a factor in social stability. This mythic construction is actually a theological claim about religions' relationship to the public good. According to this missionary line of thinking, it is good to promote religions throughout society because their influence elevates the moral character of individuals and the nation. By this logic, prison chaplaincy contributes to the public good by promoting religion and thereby shaping society for the better.

The National Chaplains' Union has maintained this perspective into the new millennium. In a 2006 publication marking the fiftieth anniversary of the union's founding, the head of the Society for the Promotion of Buddhism (Bukkyō Dendō Kyōkai, or BDK, founded in 1965), famed philanthropist Numata Toshihide (d. 2017), writes:

In recent years, our society is said to be one of material abundance yet lacking in heart, and as a reflection of this social condition, we see clearly terrible crimes beyond the scope of our imaginings. In the past, many crimes were a result of material poverty, but now I think they are caused by a poverty of the heart—a loss of perspective on the value of life and a lack of sympathy for the pain of others. As crimes like this increase, religion will play a more and more important role in cultivating spiritual abundance [*kokoro no yutakasa*] by explaining the value of the individual being, the interdependence of all life, and a way of interconnectedness that transcends ethics and morals.[54]

FIGURE 6.1 Buddhist group chaplaincy session, lecture. Photograph courtesy of the National Chaplains' Union (Zenkoku Kyōkaishi Renmei).

FIGURE 6.2 Shinto group chaplaincy session, *oharai* ritual purification. Photograph courtesy of the National Chaplains' Union (Zenkoku Kyōkaishi Renmei).

FIGURE 6.3   Christian group chaplaincy session, Christmas service. Photograph courtesy of the National Chaplains' Union (Zenkoku Kyōkaishi Renmei).

FIGURE 6.4   Buddhist group chaplaincy session, Ohigan service. Photograph courtesy of the National Chaplains' Union (Zenkoku Kyōkaishi Renmei).

These two examples were written thirty-four years apart, but the essential logic is the same. Both statements invoke the human heart as the source of personal and social evils. According to this line of thinking, religious instruction encourages spiritual transformation in the individual and fosters the values that make for good citizenship in the nation and the world. Religions can contribute to the public good by combatting the encroaching anomie, fighting the ever-worsening variety of crimes, and ensuring that social order survives these existential threats. Pointing out the mythic scale of these paeans to the chaplaincy makes them appear as exaggerations in the extreme, but these words of praise doubtless reflect the fundamental value commitments of the prison chaplaincy.

Just as the principle of public service invests the work of chaplaincy with social significance in a secular register, chaplaincy publications supplement this with a religious meaning. Numata declares that the prison chaplain is "the very figure of the bodhisattva's compassionate practice."[55] This particular example draws on a Buddhist idiom, reflecting the numerical dominance of Buddhists in the Japanese chaplaincy. Nonetheless, all sects participating in chaplaincy share the conviction that the work is religiously significant. The same fiftieth anniversary publication includes words of encouragement in a theological vein (in order) from leaders of JARO, BDK (Numata), both major sects of Shin, Tenrikyō, Sōtō, Jōdo, NASS, Nichiren, the United Church of Christ in Japan, Konkōkyō, and Shingon.[56] Thus, the chaplaincy is both a public service that endows appointees with secular honors and a form of religious practice recognized by sectarian organizations. Chaplaincy publications share two baseline assumptions: crime is in large part a religious problem in need of a religious solution; and the work of chaplaincy has religious significance as part of the ongoing struggle between good and evil, order and chaos, religion and anomie. Though the dominant lens for understanding varieties of chaplaincy in Western societies relies on notions of spiritual care and medicalized conceptions of religion's role in alleviating suffering, the official discourse of the Japanese prison chaplaincy went without such concepts and retained instead a focus on the problem of evil from the nineteenth century into the twenty-first.

To a great extent, sects shared the conviction that chaplaincy was a matter of public service and religious mission. Of course, each chaplain would have had a personal opinion about the work, but no major publications questioned the core assumption that the chaplain's role is to perform religiously meaningful work by fighting the social and existential evil of crime. However, various religious organizations or their representatives also fostered differing approaches to the particulars of chaplaincy based on divergent visions of the public good, the role of their religion in society, and the role of the chaplain in the prison. I turn next to consider some new directions in prison chaplaincy that developed in the late twentieth century. I refer to Tenrikyō, shrine Shinto, Christianity, and Shin Buddhism relying primarily on published records. My reading of these materials is also informed by fieldwork with chaplains from each of these groups.

Under the postwar volunteer chaplaincy system, only religions affiliated with either JARO or the ecumenical Federation of New Religious Organizations of Japan could enter the prisons to proselytize.[57] Religions that did not participate in either of the ecumenical unions (notably Sōka Gakkai) could not field prison chaplains. Of the groups typically categorized as new religions, Tenrikyō was the most active in prison chaplaincy.[58] The Tenrikyō prison chaplaincy incorporated that religion's distinctive tradition of communal living as a means of support for inmates facing insecurity after release.[59] This created friction with the prisons, where administrators sought to prevent chaplains from maintaining connections with their clients beyond the framework of the correctional system.

The 2017 edition of the *Chaplaincy Casebook* (*Kyōkai jireishū*)—a training material produced by the National Chaplains' Union—includes a telling anecdote from a Tenrikyō chaplain. The chaplain describes working with a juvenile inmate in a one-on-one session overseen by a guard. He asked the youth about release: "When you get out of here, where will you go?" At that moment, the guard standing by in the corner cut in: "Sensei, please don't go any further." The guard informed him that a chaplain's responsibilities extend only so far as the prison walls. The chaplain writes: "I was just about to say, 'When you get out, come on over to my place and we can talk. I will come and pick you up.'"[60] Some Tenrikyō churches operate as communes, and in cases where the church head is also a prison chaplain or a probation officer, it has not been uncommon for them to take in parolees as lodgers. The tradition of communal living is important in Tenrikyō doctrine and practice, and even though the Corrections Office does not want chaplains to maintain contact with their clients outside the prisons, in reality it does happen. There are also documented cases from the 1980s wherein Buddhist prison chaplains either accepted their clients after release into their temples as lodgers or maintained contact with former clients to help them get back on their feet.[61] In such cases, the chaplains who chose to become personally involved with their clients did so without the approval of the prison system and motivated by their own values.

The National Association of Shinto Shrines has an unusual political platform for a religious organization. The Occupation reclassified Shinto shrines from secular public institutions to private religious ones, but through the late twentieth century NASS has maintained the position that Shinto should rightfully be recognized as a public tradition rather than a religion. Nonetheless, NASS produced a Shinto prison chaplaincy for the postwar era, reflecting their newfound status as one religious organization among many. Shrine Shinto chaplains did not have a robust textual or doctrinal basis for developing chaplaincy theories in the mold of doctrinal admonition, but they emphasized ideals of ethnic unity to encourage offenders to reform.[62]

The NASS *Chaplain's Guidebook* (1999) includes the following assertion about the character of their chaplaincy activities: "Because Shinto is the source of Japanese culture, if you explain the spirit of Shinto at the root of traditional culture, mind your expressions and choice of words, and avoid criticizing other religions, then NASS prison chaplains should be quite capable of handling general chaplaincy sessions."[63] Prisons divide chaplaincy sessions between those deemed religious and those deemed general. Inmate participation in religious chaplaincy sessions is voluntary, and these sessions typically focus on either one-on-one counseling or lectures on sect doctrine (where proselytization is an accepted goal). General chaplaincy sessions, by contrast, can be mandatory, and these sessions focus on a range of topics including ethical instruction, but proselytization of a particular religious doctrine is prohibited. It is worth noting that the NASS *Chaplain's Guidebook* is, to the best of my knowledge, the only chaplaincy manual to assert that its chaplains are particularly qualified to offer general (as opposed to religious) instruction. This assertion is in keeping with NASS's broader political plat-form, according to which Shinto should belong rightfully to the public domain.

The guidebook elsewhere reinforces the idea that Shinto is not a re-ligion. In describing the appropriate attitude for Shinto chaplains, the guidebook lists several necessary qualities. The first is "the capacity to demonstrate through deep faith and broad learning that the way of the Kami transcends all forms of logic, religion, and philosophy."[64] In the same vein, the last pages of this manual include as a reference text "Twelve Virtues of the Imperial Rescript on Education."[65] In other words, the manual presents the public ethos of the prewar era as an appropriate teaching for Shinto chaplains in 1999. NASS appears to have struggled to identify what components of Shinto are religious versus those believed to be simply characteristic of a Japanese cultural ethic. Alternatively, NASS may simply have refused to designate specific components of shrine traditions as belonging to the realm of religion because to do so could be seen as conceding to the view that shrines are properly catego-rized as religious institutions. The guidebook exhibits an eagerness for NASS to be involved in the project of governance, matched only by a reluctance to identify anything Shinto as religious.

In the postwar era, Christian chaplains were once again admitted to Japanese prisons to proselytize. Protestant ministers and Catholic priests had to assimilate themselves to the Japanese form of prison chaplaincy with working conditions informed by the long tradition of doctrinal ad-monition. In general, this meant that Christian group chaplaincy sessions of both Protestant and Catholic varieties typically took the form of Bible readings about issues that could be related to the theme of correctional reform. The 1983 edition of the *Chaplaincy* journal contains the record of an Irish Catholic priest's speech to a chaplaincy conference. He had pre-viously worked as a prison chaplain near London, and he describes his disappointment with the working conditions in Japan. In London, he had been responsible for counseling inmates and, if requested, he sometimes went to visit their families. He found this work extremely fulfilling. By contrast, at the Japanese juvenile prison, many of the youths in his Bible class simply dozed through it, and even though he was fluent in Japanese, he found it hard to tell if he was getting through to them.[66] It seems he found the work conditions in Japan far more restrictive than those in the United Kingdom. He was certainly not expected to liaise with the families of his incarcerated clients in Japan.

One notable characteristic of contemporary Japanese Christian prison chaplaincy literature is that it tends to emphasize making converts out of clients to a greater degree than do Buddhist and Shinto chaplaincy texts. For example, the 2017 *Chaplaincy Casebook* includes a Protestant chaplain's representative account of his proselytization efforts to the incarcerated. His primary theme is that "the love of Jesus can change a person."[67] He concludes a sermon peppered with quotes from the Bible by saying, "Anyone can change when they accept Jesus and welcome him as their savior. They will be able to live a new life. You, too, can change and reform your life."[68] Given the prison institution's historical connection to Christianity, it is no surprise that a Christian concept of salvation can be made to support the ideals of correctional reform in Japan.

However, something perhaps unexpected becomes apparent when we add to this the example of a Japanese Catholic priest's representative essay on method from the 1993 *Chaplaincy Casebook*. This priest served as chaplain at a medical prison, and he includes an account of a deathbed conversion. He writes that his client was afraid to die. In response, the priest said, "There is still one last chance. Pray from the bottom of your heart to God for forgiveness for all of your sins. [. . .] Believe that Christ is the son of God and receive salvation. To do so, you must be baptized."[69] The priest reports that he successfully performed the baptism just two days before the inmate died. This tale is immediately followed by another story that similarly concludes in a victorious baptism (with no further comment). In both cases, there is no narrative telos beyond the push for conversion. Despite the fact that the priest served in a medical prison, there is no comment about the relationship of these baptisms to religious needs, spiritual care, correctional reform, or emotional stability.

These cases correspond with my own findings based on interviews with Japanese Christian prison chaplains and fieldwork conducted at Fuchū Prison in 2012, including observation of a Protestant minister's chaplaincy session (a Bible reading). The cumulative impression from readings and fieldwork is that Christian prison chaplains tend to focus intently and rather exclusively on the sectarian goal of converting inmates to Christianity. In an international context, this finding may be unexpected as Christian chaplains outside Japan have a long-standing tradition of spiritual care. A study of American varieties of chaplaincy notes that one defining characteristic is that US chaplains, most of whom are Christians, tend to address themselves to the spiritual health of their clients while consciously trying to avoid imposing a particular religious viewpoint.[70] By contrast, contemporary Christian prison chaplaincy in Japan does not incorporate any concept of spiritual care in a systematic or influential way. In fact, Japanese Christian prison chaplains appear not to have thought about it at all. It seems ironic, but of all the varieties of Japanese prison chaplaincy, the Christians appear to be the most eager to impose their doctrinal viewpoint and to win converts from their clients. An episode from my own experience corroborates this conclusion. In 2019, I gave a public talk about prison chaplaincy and spiritual care at the University of Tokyo to an audience that included prison chaplains. A Christian chaplain raised his hand during the Q&A to say: "Just so you know, I do not care at all about spiritual care. My only concern is to help the incarcerated to know Jesus." No matter the focus of Christian chaplains elsewhere, the introduction of Christian chaplains to postwar Japanese prisons did not lead to a reorientation of the prison chaplaincy toward spiritual care. The prison system retained the chaplaincy under the rubric of doctrinal admonition, and Christian chaplains participated in this project while introducing their own religious mission to the prisons.

As a final example of the postwar diversification of the Japanese prison chaplaincy, I take up a tenuous connection between Shin Buddhist prison chaplaincy and spiritual care. In the last decades of the twentieth century, Japanese religious discourse began to highlight a medicalized conception of religion's role in alleviating suffering.[71] This shift has been described as the rise of spirituality (*supirichuariti*).[72] The bulk of chaplains' manuals and vocational training materials remained out of step with this larger trend in religious life, but from the mid-twentieth century, some individual chaplains focused on counseling in ways that foreshadowed the later development of spiritual care practices. The most direct example of a connection between the prison chaplaincy and spiritual care is *naikan*—a form of meditative counseling based on self-reflection that Buddhist chaplains (and sometimes prison staff) practiced with the incarcerated beginning in the 1950s.[73]

A devout Shin Buddhist, Yoshimoto Ishin (1916–1988) refined the meditative counseling practice of *naikan* while serving as a prison chaplain at Nara Juvenile Prison in the 1950s.[74] He developed this practice based on an earlier Shin Buddhist meditation method known as *mishirabe* (roughly, "introspection").[75] *Naikan* practice involves directed self-reflection over one's memories for a period of isolation (typically days on end), focused on the theme of one's moral debts to others.[76] The practitioner is instructed to consider their relationships in light of three questions: What have I received from others? What have I given back in return? And what trouble have I caused others?[77] Scholars have traced the development of *naikan* from its roots in Shin Buddhism through its expansion into psychotherapy and new spirituality movements in Japan and around the world.[78] As of 2020, there is no doubt that *naikan* "belongs" in some sense to the realm of spiritual care practices. However, in its first institutionalized form, *naikan* was instrumentalized as a mechanism for reforming the hearts of prisoners in ways that situate the early practice firmly in the tradition of doctrinal admonition.

Believing in the efficacy of his new technique, Yoshimoto Ishin promoted *naikan* to the correctional field by presenting it as a secular (nonreligious) method of self-reflection. Clark Chilson has noted that by 1962, twenty-nine prisons and ten reform schools in Japan offered *naikan*, and a study conducted at Miyazaki Prison indicated that the recidivism rate for those who practiced it was a mere 14.4 percent, whereas those who did not participate reoffended at a rate of 80.3 percent.[79] A study conducted at Hiroshima Juvenile Prison in 1962 involved ninety inmates who were asked to record testimonies about *naikan*. The reported results consistently frame the *naikan* experience as a catalyst to repentance and reform.

Before *naikan*, inmates describe feeling skeptical about the procedure and resentful of their families and of society at large. Inmate 1: "Before I started *naikan*, I put my own bad deeds on a shelf and thought, 'Society is bad, my parents are bad, my family is boring.'" Inmate 2: "Regarding my own bad deeds against society, I never once felt sorry for my parents or siblings."[80] Testimonies from the middle of the *naikan* trial generally report a period of psychological and emotional turmoil as resentment was redirected toward feelings of guilt and a recognition of the evils of the self. Inmate 3: "While doing *naikan*, I heard a voice crying out from the bottom of my heart saying, 'I am sorry, I am sorry.'" Inmate 4: "Even though I hated my parents and my siblings so much, after doing *naikan* I realized that I am the one who was bad."[81] By the conclusion of the trial, inmates reported feelings of gratitude, catharsis, an increased degree of self-insight, and a resolve to reform: "I came to feel that the sensei [chaplain] was like a warm maternal presence. When I said everything I had in my heart, I felt like my evil heart was replaced with a firm determination [to do good]."[82]

As these testimonies indicate, the institutional form of *naikan* started out as part of the broader project of doctrinal admonition that defined the role for religions in the carceral system. *Naikan* was one of a variety of chaplaincy methods to harness religious resources in promoting correctional reform and fighting crime. Yoshimoto Ishin and his successors expanded the *naikan* practice beyond corrections and into the realm of psychotherapy after their apparently successful experiments with prisoners. However, as of 2020, *naikan* is no longer commonly practiced in the Japanese prison system. It is not mentioned in the 1993 or the 2017 casebook. It appears that once *naikan* succeeded in gaining a following outside the prison, it largely vacated the correctional system and relocated into the sectors of medicine and, later, spirituality. This transition was likely furthered by the fact that the key figures promoting *naikan* moved on from prison chaplaincy. Moreover, no religious organization participating in prison chaplaincy maintained *naikan* as a primary practice, and so chaplains' training materials do not generally discuss it. It is entirely possible that individual chaplains continued to conduct *naikan* with their clients. Be that as it may, the peak of *naikan* in corrections appears to have been in the 1960s. With the tentative exception of this reflective practice, there is no genealogical connection between Japanese prison chaplaincy and later forms of spiritual care practice that developed in Japan.

As this survey indicates, prison chaplaincy in late twentieth-century Japan diversified by incorporating a range of different religious motivations and practices. However, the mainstream of prison chaplaincy remained tethered to the tradition of religion-state unity characteristic of doctrinal admonition, and all of the sects who joined chaplaincy activities did so under this umbrella. Tenrikyō, Shinto, and Christian chaplains joined together with Buddhists to provide doctrinal admonition in accordance with the functionalist logic governing the chaplains' roles. Along the way, Tenrikyō chaplains could sermonize about reform in the prison chapel and then invite inmates to come to the church as lodgers after release. Shrine Shinto chaplains could promote what they saw as their tradition's rightful connections with governance and offer their contributions to the nation-state. Christians could seek converts. And some innovative Buddhists like Yoshimoto Ishin could develop and refine new forms of religious practice with their incarcerated clients. However, none of these new developments overrode the dominant tradition of doctrinal admonition and the functionalist logic governing the role of religions in the correctional system.

Conclusions

The chaplaincy in late twentieth century Japan can be understood in relation to four primary issues: the political context of religion-state relations, institutional arrangements for the appointment of chaplains, the administrative framework governing the chaplaincy behind bars, and the layers of religious significance accorded to the work. In the larger political context, ambiguity about the chaplain's role (to serve inmates or to serve the state?) can be seen as a microcosm of the ambiguous relationship between religions and the public good in society at large. The broader political issue hinged on a rift between the ideals and the reality of religion's social role. The postwar legal framework governing religion was rooted in the Occupation-era ideal of religions as civil society groups that should operate separately from the government. However, the reality was that most widely recognized forms of religious public benefit work—and social work in particular—in fact remained deeply connected to state agencies (as was the case in the prewar period). Even though there is ambiguity about religion's relationship to the public good in society more broadly, a closer examination of the chaplaincy's workings demonstrates specific normative ideas about how religions should serve the public interest in the late twentieth century.

The institutional arrangements for chaplain appointments in postwar Japan show that religions' service for the public benefit was in many ways obligatory. Even in an era of separation of religions from state, chaplains were appointed to perform public service work for the government in the prison system and without expectation of remuneration. The National Chaplains' Union operated less like a private and autonomous civil society group and more like a semigovernmental agency linking religious organizations to state agencies. Regardless of the religion-state separation ideal enshrined in the 1947 Constitution, the postwar realities in the area of social work fell far short.

Behind bars, dueling rationales governed the chaplaincy. On the one hand, chaplains were officially responsible to ensure that inmates' constitutionally guaranteed rights to religious freedom were protected. On the other hand, the management expected chaplains to serve the project of correctional reform. In the eyes of the wardens, the chaplains' job was to provide religious instruction to promote rehabilitation and to provide counseling to enhance inmate docility. Clear ideas about how religions should serve the public good in the context of the prison do exist, but so does an inherent tension between the conflicting obligations chaplains faced—to their incarcerated clients, on the one hand, and to the state, on the other. This ambiguity appears to be a product of the way the postwar settlement's promotion of religious freedom and human rights has been mapped onto the prewar model of doctrinal admonition (according to which religious workers' primary duty in the correctional system is to fight crime and serve the state). Nonetheless, the very ambiguity in the chaplain's role probably contributed to a greater degree of freedom for late twentieth-century volunteer prison chaplains in comparison to their prewar civil service predecessors. The most obvious symbol of this increased independence can be found in the rare examples of postwar chaplains who publicly challenged the death penalty.

Finally, various parties engaged in chaplaincy have invested the work with differing religious meanings. The dominant mode for understanding the religious significance of chaplaincy inherited the prewar view of crime as an existential evil against which religions must defend society. This baseline corresponds with the long-standing tradition of doctrinal admonition that has been central to prison chaplaincy in Japan since the Meiji era. On top of this foundation, the variety of religious groups who became involved in chaplaincy in the postwar era introduced their own religious motivations and sectarian perspectives to the work. Nevertheless, because all groups were required to work within the correctional system and under its functionalist agenda, no fundamental rethinking of the core chaplaincy doctrine took place. The prison chaplaincy's public discourse in late twentieth-century Japan combined a concern with the human rights of the incarcerated with a commitment to fighting crime.

The cumulative result of this history is that the prison chaplain's role was carved out between the prison management and the prisoners in a way that reproduced fundamental tensions between state and religion, public and private, government agencies and civil society. The chaplain was saddled with ambivalent responsibilities in the same way that the relationship between religion and the public good was ambiguous through the late twentieth century.

CHAPTER 7

The Dilemmas of Bad Karma

The Chaplain's Joke

Japanese prison chaplains, most of whom are Buddhist priests, have a wonderful joke that evokes the complexities of their position. *Why did you become a prison chaplain?* "Because I did something terrible in a past life to deserve it." I heard this refrain several times—more often than not outside the context of formal interviews at an *izakaya*, when the drinks were flowing, and the audio recorder was off. The sentiment behind this joke reflects hidden realities of prison chaplaincy in Japan. Virtually all of Japan's prison chaplains are appointed. They are not really "volunteers," but the position is unpaid. Though many of them embrace the work with a sense of purpose, some feel ambivalent about the position, and even those who find it meaningful recognize that the job is rife with challenges.

In this joke, karma is invoked as a gloss for the idea that none of us are the sole author of our destiny. Some situations (like appointment to the chaplaincy) are beyond our control because so much of our horizon is shaped by the web of interpersonal connections (or karmic bonds). The joke touches a nerve because assignment to the chaplaincy is often obligatory and hereditary. One source of its "sting" comes from the collective reservoir of shared frustrations associated with hierarchical kinship relations; in this case, the Buddhist idiom of past-life connections gestures to multigenerational family life in a clerical household where sect responsibilities weigh heavily. Humor offers a different perspective on the concept of karma than the one prevalent in the official prison chaplaincy literature, wherein karma is most frequently invoked as a shorthand for the idea that those in prison are getting their just deserts. This chapter returns to the anthropological distinction between dominant and demotic discourses (discussed in the introduction) to shed light on the private dimensions of chaplains' experiences—the personal lives that are typically excluded from the archival records of the chaplaincy.

Based on two years of fieldwork and interviews, I introduce the stories of chaplains and their views about this work. I argue here that the people appointed to the chaplaincy face a host of dilemmas that can be understood as refractions of the way the prevailing settlement between religions and state manifests behind bars. Chaplains are to attend to inmates' private religious concerns while avoiding political issues. They are expected to work within the system while maintaining silence about their personal views in public, and thus the delimitation of their duties compounds the problems of secrecy inherent in the Japanese prison system. This arrangement is entirely consistent with the normative role for religion as a private affair and a public benefit—a normative role that entails costs for those assigned to do religion's good works.

In previous chapters, I examined chaplains' publications to show that the dominant discourse of prison chaplaincy takes the form of doctrinal admonition. Prison chaplaincy literature typically involves variations on the theme of theodicy. Karma is invoked as an exhortation for inmates to overcome evil by purifying their hearts. The bulk of the prison chaplaincy archive conforms to this perspective. Religious instruction is framed as a potential solution to the problem of crime. Even today, the official responsibilities of the prison chaplaincy remain rooted in this tradition of doctrinal admonition.

The chaplain's joke inverts the official theology in a way that makes the logic of the chaplaincy doctrine appear absurd: the chaplain (in a former life) must have been a criminal because he is in prison now, and according to the notion of karma presented in the *Chaplain's Manual*, only bad people wind up in prison. But the chaplain, too, is a "prisoner," and so he must deserve it. The gulf between chaplaincy doctrines (public discourse) and the inversion of orthodoxy seen in the joke (private conversation) indicates there is more to the prison chaplaincy than the official story.

In a discussion of the dilemmas faced by chaplains, why start with a joke? Anthropologist Michael Jackson writes of comedy that it has the capacity to transform tragic experiences by creating a sense of distance and release as well as building intersubjective affinity: "First, the comedy restores a sense of agency. Second, it fosters a sense of emotional detachment. Third, it entails shared laughter, and thus returns us to a community of others."[1] The chaplain's joke provides the frame for what follows. The dilemmas of the chaplaincy are characterized by lack of agency. The job can be emotionally challenging. It is partly through the sharing of private conversations about the work that chaplains build relationships with one another and try to overcome the difficulties of their position. Shared humor is also part of how younger chaplains are socialized into the role, becoming insiders to the closed world of the prison.

Joking is about making connections with other people. Just as the chaplain's joke resists the dogmatic view presented in official publications, I make a case here that many dedicated chaplains go beyond the official range of their duties. Prison chaplains are, first and foremost, expected to admonish inmates and exhort them to reform. Although their primary responsibilities present obstacles, some chaplains also work to build personal connections with their incarcerated clients. It is in this secondary capacity, in big and small acts of resistance, that Japanese prison chaplains carve out a space to do work that resembles spiritual care in its intent of mitigating suffering. In the margins of the prison routine, *sotto voce*, chaplains can shift from remonstrating with offenders to cultivating relationships with them. This alternative tradition is often framed in the intersubjective idiom of karmic bonds (*en*). It is always from within the web of our existing relationships that we must make our way. As the joke recognizes, the chaplains are in the same boat as the prisoners (fig. 7.1).

The Weight of History and the Chaplain's Burden

This book so far has engaged the construction of the public-private divide as a historical problem. In Japan, since the nineteenth century, this divide has been negotiated around a concept of religion in a way that

FIGURE 7.1   Individual chaplaincy session. Photograph courtesy of the National Chaplains' Union (Zenkoku Kyōkaishi Renmei).

shapes modern religion-state relations around a tension. Somehow, religion is supposed to be both a private affair and a public benefit. The Shin sects' favored principle of complementarity between dharma and law offers an emic account of how the uneasy balancing act between religions and state is supposed to work. This ideal holds that the right kind of religion can harmonize private interests with the public good. In the postwar period, even as the specific Shin Buddhist representation of this ideal was eclipsed in public discourse, a virtually identical logic of sect-state collaboration was maintained as the Allied Occupation, the Shinto Directive, the Postwar Constitution, and the ecumenical Japanese Association of Religious Organizations reinforced the idea that religions should play a role in keeping the peace by promoting private virtues. As one by-product of this history, prison chaplaincy has been created and maintained to stand between the realms of sect and state and perform religions' private work for the public good.

The archive of prison chaplaincy materials reflects the perspectives of the sect and state organizations that commissioned these publications. Representations of chaplaincy available through archival sources overwhelmingly align with the official positions of the authorities, and this body of literature is almost as a rule highly impersonal. The story turns now to what is concealed.

The chaplain's joke can be read as a comment about how the weight of history has come down on the shoulders of individual clergy members today. The people appointed to serve in the prison chaplaincy come into a role fraught with tensions. They are faced with what I call "the dilemmas of bad karma." I use the term "dilemma" to refer to situations wherein conflicting obligations admit of no final resolution. Chaplains' competing responsibilities all too often place them in untenable positions. I explore case studies below, but a brief schematic may be helpful at the outset. Chaplains face role conflicts because they recognize coexisting duties to (1) their own value commitments, (2) their families, (3) their clients (inmates), (4) their sects and the chaplains' unions, and (5) the prison system (personally, to wardens and staff; abstractly, to the state). How can a chaplain both serve the state and heal the heart of an individual offender? How can chaplains tackle the problem of crime by looking to personal religious issues—the private troubles of individual inmates—without also working to mitigate the material factors that underlie crime as a public issue? How does being a chaplain impact a person's home life? How can a chaplain save someone on death row when the possibility of political action is foreclosed?

It is difficult to gain a sense of the ubiquity of these dilemmas from archival research because official publications conceal ambivalence. Based on my interviews and interactions with chaplains, I found that they are often painfully aware of the shortcomings in the official doctrines. Their private narratives, personal struggles, in-jokes, and occasionally heroic efforts to help marginalized people reveal a conflict between some clergy members' personal commitments to social justice and the structural limitations that consign religion to the apolitical realm of the heart. The history described in the previous chapters has created social conditions that are experienced by many of today's chaplains as their own "bad karma."

Karma as Bad Luck: "Honestly, I Did Not Want to Become a Prison Chaplain"

At the outset, I emphasize that although some chaplains declared an ambivalence about their work, more of them expressed the conviction that they found the job worthwhile. I introduce first some of the most revealing grievances to convey some of the chaplaincy's challenges, and in the next section, I turn to the stories of those who find the work personally fulfilling.

How does one become a prison chaplain in Japan today? In official literature, prison chaplains are generally described as "volunteers" (*tokushika*). The English term is deceptive. During the course of interviews, all but one chaplain related that they were recommended for the position by a senior colleague from their own religious organization. (The sole exception opted to do it completely of her own volition, and she is discussed shortly.) Some chaplains informed me that their father (and, in one case, both a father and a grandfather) had served in the prisons before them.

Japan's sectarian organizations function like extended, hierarchical kinship groups. It is common (though not universal) to see the stewardship of Buddhist temples, Shinto shrines, Christian churches, and churches of the new religions, like Tenrikyō, transmitted in a hereditary pattern from father to son (and sometimes to daughters, but typically only if no son is available to take over). The clerical vocation is, more often than not, a family tradition embedded in social expectations and a system of inheritance.[2] It is also common (though less so than it once was) to see marriages arranged within sectarian networks. I saw this dynamic playing out in several chaplains' families (sometimes with tensions between the parents' desires and the children's wishes), and the practice reinforced the sense that sectarian organizations are not merely professional networks. Sect organizations assign members of their clergy to fill open chaplaincy posts based on recommendations from within their social networks (in the same way that parents of a temple household might seek appropriate spouses for their children through a combination of formal and informal connections in the sect). In the Buddhist idiom, these arrangements are sometimes referred to as a matter of karmic connections.

If a chaplain from a particular sect retires or dies, then the host prison institution may contact the National Chaplains' Union to request a new appointment from the sect of the departed. In general, sectarian organizations make an effort to find a person whose personality or public-spirited attitude suggest they would be amenable to serving in the chaplaincy (presumably in the same way that parents would seek a spouse for their child with desirable personality traits). Most chaplains I interviewed said that they were generally glad to have been appointed. However, in some cases, the issue of appointment can be a sore point (analogous to mixed feelings about an arranged marriage). In my experience, some people feel they have been roped into serving; yet I also found that some committed chaplains do not like to hear such stories of begrudging service. At a study retreat for chaplains, surrounded by colleagues, one man described his situation with an extended reflection on the chaplain's joke:

> Honestly, I did not want to become a prison chaplain. My father was a prison chaplain for a long time. Then why did I become one? The reason I have to spend my days going in and out of prison has to do with past-life causes and connections. It feels like that. I really resisted becoming a prison chaplain, truly I did. I refused and refused.
>
> After my father died, he was awarded a commendation from the state. He did not get it until after he was dead, mind you. So after he died, the warden of the prison where he had worked came to me at the end of the year. The warden said that he had come to announce that my father had received this commendation from the Ministry of Justice. Now, I had some sense what this was about because earlier, at my father's funeral, another chaplain had already asked me if I would take over as a prison chaplain in my father's place. I flat out refused.
>
> But then it turned out that this senior chaplain had arranged it so that my succession as prison chaplain was to be announced at the ceremony for my father's award. So of course I had to go to this ceremony to receive the award on behalf of my father. When I got there, do you know what they said? At the ceremony, they said, "There is nothing so admirable as a son who takes over his father's responsibilities as a prison chaplain!" I thought, What!? I refused this outright! But it was too late—I already had my father's award in my hands! I was thinking, *But I refused*! And then I realized: oh no, I have already accepted the award. I really can't refuse to take over as prison chaplain after taking the award.
>
> There was nothing I could do. Now both my father and I have ended up spending our days in and out of prison—both of us must have done terrible things in our past lives! We must have been that kind of family in a past life.[3]

Two chaplains who sat by listening to their compatriot tell this story appeared to think it hilarious. The man telling the tale seemed less amused, and I could not decide if he was primarily joking or seriously trying to get himself fired from the chaplaincy. In either case, it is clear that the circumstances of his appointment do not constitute "volunteering." He sees his duties to the chaplaincy as an onerous burden. Nonetheless, moments later, he described the rewarding feeling he gets when former inmates approach him to thank him for helping them to get through prison. Many other chaplains similarly vacillated between complaining of the difficulties of the work and expressing gratitude for the learning opportunities their appointment provided.

The nature of the reluctant chaplain's grievance deserves clarification. In addition to being unpaid labor, the work of the chaplains can be emotionally draining, intellectually frustrating, and discouragingly fruitless. One shrine Shinto chaplain humorously bemoaned the difficulty of working with sex offenders:

> I tell them that they ought to stop offending because it will make a mess of their lives! All I can really say is "You've got to stop it!" And then they ask me, "*Sensei*, do you not have sexual desires?" And I have to say, "I am a human being! Of course I do! If I see a beautiful woman in a skirt, I might *think*, 'nice knees!' But having that thought and reaching out and grabbing someone are two totally different things![4]

If the difference between tragedy and comedy is a matter of distance, then this chaplain's humor may be interpreted as a distancing strategy: getting a laugh out of his predicament rather than being overwhelmed by it. The underlying fact remains: chaplains often work with difficult inmates without any formal training or practical experience to guide them, and this can be a source of exasperation. Another chaplain expressed the sentiment like this: "It often feels like promoting chaplaincy as a means of reform is done in vain. Too little, too late."[5]

Like most of his colleagues, the shrine Shinto chaplain is not trained as a psychologist or clinical social worker, he has no professional education or skills related to the treatment of sexual pathology, and he is not qualified to propose either pharmacological treatment or cognitive behavioral therapy. The doctrinal and practical chapters of his sect's chaplain's manual (with which he is doubtless familiar) are in fact divorced from the reality of work with incarcerated people. Leaving aside for a moment what is in the best interests of the incarcerated client, it is not fair to this man to expect him to do this work. Asking a Shinto priest to provide competent counseling to sex offenders based on his knowledge of shrine rituals and traditions is akin to asking a poet to perform brain surgery based on a knowledge of meter and verse. As unhelpful as it is arbitrary, this is a difficult situation for anyone involved.

Nonetheless, once a person is appointed as a chaplain, a range of social pressures can make it difficult to quit. A sectarian Shinto chaplain from Chiba who is in his seventies explained that complex relationships between the sects in the National Chaplains' Union place some chaplains in a bind. He related a story about a case from Hokkaido involving a chaplain's retirement from his relatively small sect. According to this account, once the sect Shinto chaplain retired, the Buddhist priests who held the other chaplaincy posts at his prison refused to appoint a replacement from the Shinto sect: "We don't need the help." The chaplain told this story to emphasize that individuals are appointed to represent their own sects in relations with the state and with other religious groups. The tale implies that there is a sense of team solidarity within one's own sect (and its chaplains' union) and a latent but ever-present competition between the sects that make up the National Chaplains' Union. The ecumenical attitude of the National Chaplains' Union has its limits. Asked about his own case, the Chiba chaplain paused:

> There are some issues . . . There is no system for retirement, and there is no pension. I have done this work until this advanced age, and I do not have anyone to take over in my place. Even if I wanted to stop, I couldn't really do it. If I quit, then [my sect] might lose our place at the prison. If I were to stop, we might not be allowed back in.[6]

The story about his own sect taking a loss in Hokkaido was a roundabout way of expressing his own dilemma. If he retires without a replacement, will his sect lose face?

Assignment to the chaplaincy takes place within ecclesiastical networks of hierarchical relationships that function like extended kinship groups. Individual clergy members must rely on the tangled web of sect connections throughout their careers. Clergy posts in a wide range of religious organizations are hereditary, and positions within the sect hierarchy often pass from father to son. Chaplaincy posts, too, are often handed down from a priest to his male heir. Because the actions of a senior member may impact the standing of his son, clergy must be extremely circumspect in their relations with the sect. Though there are many children of clergy who eagerly embrace the family tradition and its vocational path (including responsibilities like prison chaplaincy), there are others for whom these preordained arrangements represent a burden. The chaplain's joke crystallizes this sentiment. As the joke implies, an assignment to the chaplaincy can be hard to refuse and difficult to relinquish. In some cases, the appointment can be for life. Other interviews and participation in chaplains' retreats confirmed that most active chaplains are in their fifties, sixties, and seventies. After one training retreat, a middle-aged chaplain known to be a joker leaned my way and quipped about the greying audience: "The guys who come to these things are so old, usually a few of them are dead bodies!"

Mind the Gap: "The Practice of Chaplaincy and the Doctrinal Concept Are Distinct"

Whatever the conditions of appointment, many chaplains are in it for the long haul. But once they have a chaplain's manual in hand, National Chaplains' Union pin in their lapel, and a few shadowing sessions under the belt—then what? Interviews clarified that many chaplains view the official discourse with a healthy dose of skepticism. While many strive to go beyond the perfunctory performance of their duties, others pointed out that there are some chaplains who are more or less dead weight—those who show up at year-end events to receive accolades from the Ministry of Justice but rarely visit the prison at all. This is perhaps not surprising considering that the work is both unpaid and challenging.

However, in the course of my fieldwork, the chaplains who opted to spend the most time speaking with me did so because they felt they had something to say. For that reason, I focus here on some of those who expressed their commitment to doing a good job. I found that they try to improvise by focusing on the relationship with each client. *What does this person need? How can I help?* My overall impression was that those who expressed most dedication to the work embraced it with an avowed sense of personal or religious motivation. None declared a financial motivation, and none exhibited a great love for the prison system.

Rather than a comprehensive sociological overview, I pursue here the ethnographic goal of triangulation, seeking to paint a picture of what it is like to be a prison chaplain. I opt for this approach for the following reasons. First, chaplains themselves contend that no two people go about the job the same way, so individual variation is a defining feature of contemporary chaplaincy practice. Second, I focus on particular individuals because personality is so rigorously excluded from archival sources about chaplaincy, and I take the position that one of the most important things to know is how people respond to this inherited role. To this end, I introduce three chaplains who exemplify a tendency to overcome the limited horizon of the official doctrines. I have selected these case studies to represent a range of voices and approaches: a female Jōdoshū Buddhist chaplain working at Tachikawa Jail (with short-term detainees or those awaiting trial), a male Tenrikyō chaplain working at Fuchū Prison (with long-term detainees), and a male Shin Buddhist chaplain working with short-term detainees and on death row at Tokyo Jail.

I believe these chaplains' stories are representative of the prison chaplaincy as a whole in several ways. First, the chaplain's formal role is the same throughout Japan, so they face common challenges. Sect and state authorities expect the chaplains to contribute to the public benefit while refraining from involvement in politics. Chaplains are positioned between religious organizations and government agencies with responsibilities on both sides in addition to their duties to their incarcerated clients, and the case studies here show how this arrangement creates role tensions. Second, interviews suggest that the attempts these three chaplains make to transcend the limitations of their circumscribed role are representative of the ways committed chaplains go about the work. They do more than is described in chaplaincy publications, and they think about the situation of the incarcerated with a far greater degree of nuance than the official records provide. Finally, there are many chaplains who try their best to help inmates, but these three are considered effective and devoted by their peers, and so they are in that sense exemplary.

Rev. Fukai Miyoko is an unusual chaplain for several reasons.[7] When I interviewed her, she was one of only fifty-six women serving in the prison chaplaincy, and she was the only woman serving in the Jōdoshū chaplaincy. She was an ordained Buddhist priest who did not come from a temple household, and she was the only person I met who actively sought to become a prison chaplain. Fukai was born into a lay family, but she studied at the Buddhist Taisho University in Tokyo. Her college friendships with members of the Buddhist clergy sparked a lifelong interest in Buddhism. She studied under a respected scholar who happened to be a Jōdoshū priest and prison chaplain. Through him, she first became aware of prison chaplaincy when she was eighteen years old, and for some reason, the idea of this work struck a chord with her. During college, she worked part-time as a staff member at a Buddhist temple on weekends. She emphasized that it was her personal connections to Buddhist people that first attracted her to clerical work.

After graduation, Fukai pursued a career in research and education. As part of a team of researchers, she was involved in editing a Buddhist studies encyclopedia in her twenties. By her thirtieth birthday, she had taken a trip to India and returned to Japan to pursue graduate study in Buddhism. At some point, she was married briefly but separated soon after the birth of her daughter, with whom she now lives. In her thirties, Fukai received ordination in the Pure Land sect. She was working as a teacher at the time I met her.

After ordination, in pursuit of a job, Fukai said that she once phoned Utsunomiya Women's Prison (in the Tokyo area) to inquire about openings for a chaplain. She was told, "There is no way for someone to become a prison chaplain. One has to be appointed." She inquired once more through a friend who was serving in the chaplaincy, but she was told it would be impossible to get an assignment. It is not surprising that Fukai was unaware of the inner workings of the prison chaplaincy, nor is it surprising that even though she wanted to serve she could not get a post. My own impression is that virtually no one outside the prison service seems to know much about it. Like the prison system, it is a closed world.

Having been involved in the Pure Land Buddhist community for forty years, Fukai finally received an invitation through her sect to fill a chaplaincy opening at Tachikawa Jail in western Tokyo. She was over sixty by the time she got the call. She explained the circumstances of her appointment as follows:

A Jōdoshū chaplain stepped down, and I got a call from the sect one day. "Do you still want to do it?" I said yes, and they asked me to come over to Zōjōji temple to fill out the paperwork. So I did, and I became a prison chaplain. The thing is, it costs money to be a prison chaplain [fees to the union]. As you know, I am not from a temple household. So when I went to talk to them about becoming a chaplain, they said, "Are you going to be able to afford this?" And I said, "If I don't try it, then I'll never know."

The work is unpaid, right? And you have to pay to do it?

It is unpaid. You have to pay into it more than you are remunerated. But it is worth it.

I have never met someone who wanted to do this. Why would you want to do this?

I became a chaplain after the age of sixty. It was something I had wanted to do since I was eighteen. I had been wanting to do this for over forty years!

I asked Fukai if she had some religious motivation for wanting to become a chaplain, but she said she does not regard chaplaincy as a kind of religious practice (*shūkyōteki na shugyō*). Rather, she considers it "training for life" (*jinsei no shugyō*). She said she was interested in prison chaplaincy primarily because she thought this work would help her to understand people and society at a deeper level.

I observed Fukai's individual chaplaincy sessions at a small chapel at Tachikawa Jail in 2012. Inside a cramped room with a *butsudan* in one corner, Fukai met with an elderly man who had been arrested repeatedly for minor offenses. The man entered the room with a bow and then sat in a folding chair before the altar. Fukai, in black clerical vestments, stood between the man and the Buddha. After chanting the *nenbutsu* (the name of Amida Buddha), she talked to the man about his impending release. She spoke with a firm tone, but she never raised her voice: "You are to be paroled soon, aren't you? But it looks like you have been in and out a number of times for stupid [*baka*] offences. Why do you keep doing these things?"

The man stared at the floor, avoiding Fukai's gaze. When he finally spoke, I noticed that he seemed to struggle putting sentences together, and he stuttered badly: "I don't know why. I can't help it. If I have money . . . I just want to spend it right away . . . I want to do something fun." Fukai looked at him with sympathy, and I imagined that she now realized, as I just had, that this man suffered from an intellectual disability. The word *baka* now seemed like a poor choice. She tried first to speak to the man in the language of Buddhism. "Next time, before you do something bad, try to remember the face of the Buddha." His eyes remained on the floor. He said, "I don't know the face of the Buddha." Fukai nodded once and shifted focus to the family. "Where is your mother? Do you still have contact with her? Why don't you visit her when you get out? I am sure she thinks about you." The man remained impassive: "I don't know."

Fukai pressed. "You have to remember your mother. The next time, before you do something that will send you back here, please try to remember the face of your mother." The man said, "I can't remember." Undaunted, Fukai said, "You have to try. Please do your best."

When I met Fukai to talk about her work as a chaplain, we discussed this session as a representative example of her process. She insisted that the focus should not be on doctrine, but on the needs of inmates and the requirements of the particular situation:

> I have been a chaplain for seven years, and I think that whatever "doctrinal admonition" means in the doctrinal context, the actual practice of chaplaincy and the doctrine are distinct. Take the concept of the eightfold path. I think that however one may try to explain this path to people behind bars, some are not going to be able to understand it. So how do we proceed?
>
> That's why I start from everyday conversation: What was your father like? What was your mother like? I am from the Jōdoshū sect, but usually the client doesn't know the difference between Jōdo and Shin or any of the others. They don't know Kūkai [774–835, founder of the Shingon sect] from Hōnen [1133–1212, founder of Fukai's Jōdo sect]. So there is no way to begin other than by asking them to think about why they are here in prison now.
>
> There is a big gap between the doctrines of prison chaplaincy and the expectations that inmates actually have toward prison chaplains. This is something I have learned well in my years as a chaplain.
>
> There is another issue. In my own experience, 70 percent of the people I meet in prison seem to have suffered neglect from their parents when they

were small. In one of my group sessions, four out of five inmates did not receive sufficient affection from their parents—specifically from their mothers. I ask them about this: how was your childhood? Many of them were separated from their parents, and they grew up by themselves. With problems like this, we don't yet enter into the realm of Buddhist doctrine [*Bukkyō izen no mondai*].

Fukai's comments strike at the heart of a fundamental problem with the official discourse of the chaplaincy. She gestures to mitigating circumstances behind crime that fall beyond the realm of individual moral responsibility—issues beyond the doctrine's limited scope. What should a chaplain make of the fact that many people in prison suffer from intellectual disabilities? In her session, Fukai moved from invoking the face of the Buddha to the face of the mother as an exhortation to do good. The maternal image is associated with the compassion of Amida Buddha in the Pure Land tradition, but as Fukai acknowledged, even this expedient means may have been beyond the reach of this client. Some people will not be able to intellectually grasp Buddhist doctrine. This reality poses a problem for chaplaincy dogma precisely because the enterprise is premised on the educative model of punishment. How can the correctional system "correct" people who, through no fault of their own, lack the capacity to learn the lesson? Moving beyond the neurobiological realm to social history, how can a chaplain reckon with the life history of inmates who have suffered abuse and neglect from childhood? Fukai acknowledged that the majority of her clients have shared this kind of suffering, and she said bluntly that the individual client's lived experience must take priority over doctrine in chaplaincy sessions. It is important to note that she said she came to these conclusions herself over seven years on the job—she was not formally trained to think this way.

Though she expressed her motivations in terms of intellectual pursuits, Fukai exhibited concern for the incarcerated people who come to see her. I asked her what she thinks her clients want from her, and she emphasized a sense of connection that is otherwise unavailable to prisoners:

Their faces change before and after a chaplaincy session. When they leave, they smile. They have thirty minutes to talk. They can put themselves out there. They cannot do that with the prison guards. If I see them two or three times, then I feel like I can see a difference. The prison staff also says that it seems to make a difference. I think the ones who meet me two or three times must be getting something from it. Even when they are transferred to another facility, they can continue meeting with chaplains. Perhaps this is just wishful thinking?

Fukai contrasts her role as a chaplain with that of the prison guards who cannot interact with inmates with any degree of intimacy. In a separate interview, a correctional staff member from the education department at Fuchū Prison emphasized the same point, highlighting that inmates can speak more freely with chaplains than with prison staff and that chaplains provide inmates with a sense of connection to the world beyond the prison.[8] Nonetheless, even Fukai herself questioned whether her sense of the impact of her actions was anything more than wishful thinking. Without input from inmates, it is impossible to venture a judgment— but chaplains and correctional officials do appear to agree that the chaplain can offer a more intimate and sympathetic conversation partner than other correctional staff.

Though Fukai was reluctant to frame her activities within a doctrinal context, she asserted that the value of the chaplain's presence lies in the capacity to provide a sense of human contact. This theme of connection as a means to alleviate suffering represents the major countercurrent to the mainstream discourse of doctrinal admonition. It is not robustly theorized, and because it tends to emerge in the context of particular relationships, it appears to be resistant to both doctrinal systematization and institutionalization. In my experience, many chaplains talked about the importance of connecting with inmates. However, little is written about the topic in chaplains' publications, and the chaplaincy is not organized around such principles. This is what Fukai meant when she declared that the practice and the doctrine are distinct.

The disjunction between chaplaincy discourse and practice raises a larger issue. Prison chaplains do not consider their work in prisons to be a form of spiritual care (*kokoro no kea*).[9] Despite this, many prison chaplains emphasize the importance of attentive listening and extending oneself in compassion toward clients, and these practices appear similar to those of hospital and hospice chaplains (spiritual care workers) to an outside observer.[10] Nonetheless, when I asked prison chaplains whether they think of their work as a form of "spiritual care," *no one* agreed with that characterization. Many appeared never to have considered the connection. Typical responses included the following: "Isn't spiritual care for people in a hospice?" "This issue developed after the 3.11 disaster, but not in relation to prison." "Spiritual care? Hmmm. Now that you mention it [*tashikani, sō iwaretara*] . . . Perhaps there is a similarity?"

There are historical reasons that Japanese prison chaplains tend not to consider their work under the rubric of spiritual care. As the preceding chapters have demonstrated, the formal goals of Japanese prison chaplaincy developed prior to the contemporary focus on spiritual care, and the original nineteenth-century rationale for doctrinal admonition bears little similarity to the more recent history of global spiritual care trends. Concisely put, spiritual care practices focus on alleviating suffering. By contrast, the goals of doctrinal admonition (Japanese prison chaplaincy) have historically been construed within the parameters of moral instruction. It is true that in their respective vocational discourses, both hospital chaplains and prison chaplains in Japan emphasize their contributions to the goals of their institutional hosts, but most prison chaplains do not yet seem to draw the connection between hospital and prison chaplaincy themselves. The tradition of prison chaplaincy doctrine is centered on the mission of fighting the personal and social evil of crime. The job of providing spiritual care in a hospital is the domain of a hospital chaplain (*chapuren*). Japanese hospital chaplaincy developed separately from prison chaplaincy, and it is not a genealogical descendant of "doctrinal admonition." The fact that both *kyōkaishi* and *chapuren* are rendered into English as "chaplain" obscures the important distinction.

The sects involved in prison chaplaincy developed their programs as part of broader attempts to cultivate their niche as defenders of the public good. Could not a similar motivation be relevant to individual chaplains? Some of Fukai's attraction to both Buddhism and prison chaplaincy may arise from her sense that there is power in these forms. She made it clear that she considers the vocation of the Buddhist priesthood a way to do good in the world. To this extent, does it not also offer a chance to be clothed in moral authority? Fukai told me of her failed marriage and the daughter she raised alone. She made it clear that she had needed to be tough in order to provide for her child. The Buddhist path and her many Buddhist friends presented a way to move forward and take charge of her own life when things threatened to fall apart. In her capacity as a prison chaplain, she is in a position to try to help other people to get their lives on track. The work may be empowering in some ways. Nonetheless, to help inmates, Fukai relies more on her own life experience, wits, and strength of personality than she does on any doctrinal training.

Getting Personal: "People Only Want to Look on Crime from a Distance"

When I met Rev. Dōyama Yoshio, he was the head of the Tenrikyō Ōedo Branch Church in Tokyo.[11] He was also serving as prison chaplain at the nearby Fuchū Prison. According to his own estimate, he was one of only a handful of prison chaplains to serve simultaneously as a volunteer probation officer and a volunteer prison visitor.[12] These combined responsibilities meant that his life was deeply connected to the correctional system. I met with Dōyama in Tenri City, Nara Prefecture, in September 2014 to discuss his work as a chaplain. Dōyama was in his mid- to late fifties, and he came across as friendly and straightforward. I got the impression that he said exactly what he was thinking with no filter.

Like Fukai, Dōyama emphasized the disjunction between the way prison chaplains' responsibilities are officially defined and what he considers to be *the real work* of chaplaincy:

> I only have about fifteen minutes for individual chaplaincy sessions. If it were up to me, I could talk to them all day. It is not enough just to talk to them while they are in prison. To really help people, it takes more. Many people in prison tend to have intellectual disabilities. So when it comes to conversation, it can sometimes be difficult to tell how much they are comprehending. The fact of having an intellectual disability is not the individual's responsibility. Many of these people get used by others, and that is why they wind up in prison. I really think that many of the so-called perpetrators are also victims themselves.

As soon as he broached the topic of prison chaplaincy, Dōyama pushed back against the undergirding assumption of chaplaincy discourse and correctional rehabilitation. He turned to mitigating factors that contribute to crime, specifying that the issue of intellectual disability complicates any simplistic understanding of moral agency. The line between perpetrators and victims can be blurry because offenders are often themselves victims of structural injustices. Dōyama thinks incarceration is not an appropriate method for dealing with intellectually disabled offenders, and he believes there are many such people in prison. As a chaplain, what can he do?

Dōyama was working within the correctional system but doing so according to his own values. He said that religious social work was his lifework (*raifu wāku*), and he elaborated by explaining that within the Tenrikyō Church, there is a tradition of recognizing reincarnation within the same family. The biography of an individual may be connected to the biography of an ancestor who is thought to have been the prior incarnation of the same soul (*tamashii*). In Dōyama's case, he has been taught since his birth that he is the reincarnation of the paternal ancestor who founded his Ōedo Church in 1930. This past life formed the template for his own, connecting his destiny to that of his progenitor and binding them both to the web of stories that make up the collective memory of the Tenrikyō community. In Dōyama's understanding, the mission of his church, the legacy of his family, and the meaning of his life are tied to the goal of uplifting the people who live on the margins of society:

> There is a record of the past written into our souls before we are born. This record impacts the course of all of our future lives. My name is Dōyama Yoshio. The first member of the Dōyama family to become a Tenrikyō follower was my great-grandfather, Dōyama Aibei. His life has had an impact on the course of my own. Aibei came out to Tokyo with nothing but a single bag. He came out to help people in Tokyo. He spent his life helping people living at the margins of society, helping the poor. We have a record of his life in the history of our church. In Taishō 5 [1930], Aibei founded our church.
>
> When I think about his life, I think it is related to the fact that I became a chaplain at Fuchū Prison, then a VPO, then a volunteer visitor at another prison. I think there are maybe fewer than two dozen people in Japan who do all three of these jobs. Every year I picked up another. They just kept coming my way. The thing is, I kept getting recommended for these things. These aren't the kind of thing that one can apply for. It happens through nominations and recommendations. I think that there must

be some connection to my own soul's destiny [*innen*]. Aibei worked with people on the margins of society, and today, the people in prison are the ones on the margins of society.

So I feel that doing this work is my destiny. I can feel the working of God [*Kami-sama no hataraki*]—God's mind is behind this. This is the destiny of my ancestor Aibei at work in my own life. Since I was a child, people have been telling me that I was the reincarnation of Dōyama Aibei. My name has the kanji for "love" in it, like his name. As a little boy, I couldn't stand it. People thought it was feminine. But over time, I started to think that I have been very lucky thanks to him. You know, I inherited a church—the church he founded. As a young man, I was sent out to found my own church in Matsudo in Chiba. It was hard, but that was an appropriate test for me given that my destiny is tied to Aibei [because Aibei, too, founded his own church]. I was happily able to start a new church, and I even found a successor to take over.

I became a chaplain, a VPO, and then a volunteer prison visitor in 2000, 2001, and then 2003, respectively. One after another. As these piled up, I really felt like the connection to Dōyama Aibei was shaping my life. This all became my lifework [*raifu wāku*]. Of course, being a Tenrikyō priest is my lifework, but the prison work is part of my work as a priest. All of this was recorded in the destiny of my soul. As a religionist, I was raised to believe that I must fulfill my destiny. We are all supposed to live up to the destiny that is recorded in our souls as if it is written into our DNA. Realizing this goal can be very hard. I am sure that every chaplain and every VPO thinks differently about the work—but I think that my own mission has been to work with people in prison because Aibei worked with people at the margins of society.

Dōyama's story of destiny offers another variation of the theme of karma that surrounds prison chaplaincy. Unlike the chaplain's joke, which reflects a bitterness about the appointment, Dōyama saw working with the incarcerated and parolees as his vocation. For him, the work was meaningful and fulfilling because chaplaincy has a coherent connection to the tradition that he wished to uphold—but the tradition that he honored was not that of the chaplaincy, the correctional system, or the state.

Precisely because he found the work to be existentially significant, Dōyama regarded the official definition of a chaplain's responsibilities to be self-defeating. There are prison regulations (not laws) that aim to prevent chaplains from having any contact with inmates after release. Though it is technically not permitted, Dōyama was in the habit of inviting former inmates to come and live in his church with his family:

> So the other week, I told a young man, "When you get out, come to my house. We'll sort you out." He said he wants to work, so I thought we could find something for him. I told him that when he gets out, he can rent an apartment near my place. That way, when he gets frustrated or upset, he can come over, and I will talk things over with him. He could become friends with some of the people from our church, and he would be welcome at our monthly service [*tsukinamisai*]. To me, this is what it takes to lift someone up from hardship [*nanjū o sukui ageru*].

Dōyama took the mission to help marginalized people as a sacred duty. He tried to overcome what he saw as the shortcomings in the correctional and probation system by bringing his work home with him. He operated an ad hoc halfway house without support from the state.[13] When I visited Dōyama's church, I met people at the monthly service who first encountered him while they were in prison. Dōyama said that at least one of those men was living in the church at the time of my visit. Because the church also served a foster home, there may have been as many as ten people living there—most of them school-age children. Dōyama's public role as prison chaplain bled into his private life as he maintained relationships with clients outside prison walls. In his own words, he was doing this work "personally" (*kojinteki ni*)—and Dōyama was not the only one. Based on interviews, it appeared to me that Tenrikyō churches, in particular, frequently engaged in this kind of outreach work with former inmates. It was sometimes done in an official capacity as a registered halfway house, and sometimes it was just done privately or, as Dōyama said, "personally."

Despite his conviction that the personal relationship is the key to helping those who fall off the straight and narrow, when I attended his group chaplaincy session at Fuchū Prison in September 2015, Dōyama's sermon conformed to the pattern of the official chaplaincy discourse. Speaking in the Shinto chapel (there are also separate Buddhist and Christian chapels at Fuchū—Japan's largest prison), Dōyama exhorted the assembled inmates to rectify their hearts:

In Tenrikyō, we teach that in this life we are working out our past karma. [. . .] The deeds we do and the way we use our hearts are distinct from the physical body, connected to the life before and to the next. The good that we do comes back, and the evil that we do comes back too. I have come to think of this remnant as something like a savings account with the divine bank that is built into our souls. Anybody would be glad if their savings increase, right? I believe that Kami watches over us and sees how we use our hearts every day and how we behave. I think that when we act to make others happy and to help others, then our moral savings increase, and when we do the opposite, our savings are depleted. There is no point in saying, "I am too old. I can't turn it around now." Why? Because the soul continues to live, and the balance with the heavenly savings account influences one's future lives. If I put this heavenly savings account metaphor into religious language, I might be able to refer to it as virtue. I certainly hope for each of you that you will work to increase your moral savings, to develop virtue in your souls.

It appears that even Dōyama—who privately criticized the correctional system and went above and beyond the call of duty outside prison walls— was willing to play the part as written in this context. Of course, what he said was not objectionable, and one might hear a similar talk at Tenrikyō churches throughout Japan. Nonetheless, in the prison—that is, in public speech representing the chaplaincy—Dōyama completed the genre-defining exercise of chaplaincy doctrine by linking a notion of religious salvation to the goals of correctional reform. This is despite the fact that the mainstream of Tenrikyō theology emphasizes both healing the individual heart (*kokoro naoshi*) and healing the world (*yo naoshi*). Tenrikyō scriptures call for the building of a more equal society by addressing inequality in the social structure. However, in the context of the prison, just as the postwar Shin Buddhist chaplaincy doctrine eschews Shinran's antinomian tendencies, the Tenrikyō chaplain Dōyama emphasized healing the individual heart and did not discuss injustices. What is excluded is as significant as what is said. The sermon not only presents a one-sided version of his religion's core theology, it also belies the nuance of Dōyama's own beliefs about the nature of crime. This episode encapsulates the tendency for religious workers to mold their presentations to the demands of the correctional system. (See Appendix A for a full transcript of this chaplaincy session.)

Dōyama seemed to enjoy his work, but the involvement with the correctional system took up an enormous amount of time, and prison chaplaincy is unpaid. He has a wife and children at home, and I wondered how he managed to balance his responsibilities with family life. There were also signs that the stress of his endless poverty relief work might be impacting his health. He joked openly about drinking too much. He even advocated active involvement in community and social justice work as an effective hangover cure:

> Yesterday, I was hungover from a party the night before. This happens to me when I drink. I was hungover, and then I got a call from someone on the Parent Teacher Association. And you know what? As soon as I started thinking about other people and trying to do something to help out, I started to feel better! I guess working for other people must be good for my body as well as my heart. There is nothing happier than helping other people.

Tenrikyō doctrine entails a belief in the power of a pure heart and good works to contribute to good health. Dōyama found it fulfilling to help others, and he seemed to be surrounded by people who were relying on him constantly. I spent something in the range of thirty hours in his company, and I have rarely seen anyone whose cell phone rings so frequently. In this sense, he is a pillar in his community. As a result, it may be that he directed all of his energy toward the needs of others. His joke was in part to deny that this work was done at the cost of neglecting himself. Despite this, I wondered if it was not the case that his private life was being consumed by responsibilities spilling over from his public station. What did his wife and children think?

Because Dōyama was not the only prison chaplain to bring former inmates home, I asked some other chaplains what they thought of the practice in general. A shrine Shinto prison chaplain provided a contrasting view:

> I know of some chaplains who are really putting everything into it, and somehow they have created relationships between their own home life and former inmates. There are some people who have faced complicated problems because of this. We have to do [chaplaincy] in a way that doesn't make

our own lives a mess. Sometimes [former inmates whom I recognize] come
to pay their respects at the shrine. I tell them they do not have to do this,
but some still come. I try to avoid them if they come. If I did meet them,
the staff would know what was up. Even if these guys just come to me to
say, "Thank you for your help," the staff can tell where they have come
from. When I see one, I just say, "Please feel free to pay your respects at
the shrine" [but I will not engage in a conversation].[14]

The shrine priest preferred to keep a strict separation between his private
life and his duties to the prison. If one sought a theological explanation,
then his desire may be attributable partly to a Shinto priest's responsibility to maintain the purity of the shrine precincts by preventing the
intrusion of ritual pollution (*kegare*). The concept of pollution can be
applied to the perception of moral impurities, so it may be associated with
negative views of former inmates.[15] A pragmatic explanation is also possible: the chaplain may have been trying to avoid some of the difficulties
that former inmates may bring into the home.

Another Tenrikyō priest involved in chaplaincy, foster care, and halfway house work described a harrowing incident involving a parolee. At
the parolee's request, the priest permitted the man to reside temporarily
in the church, where the priest lived with family, including young foster
children. It turned out that the lodger was severely mentally ill. One day
while the priest was away, the man brandished a knife, threatened everyone in the church, attacked his host's wife, and then barricaded himself
in a bedroom. The priest's wife immediately phoned the police, but before they arrived, the rampaging parolee had hanged himself. The wife
picked up the knife and cut the dead body down from the rope.

To open one's home to parolees and former inmates cannot make life
easier. Nonetheless, Dōyama's desire to be heavily involved in the lives of
the incarcerated is consistent with the doctrines of his religion. Tenrikyō
rejects concepts of impurity, and according to the teachings, all people
should be regarded as part of one human family—the children of God
the Parent (Oyagami-sama). This ideal expands the boundaries of the intimate circle and entails a duty to help the poor and the suffering as one's
own. In this vein, Dōyama described what he saw as the Japanese public's prejudicial attitude toward parolees by referring to a line from one of
his favorite novels: "People only want to look on crime from a distance."[16]

Dōyama did not want to create distance between himself and his clients. He said that he wanted to live according to the model of his ancestor Aibei by devoting himself to helping people on the margins of society. One result was that he had to live there himself, working outside the bounds of the state's correctional program to supplement inadequate aftercare for offenders. The same shrine Shinto chaplain who worried about this kind of involvement acknowledged that it stems from an underlying structural problem:

> I think it would be better if there were more intermediary institutions between the prison and society at large. If inmates are released from prison back into society all of a sudden—with no job prospects, no place to live, and typically no contact with their family—then it is extremely difficult for them to reintegrate.[17]

In this chaplain's words, it is a "political problem" (*seijiteki na mondai*). Without any major public discourse surrounding this issue and absent any state-backed reform initiative, Dōyama and some of his colleagues in the prison chaplaincy have been left to try to solve this structural issue by addressing it "personally." This degree of commitment to religious social work entails real risks for individual chaplains and their families.

Karma as Connection: "What we Really Need in Life is the Sense of Connection"

Rev. Hirano Shunkō, discussed in the introduction to this book, was one of the people responsible for inviting me into the world of the chaplaincy. Hirano is a Shin priest and former abbot of the Honganji sect temple Chūgenji in Chiba. He was in his mid-seventies when I first met him in 2014, and he was formerly the elected chairman of the National Chaplains' Union. At that time, Hirano had been serving as prison chaplain to death row inmates at Tokyo Jail since 1981. He is highly respected by fellow chaplains for his wisdom and kindness, and he impressed me as a person of great sensitivity. I met Hirano regularly at National Chaplains'

Union meetings over two years, observed one of his group chaplaincy sessions, and visited him several times at his temple.[18] I found him to be a master conversationalist. It may be that he refined the techniques of the heart-to-heart talk over three decades of practice with people on death row.

The job of death row chaplain is an enormous burden for anyone to take on, but Hirano never said a bitter word about it. He explained that taking the work of chaplaincy seriously allowed him to grow as a person. For this reason, despite the challenges, Hirano said that his feeling toward his clients was one of gratitude. He did not always feel this way. When he was first invited to take the post on death row as a young man, he was terrified:

> Honestly, I thought, are you kidding? I was scared! I thought, can I really do this? Working with people who have committed serious felonies? Murders? At that time my mother was still alive, but she was ill. She was hospitalized. [. . .] It turned out my mother had cancer. I was very upset at that time. We knew she had about a year to live. Honestly, my head was so full of my own concerns at the time. But, in Buddhism, we call this kind of thing a karmic connection. So I asked my mother for advice. And she said, "You can't possibly go to such a scary place!" [laughs].[19]

Despite his mother's objections, Hirano did not refuse the appointment. In telling the story, he invoked the concept of karmic connection to attribute his assignment to the chaplaincy to the hands of fate. It was Rev. Watanabe Fusō, a senior colleague from the sect and a death row chaplain himself, who asked the young Hirano to join. (Watanabe later became head of the National Chaplains' Union—the same post that Hirano would go on to hold.)

Hirano was grateful that Watanabe expressed confidence in him, but initially he felt like he was out of his depth. He described his first time going to meet a death row inmate for a religious counseling session in Tokyo Jail's small prison chapel. Watanabe and a guard accompanied him:

> That first time . . . What can I say? I suppose I was very nervous. I am sure the inmate could tell I was terrified. Periodically, I would have a sudden wave of fear. Of course, I had no way to defend myself if something went wrong. [. . .]

The scene was like this. There was a *butsudan* in the corner. We started by clasping our hands and doing a prayer. And then I returned to the table, and at that moment I had a wave of fear. Just for a moment—it passed. [. . .]

The thing is, I had this idea that a death row inmate might try to do something to cause trouble. If they commit a crime while behind bars, then a new trial will start, right? So if they do something to cause a new trial, then the date of their execution could be pushed back! I started to think about this and convinced myself that I was in danger.

Is there a known case where something like that happened?

No, no. Not at all! But I was thinking, if I were him, what would I do? And that's where my fear came from. If I were on death row, maybe I would want to do something to put off my execution!

In this remarkable story, it is possible to detect the first seed of Hirano's later insight. Interacting with a person on death row disrupted Hirano's sense of himself in a way that was initially frightening. By his own estimation, *the source of his fear was that he started to imagine what it would be like to be the other person*. He spontaneously identified himself with the incarcerated person and started to imagine how he would react if he were in the other's shoes. At first, he experienced this interaction as a threat to his identity, but over time the experience came to have a different meaning for him. In recognizing that someone on death row is human like himself, Hirano began to let go of the idea that "criminals" are one-dimensional.

Whether it be construed as fate or the workings of the correctional bureaucracy, both Hirano and his first client were brought together by forces beyond their control. In Hirano's thinking, the shared situation was the result of a karmic connection. Hirano suggested that the death row inmates he counseled provided him with some of the most existentially significant experiences of his life—conversations and interactions that fundamentally shaped him as a person and a devout Buddhist. Through these connections, his thinking about other people changed, and so too did his understanding of himself and his place in the world. Hirano realized that a person is not reducible to his or her worst mistake. In his own words:

Every person I meet is different. Just because a person has committed a crime, it doesn't mean they will be similar to someone else who is behind bars for the same crime. They all think differently, and they have different personalities. But they have all lived through some adversity. Perhaps they come from dire poverty, or their parents divorced, or they couldn't cut it at school. There are many background factors involved. In the end, they have ended up living behind bars. This means that they are alone.

Contrary to the doctrinaire assumption that people commit crimes due to a spiritual problem, Hirano maintained that the course of a person's life depends largely on luck: "There are times when life seems to go our way, and times when it does not." This perspective implies that people are more than they appear to be at any one moment or in the context of any one relationship. Rather than seeing crime as emerging from a fixed personal identity, Hirano believes it to be a product of situations. In Buddhist terms, the course of a person's life is not determined by volitional action—the working of individual karma—but rather through relationships and accidents: an unfathomable karmic destiny unfolding through a tangled web of connections to others. It is not that people wind up on death row because they share common character flaws. In Hirano's view, what they have in common (besides conviction for a capital offense) is that their lives have been a struggle, they have had bad luck, and they are alone now.

The change in Hirano's perspective may in part be attributed to the peculiar working conditions of a death row chaplain. In the case of ordinary inmates, the purpose of prison chaplaincy is to promote character reform through religious instruction. However, in the context of death row, the state has abandoned the goal of educative punishment. These inmates are not to be rehabilitated but killed. Thus, the official purpose of death row chaplaincy is to promote "emotional stability." From the perspective of the institution, death row chaplaincy promotes docility. I consider the implications of this arrangement shortly, but what does this work mean for the chaplain? The absence of a correctional goal means that death row chaplains primarily serve as counselors. They have conversations with their clients to mitigate against the effects of the total social isolation on death row. In short, the chaplain is the only person responsible to engage these people as human beings. It is here that Japan's prison chaplaincy practice creates a space for work resembling spiritual care, with a primary focus on mitigating suffering. Through this work, Hirano learned to see his incarcerated clients as individuals with unique life stories and personalities.

The death row chaplain's job is to provide intimacy. Hirano's explanation of this role revolved around the themes of aloneness and connection. For people who are otherwise cut off from the world, the chaplain provides the only chance for a sense of connection to a reality beyond the prison cell:

> When they were free, they may have gone about committing crimes, but once they are inside, they feel loneliness in a different way than people on the outside do. Now you and I might feel lonely, but it is not the same. Basically, we are free. You want to go for a walk? Then you can go. But for them, for the first time, this freedom is no longer possible. They realize, I am well and truly alone now. Typically, they have been abandoned by their parents too. Now, if you take a lonely person, and they meet someone who does care about them [like the chaplain], then that is a most happy thing. In prison, the inmate might not care about rehabilitation at all. There are some people in prison who fall into despair. What they really want is to feel a connection between human hearts. The warmth of another person's heart is what these people need. Even for me, living in normal society, I might not think of the importance of the warmth that comes from another person. I might think: I want people to think well of me! I want to be recognized for doing my best! Our lives in society flow on like this. But what we really need in life is the sense of connection to other people. The role of the chaplain is to relate to the client as an equal.

Hirano tended to humanize people on death row by comparing them constantly to himself: *They think like this; I think like this too.* He invited me to imagine what it is like to be one of them: "You want to go for a walk? You can go." But if I were one of the unfortunate souls on death row, then I would lack even this simple freedom. Behind Hirano's invitation to place myself in someone else's shoes is his insight that the need for human connection is universal: the incarcerated feel it as much as anyone. The chaplain's job is to respond to this universal human need— Hirano described it as a problem of the heart (*kokoro no mondai*). He does not mean that crime arises from internal disharmony. Rather, the implication is that all people face similar existential struggles. It is just that those on death row are in a particularly extreme situation. He pressed the theme of human similarity to emphasize that the chaplain's most sacred duty is to recognize the humanity of the incarcerated: "The role of the chaplain is to relate to the client as an equal." This egalitarian way of thinking, with its focus on relieving the suffering brought on by isolation, is totally distinct from the official chaplaincy discourse and its goals of correctional reform and promoting docility. Hirano makes no attempt to "rectify the hearts" of offenders in a rigid way. Rather, he tries to extend himself as a sympathetic conversation partner.

In January 2016, I attended one of Hirano's group sessions for regular inmates (not for death row, which was closed to me), and witnessed him putting his philosophy into practice. Tokyo Jail's small chapel resembled a classroom with a *butsudan*. There, Hirano led a group of a half dozen male inmates in a reading session. The text was a small pamphlet titled *The Teaching of Buddha*. In simple language, it conveys the famous life story of Siddhartha Gautama. The men sat around a table as in a typical college seminar, and Hirano asked for volunteers to read the section "The Question of Life." One by one, the men read the story aloud. It told of the nineteen-year-old Prince Siddhartha's first voyage beyond the cloistered walls of his father's estate. Out in the world, he saw for the first time the reality of aging, illness, and death. Most versions of this story then include a fourth sight, the vision of a renunciate, but this was not mentioned. We read of Siddhartha's deepening existential crisis: "If all must die, then I too must die?" In light of the recent Coming of Age Day ceremonies held throughout Japan, Hirano asked the men what it means to become an adult.

The second Monday in January marks the coming of age ceremony for people reaching their twentieth year (Siddartha was nineteen in this version of the story). Hirano emphasized that becoming an adult is not just a matter of attending such a ceremony. He prompted the men to think: "Was there ever a time in your own life where you started to think more deeply, like Siddhartha?" After a brief silence, one of the men raised his voice. "When I was young, my father broke his neck. He was able to continue working. But he couldn't play with me outside anymore. I think from that point, my perspective on life became sad." Hirano nodded with understanding and said, "Oh, was that so. That's what your family was like . . . I had no idea." As the reading continued, I found that my mind lingered on this moment. I thought it encapsulated Hirano's approach—without pushing, he was extending himself to this man. Hirano was prepared to offer existential counseling or even simple conversation should the man choose to see him one on one. In Hirano's teaching and practice, to reach maturity is a goal: it means facing up to the reality of one's own mortality and realizing that such is our shared human destiny. This realization may open the space for new personal possibilities and new kinds of connection.

As a Shin priest, Hirano hopes that his clients will want to talk about Buddhism so that he may share Shinran's teachings about universal salvation through the power of Amida. However, he acknowledged that this rarely happens right away, and he insisted that doctrine has to come out naturally in the course of a conversation. And if a whole counseling session goes by without a mention of Buddhism, Hirano said that "even having a conversation about nothing in particular can be a kind of karmic connection." He would not force doctrine on his clients, and he recognized, "Even if I can provide someone with a kind of peace, I certainly don't have the power to save someone." He could take up religious topics if the client so desired, or he could leave religion out of the conversation entirely. He exercised judgment about how best to approach each individual so as to promote peace of mind or to build intersubjective affinity. Establishing the sense of connection takes priority over the propagation of doctrine. At the same time, Hirano suggested that the sense of connection itself was of the utmost religious significance.

Hirano's sense of the need for human connectedness was not limited to interpersonal relations. He invoked the theme of connection to suggest an extrahuman reality that can provide the kind of sustenance that significant others give—and more. Hirano has performed last rites for inmates for decades, and he experienced the problem of salvation for people on death row as a personal religious issue. In reckoning with this burden, he found it imperative to maintain a sense that Amida Buddha can provide deliverance from loneliness and suffering. Herein lies the significance of a karmic connection to the Buddha:

Shinran says that no matter what, there is a greater life beyond our human existence, and everyone is saved by this greater life. Our ailments, our suffering, our deaths—these things that come at the end of life are not the problem. They all emerge from our karmic destiny. Even people who seem to be living a pious life, praying the *nenbutsu* every day—even such people can die in pain. There are many who die in pain; people die—not praying, but cursing their own lives. [Shinran] rejects the idea that the way a person dies reflects the quality of the person. Those who die piously are not necessarily the good. And those who die fighting it are not necessarily evil.

We tend to think that the quality of a person's death reflects their fate after death, but that is because we do not realize the ultimate truth. That is why I believe in leaving salvation up to the working of Amida. We are fine as we are. There is Amida, there is hope, there is salvation. I think all we can do is believe in this. We have to leave it up to Amida. That is the nature of religion. Whether or not people realize it, I have come to believe this is what our human life is. We have to leave some things up to the Buddha.

Hirano maintains a belief in equality supported by his interpretation of Shin doctrine. Those on death row are not excluded from Amida's saving grace. There is salvation for those condemned to die "not praying, but cursing their own lives." This reading of Shinran is informed by the experience of serving on death row. Hirano's contention that the way a person dies is not an indication of the quality of that person must be understood as entailing a criticism of the death penalty. Hirano was at once both critical of the system and committed to serving within it, extending himself to those inmates who might desire his company, conversation, or counsel. Nonetheless, Hirano himself did not frame his activities under the rubric of spiritual care. Rather, his idiom for expressing his relationship to clients was the Buddhist language of karmic bonds. If his is not a ministry of presence, perhaps it is a ministry of connection. (See Appendix B for a full transcript of the interview with Hirano.)

My lasting impression of Hirano is that he is a man of great wisdom. I felt awed by his hard-earned insights into people, but at the same time, I wondered how one can best strike the balance between becoming reconciled to the world and its imperfections, on the one hand, and working to create a more just society through political action, on the other. I tried to put this question to Hirano as best I could at the time:

You mentioned that you have to treat your client as an equal. It seems that the perspective on humanity we see in Shinran implies a kind of equality. He thinks that the difference between the good and the evil is a false distinction. But this differs from the interpretation of the human that dominates in the law, no? Does not the law make a clear distinction between the good and the evil?

Yes. That's right. Society must be that way. In the end, our life in society is not designed for the salvation of the individual person. If society does not make a distinction between good and evil, it cannot survive. This is the social life of humanity. At the basis is the idea that society requires stability. That is why we need the law. There is nothing we can do about it.

But then again, we have the teaching of Buddha. Life is suffering. Of course life is tough! Of course it is hard! We cannot make the world equal through the power of the law. Why? It will not work because the law is made by human beings, and everything made by human beings changes over time. Even the law changes over time, right? It changes because it is something made by human beings. Law changes to suit the times. Reality or the truth, these do not change. For example, love [*ai*] in Christianity, or compassion [*jihi*] in Buddhism. It would be strange to claim that these change. "When your dad was around, it wasn't like this! We were not doing the *nenbutsu*! The scriptures used to be different!" That could not be because the truth does not change.

It is because the truth does not change that the teachings provide us with a sense of stability [*anshinkan*]. Think about it. If your hometown changed, you wouldn't want to go back, right? The mountains remain the same, the river remains the same, and even some of your friends stay around. In the same way, the truth doesn't change. The things made by human beings are subject to change.

In this framing, law, a product of human political compromise, is imperfect and impermanent. Religion and the values espoused therein—love or compassion—are timeless and provide refuge from the vicissitudes of political life. A tension exists between politics/engagement and religion/withdrawal. I realized only much later that Hirano's explanation of the relationship between politics and religion implicitly reproduces the Shin Buddhist distinction between two domains of law. As the public-private divide continues to be structured around a concept of religion, existential concerns that should rightly be included in political discussions— for example, concerns about our shared human destiny and what this implies for our responsibilities to the most marginalized people, those on death row—have come to *belong* to the realm of religion at the cost of forcing them into the private realm and generally excluding them from political discourse. The state recognizes that people on death row have private religious needs, and chaplains are thus the only outsiders who have contact with death row and its inhabitants. And yet even the chaplains who serve the incarcerated on death row are sworn to secrecy and forbidden from engagement with political issues. They may offer spiritual support but not political assistance. Is this because there are still effectively two domains of law? Is it that the role of religion even in the twenty-first century is to tend to private troubles of the heart but not to question sovereignty?

Like Dōyama and Fukai, Hirano strives to provide compassionate care for the incarcerated. All three of the chaplains introduced here move beyond the bounds of "doctrinal admonition" because they recognize personal moral obligations to alleviate suffering. At the same time, the official range of their responsibilities—and those of all Japanese prison chaplains—are delimited by the legal settlement that requires religion to be both a public benefit and a private affair. In effect, this arrangement means that religious workers in government institutions like the prison have little room to question the state's favored conception of the public good. If they want to make a difference in the lives of incarcerated people, then they must work within the system even if they do not support it. I close by exploring how this problem plays out on death row.

The Death Penalty and the Dharma

The worst-case scenario for prison chaplains is to be assigned to death row. Information about death row in Japan is extremely limited. The most significant recent work dealing with the death penalty is *Prison Chaplain* (*Kyōkaishi*, 2014) by freelance journalist Horikawa Keiko. This book is based on extended interviews with Watanabe Fusō (Hirano's mentor). Watanabe was a True Pure Land priest, and he served as head of the National Chaplains' Union some years before Hirano. Because the prison chaplaincy is governed by the same code of secrecy that surrounds the prison system, Watanabe agreed to talk with Horikawa only on the condition that she would not publish until after he died. When he passed away and Horikawa moved to take her findings public, she faced pressure from the Corrections Office not to publish.[20] The worst of it, she said, was that Watanabe's wife phoned to ask her to kill the story: "He never talked to me about any of this. Why would he talk to you?" The widow and family likely have their own reasons for not wanting their loved one's story to enter the public domain in connection to what may be seen as journalistic muckraking. However, the administrative drive to keep information about death row private and the attempt to prevent this journalist from taking her findings public arise from the antidemocratic regime of secrecy surrounding Japanese corrections. According to the bureaucratic rationale, the chaplain's role at an execution is not to be a witness. Rather, it is that chaplains should be present to promote an inmate's "emotional stability." The fallout from this arrangement is multifarious, and we consider now its impact on the chaplain.

Horikawa's book offers a description of Watanabe's first experience standing in at an execution. He was a junior chaplain, shadowing his mentor Shinoda. This account describes what he saw as he observed Shinoda playing the part that would subsequently become Watanabe's own role for decades:

> It was time. Prisoner Sakurai's name had been called. The legs that carried him forward were trembling slightly. Chaplain Shinoda quickly placed his hand on Sakurai's back.
>
> When the door opened, there appeared a four-mat tatami room with a small Buddhist altar. The warden and the director of general affairs were already seated. [. . .] Following Shinoda's lead, all of them together chanted a sutra and burned offerings of incense. Typically, this rite is performed for a person already dead. Now, it was being performed for a living man who would be dead in a matter of minutes. It was Watanabe's first time to see such a thing, and he felt it strange.
>
> The moment the sutra chanting was completed, there was a powerful, dry noise—*sha!* It was the sound of a deep purple curtain concealing the execution chamber next door being opened. At some point, Sakurai's arms had been bound behind his back, and he had lost the freedom of movement. He was surrounded by several guards who shuffled him in to the next room. Sakurai's body was positioned atop a small square trapdoor encircled by a white line. Already it was becoming unclear if Sakurai's body was his own or not. Just as they had rehearsed many times before, the

guards took the thick noose that hung from the ceiling and efficiently put it round Sakurai's neck. It was time.

Sakurai's face turned pale as he twisted the upper half of his body to face Watanabe and Shinoda, and with a desperate look he screamed to Shinoda, "Sensei! Please give me my last rites!"

The hands of the guards stopped moving. Everyone turned to stare at Shinoda. Watanabe was sweating. *Jōdo Shinshū doesn't have last rites for this! What's he going to do?* Without hesitation, Shinoda stepped forward before Sakurai. He looked directly into Sakurai's face. They pressed so close together their noses almost touched, and then Shinoda clasped Sakurai's shoulders with both hands and put the power of his belly into his hoarse and throaty voice.

"Get ready! Sakurai, it is time to go! You are not dying! You will be reborn! *Katsu!*"[21]

Officially, Shinoda's role in this execution was to support the emotional stability of death row inmate Sakurai. From a sociological perspective, it is reasonable to conclude that the chaplain's presence may have contributed to inmate docility in the final moments. Shinoda played a role designed to smooth state killing. Drawing on Sartre, sociologist Peter Berger famously describes the roles played by various officials in executions as the paradigmatic example of acting in bad faith. Berger writes:

> Socially constructed roles are taken as alibis [and] in the final act of the drama [. . .] those who watch over [an execution] and those who physically perform it are all protected from personal accountability by the fiction that it is not really they who are engaged in these acts but anonymous beings representing the law, the state, or the will of the people. [. . .] The excuse of such men that they have no choice is the fundamental lie upon which all bad faith rests. [. . .] The truth is that a judge can resign, a warden can refuse to obey an order, and that a governor can stand up for humanity even against the law. [. . .] The nightmare character of bad faith in the case of capital punishment [. . .] [is in its function:] the killing of a human being with precise bestiality and in such a way that nobody need feel responsible.[22]

I do not dispute Berger's structural analysis of the way that the official roles overseeing an execution have been constructed. Japanese execution rituals—with curtains for concealment and the mechanism of the gallows to distance performers from the act of killing—appear designed to eliminate the individual's sense of agentive action. However, from an anthropological perspective, it is necessary to note that the relationship between socially constructed roles and individual experiences and actions is always indeterminate.[23] It is one thing to say that an institutionalized role is structurally shot through with bad faith and another to say that individuals who fill those roles are always or inevitably acting in bad faith. For example, is it true that nobody feels responsibility to the person being executed? This is an empirical question, and it gets to the core of the chaplain's dilemma, which is really a matter of conflicting obligations. The experiences of the people working in the death row chaplaincy cannot be adequately grasped by a reductive analysis that makes of the people no more than their socially constructed role would have of them.

As Hirano Shunkō suggests, the heart of the matter lies in the bonds formed through interpersonal connections. Death row inmates typically spend years talking to their chosen chaplains before the day of their execution. When chaplains take on this connection to death row inmates, it complicates their lives in ways they cannot predict. What an individual chaplain might make of these complications depends on personality and circumstance—but no one is happier for taking on this burden.

Before graduate school, I worked for the Georgia Capital Defender, assisting lawyers defending people on death row. I was then, and remain, opposed to the death penalty. There are many reasons to be an abolitionist, but I came to this way of thinking primarily because our office worked with families of people on death row, and so I became aware of some of the impacts that the death penalty system has on people who have relationships with offenders. "Disenfranchised grief" is a term used to describe the feelings of loss, shame, isolation, and trauma that haunt family members whose loved ones are killed by the state.[24]

Before I interviewed death row chaplains in Japan, I wondered if they might not have similar perspectives to my own. The chaplains are typically the only personal connection that a death row inmate has. In Japanese, the concept of karma implied in the chaplain's joke is frequently invoked in the ubiquitous phrase *en ga aru*: literally to have a karmic connection to someone. Expressions that invoke fate are bound up with ideas about relationships—and many chaplains told me they got into the work because they had a connection to it. Sometimes this meant, "My father was the chaplain at this prison before me." The "karmic connection to the prison" joke can also be a joke about dad. But the metaphor of connection goes further than this. In Hirano's framing, the death row chaplain's role is to provide a human connection to people who otherwise would not be acknowledged at all. If the official discourse sees karma primarily as a moral law, then the private accounts of committed chaplains more often frame their responsibilities according to the theme of connection as a means of alleviating suffering.

When I set out to conduct interviews, I naively imagined that some prison chaplains might want to discuss the death penalty with me. However, when I started asking death row chaplains questions, I got responses like, "I am in no position to have a personal opinion about the death penalty."[25] What does it mean to be in no position to have a personal opinion? My first impression was that this refusal to acknowledge a personal view amounts to precisely the kind of bad faith that Berger describes. However, over time, some death row chaplains did opt to discuss their work with me—on the condition that I would not publish what they said or share it with others. *Off the record.* Eventually, I realized that the reason chaplains do not publicly criticize the death penalty cannot be reduced to bad faith. The refusal to take a public stand is not merely a matter of preserving professional protocols. If a chaplain talks publicly, he will lose access to the prison and effectively abandon the clients he feels morally obligated to help. The closer a chaplain gets to his clients, the less likely he is to support the death penalty—and the harder it becomes to express that opinion in the open. Rather than a paradigmatic case of bad faith, the chaplains' silence reflects a paradigmatic catch-22 situation. The responsibilities of death row chaplains are constructed such that this dilemma is unavoidable. In Hirano's words, "I think big social contributions and social movements are important, but in my position, I ask what the death row inmate sitting across from me wants of me."[26]

Problems of the heart are the chaplain's official responsibility—not oversight of prison management. The silence that surrounds death row in Japan is a product of the correctional system. It results equally from the fact that the only outsiders to witness executions are prison chaplains, whose duties as religious workers have been carved out in a way that precludes the possibility of activism. It attests to the cruelty of the death penalty system that it makes chaplains responsible to tend to the suffering of the incarcerated and, by the same gesture, muzzles them, making their capacity to ease suffering contingent upon their complicity with maintaining the death penalty. The price of access is silence. This settlement is a result of the way religion's role has developed over the past century, reflecting a lasting division of responsibilities between two domains of law.

In the wake of the publication of Horikawa Keiko's work, the death penalty has risen into the consciousness of religious organizations (if not the general public) as a topic of debate. Horikawa herself has been invited to speak at various chaplains' conferences. The most high profile of these events was a symposium held at Ryukoku University on July 11, 2015. The symposium was titled *The Present and Future of Religious Chaplaincy: The Religious Consciousness of the Japanese.*[27] The centerpiece of this conference featured Horikawa Keiko conducting a dialogue with the former head of the Honganji sect and honorary president of the National Chaplains' Union Ōtani Kōshin. In his closing statement, Ōtani publicly expressed his opposition to the death penalty for the first time. His closing comments were the following:

> In light of my position, this is very difficult to say, so please take this as an attempt to raise a question. The death penalty system is an extremely binary way of thinking: we cannot kill good people, but it is okay to kill evil people. I think that the distinction between good and evil is extremely ambiguous.
>
> In Buddhism, there is a basic teaching of Shakyamuni that says that you must not kill or make others kill. This falls within the range of one of the precepts. The fundamental meaning of the precepts is that they are conditions for the practice to attain enlightenment [*satori*]. I don't mean to force this upon anyone who is not a Buddhist, but even for lay Buddhist believers, there are five precepts. The first is referred to as the precept against taking life. If you look at the sutras, you will also see it expressed as the precept against taking human life. The sutras do not say who you are not supposed to kill. It doesn't matter if the person you kill is a good person or an evil person. You must not kill. You must extinguish the evil karma of killing— that is how I understand the precept.
>
> As a Buddhist, from today's symposium, I have the impression that we have been given a very important issue to think through: in reality, to what extent can we follow this precept against taking any human life?[28]

Ōtani's comments suggest an increasing degree of openness in the chaplaincy to rekindling the dormant debate about abolition. After acknowledging the difficulty of his position (both as a religious leader and as honorary leader of the chaplaincy), Ōtani criticized the death penalty system with reference to the tradition of Buddhist ethical thought. It is possible to view his statement as an instance of "doctrinal admonition" aimed at the state. Such resistance has never been the primary trend in the prison chaplaincy's history. However, it is possible that acts of criticism may come to play an important part in the world of the chaplains moving forward.

Although Watanabe asked Horikawa to hold publication of her book until after his death, when he elicited her promise, he already knew he was dying of complications from alcoholism. In a memorable scene, Horikawa presses Watanabe on the reason for his drinking. He replies: "I am sure you would be most pleased if I said something about drinking because of stress from my work as a chaplain. But the truth is I drink because I have always loved to drink since I was a kid."[29] Despite his protestations, based on Horikawa's account of his life, it is difficult to avoid the impression that Watanabe's drinking had something to do with stress relief. It may be that he found it easier to change his state of mind than his situation. He himself insisted: as long as there is a death penalty, someone will be forced to do the dirty work—having a chaplain on the scene makes it easier for the person going to the gallows, and it also helps the staff get through it by disguising the fact that we are "committing a murder."[30] In the process of doing this work, Watanabe was both traumatized and obligated to hide his ongoing burden from everyone in his life. The fact that he was responsible for easing the hearts of those on death row likely contributed to his own "problems of the heart." Thanks to Horikawa's work, Watanabe's story has inspired religious organizations to begin publicly discussing capital punishment in Japan. Whether these conversations generate the will or the political action needed to abolish the death penalty remains to be seen.

Conclusions: "A Serious Person Cannot Be a Prison Chaplain"

The prison chaplain's role in contemporary Japan exemplifies the tensions inherent in the status quo of religion-state relations. The public-private theme is relevant to both prisons and religion. Prisons are public institutions that function in part to keep punishment out of the public gaze—hence the code of secrecy to which chaplains are bound. This form of enforced secrecy is a problem because it is inherently antidemocratic and authoritarian. It is within this problematic system that religions are expected to offer a social contribution in line with state goals. The result is a chaplaincy structured around the institutional goals of rectifying the hearts of offenders and promoting inmate docility. In effect, the role of the prison chaplain as officially defined is to serve the prison more than it is to serve the inmates—even though chaplains are private "volunteers" with no public money to support them.

In the twenty-first century, both civil society and state agencies have recognized the need to increase public oversight of Japan's prison system, and the 2007 Act on Penal Detention Facilities and Treatment of Inmates and Detainees pushed in the direction of greater openness. Given this shift, it is easy to imagine an alternative arrangement wherein chaplains could contribute to the public good by facilitating oversight, especially since they are some of the only outsiders with eyes inside the prison system. However, such a role would not be consistent with the understanding that religions should remain a private affair, and the 2017 edition of the *Chaplain's Manual* gives no indication that the chaplaincy's official priorities have been reoriented.

The role of prison chaplains in Japan continues to be structured by the prevailing settlement between religions and state. Mainstream religions and the National Chaplains' Union are expected to work for the public benefit while remaining aloof from politics. Chaplains are supposed to perform the political argument that religions can contribute to the public good by promoting prosocial behavior. The official chaplaincy discourse reflects this orientation: crime is interpreted only as a private (spiritual) trouble, but never as a reflection of broader public (material) issues such as poverty. Such is the structure of doctrinal admonition. However, despite the limitations of the chaplains' formal duties, the individuals assigned to serve are not reducible to their socially constructed roles. The relationship between the inherited role and the individual who occupies it is indeterminate. In existential terms, people can always make something out of what they have been made into.

Those assigned to the chaplaincy respond to the role in diverse ways, and I chose to focus on the stories of individual chaplains in this chapter to highlight the multiplicity of meanings that the role takes on for a variety of people. Perhaps Fukai sought the appointment for the sense of moral authority it entails. Dōyama appeared to embrace the assignment with a sense of mission. Hirano seemed reconciled to the position as a matter of karmic destiny. Nonetheless, these three are representative of Japanese prison chaplaincy: first, because they face inevitable dilemmas arising from contradictions inherent in their role; and second, because they all try to go above and beyond the call of duty by developing their own style of engagement with their clients.

Like Fukai, chaplains tend to be aware of the critical shortcomings in the official doctrine. They may try to overcome these shortcomings by improvising. However, individual improvisation does not appear to contribute to a redefinition of the formal responsibilities of prison chaplaincy, and so it does not amount to a reform in the structure of chaplaincy theory and practice. Even as more chaplains come to understand their work in relation to the problem of suffering (an understanding that resonates with spiritual care chaplaincies), the prison chaplain's formal duties continue to be defined by the priorities of correctional reform and the legacy of doctrinal admonition.

In Dōyama's case, not only did he seek to provide spiritual comfort to the incarcerated, he also offered material support by inviting parolees to live in his home with his family. Dōyama regards the prison as inadequate to address the social problems underlying crime, and so he opened the doors of his church to people who slipped through the cracks of society. Some other chaplains do this too, but the work is not remunerated, and it is not without risk. It is also done privately. Dōyama was fighting alone to address a problem inherent in the social structure. The image that comes to mind is that of one person trying to stem an oncoming tide with a bucket; though, like Sisyphus pushing his boulder uphill, Dōyama insists that he finds meaning in this endless work.

Hirano emphasized the importance of cultivating personal relationships with his charges on death row in order to help them (to the extent possible) to endure. The depth of his wisdom and his understanding of the universal human need for connection are inspiring. At the same time, his position as death row chaplain has meant that he had little choice but to become reconciled to serving within the system as a condition for maintaining access to the people he feels morally obligated to help. His responsibilities make it such that he can attend to the suffering of his clients only at the price of eschewing public calls for abolition. It appears to have been the same with his mentor Watanabe, and with Watanabe's mentor Shinoda before him. The ties of relationship—karmic bonds—bind them to the system. These are the dilemmas of bad karma.

As the chaplain's joke implies, appointment to the chaplaincy is a burden—so much so that it can be glossed as bad karma. The joke reveals the great irony at the heart of the Japanese prison chaplaincy: it inverts the official theology that sees inmates only as transgressors by asserting that the prison chaplain, too, is in a position of suffering. The joke conveys a legitimate grievance, and it reveals that the official story promoted by sects and the Corrections Office provides only a partial view of the complex lived realities of prison chaplaincy in Japan.

In sum, I found that chaplains respond in a range of ways to the situation they inherit. Some treat it as a perfunctory responsibility. Some wish they could get out of it. And some, like Fukai, Dōyama, and Hirano, try to find ways to go beyond the limited range of their official duties by building relationships with inmates and trying to attend to their individual needs. It is clear that to become a prison chaplain in Japan is to inherit a range of dilemmas that resist any easy resolution. It is perhaps in response to this tension that some chaplains develop a wicked gallows humor. It seems appropriate to close by sharing another chaplain's joke unlikely to appear in official publications. In a comment about the difficulty of the work, one particularly morose death row chaplain with a biting wit said, "A serious person cannot be a prison chaplain. He'll go insane."

CONCLUSION

At the Altar of Doctrinal Admonition

A convertible altar presides over an otherwise nondescript room inside Tachikawa Jail. It is the single feature indicating that this space is the prison chapel. The altar's functionalist design allows for easy modification: a Christian cross, a Shinto *kamidana* altar, or a Buddhist *butsu-dan* can be moved into the central position while barriers conceal the other two religious symbols. My thoughts have returned to this tripartite configuration again and again over the years. The apparatus condenses the whole history of Japanese prison chaplaincy into a symbol. This is the altar of doctrinal admonition. In closing, it seems appropriate to consider what this mechanism does, the message it conveys, and the historical processes that created the possibility for it to exist.

Function. In this chapel and others like it in every Japanese correctional institution, prison chaplains and inmates gather before such altars for chaplaincy sessions. At most times, the chapel is empty. It is not a place for inmates to linger. However, at appointed times (and rarely for longer than an hour), guards will direct inmates to the chapel to access the services of the chaplains. To all those who assemble in the chapel, the altar doubtless carries multifarious personal meanings. Chaplains may chant sutras, lead Bible readings, perform rites for the spirits of departed family members or for victims of crimes, practice seated meditation with inmates, conduct Shinto purification rituals, or hold one-on-one religious counseling sessions. If one looks for continuity amid the diversity, however, it is not hard to find. Above all, chaplains are expected to admonish inmates based on religious teachings to promote reform. The guiding idea that appears everywhere in chaplaincy discourse is that doctrinal admonition can lead the incarcerated to purify their hearts and undergo a spiritual transformation that is akin to a moral rebirth and tantamount to correctional rehabilitation. The altar serves to sanctify this arrangement just as it provides the focal point for the many ritual performances dedicated to reform.

The question of whether or not this arrangement actually works—whether admonition in reality has the desired impact on the recidivism rate—is beside the point. The prison routine and religion's role therein are simply arranged *as if* it does work as intended. Then again, from another perspective, the formal conditions of the prison chaplaincy (and even the bulk of their vocational discourse) might also be seen as a mere pretext to afford dedicated clerics some space in the margins of the prison routine to connect with incarcerated clients and provide some sense of contact with the outside world. In the prison chapels today, there is a tension between the new settlement and the old. The postwar era saw the chaplaincy restructured around the baseline principles of religious freedom and separation of religions from the state—and yet prisons continued to operate under the Meiji-era Prison Act until the new millennium. Even after the legal framework governing prisons was reformed, the task of the trans-sectarian committee writing the new *Chaplain's Manual* in the 2010s was to maintain a tradition that somehow balanced respect for the human rights of the incarcerated with the long-standing ideal of harmony between religious teachings and the political authority of the state. The contemporary chaplaincy combines a concern for the individual client's "religious needs" with an inherited statist perspective on the relation between religion and law. That perspective is one that calls to mind the medieval maxim about the dharma and the law of the sovereign as "two horns on an ox" or "two wheels on a cart." The preface of this book opened with one chaplain's assessment of his position astride the proverbial "ox cart" of religion-state relations: in reality, heading to the prison to stand before the altar of doctrinal admonition week after week is "a difficult thing to do."

Form. The convertible nature of the chapel's altar conveys its fundamental message about the normative role for religion behind bars. Beneath the personalized meanings that prisoners and chaplains may attach to it, the prison chapel's altar is a symbol of the prevailing settlement between religion and state that uneasily combines an ideal of religious freedom with administrative demands for a functionalist form of religious instruction to rectify the hearts of offenders. Legally, the rationale for offering chaplaincy sessions to inmates is grounded in the constitutional requirement to protect religious freedom. It is in accordance with this principle that inmates may choose whether or not to meet with chaplains and which religion they prefer. For a Shinto session, one can use the *kamidana*. If an inmate wants to meet with a Protestant minister, there is a cross for that. Buddhism is also on offer. Participation is voluntary, but it is often encouraged. The chaplains themselves are not state employees, but volunteers, as required by the legal separation of religion from state.

Nevertheless, the formal goals of doctrinal admonition remain tethered to the state's purposes of correctional rehabilitation and promoting inmate docility. The individual inmate has the right to participate in a state-approved religion—but the religions on offer in prisons are expected to conform to the objectives of corrections. Prison management and religious organizations expect the chaplains to share the prison's goal of promoting prosocial values to encourage good citizenship. The altar, by its variability, conveys the message that any of the three major religions recognized by the prison can and should teach a doctrine to maintain social order.

History. To respect historical priority, the first aspect of the altar to consider is the *butsudan*. The idea that moral edification is essential to good governance and social stability has deep roots in the Japanese Buddhist tradition. Since the dawn of Japan's written history, Buddhism has been ideologically and institutionally connected to governance, from ancient rites to protect the emperor and the realm to the Tokugawa-era temple certification system that relied on Buddhist clergy to monitor the population and prevent the spread of the Christian heresy. These traditional roles for Buddhist temples as defenders of society did not simply disappear in a puff of steam with the Meiji Restoration of 1868 or vanish in an atomic flash in 1945. For more than a millennium, Buddhist institutions were part of the architecture of rule, and the processes of modernization did not erase this history.

From the nineteenth century, the Japanese imported and refined new forms of knowledge, governance, science, and technology as part of a na-

tional campaign under the banner of "civilization and enlightenment."
All sectors of society sought ways to contribute to the nation with a sense
of collective destiny, but for Buddhist temples, the need to demonstrate
their social utility was particularly acute. The modern era brought for the
first time threats of extinction—first at the hands of domestic nativists
and next through competition from newcomer Christian missionaries
who poured into Japan from overseas. Survival depended on carving out
new roles in a rapidly changing society. It may be a truism that it is always easier to find a new job if one can leverage an established skill set,
but this principle certainly applied for the Meiji-era Buddhists.

Prison institutions and the legal framework that relies on a concept
of religion to organize social life were first developed in Western, predominantly Christian societies before being imported to Japan in the
nineteenth century through global processes of colonial expansion and
international competition. The Meiji modernization regime began to invest
in building a modern carceral system in 1872, creating a new institution to
promote social stability through the moral edification of the emperor's
imprisoned subjects. As the carceral system developed through the 1870s
and 1880s, Japanese society also adapted a concept of religion in both
legal and popular discourse with enormous philosophical and political
implications. At the level of doctrine, the encounter with Western
thought spurred Japanese Buddhists to develop new understandings of
interiority and the meaning of faith while also grappling with the challenge of scientific rationalism. At the level of politics, religion became a
key term for negotiating the public-private divide, and the central issue in
conversations about the social role for religion was always framed around
the question of how religion might contribute to society. Seizing the moment, Buddhist activists from the powerful Shin sects saw the brand-new
prisons as a golden opportunity to demonstrate the potential of their
teaching to serve the national interest. These entrepreneurs adapted their
indigenous Buddhist tradition to the prisons with great success. Buddhist
ideas about the role of the dharma in maintaining social order became
foundational to the Japanese version of a religion-based reform program. The ideal of harmony between temples and the government informed their vision of religion-state relations. This tradition combined
with the "inward turn" characteristic of modern Japanese Buddhist
thought and converged with the prison's subjectivist focus on the hearts

of the incarcerated to produce the new role of doctrinal admonition. It is this job that we recognize today under the rubric of prison chaplaincy.

By the 1890s, many Japanese prisons featured *butsudan* of their own. In the same decade, reform-minded Protestants who had established a foothold in the prison service pursued an alternative path for the development of prison chaplaincy, but the Shin sects lobbied the Diet on the grounds that the foreign religion and its associated reformist tendencies threatened to disrupt harmony between the established religion (Buddhism) and the state. This campaign for control of prison religion succeeded, and by the turn of the twentieth century, Shin Buddhist sects grasped a monopoly over prison chaplaincy. Rotating cohorts of Shin clerics were thereafter appointed as civil servants with responsibility over the prison chaplaincy until 1945. For more than half a century, inmates throughout Japan were required to assemble before Buddhist altars to listen to Shin chaplains give dharma talks about the moral law of cause and effect. The central message was a rationalized Buddhist ethic tailored to the correctional system: to commit crime is bad karma; to reform is to purify the heart; imperial subjects owe a debt of gratitude to the emperor and society to be repaid through good conduct and productive labor to benefit the national community.

After the war, the Allied Occupation abolished the civil service prison chaplaincy and the single-sect monopoly. Rather than abandoning prison chaplaincy, however, the Occupation forced its diversification and privatization by imposing American-style principles of religious freedom and religion-state separation. A wide range of religious organizations collaborated with the Corrections Office to produce a trans-sectarian and all-volunteer prison chaplaincy. Representatives from Buddhist sects, Christian churches, Shinto shrines, and new religions found themselves appointed to serve in the prisons, and the decor of prison chapels was updated accordingly. Thus, the *kamidana* and the cross joined the *butsudan* as permanent fixtures of postwar prison chapels (prewar-era prisons also featured *kamidana*, though not in the chapels, which were a Buddhist space). Under the Postwar Constitution, inmates could now decide whether or not to engage with prison chaplains. The message of chaplaincy was updated too: committing crime is still bad karma (to the Buddhist chaplains), but it can also be seen as sin (by the Christians) or as pollution (from a Shinto perspective). Nonetheless, in every doctrinal lens on offer in the chapels, crime is seen as an ethical transgression rooted in disharmony of the individual heart, and religious instruction is thought to be a solution to this problem. Citizens owe a debt to society (now a constitutional democracy), and this debt must be repaid through good conduct and productive labor to benefit the national community.

Underlying the cultural and legal transformations of the modern era has been a long-standing theme in religion-state relations that sustains the role for religions in the prison system. Even as prison chapels were redecorated and participation was made voluntary, baseline assumptions about the role of religions in society remained constant: religions should elevate the morals of the populace to benefit the nation. It does not require a great leap of the imagination to see that prisons have the very same role. In modern Japan, both prisons and religions have been connected to strategies of governance that rely on processes of moral edification to promote the values of good citizenship. In line with this enduring ideal, prison chaplaincy's core practices remained intact, and the scope of reforms never interfered with this foundational principle.

These are the historical conditions that made possible the tripartite altar at Tachikawa Jail. The altar is a symbol of the way the postwar religion and state settlement (with its provisions for religious freedom and religion-state separation) was grafted onto an enduring foundation of religious statism that remained particularly entrenched in the prisons. In fact, the idea that the purpose of doctrines is to serve the interests of governance was not a modern innovation, but rather a feature of the Japanese Buddhist tradition dating from ancient times. The model of prison chaplaincy that developed in Japan was the product of a nineteenth-century marriage between deeply rooted Buddhist political ideals and the prison's agenda of reforming troubled souls. Doctrinal admonition is the child of this particular union of religion and state. When the chaplaincy was diversified in the postwar period, the varieties of prison chaplaincy were all shaped by the mold of the dominant tradition of doctrinal admonition, which bore the engrained influence of Shin Buddhism's long monopoly over religion-based reform programs from the turn of the twentieth century until the end of World War II.

In the secular democratic societies of Japan, Europe, and North America, the percentage of the population who avow commitments to religious organizations continues to decline, but chaplaincies focused on individualized spiritual care and a medicalized concept of religion appear to be on the rise. And yet a concern with spiritual health or religious individualism is never all there is to chaplaincy: chaplains who work with the military are expected to contribute to combat readiness; chaplains in hospitals can smooth the host institution's operations by dealing with emotional fallout that doctors and nurses are ill-equipped to handle; and chaplains in prisons are responsible to contribute to reform and inmate docility. The case of doctrinal admonition in Japan is distinguished from those other varieties of chaplaincy that center around spiritual care practices. Although Japanese prison chaplaincy shares with other chaplaincies the goal of contributing to the host institution's objectives, its vocational discourse has never aimed to justify or even explain this role by appealing to a formal concept of spiritual care (even when some individual chaplains have worked to mitigate the suffering of prisoners in ways that resemble spiritual care to outside observers). Rather, since its inception more than a century ago, Japanese prison chaplaincy has retained a focus on the social pathology of crime and emphasized religion's role in defending the nation and fighting evil.

This case study shows that a form of chaplaincy developed in a non-Christian society on a trajectory that radically diverges from the notions of spiritual care that usually form the basis for understanding chaplaincy work. The question now is, Is it possible to have a form of chaplaincy without spiritual care? If we can forego the idea that chaplaincy, in its essence, focuses on the problem of suffering, then the answer would appear to be in the affirmative, because Japanese prison chaplains share many important commonalities with spiritual care chaplains around the world. They operate within a modern and ostensibly secular institution of governance. Their role is structured and delimited by the religion and state settlement encoded in constitutional law. They perform religion's private work for the public benefit under the rubric of a managerial regime that adopts a functionalist approach to religion as one strategy for maintaining social order. This study shows that a non-Christian society's religion and state settlement and the form of chaplaincy it underwrites can be structured by assumptions about the relationship between political and religious authority inherited from local traditions—and these may differ significantly from arrangements in societies where the dominant legal and cultural tradition is informed more by Christianity.

Spiritual care and doctrinal admonition have different roots. The contemporary phenomenon of spiritual care is descended from the pastoral practices of parish priests in European societies, wherein the cleric attended to the needs of a congregation as a shepherd tended to a flock. By contrast, doctrinal admonition started out as an expedient means for imperiled Buddhist temples to prove their continued value to the state in line with their traditional role as firewalls against heresy. When punishment by deprivation of liberty was adopted in 1872 and Christianity tacitly permitted the following year, doctrinal admonition evolved into prison chaplaincy because Buddhist priests shifted their focus from admonishing illegal Christians (who were illegal no longer) to admonishing incarcerated Japanese for all manner of conduct defined as criminal by the state. By its own official account, the Japanese prison chaplaincy was born the moment one Buddhist cleric turned his attention from admonishing detained "heretics" to admonishing incarcerated "criminals." Since that time, the chaplain's responsibility to mitigate the suffering of clients has been considered ancillary (if it has been considered at all) to the primary duty to serve the host institution's purposes of facilitating governance.

If the ascendance of spiritual care chaplaincies (even in Japan) represents a rise in religious individualism, then the maintenance of doctrinal admonition represents the endurance of religious statism. This orientation explains why prison chaplaincy publications spend far more time discussing crime as a social problem than they do considering the perceived religious needs of inmates. The historical background for this arrangement lies in the legacy of connections between the Buddhist temple institutions and the architecture of government. In the contemporary era, institutional connections between religious organizations and government agencies continue to define religion's works for the public benefit in fields of social work, including chaplaincy. All mainstream Japanese religions today embrace the values of public service to the community and the nation, and the chaplains are appointed representatives of their religious organizations whose task is to fulfill religion's normative social role.

The topic of appointment returns to the theme of karmic connections. The chaplain's role is generally inherited through religious organizations that function like a hybrid between extended kinship groups and political lobbies invested in preserving their own traditions. The kinship element is readily apparent from the perspective of the individual cleric; in the Buddhist idiom, the sect is a network of intersubjective bonds. When a person (usually a man) is assigned, under the weight of collective expectation, to serve in the prison chaplaincy, he enters a tradition with a century and a half of history structuring the appointed role and assumes a place in a particular lineage. In this sense, the matter of assignment is sometimes glossed as karmic destiny. Individuals are, of course, free to make of the role what they will, but embedded normative expectations are not so easy to shift. The source of those normative expectations becomes clear if one zooms out from the individual biography to the broader contours of history and social structure to examine how sects have functioned like political lobbies. From this bird's-eye view, the chaplaincy looks like one institution that links two other institutions—prison and sect—as well as two sectors of society—religion and state. Though it is seldom clear from the perspectives of individual chaplains, they occupy positions in an ongoing, complicated game of political negotiations between religious organizations and state agencies over the contours of the public-private divide.

The individual chaplain's vocational biography can be situated in history with reference to the major questions addressed in this study: What is the social function of doctrinal admonition? Whose interests are served by framing crime as a religious issue in this way? Why does doctrinal admonition endure? What are its consequences? The official story of the chaplaincy offers one explanation: a narrative of humanist progress that interprets the history of corrections as a trajectory of increasing benevolence where religion's essential altruism drives the chaplaincy's creation and maintenance. While recognizing that the development of prisons in Japan was no doubt a civilizational project, I have resisted a narrative of progress and essentialist assumptions about the nature of religion and its social role. Instead, I have argued that the prison chaplaincy's development was motivated by a convergence of sectarian and state interests. Doctrinal admonition functions to support the state's correctional program while simultaneously promoting the moral authority of religious organizations by creating connections to the government. It is not hard to see vested interests at work here.

Throughout, I have returned to the Shin Buddhist ideal of complementarity between two domains of law as the undergirding rationale for the creation and expansion of the Japanese prison chaplaincy. The essential idea holds that the right kind of religion can harmonize private interests with the public good as defined by the political authorities. "Good" religions have a duty to make a social contribution to the nation state, and it is in the government's interests to promote these desirable religions as a public benefit. Shin lobbyists and thinkers invoked this ideal of harmony between sect and state during late nineteenth-century and early twentieth-century debates about the role of religion in society, and the earliest chaplaincy publications relied on this idea as their doctrinal basis. Even in the postwar era, the idea that crime is a religious problem persisted because it proved important to the political maneuvering of a range of religious organizations (not just Shin) as they sought to position themselves as guardians of the public good. The architects of policy—both SCAP and their successors in the Japanese government—were amenable to this arrangement, because it frames the role for religion as working to facilitate governance and benefit the nation. Under the Postwar Constitution, various sects were called upon to contribute to the correctional program on a voluntary basis to avoid running afoul of the constitutional requirement for religion-state separation. Though this call was described as an accommodation to religious freedom, from the perspective of the Corrections Office, the shift to a diversified, all-volunteer chaplaincy had the effect of harnessing more sectarian networks and their human resources for the carceral project, thereby expanding the pool of cheap labor while simultaneously cutting expenditures. On the human side, this arrangement had costs for inmates (whose religious freedom was still curtailed by the chaplaincy's limitations) and for the clergy assigned to serve as chaplains (who were pressed into doing onerous work without remuneration). The interests of the frontline clergy assigned to prisons were not necessarily the same as those of the sectarian hierarchies responsible to dispatch staff to fill chaplaincy posts.

By responding to shifting demands from the government, sects like Shin managed to survive crises like the anti-Buddhist movements and the Occupation while holding on to some of their moral authority. Whether the threat was Christian heresy, Marxist thought crimes, crimes against peace, or mundane forms of criminal behavior, religions invested in prisoner outreach to demonstrate their capacity to fight crime and thereby contribute to the nation. The prison chaplaincy and its unifying notion that crime is a religious, not a structural, problem have endured because of a confluence between the function of the prison and the way the social role for religion has been negotiated in Japan. The heart of the matter is that normative expectations for religions require them to remain a private affair while also offering some form of public benefit. Thus, preaching private virtues to the incarcerated in service to the state's goals of correctional reform has been one paradigmatic example of religious work for the public benefit in Japan.

What are the consequences of this history for the present? The public-private theme is important not only for understanding how the role for religions is continually renegotiated in contemporary society. It is also connected to the problematic secrecy that surrounds the Japanese prison system—a public institution that functions in part to make punishments invisible to the public gaze. Both the privatization of religion and the prison's privatization of punishment are underlying causes of the gap between the official public representations of chaplaincy and the actual experiences of chaplains, which tend to be concealed. The postwar model of volunteer chaplaincy operates on the principle of public service and its concomitant assumption that personal, private interests must be subordinated in the name of the public good and the duties of public station. Chaplain Watanabe Fusō—who stated in his last days in no uncertain terms that he viewed the death penalty as murder—served for half a century on death row while dutifully keeping his thoughts to himself. So who gets to decide what constitutes the public good? Prison is not a democracy run by the prisoners, and the answer is not the chaplains themselves.

Through case studies drawn from fieldwork, I introduced the gulf between the official chaplaincy discourse (which remains myopically focused on rectifying offenders' hearts) and the individual chaplains who try to find ways to help people—often by going above and beyond the call of duty (in extreme cases, even inviting former inmates to come and live with them after release). Chaplains are not blind to social injustices, and so they experience the limitations of their role as a frustration. They try to grapple with the messy realities that spill beyond the neatly circumscribed boundaries of doctrinal orthodoxy. However, in general, chaplains do not understand themselves to be in a position to promote structural changes to the correctional system. They improvise collectively—but also alone—in the context of relationships with individual clients. In the chaplain's idiom, they operate based on karmic connections. This private domain of intersubjective bonds is a realm where many chaplains do significant good works. Yet it is distinct from the public domain of political action, which sectarian organizations, the correctional bureaucracy, and the National Chaplains' Union expect chaplains to avoid because of the inherent risk of creating conflict between religion and the state.

Those assigned to the chaplaincy are responsible to deal with inmates' problems of the heart. Such is the role of religions in Japan's prisons: to harmonize the private realm of values, aspirations, and the conscience with the priorities of the public authorities. The delimitation of religions' concerns in this way is a product of Japan's history of religion-state relations. This settlement comes down on the shoulders of today's chaplains, bequeathing to them a host of dilemmas and the difficult dual task of serving the warden and the incarcerated client. The prison chaplain's role—defined by the work of doctrinal admonition—is a manifestation of the ideal of harmony between sects and state. This ideal underlies the doctrines of the chaplaincy, political negotiations about the role of religions in society (and in the prisons), and the personal dilemmas faced by clergy members called upon to enter prisons and perform religions' private works for the public benefit. The case of the prison chaplaincy shows that, despite the personal costs and internal tensions, statism is an enduring feature of mainstream religious life in modern Japan. And in every prison chapel across the country, an altar of doctrinal admonition stands as a testament to this persistent orientation.

APPENDIX A

Tenrikyō Group Chaplaincy Session Field Notes Autumn Festival of Souls (Aki no Mitama Matsuri)

Conducted at Fuchū Prison, September 2015

On an early autumn morning in September 2015, I attended a Tenrikyō group chaplaincy session at Fuchū Prison. This session was to mark the Autumn Festival of Souls (Aki no Mitama Matsuri). After we checked in with the education and rehabilitation department office, I followed the three chaplains and a guard assigned as our escort to a room marked with the words "Shinto chapel." Fuchū Prison features three chapels: one for Christianity, one for Buddhism, and one for Shinto. The front of the room was covered in tatami mats, but in the rear, the flooring was bare. Six inmates were waiting, seated on the tatami, when we arrived. I entered through a rear door and sat behind the inmates on a folding chair next to a guard.

The three chaplains filed in from the front of the room between the inmates and a simple *kamidana*. As the three chaplains entered, the guard seated to my left called out the orders "Bow!" and "At ease!" The six inmates moved in synchrony with these commands, and the chaplains bowed in return.

The chaplains stood before the *kamidana*. Between them and the altar, there were four small offertory tables laid out with various ritual implements and offerings: two wooden wands with white paper streamers (*ōnusa*) to be used in the purification ritual (*oharai*); a white clay sake bottle (empty); white cup-shaped objects stacked into a pyramid; and a white plastic ball resembling mochi. The sacred mirror was visible within the *kamidana*, reflecting the flourescent overhead lights of the room. Above the *kamidana* and its mirror, a calligraphic print hung over our heads displaying the characters for "Shinto."

Rev. Dōyama Yoshio, the chaplain leading the session, sat in the middle and produced a scroll inscribed with a prayer of purification. He began to read:

> We announce with trepidation that here in Fuchū Prison we humbly venerate from afar Tenri Ō no Mikoto who resides at the Jiba [the headquarters of Tenrikyō in Nara Prefecture]. On this day, we conduct the rites of the Festival of Souls as a chaplaincy session to mark the anniversaries of the passing of loved ones [of those assembled here]. To that end, we humbly request that those assembled here—beginning with the supplicants, each having been purified by the breeze of the hemp wands and having received the refreshing purification of the heavenly hemp thread—may be permitted to perform beautifully the rites of this ceremony.[1]

When this reading was completed, all those assembled performed the Tenrikyō ritual for greeting the divinity: bow once (in greeting); clap four times; bow once more deeply (in veneration); clap four more times; and bow one final time (in closing). Next, the other two chaplains took up the purification wands laid out on the table before the altar, and they waved these in sweeping arcs over the heads of the inmates. As each wand whooshed through the still air of the room, the paper streamers made rustling sounds like leaves in a breeze. The waving of the wands, combined with a prayer for purification, is thought to have the power to exorcize ritual impurities (*tsumi kegare*).

Once the purification rite was complete, a second chaplain took center stage. He produced a scroll bearing the title "Fuchū Prison Service Prayer." He read:

> On the occassion of this chaplaincy session at Fuchū Prison held to mark the anniversaries of the passing of loved ones, with those assembled here

having been purified by the heavenly hemp thread, before the spirits, I, chaplain of Fuchū Prison, humbly announce:

As distant clouds rising obscure the clear light of the moon passing
through the sky, and as a tempest lays waste to the proud, blossoming
treetops of a spring mountain, bringing grief—Spirits, you too were un-
able to escape the ways of this world, and from the time you passed
away for rebirth, morning and night, those assembled here have missed
you in their hearts. They think upon days past constantly and never forget you even for a moment, and because they will always remember
you, we have planned at this time, on this auspicious day, to conduct
the rites of the Autumn Festival of Souls.

Therefore, we humbly ask you to consent in peace and with ease that
from this day forward you will reside within the hearts of these assembled here; keep their bodies healthy; keep them free from things that
would be cause for guilt; keep them free from worry; guard them at
night; guard them by day; keep watch; and lead them towards happiness. With trepidation, so do we humbly pray.[2]

Once he finished the prayer, the chaplain invited the inmates, in turn, to
approach the altar to greet the divinity. One by one, the men approached
and kneeled before the altar in the formal *seiza* position, bowed once (in
greeting), clapped four times, bowed more deeply (in veneration), clapped
four more times, and then bowed (in closing). As each man stepped up,
one of the chaplains confirmed his name and the name of the departed
relative's spirit (*mitama*) that the inmate wished to memorialize. "You are
Mr. So-and-so? Okay. And you are here for your mother, Mrs. So-and-so,
correct? Okay." (One of the chaplains said later that inmates sometimes
ask chaplains to perform rituals for the spirits of victims of their own
crimes. But on this day, four of the inmates were there for their fathers
and the other two for their mothers.) Once each inmate had taken his
turn at the altar, the first chaplain, Dōyama, returned to the central position before the altar and began the sermon.[3]

"Thank you all for coming here today to memorialize your parents
in this Autumn Festival of Souls. I am sure that their spirits must be
pleased seeing your sincere prayers. The Autumn Festival of Souls corresponds roughly to the Buddhist Higan holiday. We are here to venerate the spirits of our ancestors and parents and those with whom we have

some close connection [*en*]. The theme for today's sermon will be the Tenrikyō view of life and death.

Here in this room right now, we have three chaplains, six inmates, one guard, and one guest, a student researching about chaplaincy. So that means there are eleven people in this room right now. We have all had very different lives, but I am sure we also all share at least one or two important things in common: we have all received life from our parents who created us, and one day, each of us will certainly die.

In Tenrikyō, we believe that our physical body is a thing borrowed [*karimono*] from Kami. Our doctrine holds that the only thing that is truly our own is our hearts [*kokoro*]. Our souls [*tamashii*] cannot be seen, but Kami has lent our souls these physical bodies so that we could return to this world. In Tenrikyō, this doctrine is known as the "principle of a thing lent and a thing borrowed" [*kashimono karimono no ri*]. We also believe that death is really departing for rebirth [*denaoshi*]. Life is not something that just goes around one time. Dying is the start of a new life.

In that case, our ancestors will return to this world for rebirth when they pass away. This means that they are not in this altar [*kamidana*] or in a Buddhist altar [*butsudan*] or in the grave. So why do we go to visit graves or come to events like today's Festival of Souls? Isn't it a waste of time to memorialize the departed souls of people who have returned to this world already?

It is not so. All of us have been born into this world precisely because we had parents who gave us life. If our parents or grandparents had not existed, then we would never have been born, right? So it is thanks to the lives of our ancestors that we are all able to be here today. Clasping our hands in prayer and venerating those parents and ancestors is a very important thing. I believe that they will be happy to see that we pay our respects, and I also believe that this attitude towards our ancestors is connected to making our own lives shine. In that sense, I believe that the spirits will certainly be pleased to see that all of you have come here today to listen to a chaplain discuss religion. By developing a grateful heart, we can please the spirits, and I am sure if your parents are still alive, then they will be pleased too.

Therefore, I would like to emphasize that although you have come to hear Tenrikyō chaplains today, I also think it would be good for you to listen to chaplains from other religions too. Christianity, Buddhism, Shinto. All of these religions have the power to make our hearts better, and if we can change for the better by listening to these teachings, then our growth will also please the spirits.

So far I have been talking about the value of cultivating gratitude towards the spirits. Now I would like to discuss methods for making our own lives better. I mentioned earlier that in Tenrikyō we teach that we have souls of our own and bodies borrowed from Kami, and we are re-born over and over into this very world. If that is the case, then doesn't it mean that our deeds are recorded in our souls? When we pass away for rebirth, this record is not extinguished. I believe it remains [over the course of many lifetimes] and builds upon itself.

In Tenrikyō, we teach that in this life we are working out our past karma [*innen nasshō*]. I just mentioned that the deeds we do and the way we use our hearts are distinct from the physical body, connected to the life before and to the next. The good that we do comes back, and the evil that we do comes back too.

I have come to think of this [remnant] as something like a savings account with the divine bank [*Kami-sama ginkō no chokin tsūchō*] that is built into our souls. Anybody would be glad if their savings increase, right? I believe that Kami watches over us and sees how we use our hearts every day and how we behave. I think that when we act to make others happy and to help others, then our moral savings increase, and when we do the opposite, our savings are depleted. There is no point in saying 'I am too old, I can't turn it around now.' Why? Because the soul continues to live, and the balance with the heavenly savings account influences one's future lives. If I put this heavenly savings account metaphor into religious language, I might be able to refer to it as virtue [*toku*]. I certainly hope for each of you that you will work to increase your moral savings, to develop virtue in your souls.

In Tenrikyō, we share the collective goal of trying to realize an ideal world [where people can enjoy the] joyous life [*yōki gurashi to iu sekai*]. The joyous life means making a world where all people help each other and live in cooperation. There are, however, ways of the heart that obstruct the goal of joyous living, and in Tenrikyō we teach that these obstructions are the eight dusts [*yatsu hokori*]: miserliness, greed, hatred, self-love, grudge-bearing, anger, covetousness, and arrogance.

These dusts build up every day, but we call them dusts because through some simple cleaning they can be taken care of. However, if the dusts build up too much, it becomes difficult to clean them up. For this reason, we are taught that it is important to clean the dusts from one's heart every day.

I was once the chaplain for a man who had been in this prison for eighteen years. Eighteen years means he was one step away from the death penalty, right? He came to see me diligently for a long period of time. He even recommended to other inmates around him that they come to meet with Tenrikyō chaplains. In Tenrikyō we have the teaching that helping others is the way to help oneself [*hito o tasukete wagami tasukaru*]. I think he probably wanted to help as many others in prison as he possibly could. This man was eventually released from prison, and I hear that he returned to his hometown, where he is now working and doing well.

However, unfortunately, I have also known people who wound up institutionalized again soon after their release. Some came back here, some were sent to other prisons. I know a number of cases like this. I heard from one of them that he felt he just couldn't stop himself. If I put it in the language of the eight dusts, he was struggling with covetousness, that was the cause. He couldn't control himself. For that reason he has been in and out of prison a number of times.

Everyone, please think about this. You may believe that the crime you committed hurt no one, caused no injury, but what about the ancestral spirits who watch over you? Don't you think they would be saddened by your crimes? I think they would much rather see you living a joyous life. I am sure, for example, that they are pleased to see you coming to see chaplains today.

I will close now by praying for each and every one of you that every day you will steadily devote yourselves to practicing ways of the heart that will bring joy to others and that will help others; that you will increase your balance with the heavenly bank; and that you will live in such a way as to cultivate virtue in your lives."

When the chaplain had finished his speech, the guard once again called out "Bow! At ease!" The inmates and the chaplains exchanged bows, and the session ended.

APPENDIX B

Interview with Hirano Shunkō, Death Row Chaplain at Tokyo Jail

October 3, 2014

Hirano Shunkō is a Shin Honganji sect priest and the former head of the National Chaplains' Union.

Adam: I'd like to ask you about the role of the prison chaplain. You mentioned earlier that you feel gratitude toward your clients. To someone who doesn't know about chaplaincy, this sounds surprising. Can you please explain how this relates to your role as a chaplain?

Hirano: It is not easy to put this concisely. Every person I meet is different. Just because a person has committed a crime, it doesn't mean they will be similar to someone else who is behind bars for the same crime. They all think differently, and they have different personalities.

But they have all lived through some adversity. Perhaps they come from dire poverty, or their parents divorced, or they couldn't cut it at school. There are many background factors involved. In the end, they have ended up living behind bars. This means that they are alone. When they were free, they may have gone about committing crimes, but once they are inside, they feel loneliness in a different way than people on the outside do. Now you and I might feel lonely, but it is not the same. Basically, we are free. You want to go for a walk? Then you can go. But for them, for the first time, this freedom is no longer possible. They realize, "I am well and truly alone now." Typically, they have been abandoned by their parents too.

Now, if you take a lonely person, and they meet someone who does care about them [like the chaplain], then that is a most happy thing. In prison, the inmate might not care about rehabilitation at all. There are some people in prison who fall into despair. What they really want is to feel a connection between human hearts. The warmth of another person's heart is what these people need.

Even for me, living in normal society, I might not think of the importance of the warmth that comes from another person. I might think: I want people to think well of me! I want to be recognized for doing my best! Our lives in society flow on like this. But what we really need in life is the sense of connection to other people. The role of the chaplain is to relate to the client as an equal. Perhaps calling this a responsibility is overstating the case.

Now, having said that, I cannot claim to get along with everyone I meet. Of course, some personalities match better than others. But I hope to give them a sense of the warmth that comes from knowing another person cares about them. It takes time and perseverance. When I meet with them, this is what I think is most important. I cannot control whether or not they will reform. That is up to them when they get out into society. But I think that if they realize the importance of the warmth that comes from connecting with other people, then they can really think about what it means to be human.

Most of the inmates I meet are on death row, but I also work with normal inmates. These normal inmates will get out and return to society, so I hope they think about the meaning of being in prison. So I try to get to this point, but of course it takes time, and I tell jokes along the way . . . Whether or not a person has committed a crime, the saddest thing for a human being is loneliness. To have no one to speak to.

Adam: Do you get the impression that people in prison are generally abandoned by society? In that case, is the job of the chaplain to provide human contact?

Hirano: I think so.

Adam: How long have you been working with people on death row?

Hirano: I started out as a chaplain in 1981.

I work primarily with people whose death sentences have been confirmed and with people whose cases are being appealed or awaiting confirmation from the Supreme Court. We have prisons and also jails [*kōchisho*, sometimes translated as detention houses], and the two are different. There are jails in Nagoya, Osaka, Hiroshima, and Fukuoka. There are seven jails in Japan, and I am at Tokyo Jail, which is the largest death row in Japan. [Death rows are located in jails.] Death row inmates are not the same as regular inmates because they are not serving a sentence designed to rehabilitate them. It can take up to seven years for a death sentence to be carried out after it has been confirmed.

In addition to death row inmates, there are also people serving shorter sentences who do labor at Tokyo Jail. For the regular inmates, I provide group chaplaincy sessions. For the death row inmates, I provide one-on-one sessions.

Adam: Why did you become a chaplain?

Hirano: I was recommended by Watanabe Fusō! He asked me if I would be willing to serve as a death row chaplain at Tokyo Jail. We are from the same sect, so I knew him from around.

Adam: What did you think?

Hirano: [laughs] Honestly, I thought, are you kidding? I was scared! I thought, can I really do this? Working with people who have committed serious felonies? Murders? At that time my mother was still alive, but she was ill. She was hospitalized. My father died when I was young, and my mother was ill in the early 1980s. It turned out she had cancer. I was very upset at that time. We knew she had about a year to live. Honestly, my head was so full of my own concerns at the time. But, in Buddhism, we call this kind of thing a karmic connection [*en*]. So I asked my mother for advice. And she said, "You can't possibly go to such a scary place!" [laughs]

Adam: [laughs] So then you said you would do it?

Hirano: Well, I was asked by my *senpai* [mentor], and to an extent I felt glad that he had the confidence in me.

Adam: When you finally began, was your experience different from what you expected?

Hirano: My first session, I went in, and I met a death row inmate in a three- or four-mat room. A guard came with us too. Actually, I was with Watanabe. It was the two of us. But that first time . . . What can I say? I suppose I was very nervous. I am sure the inmate could tell I was terrified. Periodically, I would have a sudden wave of fear. Of course, I had no way to defend myself if something went wrong. The guard was there, but I was basically defenseless, sitting right across from an inmate.

The scene was like this. There was a *butsudan* in the corner. We started by clasping our hands and doing a prayer. And then I returned to the table, and at that moment I had a wave of fear. Just for a moment—it passed.

Adam: I suppose the prison is a scary place.

Hirano: Yes, that's right. The thing is, I had this idea that a death row inmate might try to do something to cause trouble. If they commit a crime while behind bars, then a new trial will start, right? So if they do something to cause a new trial, then the date of their execution could be pushed back! I started to think about this and convinced myself that I was in danger.

Adam: Is there a known case where something like that happened?

Hirano: No, no. Not at all! But I was thinking, if I were him, what would I do? And that's where my fear came from. If I were on death row, maybe I would want to do something to put off my execution!

Adam: It sounds like working with death row inmates is more complex than working with normal inmates. What do you think your clients want from you? Particularly people on death row?

Hirano: I think they are looking for emotional stability [*shinjō no antei*], like it says in the book [points to either the *Chaplain's Manual* or Horikawa's book—not clear which one]. That's what the inmates want. This is something that is provided from the perspective of religion. This is what they hope to get from us chaplains. Now, there are certainly problems with the death penalty system, and Horikawa's book presents the perspective of the abolition movement. But nonetheless, the people on death row are looking for some peace. The prison staff cannot engage with the hearts of the inmates. So that is what is expected of us religionists.

Adam: So the job of religionists is to support the peace of the hearts of the inmates? Is this a kind of psychological support?

Hirano: In Japan, the relationship between religions and politics is strange. Religionists cannot be state employees, and state employees cannot discuss religion. So our job is defined as providing support to the hearts of the people on death row. That role is the role of a religionist, and chaplains are private volunteers. The government cannot pay religionists for this kind of work.

However, inmates can make requests for a Buddhist or a Christian chaplain, and the prison is permitted to meet these requests. The whole system works on requests from the inmates. This is the law. The country has to acknowledge that there are problems of the heart [*kokoro no mondai*], but the government cannot present a Buddhist or a Christian perspective. Private prison chaplains exist to answer to this need.

Adam: What do you do in order to meet that need? For example, do you read the *Tannishō* with inmates?

Hirano: Well, we try to talk with people while keeping religion as the backbone for the conversation. Of course, there are people in jail who don't know anything about religion. So I might go in and offer to teach about Jōdo Shinshū and Shinran and Buddhism. We might discuss the *Tannishō* or the *Kyōgyōshinshō* [Shinran's major doctrinal treatise]. I might quote these particular texts, but there is no set program of always reading the *Tannishō*.

Adam: So there is a great deal of leeway for the chaplains to talk about different things?

Hirano: Yes, that's right.

Adam: It sounds like people on death row don't have contact with anyone but lawyers and chaplains.

Hirano: That's right, they have no contact with anyone at all.

Adam: I read that prison guards used to be able to talk with death row inmates, but that this practice was abandoned in the 1970s on the grounds that it may disrupt the inmates' peace of mind. I imagine this must reflect the loneliness of people on death row. When they meet you, what do they want to talk about? Do they want to talk about religion? According to Horikawa's book, Watanabe found that many of his clients just wanted to discuss worldly affairs or to engage in small talk.

Hirano: Horikawa has only described things from the Shōwa 30s [1955–1965] in that book. You know we have an obligation to maintain secrecy [*shuhi gimu*]. Watanabe had the same responsibility, so he asked Horikawa not to publish it until he died, and he asked her to keep the book focused on things that happened a long time ago. She knows a lot more than was published in the book. In my experience, occasionally people do want to talk about something like the *Tannishō,* but some people just want to talk about baseball—*How was the game last night?* Horikawa mentions that Watanabe used to bring books for people, but that's forbidden these days.

Adam: What about religious books, sutras, or a Bible?

Hirano: Yes, those are permitted. We usually read sutras together at the beginning of a chaplaincy session. There are some books that are permitted and some that are not. Religious books are generally permitted. During a chaplaincy session, we are permitted to bring in resources so long as they are not regarded as dangerous. But we are not going to take requests from inmates to bring in certain pamphlets.

Adam: What kinds of sutra literature do you read with the inmates?

Hirano: I always use the same things. I use the *Sanbutsuge*, *Jūseige*, and *Bussetsu muryō jukyō*. These are basic scriptures in Jōdo Shinshū. I take small selections and read them together with the inmates. I can't do *Shōshinge* because it takes twenty minutes to read, so unless the inmates request it, I will read a shorter sutra to save more time to talk. *Jūseige* takes about five minutes to read.

Adam: How long do you have with the inmates?

Hirano: Usually individual chaplaincy sessions run for about an hour. The prison considers one hour to be quite long, but the staff are quite understanding with me. I have heard that other chaplains may only have thirty or forty minutes.

Adam: So you begin with a sutra reading and then have a conversation?

Hirano: That's right. They want to talk. They don't have anyone to talk to throughout the day, so usually they have something they want to discuss. If they don't, then I try to raise something to talk about, but it can be difficult to try to raise religious topics with people.

Adam: How many clients do you see?

Hirano: [laughs] Don't write the number, okay? [redacted]

Adam: Do the clients meet with many chaplains or only with you?

Hirano: Some meet with many chaplains and others only with one. I think those who meet with many chaplains don't continue for too long. I think eventually people decide which teaching appeals to them, or they decide which chaplain they like best, and then they continue with that chaplain.

Adam: I get the sense that chaplains have responsibilities at various levels: to the facility, to the client, to the union, and to the sect. You men-

tioned that the facility wants the chaplain to support the inmate's emotional stability, but I wonder how you balance this responsibility with the
other responsibilities to the sect and the client, for example?

Hirano: When it comes to the balance, sometimes I am left with a feeling of dissatisfaction about my own performance. Of course, I am a Shin
priest, so if a chaplaincy session ends, if we go one hour and I haven't
talked at all about Jōdo Shinshū or Shinran, I do feel disappointed. But
I think [doctrine] has to come out naturally in the course of a conversation. For example, we might discuss our understanding of Shinran.

People on death row do not have a tomorrow. You can't say, "See you
next time." Death row is not that world. If we end without discussing
the most important thing together, then I feel like, "Oh no, was that
okay?" So I have banned myself from using the phrase, "We will discuss
that next time!" Watanabe used to say the same thing [he did not want
to put things off for next time]. Although, recently, I have started to feel
that it might be okay to try to put off some [important] topics for another
session . . . But then, of course, if I hear that someone has been executed,
and I have left something unsaid, I regret it.

I have started to think that even having a conversation about nothing in particular can be a kind of karmic connection. Of course, if someone wants to hear about *nenbutsu*, then I am ready to go. But if that doesn't
happen, I realize it's not up to me to save someone. There is always a karmic connection [to the Buddha]. Even if I can provide someone with a
kind of peace, I certainly don't have the power to save someone. Amida
does the saving, not human beings. If salvation through the power of
Amida is assured, then it is not for me to worry about whether or not I
have been able to save someone myself.

This is getting a little bit deeper, but are you familiar with the
Tannishō? Chapter 15 describes the human desire to die peacefully with a
nenbutsu prayer on our lips. Long ago, Eirokusuke painted an image called
Dying Peacefully [*Tatami no ue no dai ōjō*]. I think this painting reflects
the common conception of the ideal death that is discussed in chapter 15
of the *Tannishō*. [Chapter 15 deconstructs this natural desire as something
that emerges from human ignorance.]

In Buddhism, we have the concept of karma [*gō*]. My life does not
come from nowhere; it exists in an endless repeating cycle. Human life

did not just arise out of nothing. There is a larger life span that continues forever in succession. Karmic connections to that greater life appear as individual lives. Even the present situation, what we call our reality, is made up of karmic connections.

Now, there are times when life seems to go our way, and times when it does not. [Chapter 15 of the *Tannishō* says that] we can't say that for a person to die peacefully while chanting the *nenbutsu* is proof that they have been saved. Human beings might think so. We tend to think that we want to die peacefully, to die peacefully with a prayer on our lips. This is how people think. But this tendency is precisely what Shinran denies completely.

Shinran says that no matter what, there is a greater life beyond our human existence, and everyone is saved by this greater life. Our ailments, our suffering, our deaths—these things that come at the end of life are not the problem. They all emerge from our karmic destiny. Even people who seem to be living a pious life, praying the *nenbutsu* every day—even such people can die in pain. There are many who die in pain; people die—not praying, but cursing their own lives. [Shinran] rejects the idea that the way a person dies reflects the quality of the person. Those who die piously are not necessarily the good. And those who die fighting it are not necessarily evil.

We tend to think that the quality of a person's death reflects their fate after death, but that is because we do not realize the ultimate truth. That is why I believe in leaving salvation up to the working of Amida. We are fine as we are. There is Amida, there is hope, there is salvation. I think all we can do is believe in this. We have to leave it up to Amida. That is the nature of religion. Whether or not people realize it, I have come to believe this is what our human life is. We have to leave some things up to the Buddha.

For me, as a chaplain, I realized [over time] that my clients are not going to come to me to thank me for saving them. They are not going to say, "Oh Hirano, thanks to you, I feel totally prepared to head to the gallows!" That is not going to happen. Shinran knew this, and that is why I believe he was a great thinker. He understood that human beings are complacent and that we try to live by relying on our own judgments even unto the very last. That's what I feel as a chaplain. I can't accomplish anything by my own power. It is not thanks to me that people will be saved.

Shinran knew that each human being lives bearing the karma of his own past.

Adam: Is this understanding of chaplaincy not related to the Shin doctrine of salvation of the evil person [*akunin shōki*]? You just mentioned that Shinran's perspective transcends a worldly understanding of good and evil.

Hirano: That's right. Amida wants to save every human being. That is the nature of the primal vow [*hongan*]. So, no matter how a person dies, Amida wants to save that person. Now, the way [Shin doctrine] conceives of good and evil differs from the perspective of society at large. The worldly interpretation differs from [the doctrinal meaning of] "salvation of the evil person." In the doctrinal meaning, a "good person" refers to one who believes in the power of the self to attain salvation. The evil person, in this context, means the person who realizes the limited power of the self. [Doctrinally, people convinced of their own goodness are more ignorant than those who realize the limitations of the self.] Because of the complex nature of this doctrinal term, I actually avoid using it. I prefer to talk about awakening to the significance of life. I think the aim is to realize that there is the external force of the primal vow working for the salvation of human beings.

Adam: I get the impression that this doctrinal perspective you mentioned is related to your approach to counseling. You mentioned that you have to treat your client as an equal. It seems that the perspective on humanity we see in Shinran implies a kind of equality. He thinks that the difference between the good and the evil is a false distinction. But this differs from the interpretation of the human that dominates in the law, no? Does not the law make a clear distinction between the good and the evil?

Hirano: Yes. That's right. Society must be that way. In the end, our life in society is not designed for the salvation of the individual person. If society does not make a distinction between good and evil, it cannot survive. This is the social life of humanity. At the basis is the idea that society requires stability. That is why we need the law. There is nothing we can do about it.

But then again, we have the teaching of Buddha. Life is suffering. Of course life is tough! Or course it is hard! We cannot make the world equal through the power of the law. Why? It will not work because the law is made by human beings, and everything made by human beings changes over time. Even the law changes over time, right? It changes because it is something made by human beings. Law changes to suit the times. Reality or the truth, these do not change. For example, love [*ai*] in Christianity, or compassion [*jihi*] in Buddhism. It would be strange to claim that these change! "When your dad was around it wasn't like this! We were not doing the *nenbutsu!* The scriptures used to be different!" That could not be because the truth does not change.

It is because the truth does not change that the teachings provide us with a sense of stability [*anshinkan*]. Think about it. If your hometown changed, you wouldn't want to go back, right? The mountains remain the same, the river remains the same, and even some of your friends stay around. In the same way, the truth doesn't change. The things made by human beings are subject to change.

Adam: Do you have this conversation with your clients?

Hirano: I do.

Adam: How do they respond?

Hirano: The response changes by the person. Some say they have never heard or considered such things. For example, some say they have never considered that their situation arises from an unequal society. They might say, "So that is why I hate such and such a person! The world is not a perfect place, and so it is not purely my fault that I have committed a crime." I try to get them to consider the idea that there is a world not entirely defined by profit and loss or by good and evil.

I tell them about myself too. I tell them that I used to fight with my parents [as a young man]. In my heart, I even became so angry some-times that I wanted to kill them! [laughs] I tell them that sometimes when I am overwhelmed, I cry. If you are going to have a completely open in-teraction with someone, then it is like you are both naked. [laughs] In order to do this kind of counseling, I have to put myself out there too. That is the role of the counselor.

So one cannot begin with the idea that people in prison are fundamentally different from yourself. I try to begin by acknowledging that the same things that trouble them have troubled me. And not just in the past tense! I think it is important to be able to say such things.

Adam: I imagine that people on death row do not have many people around them who recognize their humanity. They do not meet many people, and they don't have anyone to rely on. It must be one of the important roles for the chaplain to provide this kind of human connection.

Hirano: [inhales deeply] Yes. That's right.

Adam: There is one last thing. What do you make of the previous chaplains who were persecuting thought criminals? How does that look now?

Hirano: That is how history moves [*sore wa rekishi no nagare desu yo*]. At one time, things are open, and then later society becomes repressive. And then, when things open up again, we can look back critically on the past.

Notes

Preface

1. The Japanese correctional system recognizes a distinction between *ippan kyōkai* and *shūkyō kyōkai*.

2. The rationale for the distinction between general and religious chaplaincy rests on the legal framework governing religion in Japan. Religious chaplaincy cannot be compulsory due to the constitutional provisions for religion-state separation and for religious freedom. General chaplaincy may be compulsory, as it was in this case, because it is officially nonreligious. It is typical for religious workers like this Shingon priest to conduct both types of chaplaincy sessions. There is ambiguity about what kinds of activities are considered appropriate for general chaplaincy. Why is copying the *Heart Sutra* not considered a religious activity? Is it simply that the warden does not consider it to be religious?

3. Fukkyō Kenkyūsho, *Kyōkaishi kyōhon*, 193–96.

Introduction

1. The expression "just deserts" is probably the last abode in the English language of the archaic word "desert" meaning "things deserved."

2. Kuroda and Stone, "The Imperial Law and the Buddhist Law," 283.

3. Lawson, "Reforming Japanese Corrections," 132. Lawson provides a detailed account of the Act on Penal Detention Facilities and Treatment of Inmates and Detainees.

4. On the anti-Buddhist movements, see Grapard, "Japan's Ignored Cultural Revolution"; Ketelaar, *Of Heretics and Martyrs*; Yasumaru, *Kamigami no Meiji ishin*; and Iwata Mami and Kirihara, *Kami to hotoke no bakumatsu ishin*. On the ending of the ban on Christianity, see: Nosco, "Experiences of Christians," 85–97. State Shinto is a major topic in studies of religion and state in modern Japanese history, and a small selection of major works includes Hardacre, *Shinto and the State*, and *Shinto*; Murakami, *Kokka Shintō*; and Shimazono, *Kokka Shintō to Nihonjin*. The study of Japanese new religions

is a subdiscipline in its own right. Some important works include Baffelli and Reader, *Dynamism and the Ageing*; Dorman, *Celebrity Gods*; Hardacre, *Kurozumikyō*, and *Lay Buddhism*; Inoue Nobutaka, *Kyōha Shintō no keisei*, and *Shinshūkyō jiten*; McLaughlin, *Human Revolution*; Murakami, *Shinshūkyō: Sono kōdō to shisō*; Staemmler and Dehn, *Establishing the Revolutionary*; Stalker, *Prophet Motive*; Yasumaru, *Nihon no kindaika to minshū shisō*. On the rise of spirituality in Japan, see Shimazono, *From Salvation to Spirituality*.

5. Fujiwara, "Introduction"; Reader, "Secularisation, R.I.P.? Nonsense."

6. Along these lines, Sullivan argues that chaplains are the "priest[s] of the secular." Sullivan, *Ministry of Presence*, 3.

7. Article 28 guarantees religious freedom "within limits not prejudicial to peace and order, and not antagonistic to their duties as subjects." See National Diet Library (website), The Constitution of the Empire of Japan.

8. There is a general understanding that the prewar regime relied on symbols, myths, and rituals drawn from the Shinto tradition to bolster its own legitimacy. Shimazono Susumu represents the view that the term "State Shinto" is an apt description of the dominant ideological mode that prevailed between at least the 1920s until 1945 (Shimazono, "State Shinto and the Religious Structure"; Shimazono and Murphy, "State Shinto in the Lives of the People"). However, there is much debate about whether this arrangement amounted to a form of state religion and the extent to which policies actually favored shrine priests themselves. This line of critical reappraisal can be found in Sakamoto Koremaru, *Kokka Shintō saikō*.

9. Articles 20 and 89 of the Postwar Constitution. See Kantei (website), Constitution of Japan.

10. Thomas, *Faking Liberties*.

11. Nakao, "Jigan hishin," 5. I received a photocopy of this interview at my first *Chaplain's Manual* committee meeting. The Corrections Office is responsible for the centralized management of the Japanese prison system, and the chair of the *Chaplain's Manual* committee meeting, Kondō Tetsujō, distributed this interview to introduce the Corrections Office's normative expectations for prison chaplains. The interview forms the preface of a memoir by the Jōdoshū prison chaplain Otoyama Nyoun.

12. For a concise summary of Yoshida's position, see Shigeta, "Yoshida Kyūichi." Shigeta notes that Yoshida takes the so-called New Buddhism (*shin Bukkyō*) faction as representative of Buddhism's social outreach, but I believe the same can be said for Buddhist social welfare projects generally, and this expanded reading would include prison chaplaincy and probation works. For Yoshida's approach to the social history of religion, see his studies of Buddhism and society included in Yoshida, *Nihon kindai Bukkyō shakaishi kenkyū*. In recent years, the field of modern Japanese Buddhist history has expanded into a subdiscipline in its own right. For a broad introduction to the topic, see Ōtani et al., *Kindai Bukkyō sutadīzu*.

13. Yoshida, *Kiyozawa Manshi*. Yoshida's classic biography of Kiyozawa Manshi contributed to the scholarly interpretation of Kiyozawa's *seishinshugi* movement as an exemplary case of the modernization of Japanese Buddhism.

14. Yoshida devoted his scholarly career to two primary research areas: the historical study of modern Japanese Buddhism and the historical study of social work in Ja-

pan. For his foundational studies of social work, see Yoshida, *Gendai shakai jigyōshi kenkyū*, and *Nihon shakai fukushi shisōshi*. On the intersection between Buddhism and social welfare specifically, see Yoshida and Hasegawa, *Nihon Bukkyō fukushi shisōshi*.

15. On the *seishinshugi* movement in English, see Blum and Rhodes, *Cultivating Spirituality*.

16. The term *kyōke* appears in the *Larger Sutra on Amitāyus* (*Daimuryōjukyō*). One of the Pure Land tradition's three most important sutras, this sutra is given pride of place in Shin Buddhism. The word *kyōke* first appears in a later section of the *Larger Sutra* known as "Discourse on the Five Evils" (*goakudan*). This section is found only in Chinese versions of the sutra. Here, the Buddha offers a description of our imperfect world as a contrast to the bliss of the Pure Land. These passages have been read in the modern Shin tradition as evidence of the fundamentally corrupt nature of humanity (for an example of a modern Shin reading of "Discourse on the Five Evils," see Toyohara, *Daikyō goakudan no ohanashi*). The term *kyōke* appears in three instances: parents *admonishing* their children; Buddhists *proselytizing* to nonbelievers; and Buddhists *remonstrating* with the ruler to prevent the secular authorities from violating the dharma. The sutra has been translated into English in Gómez, *Land of Bliss*, and in Inagaki and Stewart, *Three Pure Land Sutras*. Nakamura Hajime's dictionary of Buddhist terms, *Bukkyōgo daijiten*, gives a simple definition of *kyōke*: "to teach and remonstrate" (*oshiesatosu*). I have expanded upon this definition in my translation (as "doctrinal admonition") by reading *kyō* in the nominal sense of "doctrine" because this reading more completely captures the meaning of remonstrating based on the Buddhist teaching.

17. The term *kokoro* can be translated as heart, mind, soul, spirit, consciousness, or self. For an analysis of the multivalent meanings of this concept, see Sagara, *Kokoro*. I choose to translate the term as "heart" in part because the ubiquitous chaplains phrase *kokoro no mondai* seems to translate into English best as "problems of the heart." The word "heart" also seems to carry the implications of internality and privacy that I want to highlight as essential to chaplaincy discourse. On the significance of this concept to Japanese Buddhist thought, see Bukkyō Shisō Kenkyūkai, *Kokoro*. In addition to *kokoro*, Buddhist chaplains employ a host of terms to express the concept of karma: law of cause and effect (*inga ōhō*) and bonds (*en*) are the two most prominent examples that recur throughout this study. In translating *en* as "bonds," I follow Rowe, *Bonds of the Dead*.

18. The concept of karma has a long history, and with no exaggeration, it may be said to be foundational to all Buddhist cosmologies, soteriologies, theories of subjectivity, and ethical doctrines. Buddhist conceptions of karma take various forms, from the Pali *Dhamapadda* to the "three mysteries" (*sanmitsu*) of Shingon (see Hakeda, *Kūkai*); medieval conceptions of the four debts (*shion*; see Ruppert, "Sin or Crime?"); the Pure Land doctrine of "merit transfer" (*ekō*; see Nara, "May the Deceased Get Enlightenment!"); beliefs in familial or blood-based karmic ties (*en*) as are found in some Japanese new religious movements (see Hardacre, *Kurozumikyō*, 30–31; and Kisala, "Contemporary Karma"). There are numerous interpretations of the doctrine of karma even within the relatively limited range of Japanese Buddhism, and this book adds to this list by considering theories of karma generated by and for the prison chaplaincy. For a creative reinterpretation of the concept of karma and rebirth as a mode of ethical reflection with parallels in diverse cultural regions, see Obeyesekere, *Imagining Karma*.

19. Berger defines theodicy as follows: "Every nomos [moral order] is established, over and over again, against the threat of its destruction by the anomic forces endemic to the human condition. [. . .] Anomic phenomena must not only be lived through, they must also be explained [. . .] in terms of the nomos established in the society in question. An explanation of these phenomena in terms of religious legitimations, of whatever degree of theoretical sophistication, may be called a theodicy" (*Sacred Canopy*, chap. 3, "On Theodicy," esp. 53). See also Berger and Luckmann, *Social Construction of Reality*.

20. McMahan, *Making of Buddhist Modernism*. McMahan interprets Buddhist modernism as a product of hybridization between Buddhist traditions and the dominant cultural and intellectual forces of modernity that trace their roots to the European enlightenment (including rationalism, scientific discourses like psychology, and a form of romanticism associated with modern literature). It is possible to identify similar trends in Japanese Buddhist modernism, but a nuanced picture of the modernization of Buddhism in Japan also necessitates consideration of Buddhism's hybridization with the ideologies of nationalism and modern strategies of governance. Buddhist nationalism and Buddhist statism are important dimensions of Japanese Buddhist modernism.

21. On governmentality, see Foucault, *Security, Territory, Population*, 108–9. On the distortions that have arisen because of the Weberian framing of the Mahayana as an inherently irrational, otherworldly, and antimodern, degenerate form of Buddhism, see Ivy, "Modernity." Contrary to this caricature of East Asian Buddhism, the case of the prison chaplaincy represents a deliberately (self-consciously) rationalized, this-worldly, and modern form of Mahayana Buddhism.

22. This is Foucault's genealogical interpretation of the birth of the prison (Foucault, *Discipline and Punish*). I discuss this line of thought at length subsequently in this chapter.

23. On chaplaincy and spiritual care in the Japanese hospice, see Benedict, "Practicing Spiritual Care." For a representative discussion of chaplaincy and spiritual health in the United States, see Sullivan, *Ministry of Presence*.

24. The Religions and Social Contribution Research Group (Shūkyō to Shakai Kōken Kenkyūkai) continues to publish on the topic of religions' public benefit work in the contemporary period. For a study of religious care work in Japan, see Kasai and Itai, *Kea to shite no shūkyō*. Another important recent work on religion's social contributions is Inaba and Sakurai, *Shakai kōken suru shūkyō*. In general, the basic political orientation of these works is to assert the continued vitality and importance of religion (and thus religious studies as a discipline) to Japanese society. In the larger twentieth-century historical context, the idea that religions can and should yield a social contribution is a long-standing theme in Japanese religious life.

25. The same tendency has been noted by others: Garon, *Molding Japanese Minds*; Ives, "Mobilization of Doctrine"; and Rogers and Rogers, "Honganji: Guardian of the State."

26. See the 1886 Honganji sect charter reproduced in Honganji Shiryō Kenkyūsho, *Honganji shi* (2019) 3: 177–80 (the term *nitai sōshi* appears in Article 2 on 177). The political significance of this ideal is discussed in Kondō, *Tennōsei kokka to seishinshugi*, 16–17.

27. Despite the fact that some new religions like Tenrikyō and Konkōkyō have long been active in prison chaplaincy and other social welfare endeavors, in mainstream Japanese society, adherents of new religions are sometimes still subjected to prejudice. See McLaughlin, "Did Aum Change Everything?"

28. Durkheim, *Elementary Forms*. Durkheim's term is "social cohesion."

29. Foucault, *Discipline and Punish,* and *Security, Territory, Population.*

30. Foucault, *Birth of the Clinic.*

31. Asad, *Genealogies of Religion*, and *Formations of the Secular.*

32. Cf. Edward Said's approach: "Unlike Michel Foucault, [. . .] I do believe in the determining imprint of individual writers upon the otherwise anonymous collective body of texts constituting a discursive formation" (*Orientalism*, 23).

33. Jackson, *Politics of Storytelling*. See also Arendt, *Human Condition.*

34. Jackson introduces the disjuncture between dominant and demotic modes of storytelling (*Politics of Storytelling*, 45).

35. Jackson, citing Habermas, writes: "the lifeworlds and voices of marginalized *classes* also tend to be privatized by being denied public recognition" (*Politics of Storytelling*, 31–32).

36. On the manifold problems arising from the secrecy surrounding the Japanese justice system, see Johnson, *Japanese Way of Justice.* For an analysis of the antidemocratic regime of secrecy surrounding the death penalty in Japan, see Johnson, "Japan's Secretive Death Penalty." For an overview of the management of crime in Japan, see Johnson, "Crime and Punishment in Contemporary Japan."

37. The most notable work of this kind is Horikawa, *Kyōkaishi.*

38. The public-private divide is central to negotiations surrounding political structure, kinship relations, power dynamics, gender roles, communicative styles, and presentations of selfhood. For a comparison of the public and private dimensions of selfhood in Japan and the United States as a key feature in communicative styles, see Barnlund, *Public and Private Self in Japan and the United States.* For a discussion of the public-private division as a major feature of ancient myths and their construction of gender relations and political authority, see Hardacre, *Shinto*, 61–64. In a study of modern history, Shimazono Susumu argues that the structure of religion-state relations was defined by the elevation of Shinto in the public realm and the concomitant requirement for religions to withdraw into private life (*Kokka Shintō to Nihonjin*). The public-private divide is a key concept for understanding chaplaincy because the chaplain's role is to stand between the public authorities and the private realm of religion (which in chaplaincy practice overlaps with the intimate sphere of reflective introspection, the emotions, the formation of conscience, and, of course, interpersonal bonds).

39. Horikawa cites the example of chaplains being stripped of their visitation privileges and banned from the National Chaplains' Union because of outspoken criticism of death row (*Kyōkaishi*, 236). My own interviews confirmed that chaplains are familiar with such cases.

40. Ito, "I Became an Accessory to Legal Murder."

41. For the chaplaincy, crime covers the shifting range of behaviors that the political authorities designate as illegal and thus subject to criminal penalties. Being a Japanese Christian was illegal in 1871; being a Marxist activist was a criminal act in 1933;

armed robbery was then and is still now a crime. For an introduction to theories of crime, see Gottfredson and Hirschi, *General Theory of Crime*. The definition of crime is a complex topic in the fields of sociology and criminology—analogous to the fraught issues surrounding attempts to define "religion" in the field of religious studies. For my purposes, what counts most in the correctional system is that there are normative definitions of both crime and religion that are enforced with the full power of the state's monopoly on the "legitimate" use of violence. In the following pages, the story that unfolds shows that the most effective religious lobbyists who backed the expansion of prison chaplaincy (and chaplains themselves) had a lot to say about how the legal definition of religion should be constructed, but they did not attempt to renegotiate the boundaries of crime: the prevailing perspective was that proper religions should fight crime (however the public authorities might choose to define the latter).

42. In addition to Foucault's account (*Discipline and Punish*), another touchstone contribution to the history of prisons is Morris and Rothman's *Oxford History of the Prison*. This work offers a fairly comprehensive review of the history of prisons in Western societies, but since its publication in 1995, the field of prison studies has expanded beyond the borders of the Euro-American world.

43. There are a number of major studies of prison religion in Europe, of which I list a small sampling here: on prison religion in Germany, Italy, and Switzerland, see Becci, "Religion's Multiple Locations in Prisons"; on prison religion in Eastern Germany in particular, see Becci, *Imprisoned Religion*; and on relations between the Anglican Church and other faiths involved in the British prison system, see Beckford and Gilliat-Ray, *Religion in Prison*.

44. Sullivan, *Prison Religion*.

45. Dubler, *Down in the Chapel*.

46. See Beckford et al., *Muslims in Prison*, especially chap. 7, "Prison Imams."

47. Gibson, "Global Perspectives on the Birth of the Prison," 1051. Since Gibson's review article was published, other studies of prisons beyond the West have continued to expand the horizon of the field of global prison history. For example, on prisons in China, see Kiely, *Compelling Ideal*. Chapter 4 discusses the influence of Buddhism in the Chinese prison system, highlighting the way the principle of cause and effect (karma) was applied in the context of corrections. Another example of this growing body of literature is Schull, *Prisons in the Late Ottoman Empire*.

48. See Sullivan, *Ministry of Presence*, ix: "A significant amount of religious work is performed by chaplains who do not necessarily routinely publicly identify themselves with a particular religious community but who do their work rather within secular institutions caring for persons with whom they may not share a common religious creed or practice. Their clients are persons with whom they are temporarily brought together for other reasons—reasons such as war, sickness, crime, employment, education, or disaster—persons who may be of any religious affiliation or none. These professional encounters are spread across the secular landscape of contemporary life."

49. On the varieties of chaplaincy in the United States, see Sullivan, *Ministry of Presence*. For a study of Muslim prisoners in France and the United Kingdom (with discussions of chaplaincy and prison imams), see Beckford et al., *Muslims in Prison*. For an extensive bibliography of prison chaplaincy materials covering the United Kingdom,

Canada, France, and the United States, see Beckford et al., "Prison Chaplaincy: A Selective Bibliography."

For a study of military chaplaincy in multiple nations, see Brekke and Tikhonov, *Military Chaplaincy*. On Japan specifically, see Micah Auerback's essay in the same volume, "Paths Untrodden in Japanese Buddhist Chaplaincy to the Imperial Military." For evidence of the proliferation of chaplaincy around the world, see the websites of the following international organizations: International Prison Chaplains Association (https://www.ipcaworldwide.org), International Association for Spiritual Care (https://ia-sc.org), and International Association of Chaplains in Higher Education (http://www.iache.org), all accessed April 23, 2019. For information about chaplaincy in Europe, see Eurel Project, "Chaplaincy," accessed April 24, 2019.

50. On this topic, see Roemer, "Religion and Subjective Well-Being in Japan."

51. Sullivan cites the example of the US Army spiritual fitness program: "The army's new spiritual fitness program is explicitly founded in positive psychology, a newish branch of psychology focused on human flourishing" (*Ministry of Presence*, 26).

52. One of the most interesting analyses of this phenomenon is Hurd, *Beyond Religious Freedom*. See Hurd's discussion of "two faces of faith" (22–23).

53. See Sullivan, *Impossibility of Religious Freedom*, 1: "Many laws, constitutions, and international treaties today grant legally enforceable rights to those whose religious freedom is infringed. [. . .] A commitment to religious freedom is a taken-for-granted part of modern political identity in much of the world. Certainly this is so in the United States. Even most of those whose own personal stance is fiercely secular would include the right to religious freedom among those rights fundamental to a free democratic society."

54. On US military chaplaincy, see Waggoner, "Taking Religion Seriously in the U.S. Military."

55. For a discussion of this literature, see Becci, "Religion's Multiple Locations in Prisons." On the same theme, Sullivan refers to a US Department of Justice survey conducted in 2004, which concludes that faith contributes to crime prevention (*Prison Religion*, 14). For an overview of prison religion in Japan, see Akaike and Ishizuka, *Kyōsei shisetsu ni okeru shūkyō*.

56. Sullivan, *Ministry of Presence*, 174.

57. Sullivan, *Ministry of Presence*, 178.

58. Sullivan, *Ministry of Presence*, 188: "[For Muslim chaplains], presence is understood to be the will of Allah, as exemplified by the Prophet."

59. See Kasai, "Introducing Chaplaincy," as well as Kasai and Itai, *Kea to shite no shūkyō*. See also the entry for *bihara* in Nihon Bukkyō Shakai Fukushi Gakkai, *Bukkyō shakai fukushi jiten*, 254. On bedside religious caregivers, see Suzuki, "Rinshō shūkyōshi no tanjō."

60. Benedict, "Practicing Spiritual Care."

61. On the role of religions in the tsunami recovery effort, see McLaughlin, "In the Wake of the Tsunami." On the place of spiritual care in those efforts, see Takahashi, "Ghosts of Tsunami Dead."

62. On CPE, see Kasai, "Introducing Chaplaincy to Japanese Society."

63. Takahashi, "Ghosts of Tsunami Dead," 194.

64. The term *kokoro no kea*—literally "care for the heart"—indicates that the problem of suffering is fundamental.

65. See the report by Murase et al., "Kanwa kea byōtō."

66. The number of chaplains cited here reflects the official count presented on the National Chaplains' Union's website. See Zenkoku Kyōkaishi Renmei, http://kyoukaishi .server-shared.com, accessed March 20, 2018. The number of correctional facilities is based on Kyōseikyoku, *Kyōsei no genjō*, 15. The prison population statistic is based on official data from a 2018 Ministry of Justice white paper on crime (Hōmushō, *Hanzai hakusho 2018*).

67. Bandō et al., "Keiji shisetsu ni okeru shūkyō isshiki," 3–4.

68. I have not been able to locate any public statistics about the presence or absence of chaplains at executions, but I have heard from multiple informants that all death row inmates are encouraged to accept a chaplain's accompaniment.

69. For example, the International Prison Chaplains' Association (IPCA) noted in a personal communication (from April 2, 2019): "IPCA Europe has a mailing list with about 500 names of prison chaplains from around Europe, but we do not have a complete list over countries or all the other prison chaplains who are not on our lists. Many different churches have prison chaplains here in Europe and I do not think that anyone has the type of information which you are asking for. In some countries they might be organized nationally or in different regions, in other countries they might not be organized. I live in Norway and the Norwegian Church (DNK) have 36 and the Salvation Army (TSA) have 8. All prison chaplains, part-time or full-time, have prison chaplaincy as a paid "job" [through] DNK or TSA. There are other churches that visit prisons on a regular basis but without prison chaplains as paid jobs." For more information on prison chaplaincy around the world, see the website of the International Prison Chaplains' Association, https://www.ipcaworldwide.org, accessed July 23, 2020.

70. Pew Research Center, "Religion in Prisons," appendix A. See also the American Correctional Chaplains Association website, http://www.correctionalchaplains.org, accessed July 30, 2020.

71. For a statistical overview of religion in the United States, see Pew Research Center, "Religious Landscape Study." For an overview of increasing secularization in Japan, see Ama Toshimaro, *Nihonjin wa naze mushūkyō na no ka*; and Reader, "Secularization R.I.P.? Nonsense."

72. In English-language studies of Japanese religions, this trend bears the influence of Kuroda Toshio. For a general overview of his approach and key concepts, see Kuroda and Stone, "The Imperial Law and the Buddhist Law"; and Kuroda, *Ōbō to buppō*.

73. On the *Sutra of Golden Light*, see Sango, *Halo of Golden Light*. On "rites to pacify and protect the state," see Grapard, "Institution, Ritual, and Ideology."

74. Hur, *Death and Social Order*, 24.

75. Hur, *Death and Social Order*, 26.

76. On the anti-Buddhism movements, see Ketelaar, *Heretics and Martyrs*.

77. On the Great Promulgation Campaign, see Hardacre, "Creating State Shinto"; *Shinto and the State*, 42–58; and *Shinto*, 376–81. See also Ogawara, *Daikyōin no kenkyū*; and Miyake, *Sanjō kyōsoku engisho shiryōshū*, and *Sanjō kyōsoku to kyōiku chokugo*.

78. A general history of Japan's transition from the Tokugawa shogunate to the modern nation-state (i.e., the process of modernization) is covered in Jansen et al., *Cambridge History of Japan: Volume 5, The Nineteenth Century*.

79. On Shimaji, see Krämer, *Shimaji Mokurai*; and Yamaguchi, *Shimaji Mokurai*. Shimaji's form of Buddhist modernism—the compromise he advocated for—may be comparable in some ways to Catholic modernism as described by James Chappel: "If secular modernity is a state-sanctioned condition of religious freedom, religious modernism can be understood as the set of tactics that religious communities use to conceptualize, mobilize within, and shape that modern settlement. In other words, the 'privatization' of religion in a modern setting seldom leads to depoliticization but rather leads toward new forms of public intervention that can be legitimated in the name of th[e] sacred private sphere" (*Catholic Modern*, 5).

80. On *kokoro* in Japanese religious discourse, see Hardacre, *Kurozumikyō*, 19–21. For a historical overview of the concept of *kokoro* from ancient times to the present, see Sagara, *Kokoro*. Today the character 心 can be read as *shin* or as *kokoro* depending on context. *Shin* is the Japanized version of the Chinese reading. *Kokoro* is regarded as an indigenous Japanese word assigned to the character. The term *kokoro* can be found in the earliest Japanese court poetry collection, the *Manyōshū*, where it appears as an expression for empathy and an aesthetic sensibility (Sagara, *Kokoro*, 18–20). Like the Japanese poetic tradition, the tradition of Japanese ethical thought has long valued purity of heart as an ideal. With each historical period, the dominant mode for expressing these values has shifted: in the ancient period, the pure, bright heart (*kiyoki akaki kokoro*) was esteemed; in the medieval, it was the honest heart (*seichoku no kokoro*), and in the early modern, the ideal heart was typically expressed as sincere (*makoto*; Sagara, *Kokoro*, 68). Much of this language has been adopted into the vocabulary of the modern Shinto priesthood. By the modern period, literary intellectuals like Natsume Sōseki (1867–1916) and Watsuji Tetsurō (1889–1960) employed the language of *kokoro* in relation to the concept of conscience (*ryōshin*; Sagara, *Kokoro*, 101–12). *Kokoro* has long been an essential conceptual tool for thinking about the nature of the human in Japan. Where the cultivated heart has been regarded as an ideal, the uncultivated heart has often been regarded as a source of trouble. For example, in Genshin's (942–1017) *The Essentials of Rebirth in the Pure Land* (*Ōjō yōshū*), we find this admonition: "If you would master your heart, do not take your heart as master" (quoted in Sagara, *Kokoro*, 60).

81. There are many important works on the development of the concept of religion (*shūkyō*) in modern Japan. Hoshino Seiji's pathbreaking genealogical study of modern religious discourse, *Kindai Nihon no shūkyō gainen*, highlights the role of religionists in constructing a transcendent concept of religion bound up with matters of civilization, ethics, and modern subjectivity.

82. There is a wide range of literature on *shinzoku nitai*. See, for example, Hirata, *Shinshū shisōshi ni okeru "shinzoku nitai"*; Itō Chōjirō, *Shinzoku nitai kan shū*; and Yamazaki, *Shinshū to shakai*. Yamazaki has the most comprehensive bibliography on the topic.

83. Hoshino, *Kindai Nihon no shūkyō gainen*, 11–13.

84. Quoted in Kuroda and Stone, "The Imperial Law and the Buddhist Law," 277. For the original text in Japanese, see Kuroda, *Ōbō to buppō*, 34.

85. Kuroda and Stone, "The Imperial Law and the Buddhist Law," 283.

86. The chaplaincy is not unique in this regard. See Ives, "Mobilization of Doctrine"; and Rogers and Rogers, "Honganji: Guardian of the State." For a Shin Buddhist perspective on the sect's collaboration with the wartime authorities, see Senji Kyōgaku Kenkyūkai, *Senji kyōgaku to Shinshū*. On the same topic, see Ōnishi, *Senji kyōgaku to Jōdo Shinshū*.

87. In contrast, Melissa Curley and James Mark Shields have published recent studies that cover the Buddhist left, and these provide a significant contribution to the understanding of the internal diversity of modern Japanese Buddhism (Curley, *Pure Land, Real World*; Shields, *Against Harmony*). In highlighting politically engaged (and often progressive) Buddhists, both studies represent minority reports. In this book about prison chaplaincy, I try to reckon with the conservative doctrinal orthodoxies that the Shin sects and others created as they sought to provide a rationale for their prison outreach programs. The official doctrines of the prison chaplaincy are rooted in the mainstream dogmas against which progressive Buddhists were reacting.

88. Botsman, *Punishment and Power*.

89. Akashi Tomonori, *Kangoku no kindai*.

90. Shigeta, *Aku to tōchi*.

91. Maxey, *Greatest Problem*.

92. Josephson, *Invention of Religion*.

93. Jaffe, *Neither Monk nor Layman*.

94. Krämer, *Shimaji Mokurai*.

95. Thomas identifies multiple approaches to religious freedom in prewar Japanese political discourse: "*Statist* approaches gave preference to the governmental prerogative to grant or rescind religious freedom based on the state's perception of the public good. *Corporatist* approaches prioritized customary privileges for Buddhism as Japan's majority religion. Finally, *latitudinarian* approaches treated religious freedom as a civil liberty devolving upon individuals rather than groups. [. . .] Religious freedom was many things to many people" (*Faking Liberties*, 51–52). Thomas also identifies a fourth model advocated by Shin priests: *complementarity*. See the discussion of Shin advocacy for a system of "officially recognized religions" (*kōninkyō*) on 56–57, 63–67. In this study of prison chaplaincy, I focus on the influence of Shin advocacy for the ideal of complementarity between religion and state because this position became the dominant pattern for negotiating religion-state relations behind bars.

96. Garon, *Molding Japanese Minds*.

97. Nakanishi, *Bukkyō to iryō fukushi*.

98. Ogawara, *Kindai Nihon no sensō to shūkyō*, and *Nihon no sensō to shūkyō*.

99. Akazawa, *Kindai Nihon no shisō dōin*.

100. Some works of English-language scholarship have previously investigated the connection between Buddhism and nationalism in relation to the war. See, for example, Heisig and Maraldo, *Rude Awakenings*; and Victoria, *Zen at War*. The present study does not focus on the war specifically, and I do not address questions of Buddhist "war responsibility," preferring instead to highlight how the connection between religious organizations and state agencies has been a stable characteristic of religious work for the public benefit from the Meiji era to the present.

1. Defend the Dharma, Admonish the Heretics

1. *KKHN* 1: 32.

2. *One Hundred Years of Prison Chaplaincy* briefly refers to Sekimon Shingaku preaching in the Tokugawa-period stockades as a precursor to prison chaplaincy (*KKHN* 1: 31). Daniel Botsman interprets the stockade not as a forerunner to modern prisons but rather as a supplement to the bakufu's model of exercising power through enforced status hierarchy, public spectacle, and physical punishments. To put it another way, even though the stockade grounds were eventually converted into a prison, the stockade itself does not appear to have greatly influenced the prison system's development—in part because the stockade was not connected to the "civilizational" project of modernization (*Punishment and Power*, 85–114). In the same vein, Shin sectarian accounts (and the chaplains I met at the *Chaplain's Manual* committee meetings) do not consider the Shingaku preachers who attended the stockades to be historically significant to the subsequent development of prison chaplaincy. This is no doubt because Sekimon Shingaku preachers are not part of the Shin Buddhist lineage. Concerning Sekimon Shingaku preachers in the stockades, also see Umemori, "Shingaku to iu tekunorojī."

3. For representative postwar studies in Japanese, see Kataoka Yakichi, *Nagasaki no Kirishitan*, as well as *Nihon Kirishitan junkyōshi*, and *Urakami yonban kuzure*. For an overview of the Christianity ban and its relationship to "folk religion," see Murai, *Kirishitan kinsei to minshū no shūkyō*. Influential prewar studies include Anesaki, *Kirishitan kinshi no shūmatsu*, and *Kirishitan shūmon no hakugai to senpuku*; and Urakawa, *Kirishitan no fukkatsu* (*KF*). Also of the prewar era, Tokushige's *Ishin seiji shūkyōshi kenkyū* (*ISSK*) provides a different perspective on the event, highlighting the Buddhist remonstrators who tried to force the Christians to convert.

4. For a discussion of relevant diplomatic issues in English, see Burkman, "The Urakami Incidents and the Struggle for Religious Toleration," 143–216; and Maxey, *Greatest Problem*. On the theological considerations surrounding the interaction between the Catholic Church and the newly discovered underground Christians, see Turnbull, "Diversity or Apostasy," 441–54. For a different perspective, see Nosco, "Experiences of Christians."

5. *ISSK*. Tokushige's use of the term "doctrinal admonition" to refer to the handling of illegal Christians was the impetus for my investigations into the connection between the last persecution of the Urakami Christians and the prison chaplaincy's subsequent development.

6. For a concise summary of the social roles played by Buddhist temples in past and present, see the entry for *jiin no kinō* (functions of temples) in Ono et al., *Shukusatsuban: Nihon shūkyō jiten*, 243–71. On the role of Buddhism in the management of illness, see Nakanishi, *Bukkyō to iryō fukushi*.

7. For a discussion of the role of anti-Christianity in unifying the shogun's realm, see Hur, *Death and Social Order*.

8. On perceptions of Christianity, see Josephson, *Invention of Religion*, chaps. 1 and 2. On the perception of Christianity as an ideological weapon, see Bakumatsu idealogue Aizawa Seishisai's *New Theses* (*Shinron*) of 1825, translated in Wakabayashi, *Anti-Foreignism*

and Western Learning. For Wakabayashi's introduction to Aizawa's view of Christianity as a weapon of colonialism, see pages 13–14.

9. On the history of Nagasaki Christians, see Kataoka Yakichi, *Nagasaki no Kirishi-tan* and *Urakami yonban kuzure.* The term "underground" (*senpuku*) is used to describe Japanese Christians who practiced their faith below the radar of the political authori-ties during the period of prohibition. After making contact with foreign priests in 1865, some members of this underground community chose to rejoin the Catholic Church, but others elected to continue their own form of independent Christian practice, and this latter group is known as the hidden Christians (*kakure Kirishitan*; see Turnbull, *Kakure Kirishitan*). In other words, there is a meaningful distinction between the terms "underground Christians" and "hidden Christians." During their centuries of isolation from the Catholic Church, the underground Christians produced an oral tradition based on a combination of local folklore and Catholicism. Christal Whelan has translated their major text, *Tenchi hajimari no koto,* into English (*Beginning of Heaven and Earth*). A col-lection of primary documents pertaining to the underground Christians is included in Tanigawa, *Minkan shūkyō,* beginning on 761.

10. Kataoka Yakichi, *Urakami yonban kuzure,* 20.

11. For a concise overview of Nagasaki history based on the city's official record, see Nagasaki Shinbunsha, *Wakaru wakaran: Shin Nagasaki shishi.*

12. Kataoka Yakichi, *Urakami yonban kuzure,* 20.

13. Kataoka Yakichi, *Urakami yonban kuzure,* 28.

14. Kataoka Yakichi, *Urakami yonban kuzure,* 28. Ōura Church is now recognized as a minor basilica.

15. Kataoka Yakichi, *Urakami yonban kuzure,* 20–31.

16. Kataoka Yakichi, *Urakami yonban kuzure,* 32–34.

17. Kataoka Yakichi, *Urakami yonban kuzure,* 32–34.

18. Kataoka Yakichi, *Urakami yonban kuzure,* 39–42.

19. This paragraph's overview of the broader political context surrounding the events in Urakami draws on Yasumaru, "Kindai tenkanki ni okeru shūkyō to kokka," 490–540.

20. The orders separating Buddhas from Kami (*shinbutsu bunri rei*) are reproduced in Miyachi Masato, "Shūkyō kankei hōrei ichiran," 425.

21. On the *haibutsu kishaku* movement, see Ketelaar, *Of Heretics and Martyrs,* and Yasumaru, *Kamigami no Meiji Ishin,* 85–118.

22. See Grapard, "Japan's Ignored Cultural Revolution."

23. *ISSK*: 158.

24. The ban on Christianity was reiterated on March 15, 1868. For a chronology of the Meiji government's orders related to religion, see Miyachi Masato, "Shūkyō kankei hōrei ichiran," 425.

25. *ISSK*: 168–69. The order is reproduced in Miyachi Masato, "Shūkyō kankei hōrei ichiran," 426.

26. The order is reproduced in Miyachi Masato, "Shūkyō kankei hōrei ichiran," 427.

27. See Kataoka Yakichi, "Urakami isshūtō ikken kaidai," 762.

28. Kataoka Yakichi, "Urakami isshūtō ikken kaidai," 761–62.

29. *ISSK*: 182–83.

30. *ISSK*: 186.
31. *ISSK*: 187.
32. *ISSK*: 190–92.
33. *ISSK*: 193. The letters written by the Shin sects differ slightly in wording, but they all make the same request.
34. The circular is reproduced in Miyachi Masato, "Shūkyō kankei hōrei ichiran," 427.
35. *ISSK*: 407–8.
36. *ISSK*: 408.
37. *ISSK*: 195.
38. *ISSK*: 411.
39. *ISSK*: 411.
40. *ISSK*: 535.
41. *KF* 2 is a collection of testimonies taken from each of the internment locations.
42. Tsukada, "Meiji shoki no shūkyō kyōkaishi kō," 74.
43. Yoshida, *Nihon kindai Bukkyō shakaishi kenkyū* 5: 204–5.
44. *ISSK*: 598.
45. *ISSK*: 537.
46. On Urakawa Wasaburō, see the entry under his name in Nihon Kirisutokyō Rekishi Daijiten Henshū Iinkai, *Nihon Kirisutokyō rekishi daijiten*.
47. *KF* 2: 730.
48. *KF* 2: 695.
49. *KF* 2: 699.
50. In what follows, I refer to the discussion of Matsumoto's journal in *ISSK* beginning on 550. Excerpts from Matsumoto's journal are also included in Tokushige, *Meiji Bukkyō zenshū* 8: 465ff.
51. *ISSK*: 550.
52. *ISSK*: 550–51.
53. For the text of this admonition session, see *ISSK*: 552–61.
54. *KF* 2: 741–45.
55. *ISSK*: 559.
56. See the Honganji sect documents in *ISSK*: 418–19. The idea that Christianity was spreading "like a disease" was the baseline assumption of the threat mentality that Buddhist authorities and political leaders adopted toward the forbidden sect at this time.
57. Chūeimon's account is reproduced in *KF* 2: 706–9.
58. *KF* 2: 708.
59. *KF* 2: 741–45. Tokushige also describes Masa's story. His version is essentially a summary of Urakawa's account (*ISSK*: 599–602).
60. *KF* 2: 745.
61. *KF* 2: 688–89.
62. *KF* 2: 519.
63. *KF* 2: 692.
64. *KF* 2: 743. Of the fifty exiled to Daishōji, forty-five returned to the church after release. The remaining five died.
65. *KF* 2: 752–53.

66. Kataoka revised these statistics based on subsequent research to arrive at a total of 3,384 exiles. See Kataoka Yakichi, *Urakami yonban kuzure*, 286–87.

67. During the underground years, the illegal Christians of Urakami (and elsewhere) routinely trampled the *fumie*—a Christian icon used by bakufu officials to test for the presence of Christians, who presumably would be unwilling to tread on the image. On the prevalence of this practice in Urakami, see Kataoka Yakichi, *Fumie, Kakure Kirishitan*, 49–50.

68. The example translated here is from *ISSK*: 567. Two other certificates of conversion from the earliest days of the persecution are included in *KF* 1: 551–53.

69. See the Honganji sect *Chaplain's Manual.* Jōdo Shinshū Honganji-ha Kyōkaishi Hikkei Hensan Iinkai, *Jōdo Shinshū Honganji-ha kyōkaishi hikkei*, 257.

70. According to one report in a Catholic magazine, as recently as 2008, descendants of people who had committed apostasy during the persecution claimed that they continued to suffer "unrelenting criticism." It is not possible to know how seriously to take this account without more evidence, but the fact that the Stories of the Journey continue to be important in the Japanese Catholic community is beyond question. See the report in *Catholic Weekly*, "Pilgrims Visit Site of Nagasaki Christians' Exile."

2. The Way of Repentance and the Great Promulgation Campaign

1. *NKKS* 1: 146.

2. The term "civil religion" is borrowed from Bellah, "Civil Religion in America."

3. The most widely read history detailing the connection between Christianity and carceral programs is probably still Michel Foucault, *Discipline and Punish.* In his telling, the Euro-American prison (as a reformatory) traces its lineage to the monastery as an institution for spiritual purification.

4. Some of the major works in English to discuss the campaign include Hardacre, "Creating State Shinto"; Ketelaar, *Of Heretics and Martyrs*; Jaffe, *Neither Monk nor Layman*; Maxey, *Greatest Problem*; and Krämer, *Shimaji Mokurai.*

5. The Department of Divinities was the highest organ of state in name only. The Department of State was really in charge. On the Department of Divinities, see Sakamoto Koremaru, "Nihon-gata seikyō kankei no keisei katei," 19.

6. Miyachi Masato, "Shūkyō kankei hōrei ichiran," 431. See the entry for *senkyōshi* in Sonoda and Hashimoto, *Shintō shi daijiten*, 599; and also in Miyachi Naokazu and Saeki, *Shintō daijiten*, 862.

7. Miyachi Masato, "Shūkyō kankei hōrei ichiran," 432.

8. The overarching conception of the good appears to derive more from Confucian discourse than from either Buddhist or Shinto theories.

9. Yasumaru, *Kamigami no Meiji ishin*, 122–23.

10. See Tokoyo Nagatane, "Shinkyō soshiki monogatari: Ue no maki," as reproduced in *STK*: 361–422 (esp. 364).

11. For an authoritative study of Shimaji Mokurai in English, see Krämer, *Shimaji Mokurai.*

12. In 1863, the stated aim of serving the sovereign was not yet tantamount to opposing the shogunate, whose officials also voiced support for "revering the emperor." Nonetheless, Honganji's early show of support for imperial authority paved the way for their subsequent support of the restorationist cause. See HSK 3: 8–9; Honganji Shiryō Kenkyūsho, *Honganji shi* (2019) 3: 89–90.

13. Honganji Shiryō Kenkyūsho, *Honganji shi* (2019) 3: 4.

14. Soon after the Restoration, the other major branch of Shin, the Ōtani sect, shifted its allegiance from the doomed shogunate to the restorationist cause and similarly offered financial support for the new regime. In the Meiji period, because of the Honganji sect's closer relationship to the Meiji government, the Ōtani sect appears to have followed Honganji's lead in defining its relations with the state. See Ketelaar, *Of Heretics and Martyrs*, 72–73.

15. HSK 3: 28–30. For an overview of Shin rejection of Kami worship and the problems it caused under the Meiji regime, see Kashiwahara, *Shinshū shi Bukkyō shi no kenkyū: Kindai*, 21–39. Although Shin fared relatively well overall, this was not the case in all domains. When overzealous local authorities took it upon themselves to force temple mergers and closings, Shin temples, too, felt the impact of the anti-Buddhist campaigns. In Sado, for example, local authorities sought to reduce the number of temples from 500 to 80. In Toyama, the situation was even worse. Some 1,630 temples, roughly 1,330 of which were Shin, were to be reduced such that each of the eight recognized sects could have only 1 temple to represent it. Because most of these Shin temples were staffed by married priests, many with children, this draconian policy risked forcing hundreds of temple families into destitution (HSK 3: 32–45). For more on the Shin sects' responses to temple abolitions and mergers, see Akamatsu Toshihide and Kasahara, *Shinshū shi gaisetsu*, 430–33.

Such policies resulted in public outcry, and temples petitioned regional and central authorities to beg for reprieve. Honganji agents Shimaji Mokurai and Ōzu Tetsunen (1834–1902) petitioned the central government, protesting the capricious nature of domainal policies toward Buddhists. The state responded by establishing the Office of Temple Affairs within the Civil Ministry (Minbushō) to oversee relations between the central government and the Buddhist sects in August 1870. With the founding of this office, regional authorities could no longer force the closure of Buddhist temples. Thanks in part to Honganji's effective lobbying, the social position of Buddhist sects was gradually becoming more stable. For a summary of Shin peasant revolts surrounding the Restoration and its aftermath, see Akamatsu Toshihide and Kasahara, *Shinshū shi gaisetsu*, 434–43. For more on Shimaji and Ōzu's petition, see HSK 3: 54–56. On the Office of Temple Affairs, see Honganji Shiryō Kenkyūsho, *Honganji shi* (2019) 3: 108–9.

16. For a discussion of Kōnyo's last testament, see HSK 3: 23–27; also Honganji Shiryō Kenkyūsho, *Honganji shi* (2019) 3: 5–7. The root concept of two levels of truth (also *shinzoku nitai*) can be attributed to Nagarjuna's (Ryūju; d. 250 CE?) writings, where the concept differentiates levels of truth and relates primarily to the nature of knowledge. Its primary meaning in Shin Buddhism, while related, takes on a marked political significance, designating two domains of law (the worldly and the dharma). On the gestation of this concept, see Yamazaki, *Shinshū to shakai*, 13. Important works in the extensive bibliography covering *shinzoku nitai* in the Shin tradition include Hirata,

Shinshū shisōshi ni okeru "shinzoku nitai"; Kangakuryō, *Jōdo Shinshū to shakai*; and Itō Chōjirō, *Shinzoku nitai kan shū*. These works primarily engage with the problem of religion and state relations (that is, politics rather than epistemology).

17. Rennyo sought to curb the excesses of violent rebellions perpetrated by Shin Buddhists against the rulers (*ikkō ikki*) and to unify the Shin temples under the central Honganji temple's authority. In seeking a rapprochement, he argued that Shin Buddhists should "bow to the law of the sovereign and keep the dharma deep in the heart" and "make the law of the sovereign the foundation (*ōbō o moto to shi*) and prioritize righteousness (*jingi*)." The original text is from one of Rennyo's letters (*Gobunshō*) dated to the twenty-seventh day of January 1476. The key sentence is quoted in an oft-cited essay by Kuroda, *Ōbō to buppō*, 34–35. The same sentence is cited in Yamazaki, *Shinshū to shakai*, 20–21. The letter's full text can be found in the current edition of the Honganji scriptures (Jōdo Shinshū Honganji-ha Sōgō Kenkyūsho, *Jōdo Shinshū seiten*, 1159). For a concise discussion of Rennyo's politics, see Akamatsu Toshihide and Kasahara, *Shinshū shi gaisetsu*, 304–12.

Rennyo himself does not use the term *shinzoku nitai*. Neither did the Shin school's founder Shinran (1173–1263) use this term, though early modern sect thinkers interpreted both Shinran's and Rennyo's writings through this lens. For a discussion of this issue, see Yamazaki, *Shinshū to shakai*. Also on Rennyo, see Blum and Yasutomi, *Rennyo and the Roots of Modern Japanese Buddhism*; Dobbins, *Jōdo Shinshū*; and Rogers and Rogers, "Honganji: Guardian of the State."

18. Both major Shin sects invoked the two domains of law doctrine as they sought to renegotiate their relationship to the state by articulating the idea that a private sphere for Buddhist commitments was a requirement for human flourishing. The sects adopted this shared language because they traced their lineages to the common ancestor Rennyo. On Honganji's and Ōtani's declarations of loyalty to the sovereign, see Akamatsu Toshihide and Kasahara, *Shinshū shi gaisetsu*, 452–53. Also on the politics of Meiji-era Shin sects, see Kashiwahara, *Shinshū shi Bukkyō shi no kenkyū: Kindai*, 44–52.

19. *STK*: 231–32.

20. On the doctrinal logic underlying Shimaji's position, see Fujii Takeshi, "Shinzoku nitairon," 223–27.

21. The most comprehensive discussion of the Great Teaching Institute is Ogawara, *Daikyōin no kenkyū*. For an example of a Buddhist petition to open the Great Teaching Institute, see "Daikyōin sōritsu kenpaku," reproduced in Yoshida, *Nihon kindai Bukkyō shi kenkyū*, 80.

22. On the Great Teaching Institute examinations and the selection of the national instructors, see Ogawara, *Daikyōin no kenkyū*, 45–58. Exceptions were made, for example, for certain high-ranking priests who were automatically granted elevated status within the new system without having to sit examinations.

23. Akamatsu Toshihide and Kasahara, *Shinshū shi gaisetsu*, 447

24. HSK 3: 72. Ketelaar offers much higher numbers of national instructors based on an 1880 record from the Bureau of Shrines and Temples: "103,000 doctrinal instructors, over 81,000 of whom were members of the Buddhist sects. The largest single group were the Shin Buddhists at almost 25,000 members" (Ketelaar, *Of Heretics and Martyrs*, 105). The source chart appears in Yoshida, *Nihon kindai Bukkyō shi kenkyū*, 133.

25. Under the Institute, the three teachings were further elaborated into two curricula: the eleven topics (*jūichi kendai*) and the seventeen topics (*jūnana kendai*), or, when taken together, the twenty-eight topics (*nijūhachi kendai*). For a complete listing of these teachings, see Miyake, *Sanjō kyōsoku to kyōiku chokugo*, 36. Miyake also offers the most up-to-date overview of Buddhists' role in the Great Promulgation Campaign (see part 1, chaps. 1 and 2). The lists of eleven and seventeen topics are translated into English and discussed in Maxey, *Greatest Problem*, 118–21.

26. *Shoshū sekkyō yōgi* is reproduced in Miyake, *Sanjō kyōsoku engisho shiryōshū*, 51–64 (Shin is covered in 60–61). For translations of the three teachings, see Hardacre, "Creating State Shinto," 45. For the original text promulgating the three teachings, see Miyachi Masato, "Shūkyō kankei hōrei ichiran," 446.

27. Quoted in HSK 3: 74.

28. Yoshida provides an extended discussion of the Buddhist curriculum for the Great Promulgation Campaign and of the campaign's collapse. See Yoshida, *Nihon kindai Bukkyō shi kenkyū*, 77–88. The major evidence for these Buddhist curricula exists in the form of study guides that sects produced to prepare their clergy for Great Teaching Institute examinations. *ISSK*: 233–42 (esp. 238) discusses such texts with reference to the Honganji priest Akamatsu Kaion (1828–1896). Akamatsu is discussed in footnote 31 below.

29. For a discussion of Buddhist responses to the three teachings, see Miyake, *Sanjō kyōsoku to kyōiku chokugo*, 38. See also *ISSK*: 233–42.

30. See the "Daikyōin" entry in Miyachi Naokazu and Saeki, *Shintō daijiten*, 890.

31. This text is *Buppō tsūron jūroku-dai kōkai* (An explication of the sixteen subjects of the general Buddhism [curriculum]), published by Akamatsu Kaion in 1875. Through the 1880s he served as prison chaplain in Ibaraki, Ehime, and Osaka. For biographical information, see the encyclopedia entry under his name in Ryūkoku Daigaku, *Bukkyō daijirui*, vol. 1.

32. Akamatsu's study guide covers eight of the general Buddhism exam subjects: all phenomena are dependent and co-arising; the law of cause and effect; the four noble truths and karmic destiny; action based on delusory understanding brings good or evil effects; formation, duration, destruction, and emptiness; all things possess buddha-nature; discourse on morality based on the precepts at a level comprehensible to the audience; and various sectarian doctrines. Akamatsu Kaion, *Buppō tsūron jūroku-dai kōkai*, 3. For a discussion of Akamatsu's study guide and similar texts, see *ISSK*: 238–39.

33. Daniel Botsman provides a detailed account of the development of Meiji prison institutions in *Punishment and Power*.

34. Botsman, *Punishment and Power*, 146–62.

35. Ohara translated and quoted in Botsman, *Punishment and Power*, 154. The original text is available in a reprint published by the Japanese Correctional Association. See Ohara, *Kangoku soku narabi ni zushiki*.

36. *KKHN* 1: 32.

37. The terminology for prisons was in flux in this period. In 1876 the government issued an order that each carceral facility be named as a penal office (*chōekisho*) or a prison office (*shūgokusho*). Later, "prison" (*kangoku*) became the most widely used term.

38. Botsman, *Punishment and Power*, 160.

39. Botsman, *Punishment and Power*, 160.

40. *NKKS* 1: 12–13. On the development of the objectivism/subjectivism dichotomy, see Umemori, "The Modern Penitentiary System in Meiji Japan," 734–68.

41. Foucault, *Discipline and Punish*, 16.

42. *KKHN* 2: 2–16.

43. *KKHN* 2: 3.

44. Quoted in Tsukada, "Meiji shoki no shūkyō kyōkaishi kō," 75; also reproduced in *KKHN* 1: 525.

45. *KKHN* 2: 4.

46. *KKHN* 2: 7. See also Tsukada, "Meiji shoki no shūkyō kyōkai-shi kō," 74. Tsukada reproduces the text from a memorial stone on the grounds of the rebuilt temple. This stone makes reference to Ugai's work with the Urakami Christians. This temple would have been in Owari domain.

47. *KKHN* 2: 11–16.

48. *KKHN* 1: 346. *One Hundred Years of Prison Chaplaincy* presents Minowa Taigaku's story as the origin of prison chaplaincy at Fuchū Prison.

49. *KKHN* 1: 33, 348.

50. Taigaku's petition and the response are discussed in Ogawara, *Daikyōin no kenkyū*, 131–32. See also *KKHN* 1: 348–52 and *KKHN* 2: 12.

51. *NKGS* 2: 752. See also *KKHN* 1: 354. From 1875, the Great Teaching Institute disassociated itself from prison proselytization and passed responsibilities for coordinating with chaplains to its subsidiaries, the "middle teaching institutes" (most often temples and shrines).

52. *KKHN* 2: 13–14.

53. *KKHN* 2: 14.

54. *KKHN* 1: 34.

55. *KKHN* 1: 353.

56. Both petitions are reproduced in *STK*: 234–48. For a summary of Shimaji's activities and the Shin sects' campaign for independence from the Ministry of Doctrine, see Akamatsu Toshihide and Kasahara, *Shinshū shi gaisetsu*, 448–52.

57. My interpretation here follows Krämer, *Shimaji Mokurai*. Shimaji favored religion and state separation, but that perspective is distinct from advocacy for individual religious freedom. After the Christian educator Uchimura Kanzō (1861–1930) refused to bow to a portrait of the emperor, Shimaji eagerly criticized him in the press—the underlying idea being of course that Christianity was incompatible with the duties of Japanese subjects. For Shimaji's reaction to Uchimura, see Akamatsu Toshihide and Kasahara, *Shinshū shi gaisetsu*, 467–68.

58. See the entries for each penal institution listed in *KKHN* 1: 333–822.

59. Tsuchiya and Tsuji, *Meiji Bukkyōshi gaisetsu*, 68.

60. The appearance of a variety of prison preachers during the 1870s and 1880s is a fascinating example of grassroots religious activism. Unfortunately, because of the decentralized nature of this activism, documentary sources detailing the work of the early prison preachers are extremely limited. Any account of prison chaplaincy in Japan will inevitably be colored by the fact that most available textual evidence has been preserved by the Shin sects who eventually achieved a monopoly over the prison chaplaincy.

61. See, for example, documents from 1875 cited in the timeline included in Zaidan Hōjin Zenkoku Kyōkaishi Renmei, *Ayumi tsuzukeru shūkyō kyōkai*, 83.

62. See *KKHN* 1: 36; *NKGS* 2: 799; Zaidan Hōjin Zenkoku Kyōkaishi Renmei, *Ayumi tsuzukeru shūkyō kyōkai*, 83. See the detailed regulations covering prison chaplains in *NKGS* 2: 834–35.

63. *KKHN* 1: 36.

64. *KKHN* 1: 36–37.

65. Article 28 guarantees Japanese subjects religious freedom "within limits not prejudicial to peace and order, and not antagonistic to their duties as subjects." See National Diet Library (website), The Constitution of the Empire of Japan.

66. *NKGS* 2: 834–35; Zaidan Hōjin Zenkoku Kyōkaishi Renmei, *Ayumi tsuzukeru shūkyō kyōkai*, 84.

67. Zaidan Hōjin Zenkoku Kyōkaishi Renmei, *Ayumi tsuzukeru shūkyō kyōkai*, 84.

3. The Ideal of Harmony between Dharma and Law

1. Yamaori, *Nihon shūkyōshi nenpyō*, 488.

2. National Diet Library (website), The Constitution of the Empire of Japan.

3. The concept of the national polity holds that there is a national essence according to which the emperor of Japan is like a father to his subjects. The state began systematically promoting the idea of a national polity and the imperial ideology surrounding it in the wake of the promulgation of the Meiji Constitution and the Imperial Rescript on Education. For a general introduction in English to the Imperial Rescript on Education, see de Bary et al., *Sources of Japanese Tradition, Volume 2*, 780.

4. In an influential work published in 1970, Murakami Shigeyoshi advances the "State Shinto" (Kokka Shintō) thesis as a master narrative of religion and state relations in prewar and wartime Japan. Based on the Allied Occupation's view of Shinto, Murakami's interpretation holds that State Shinto was a state-imposed religion and an ideological driver responsible for propelling Japanese imperialism and militarism, leading the nation to total war and defeat (*Kokka Shintō*, i). Murakami maintains that the Meiji Constitution and the Imperial Rescript on Education laid the foundations of State Shinto ideology (79).

State Shinto is a topic of ongoing debate. Shinto scholars largely reject the notion that Shinto was uniquely responsible for Japanese imperialism, and they are committed to distinguishing the shrine priesthood from state projects that, in their view, co-opted Shinto shrines, symbols, and rites. For a reconsideration of State Shinto along these lines, see Sakamoto Koremaru, *Kokka Shintō saikō*. On the other hand, Shimazono Susumu, a leading proponent of a revised version of Murakami's thesis, argues that the public-private divide in prewar Japan was fundamentally formed around the principle that Shinto was the dominant public tradition whereas religion was subordinated and required to withdraw into the private realm (Shimazono, *Kokka Shintō to Nihonjin*). For summaries in English of the State Shinto debate, see Okuyama, "State Shinto in Recent Japanese Scholarship"; and Hardacre, *Shinto*, 355–59.

In my view, the pre-1945 public ethic appears to bear a clear ideological component expressed through symbols, rhetoric, and rites drawn from Shinto. Government agencies promoted an ethic of loyalty to the sovereign and a supporting ideology through the mass media, public rituals, and the education system. (See, for example, Fujitani, *Splendid Monarchy*; Gluck, *Japan's Modern Myths*; and Miyake, *Sanjō kyōsoku to kyōiku chokugo*). Religious groups were certainly pressed to identify their role in society with reference to the private realm of beliefs, aspirations, and the conscience. However, Shinto priests do not appear to have been more nationalistic as a class than representatives of other religions, including Christianity and Buddhism. Moreover, the idea that a state-authored Shinto ideology was a monocausal factor driving the course of history is reductive and simplistic. The fact is that prewar religious groups (not just Shinto shrines) competed with each other for closer relations to state agencies, and the prison chaplaincy was one product of such competition.

Shin Buddhist priests (not Shinto priests) dominated the prison chaplaincy before 1945, and the chaplaincy records hardly broach the topic of Shinto before the 1930s. The Shin Buddhists were not primarily invested in the myths and symbols of Shinto, but rather hoped to show that their brand of Buddhism contained resources that could contribute to national strength if the private realm of religious beliefs were delegated to their care. The Buddhist prison chaplaincy cannot be interpreted as an instance of State Shinto; it was created as a result of the Shin sects' attempts to marry their tradition to the state. This case study adds nuance to the picture of prewar religion and state relations by showing that Buddhist sects succeeded in linking themselves to the state in the arena of the prison system. They did so for their own reasons and not because they were compelled to by blind loyalty to a putative State Shinto ideology.

5. For an overview of Honganji's constitution and the relationship between sect bylaws and constitutional law, see Hirano Takeshi and Honda, *Honganji hō to kenpō*, part 1; on the Department of State's order for sects to produce their own institutional charters, see especially 70–74.

6. The impending implementation of a national constitution with a guarantee for a degree of religious freedom meant that Buddhist sects needed to organize themselves as teachers of a doctrine (*oshie*) that would appeal to lay persons. For some sects, like Sōtō Zen, this meant a dramatic reorientation, as the inherited doctrine was focused on full-time monastics and not lay people. Shin sects had some advantage among Buddhist groups due to their established tradition of doctrines and proselytization rhetoric aimed at lay followers.

7. Under the early-Meiji Ministry of Doctrine, the state recognized only a limited number of Buddhist sects, and by June 1873, the government appointed the patriarch of the Honganji sect, Myōnyo (1850–1903), to head all four major branches of Shin Buddhism (Honganji Shiryō Kenkyūsho, *Honganji shi* [2019] 3: 112). The other Shin sects eventually achieved independence from Honganji, but through the 1880s, Honganji retained broad influence over all Shin sects (including the Ōtani sect) because of Honganji's closer relationship with the state. The reason for the preferential treatment afforded to Honganji was no doubt related to their extensive financial contributions to the restorationist cause (as described in chapter 2).

8. The sect charter is reproduced in Honganji Shiryō Kenkyūsho, *Honganji shi* (2019) 3: 177–80 (Article 2 appears on 177). The charter also appears in Hirano Takeshi and Honda, *Honganji hō to kenpō*, 74–80. The political significance of article two is discussed in Kondō, *Tennōsei kokka to seishinshugi*, 16–17.

9. In the Meiji period, the public-private divide was interpreted broadly to correspond to a division between secular ethics (*sezoku rinri*, *dōgi*, or *dōtoku*) and religion (*shūkyō*). Meiji intellectuals wrangled over the nature of the distinction between religion and ethics. The influential conservative philosopher Inoue Tetsujirō held that a nationalist ethics should rightfully take precedence over religious commitments, and he criticized Christianity on these grounds as incompatible with the moral duties of Japanese subjects (*Kyōiku to shūkyō no shōtotsu*, 1893). In contrast, the Shin reformer Kiyozawa Manshi considered morality grounded in religion to be superior to a worldly ethics because religion transcends the limited self, whereas ethics does not. Shigeta Shinji interprets the history of prison chaplaincy in the Meiji era against the backdrop of larger debates about the relationship between ethics and religion with reference to Inoue and Kiyozawa (*Aku to tōchi*). On Inoue, see Hoshino, *Kindai Nihon no shūkyō gainen*, 159–61.

10. *NKKS* 1: 138–46. Thirty-six chaplains from the Kantō region attended the conference: twenty-two from Honganji, five from Ōtani, two from Sōtoshū, one each form Shinshū Takada-ha and Jōdoshū, and three identified ambiguously as hailing from Confucian traditions—most likely Sekimon Shingaku preachers. I have unfortunately not been able to find information about the chaplains from groups beyond Shin. This is perhaps because once Shin achieved dominance, other groups were forced out and so have not preserved the history of their early chaplains. In any case, the chaplains at this conference sought to reach a consensus about common principles. They voted in favor of the following propositions: that there would be no chaplains under thirty years of age; that the purpose of conducting death row chaplaincy was to lead the inmate to "peace of mind" (the word is the theologically loaded term "heart of peace" that appears in the 1886 Honganji sect charter, but I translate it idiomatically here). Furthermore, during chaplaincy sessions, jokes and humorous stories were not to be permitted.

11. *NKKS* 1: 147–61. This was a week-long chaplains' conference held from October 2, 1892, at the Honganji Senkyōin in Kyoto. Forty-two chaplains attended, the majority affiliated with the host denomination of Honganji.

12. Group chaplaincy (*shūgo kyōkai*) included sessions on days off, regular Sunday and after-work meetings, funerals, orientations for newly admitted inmates, and prerelease sessions. Individual chaplaincy (*kojin kyōkai*) sessions were also divided into types based on categories of inmates. These included separate sessions for new inmates, mourners, the sick, "extremely evil" inmates, those in solitary confinement, and those on death row.

13. *NKKS* 1: 157–58. Other questions included: "What does the inmate read or pay attention to when he reads? How is the inmate's attitude toward prison staff? Do the inmate's words accord with his deeds? With whom among the other inmates is the inmate close? How does the inmate think about his work? What is the state of the inmate's correspondence with the chaplain? How is the inmate's attitude after meeting with the

chaplain? [. . .] Does the inmate have financial resources? What are the inmate's goals for his future?"

14. *NKKS* 1: 164. The list of topics reads as follows. Group chaplaincy: preach the law of cause and effect. Periodic chaplaincy: preach the principles of grace and kindness. New admissions: explain the rules of the prison. Prerelease: explain the Way for human beings. In the workshop: Encourage the inmates to abide by prison regulations. In the cell: preach about religious peace of mind. For those under punitive restriction: preach so as to invite inmates to the Way of repentance. For the sick: offer psychological refuge. For special occasions: preach in accordance with the needs of the hour.

15. The record of this Kyushu conference appears in *NKKS* 1: 161–73. For the resolution to request designated chapel spaces, see *NKKS* 1: 163. Fifteen chaplains, all from either the Ōtani or the Honganji sect, attended this conference. It took place after the founding of the Tokyo and Kyoto chaplains' offices, and the chaplains in Kyushu appear to have had access by this time to previous conference records. The Tokyo conference record was published in May 1892 in the recently established *Prison Chaplaincy* journal. See *KGKK*, vol. 1.

16. *NKKS* 1: 163.

17. The donations are listed in *NKKS* 1: 235–62. The majority of these donations are from the Shin Buddhist sects, but some other Buddhist sects also donated items.

18. Fujioka, *Kangoku kyōkaigaku*, 41–42.

19. Fujioka, *Kangoku kyōkaigaku*, 42.

20. Fujioka, *Kangoku kyōkaigaku*, 43.

21. The Abashiri prison chapel building itself is not listed in the Shin donations register, but the register indicates that the Shin sects donated a wooden Buddha image, Buddhist ritual paraphernalia, and sutras (*NKKS* 1: 261). For the history of Abashiri Prison, see Shigematsu, *Shiryō: Hokkaido kangoku no rekishi*. For more images of the chapel, see Abashiri Prison Museum, "Kyōkaidō." http://www.kangoku.jp/exhibition_facility_kyoukaidou.html, accessed July 30, 2020.

22. This statistic is cited in Shigeta, *Aku to tōchi*, 221.

23. *KGKK* 1: 1. This journal provided a forum for chaplains to communicate about their methods, their vision for the future of the vocation, and the problems they faced in their work. It was also circulated for prisoners to read. Each edition contains transcripts of prison chaplaincy sessions. It is sometimes unclear whether these are transcribed sermons given in prisons or whether they were written to be circulated as texts rather than performed. The journals also include excerpts from famous doctrinal texts, karma tales (*setsuwa*), selections from a serialized overview of Buddhist doctrine, various short essays, letters to the editor featuring questions submitted by chaplains, and reports on events of interest that took place both within and beyond prison walls. An index to the complete run of the *Prison Chaplaincy* journal (1892–1893) in Japanese with English translations is included in my dissertation. See Lyons, *Karma and Punishment*, Appendix A (from 326).

24. The summary of Shimaji's essay in this section follows *KGKK* 1: 2–6. Unlike some other entries in the journal, no location is given for Shimaji's contribution, so this text is likely not a transcription of a talk first delivered in a prison but rather a written sermon intended for circulation among prisoners.

25. *kōkai no kokoro* "heart of repentance."

26. *KGKK* 1: 6.

27. There are other instances in the literature where the chaplain is explicitly compared to the bodhisattva. *KKHN* 1: 196–97.

28. The summary of Ōta's article in this section follows *KGKK* 2: 9–14.

29. See Goldsmith, "History from the Inside Out." Larry Goldsmith argues that prison chaplains, prison officers, and prisoners together contributed to reforming early nineteenth-century prisons in Massachusetts. See also Graber, *Furnace of Affliction.* Jennifer Graber's study of prison religion in antebellum America highlights conflicts between Protestant reformers (including prison chaplains) and state officials who disagreed over the prison's purpose: the former favored inmate reformation whereas the latter emphasized order and profit. For yet another example, see Nilsson, "The Practise of Pastoral Power." Roddy Nilsson argues that by the late nineteenth century, Swedish prison chaplains became increasingly concerned with social and structural factors underlying crime (even before psychiatrists and criminal psychologists began to weigh seriously the role of these factors in criminogenesis). These studies indicate that chaplains in other societies thought about and wrote about the suffering of the incarcerated and then mobilized to promote reforms. By contrast, Shin Buddhist prison chaplains did not play a similar role in nineteenth-century Japan.

30. Mills, "Professional Ideology of Social Pathologists."

31. Mills, *Sociological Imagination.*

32. The summary of Murakami's article in this section follows *KGKK* 7: 5–10.

33. All chaplains were probably male until at least 1908. Female prison chaplains were based from that year at a women's prison in Tochigi—the first specialized women's prison in Japan. Ikeda Masa may have been the first female chaplain. Her name appears under the entry for Tochigi Prison (*KKHN* 1: 386).

34. On gender dynamics in Japanese Buddhism, see Ruch, *Engendering Faith.* See Ives, "Mobilization of Doctrine," for another variation of the male/female dyad applied to the relationship between the state and the dharma. This tradition can be seen from the very origins of Shin Buddhism. Even one of Shinran's hymns venerates Prince Shōtoku as a combined mother-father figure: "like a father, never leaving us / And like a mother, always watching over us." See Shinran's *Hymns in Praise of Prince Shōtoku,* Hymn 84 in Hirota, *Collected Works of Shinran* 1: 418.

35. The standard reference work is Nihon Kirisutokyō Shakai Fukushi Gakkai's *Nihon Kirisutokyō shakai fukushi no rekishi* (History of Japanese Christian social welfare), published in 2014.

36. On Christianity in Hokkaido, see Fukushima, *Hokkaidō Kirisutokyōshi.* Four Japanese Protestants in particular are remembered for their groundbreaking prison reform work in Hokkaido: Arima Shirosuke, Tomeoka Kōsuke, Ōinoue Terusaki (1848–1912), and Hara Taneaki (1853–1942). Each of these figures is the subject of a major biography in Japanese. On Arima, see Miyoshi, *Arima Shirosuke.* On Tomeoka, see Murota, *Kindai Nihon no hikari to kage,* and *Tomeoka Kōsuke no kenkyū.* On Ōinoue, see Narita, *Kangoku bēsubōru.* On Hara, see Kataoka Yūko, *Hara Taneaki no kenkyū;* and Ōta, *Kaika no Tsukiji.* For a concise account of Christians' role in the prison service in English, see Botsman, *Punishment and Power,* 191–93. For an overview of the history of chaplaincy in Hokkaido, see Hokkaidō Kyōkaishi Renmei, *Kaidō hyakunen.*

37. Miyoshi, *Arima Shirosuke*, 70. See also Miyoshi's chronology of Arima's life: 270–71.

38. Miyoshi, *Arima Shirosuke*, 72.

39. Miyoshi, *Arima Shirosuke*, 71–73.

40. Miyoshi, *Arima Shirosuke*, 82. At this time, there were few Christians in the prison service, so the number of Protestant chaplains in Hokkaido was exceptional.

41. For a study of the journal *Prison Chaplaincy Series* (*Kyōkai sōsho*), see Murota, *Kindai Nihon no hikari to kage*, 15–45. The journal was titled *Compassion* (*Dōjō*) until issue 5. Murota writes that there are no known extant copies of *Compassion* (*Kindai Nihon no hikari to kage*, 21).

42. Miyoshi, *Arima Shirosuke*, 87–98.

43. Miyoshi, *Arima Shirosuke*, 271.

44. Miyoshi, *Arima Shirosuke*, 108–9.

45. Andō, *Sugamo kangoku kyōkaishi funjō tenmatsu*, 1.

46. The year 1898 must have been very productive for Tomeoka. In addition to his involvement in the high-profile public dispute about prison chaplaincy, he also published one of the first treatises in the Japanese language on the role of religions in social work, *Jizen mondai*—with the English subtitle *The Charity Problem*. This work is now regarded as a classic.

47. Arima repeated this request in a letter dated September 5, 1898. The letter invokes the terms ethics (*dōgi*) and religion (*shūkyō*). Arima declares that he will emphasize ethical instruction over religious instruction in the prison. The letter is reproduced in *KKHN* 2: 131.

48. Andō, *Sugamo kangoku kyōkaishi funjō tenmatsu*, 4–6.

49. Andō, *Sugamo kangoku kyōkaishi funjō tenmatsu*, 6.

50. Andō, *Sugamo kangoku kyōkaishi funjō tenmatsu*, 6–13.

51. Andō, *Sugamo kangoku kyōkaishi funjō tenmatsu*, 8.

52. Andō, *Sugamo kangoku kyōkaishi funjō tenmatsu*, 8–9.

53. Andō, *Sugamo kangoku kyōkaishi funjō tenmatsu*, 10.

54. Andō, *Sugamo kangoku kyōkaishi funjō tenmatsu*, 13.

55. Andō, *Sugamo kangoku kyōkaishi funjō tenmatsu*, 15–17.

56. Andō, *Sugamo kangoku kyōkaishi funjō tenmatsu*, 17.

57. Andō, *Sugamo kangoku kyōkaishi funjō tenmatsu*, 18–19. Ishikawa's letter to Home Minister Itagaki is also reproduced in *KKHN* 2: 140.

58. Andō, *Sugamo kangoku kyōkaishi funjō tenmatsu*, 19. *KKHN* 2: 140.

59. Andō, *Sugamo kangoku kyōkaishi funjō tenmatsu*, 27–30.

60. Andō, *Sugamo kangoku kyōkaishi funjō tenmatsu*, 27–30 (esp. 27).

61. Andō, *Sugamo kangoku kyōkaishi funjō tenmatsu*, 30–33. See also Ezure, "Sugamo kyōkaishi jiken to sono ato no bukkyōkai no dōkō."

62. On the role of the press, see Ezure, "Sugamo kyōkaishi jiken to sono ato no bukkyōkai no dōkō." For the most comprehensive account of the Sugamo Prison Chaplain Incident and its aftermath, see Yoshida, *Nihon kindai Bukkyō shakaishi kenkyū* 5: 415–39.

63. *KKHN* 2: 139. The Japanese term for the immigration issue at this time was *naichi zakkyo*. The Ōtani sect also took umbrage to Arima's ouster of their chaplains not least

because they had been investing approximately 30,000 yen per annum in maintaining the prison chaplaincy while waiting for the state to take greater responsibility for chaplains' salaries.

64. On the connection between the Sugamo Prison Chaplain Incident and debates about religious freedom, see Thomas, *Faking Liberties*, 53–55.

65. Miyoshi, *Arima Shirosuke*, 118–19.

66. Miyoshi, *Arima Shirosuke*, 119. It bears noting that women, minors, soldiers, sailors, police officers, teachers, pupils, and priests were still prohibited from voting at this time. Support from the Buddhist sects could have been moral and financial, but it could not have taken the form of getting ordained priests to vote for particular candidates. The law granting suffrage to all males twenty-five and older was not enacted until 1925.

67. Miyoshi, *Arima Shirosuke*, 119–20. Yoshida notes that some Buddhists thought it was ill-advised for Ishikawa and others to have turned the dispute about prison chaplaincy into a political issue (*Nihon kindai Bukkyō shakaishi kenkyū* 5: 439).

68. Miyoshi, *Arima Shirosuke*, 120.

69. The 1969 edition of the Honganji sect official history provides an overview of the sect's prison chaplaincy activities culminating in the appointment of chaplains to the civil service (see HSK 3: 370–84). The 2019 version of the sect history is similar but extends the history to the Taishō era (1912–1926); see Honganji Shiryō Kenkyūsho, *Honganji shi* (2019) 3: 364–72.

70. On the number of chaplains, see Zaidan Hōjin Zenkoku Kyōkaishi Renmei, *Ayumi tsuzukeru shūkyō kyōkai*, 85. The number of salaried chaplains gradually increased, first to 191 in 1935 and then to 230 in 1940. For more details, see *SSKS*: 42, 45. The Taishō-era pay scale for prison chaplains is printed in *KKHN* 1: 58. The highest-paid chaplains (those of the first rank) in 1918 made 1,500 yen per year. The Shōwa-period pay scale is printed in *KKHN* 1: 72. The highest-paid chaplains in 1931 earned 2,770 yen per year. Public funding for Buddhist chaplaincy complicates the picture of State Shinto during the imperial period because it shows that Shinto priests were not the only clergy to draw a government salary for labor in the name of state ideology (on the financing of shrine Shinto, see Murakami, *Kokka Shintō*, 173–79; in English, see Hardacre, *Shinto*, 425–28 and Appendix: Shrine Funding, from 551–56).

71. The turnover of rotating appointments is traceable in the lineage lists for chaplains at each correctional facility recorded in *One Hundred Years of Prison Chaplaincy*. For example, see the list of chaplains associated with Fuchū Prison in *KKHN* 1: 358–60. On the chaplaincy career path, see Fujii Eshō, *Shikeishū monogatari*, 2.

72. See Shigeta, *Aku to tōchi*, 295–307.

73. Eventually, prison chaplains were also stationed in Japan's colonial prisons. See *KKHN* 2: 299–387. For pragmatic reasons, I limit my discussion of chaplaincy in imperial Japan to the "Inner Territories" (*naichi*)—see chapter 4.

4. Thought Crimes and the Opium of the Masses

1. The English word "thought crime" enters the lexicon through George Orwell's dystopian novel *Nineteen Eighty-Four* (published in 1949), but the Japanese equivalent

predates Orwell. In Japan, thought crime was not a matter of fiction, it was a legal term—a category of crime defined by the 1925 Peace Preservation Law. The term *shisōhan* does not appear in the text of the law, but government officials started using it soon after the law was passed.

2. SKK 1: 6.

3. Steinhoff, *Tenkō*. Patricia Steinhoff's work is the classic study of *tenkō* in English. It is based on a largely unrevised dissertation submitted in 1969. Steinhoff does not analyze the chaplaincy, and the records that I discuss in this chapter, drawn from the postwar official history of prison chaplaincy, were largely unavailable when Steinhoff conducted research on *tenkō* in the 1960s. In 2019, Max Ward published an up-to-date history of thought crimes and forced conversions focused on the procuracy. See Ward, *Thought Crime*. Religion is not a primary variable in either of these prior studies. For pragmatic reasons, I limit the scope of my analysis in this chapter to the topic of thought crimes in the "Inner Territories" (*naichi*) of imperial Japan, but it bears noting that chaplains were also involved in the forced conversion of thought criminals in Japan's colonial territories. On the Korean case, see Hong, *Senjiki Chōsen no tenkōshatachi*; and Nagata, "Fashizumuki no shisō, shūkyō tōsei."

4. For the Honganji sect's official account of the Russo-Japanese War, see HSK 3: 475–90. For its account of military chaplaincy, HSK 3: 365–70. For a secondary work covering Shin military chaplaincy, see Ogawara, *Kindai Nihon no sensō to shūkyō*, 162–77. In English, see Anderson, *Nishi Honganji and Japanese Buddhist Nationalism*, for a discussion of Honganji's involvement in the Russo-Japanese War. On Japanese Buddhist military chaplaincy, see Auerback, "Paths Untrodden in Japanese Buddhist Chaplaincy to the Imperial Military."

5. For an overview of the Taishō period, see Suetake, *Taishō shakai to kaizō*. The Taishō era was a time of intellectual and cultural transformation as urbanization, industrialization, mass media expansion, and the generational passing of the leaders who had ushered in the Meiji Restoration bequeathed both new possibilities and, according to one watchword of the times, "confusion" (*konmei*).

6. Akazawa, *Kindai Nihon no shisō dōin*. Akazawa Shirō's work is a classic study of early twentieth-century religion-state relations, and it provides a detailed analysis of the connections between government policy and civic groups devoted to moral suasion and the promotion of a conservative brand of self-cultivation thinking (*shūyō shisō*). See chapter 1 for Akazawa's take regarding the Promulgation on Promoting the National Spirit.

7. Akazawa, *Kindai Nihon no shisō dōin*, 109. The original source is a report from the *Chūgai nippō* journal from February 22, 1924: "Shusho no shūkyōka shōtai kai."

8. Akazawa, *Kindai Nihon no shisō dōin*, 17–26. I follow Garon in translating *kyōka* as "moral suasion" (*Molding Japanese Minds*). For a comprehensive overview of moral suasion groups that flourished during the 1920s, see the Zenkoku Kyōka Dantai Rengōkai's *National Directory of Moral Suasion Groups* (*Zenkoku kyōka dantai meikan*) published in 1929. For a comprehensive overview of the social welfare organizations of the time, see the Chūō Shakai Jigyō Kyōkai's *National Directory of Social Welfare Organizations* (*Zenkoku shakai jigyō dantai meikan*) published in 1927.

9. Nakanishi Naoki provides a history of Buddhist social work, tracing a trajectory from early "moral suasion and relief work" (*kanka kyūsai jigyō*) in the Meiji period

to "social work" (*shakai jigyō*) by the Taishō period (Nakanishi, *Bukkyō to iryō fukushi no kindaishi*). Nakanishi emphasizes that social welfare work and moral suasion campaigns were intertwined. He also notes that some Buddhist social welfare activists like Kujō Takeko (1887–1928, a member of the Nishi Honganji branch of the Ōtani family) were committed to promoting respect for the individual. Kujō insisted that religion must not be reduced to a strategy of governance—a thinly veiled critique of the direction taken by both state and sect leadership.

10. Akazawa, *Kindai Nihon no shisō dōin*, 32. The examples of virtues cited here are introduced in reference to the leader of a women's group, but Akazawa cites a wealth of data to show that civic groups in the 1920s emphasized self-cultivation as opposed to political change as the strategy for obtaining a better life.

11. Chaplains themselves were tasked with laying the groundwork for inmates' release. They were responsible to investigate an inmate's family situation, and after release, they would visit the parolee and family once a month or so, offering counseling and encouragement and exhorting them to do good. The Prison Act of 1908 provided legal recognition of prison chaplains' role in probation programs. Under these changes, probation programs received some degree of funding from prison budgets. For an overview of the history of the Japanese probation system, see *KKHN* 1: 294–330.

12. In 1908, the first Probation Works conference was held, and 46 probation groups were represented by 73 individuals. More than half of those in attendance were prison chaplains. Around that time, there were between 12,000 and 13,000 individuals being paroled each year. The number of parolees accelerated with the amnesty following the death of Emperor Meiji, when over 24,900 individuals were paroled. Another 43,700 were released for the enthronement of the Taishō emperor in 1915. To prepare for the amnesty, the Home Ministry and the Ministry of Justice encouraged private groups including Buddhist temples to sponsor the creation of probation groups beginning in 1913. See *KKHN* 1: 308–312.

13. *KKHN* 1: 308.

14. The Taishō period saw a boom in interest in religious figures as biographies of Shinran and Christ presented them as relatable human beings grappling with the kinds of personal and existential dramas depicted in popular novels of the day. A well-known example is Kurata Hyakuzō's humanizing depiction of Shinran in the 1916 novel *A Priest and His Disciples* (Kurata, *Shukke to sono deshi*). On Kurata Hyakuzō's Shinran, see Ama Michihiro, "Shinran as 'Other.'" See also Ōsawa Ayako's essay on the various interpretations of Shinran among Kiyozawa Manshi's followers ("*Tannishō* no dokkai to Shinran zō"). Kiyozawa was perhaps the most influential Shin modernist thinker; his works synthesize traditional Shin Buddhist doctrines with imported Western philosophy to produce a romantic and psychologized vision of human subjectivity that rests on an interpretation of the problem of evil. See Shigeta, "Hōhō to shite no Kiyozawa Manshi." In general, modernist religious literature (including works by Kurata and Kiyozawa) contributed to strong interest in personal narratives of religious experience and conversion. There was also a burgeoning of interest in the *Tannishō*, a medieval record of Shinran's statements that became central to Shin identity and proselytization in the modern period. On modernist interpretations of the *Tannishō*, see Koyasu, *Tannishō no kindai*.

15. The language of existentialism is of course anachronistic. Nonetheless, I follow the authoritative *One Hundred Years of Prison Chaplaincy* in referring to chaplains' approach to the thought criminals as existentialism (*jitsuzon shugi*). The reasons are discussed later in this section. See *KKHN* 2: 148.

16. Chikazumi Jōkan has only become a topic of scholarship relatively recently. Though he had been largely forgotten, pioneering studies have demonstrated that Chikazumi was a major player in the intellectual and cultural circles of Shin Buddhism in early twentieth-century Tokyo. See Iwata Fumiaki, *Kindai Bukkyō to shōnen*; and Ōmi, *Kindai Bukkyō no naka no Shinshū*. For a detailed review of these two monographs in English, see Schroeder, "Historical Blind Spots." For more on the legacy of Kiyozawa's followers in English, see Schroeder, *After Kiyozawa*.

17. Washington, "Fighting Brick with Brick."

18. In writing to an audience of chaplains, Chikazumi emphasized that a prison chaplain must constantly engage in critical self-reflection (*jisei*)—the idea being that a chaplain must cultivate "character" (*jinkaku*) to be capable of encouraging inmates to reform. The emphasis on the chaplains' character (in addition to his worldly qualifications, or *shikaku*) was a common theme in chaplains' journals by the 1920s. The implication is that a chaplain should be a mature person, capable of supporting the growth of inmates, who were seen as immature. Chikazumi's work in chaplains' journals is mentioned in *KKHN* 1: 149. The term *jinkaku* was central to Chikazumi's broader project. See Ōmi, *Kindai Bukkyō no naka no Shinshū*, 118–46.

19. Chikazumi, *Zangeroku*, 2–3. The topic of repentance was important in Taishō-period religious literature beyond the realm of Shin Buddhism. Nishida Tenkō (1872–1968), founder of Ittōen, published *Zange no seikatsu* (1921), describing conversion through repentance. The book became a best seller.

20. On Chikazumi's use of the term *kyūdō*, see Iwata Fumiaki, *Kindai Bukkyō to shōnen*, 59–68.

21. Niwa Fumio's 1956 novel *The Buddha Tree* is an example of a Shin Buddhist (semiautobiographical) novel premised on the inability of the individual to overcome worldly (sexual) desire. Repentance narratives in modern Shin Buddhist literature are a rich topic for further research.

22. *KKHN* 1: 196. Aside from this one-line reference to Chikazumi's resignation from the prison chaplaincy in *One Hundred Years of Prison Chaplaincy*, I have seen only one other concise written reference to this fact, in a speech titled "A Step Toward Abolishing the Death Penalty," given by the postwar leader of the correctional field Masaki Akira (1892–1971) at the annual chaplains' meeting. Masaki's speech is recorded in the first edition of the postwar *Chaplaincy* journal published in 1963 (ZHZK 1: 59). It is possible that Chikazumi may have quietly resigned without making a public statement and that knowledge of this incident was passed down by word of mouth among the chaplaincy before eventually finding its way into the official history prepared by and for the Shin prison chaplains.

23. For a history of the early years of the Japanese Communist Party, see Steinhoff, *Tenkō*, 63–83. See also Beckman and Okubo, *The Japanese Communist Party: 1922–1945*.

24. The text of the law is reproduced in Okudaira, *Chian iji hō*, 51.

25. On the founding of the Special Higher Police, see Ogino, *Tōkkō keisatsu taiseishi*, 58–63. The records of the Special Higher Police have been republished in Akashi Hirotaka and Matsuura, *Shōwa tokkō dan'atsushi* (8 vols).

26. Thought crimes, *tenkō*, and the Special Higher Police have become a subfield of study. A sample of representative works includes Cullen, "Comparative Study of Tenkō"; Garon, "State and Religion in Imperial Japan, 1912–1945"; Hasegawa, *Tenkō no meian*; Honda, *Tenkō bungaku ron*; Hoston, "Emperor, Nation, and the Transformation of Marxism," and *"Tenkō*: Marxism and the National Question"; Itō Akira, *Tenkō to tennōsei*; Kojima Nobuyuki, "Tokubetsu kōtō keisatsu ni yoru shinkyō no jiyū seigen"; Mitchell, *Thought Control*; Odanaka, *Chian seisaku to hō no tenkai*; Ogino, *Tōkkō keisatsu taiseishi*, and *Shōwa Tennō to chian taisei*, as well as *Tokkō keisatsu*; Okudaira, *Chian iji hō*; Sasaki, "Shihōshō no tenkō yūhatsu seisaku"; Steinhoff, *Tenkō*; and Yoshimoto and Wake, "On Tenkō."

27. For a record of this conference, see Nihon Shūkyō Konwakai, *Gotaiten kinen Nihon shūkyō taikai kiyō*, 445. The same record of the conference is reprinted in *SBK* 6: 445. See also Akazawa, *Kindai Nihon no shisō dōin*, 35–36.

28. Akazawa, *Kindai Nihon no shisō dōin*, 169–98; Kondō, "Kindai Nihon ni okeru marukusu shugi to Bukkyō (jō)," 54–86.

29. The *Chūgai nippō* journal articles are reprinted as *Marukishizumu to shūkyō, shijō tenkanki no shūkyō* reprinted in *SBK* 8.

30. Miki, "Bungei to shūkyō to puroretaria undō," in *SBK* 8: 18–25 (esp. 21–22).

31. Kamichika, "Shūkyō fujin dantai no hihan sono ta," in *SBK* 8: 204–12 (esp. 205).

32. Kamichika, "Shūkyō fujin dantai no hihan sono ta," in *SBK* 8: 206–7.

33. Kamichika, "Shūkyō fujin dantai no hihan sono ta," in *SBK* 8: 212.

34. *Han shūkyō tōsō no hata no shita ni* is reproduced in *SBK* 7. The mission statement is given in the foreword (on the first page, which is unnumbered).

35. Akazawa, *Kindai Nihon no shisō dōin*, 190.

36. For a representative work by scholars and clerics criticizing the anti-religion movements, see Uno, *Hanshūkyō undō no hihan*. On reactions to the anti-religion movements, see Akazawa, *Kindai Nihon no shisō dōin*, 190–97. There is reason to believe that a range of religious leftists were inspired by Marxist thought: the Social Christianity Movement (known by the English initials SCM, also known as the Student Christian Movement) and the Buddhist Youth League (Shin Bukkyō Shōnen Dōmei) were two leftist religious movements that tried to blend socialist thought with religion, aiming for reform within their own traditions. For two recent studies that take up the Buddhist left, see Curley, *Pure Land, Real World*; and Shields, *Against Harmony*.

37. For a recent study of the government's approach to soliciting the conversion statements, see Sasaki, "Shihōshō no tenkō yūhatsu seisaku."

38. *KKHN* 1: 166–67.

39. *KKHN* 1: 170.

40. In a classic article about prison chaplains and *tenkō*, Tonohira Yoshihiko writes that the prison system adopted a carrot-and-stick approach. The chaplains promised spiritual well-being and education, while the Special Higher Police (and corrections officers) employed torture to effect *tenkō*. See Tonohira, "Tenkō to Bukkyō shisō."

41. A complete list is available in *KKHN* 1: 173. Ono Yōichi was the pen name of former thought criminal and later probation officer Kobayashi Morito. See Kobayashi Morito, *Kyōsantō o dassuru made*.

42. This information is drawn from *KKHN* 1: 171–75.

43. *KKHN* 1: 176. Unfortunately, *KKHN* does not identify the speaker or the source of the quotation. It appears to be from a lecture directed to chaplains. I have not been able to identify the unnamed professor. A number of prominent academics were involved in the study of "thought crime." See, for example, specialized works in criminal psychology from this period (Kikuchi, *Hanzai shinri*, and *Shisō hanzai no sho mondai*, both published in 1934) and studies of criminology (Sakamoto Hideo, *Shisōteki hanzai ni taisuru kenkyū*, 1928).

44. Lest the *tenkō* program be misinterpreted as irrelevant to the postwar prison chaplaincy, I note here that the official postwar history of the chaplaincy (a product of the Cold War era) reports this professor's theory that Marxists are merely religiously misguided with untempered approval: "It is not possible to lead people to develop a [moral] personality without cultivating religiosity. From its origins, the prison chaplaincy's creed has always held that the fundamental goal is to awaken religious faith" (*KKHN* 1: 177).

45. Sano Manabu and Nabeyama, "Kyōdō hikokudōshi ni tsuguru sho." Sano's prison diary is also of interest. It includes his account of "purifying his heart" by reading the Japanese classics, including the *Kojiki* and *Nihon shoki* (Sano Manabu, "Gokuchū koten ni yorite kokoro o arau"). Nabeyama also wrote a memoir about abandoning the Communist Party (*Watashi wa Kyōsantō o suteta*).

46. Steinhoff, *Tenkō*, 6.

47. *KKHN* 1: 176. Sano Manabu went on to write extensively about religion for the rest of his life, and he produced such works as *Shinran and Rennyo* (*Shinran to Rennyo*, 1949) and *Communism and Buddhism* (*Kyōsanshugi to Bukkyō*, 1953).

48. See *KK* and *KKHG*. The sheer volume of early twentieth-century chaplaincy publications makes a systematic assessment difficult. *Chaplaincy Studies / Chaplaincy and Probation* alone amounts to more than 10,000 pages. However, taken as a whole, the boom in chaplaincy studies indicates that, by the 1920s, there was an established tradition within Shin circles and correctional circles of thinking about crime as a religious problem. This is consistent with the fact that the dominant educative model of punishment relies on the assumption that crime is primarily a problem of the individual heart. On the history of the Prison Chaplaincy Training and Research Institute, see *KKHN* 1: 103–15. On the history of chaplains' journals, see *KKHN* 1: 143–47. An index to the complete run of *Chaplaincy Studies / Chaplaincy and Probation* (1925–1943) is included in my dissertation. See Lyons, *Karma and Punishment*, Appendix B (from 333).

49. *KKHN* 2: 156.

50. *KKHN* 2: 150–55.

51. Saotome, *Tenkōsha no shuki*, 1–3.

52. Kojima Yuki, "Daihi no mite ni sugaru made," 43–73.

53. Kojima Yuki, "Daihi no mite ni sugaru made," 51.

54. Kojima Yuki, "Daihi no mite ni sugaru made," 52.

55. Kojima Yuki, "Daihi no mite ni sugaru made," 56.

56. Kojima Yuki, "Daihi no mite ni sugaru made," 58.
57. Kojima Yuki, "Daihi no mite ni sugaru made," 68.
58. Kojima Yuki, "Daihi no mite ni sugaru made," 72.
59. Hayashida, "Bukkyō to tenkō no mondai," 124. On the concept of worldly benefits, see Reader and Tanabe, *Practically Religious.*
60. SKK 1: 18. For more on Osabe Kingo see SKK 3: 467. Osabe served on the Supreme Court from 1963 until his death in 1971.
61. SKK 1: 18–19.
62. Okudaira, *Chian iji hō*, 268–76. The bill was not without its opponents. A member of the Diet spoke out against it and the harms of excessive surveillance by referring to the case of Jean Valjean from Victor Hugo's *Les Misérables* (Okudaira, *Chian iji hō*, 276).
63. On the history of juvenile delinquency in Japan, see Ambaras, *Bad Youth.*
64. *KKHN* 1: 323.
65. Hoseikai published its own pamphlets on thought crime and the 1936 law for distribution to its members. See Hoseikai, *Shisōhan no hogo o chūshin to shite* (1935) and *Shisōhan hogo kansatsu hō taii* (1936). Shōtokukai was another civic group working on the probation of thought criminals, and they too produced a journal to commemorate the one-year anniversary of the Thought Criminals Protection and Surveillance Law. See Shōtokukai, *Tokushū: Shisōhan hogokansatsu hō* (1937).
66. See Kobayashi's postwar memoir (*Tenkōki no hitobito*) as well as a volume he edited about the probation programs for thought criminals (*Tenkōsha no shisō to seikatsu*, published in 1935).
67. *KKHN* 1: 327.
68. For parole placements, it was preferred to place women in the family home (if possible), while men were frequently sent to the custody of Buddhist or Shinto civic groups and halfway houses. There is also evidence that the Probation Office preferred to keep paroled couples together on the rationale that married life was conducive to solidifying *tenkō*. See SKK 1: 20–21.
69. See Rolston, "Conversion and the Story of the American Prison."
70. *KKHN* 2: 81–82. For a biography of Kariya, see *KKHN* 2: 81–88.
71. Interview with a Shin prison chaplain, April 19, 2015.

5. War Crimes and the Discovery of Peace

1. For the full text of the Constitution of Japan, see Kantei (website), Constitution of Japan. The articles referred to in this chapter are as follows:

Article 9. Aspiring sincerely to an international peace based on justice and order, the Japanese people forever renounce war as a sovereign right of the nation and the threat or use of force as means of settling international disputes. In order to accomplish the aim of the preceding paragraph, land, sea, and air forces, as well as other war potential, will never be maintained. The right of belligerency of the state will not be recognized.

Article 20. Freedom of religion is guaranteed to all. No religious organization shall receive any privileges from the State, nor exercise any political authority. No person shall be compelled to take part in any religious act, celebration, rite or practice. The state and its organs shall refrain from religious education or any other religious activity.

Article 89. No public money or other property shall be expended or appropriated for the use, benefit or maintenance of any religious institution or association, or for any charitable, educational or benevolent enterprises not under the control of public authority.

2. Other important ecumenical groups include the Federation of New Religious Organizations of Japan (Shin Nihon Shūkyō Dantai Rengōkai) founded in 1951 and the Japanese Buddhist Federation (Zen Nihon Bukkyōkai) founded in 1957. On the pacifist commitments of Japanese new religions in particular, see Kisala, *Prophets of Peace*. On the repackaging of religious freedom as a fundamental human right under the Occupation, see Thomas, *Faking Liberties*, part 2. On religious freedom and postwar constitutional politics, see O'Brien and Ohkoshi, *To Dream of Dreams*.

3. See MacArthur's own account of his role in the Occupation in his autobiography (*Reminiscences*, 269–324).

4. See *SSKS*: 48. Ultimately, Minister of Justice (Shihō Daijin) Iwamura was released without being prosecuted in 1948. SCAP issued SCAPIN 93 (CIE) on the October 4, 1945: "Removal of Restrictions on Political, Civil and Religious Liberties." This and a subsequent order issued on October 15 initiated the release of political prisoners, pacifists, Marxists, and religionists who had been incarcerated as thought criminals under the Peace Preservation Law. The orders regarding political prisoners are cited in Woodard, *Occupation of Japan and Japanese Religions*, 291–92.

5. *SSKS*: 48.

6. Former editor of the *Military Police Journal* John G. Roos provides a detailed account of the Occupation's management of Sugamo based on declassified documents (Roos, *In a Prison Called Sugamo*). For an account of Sugamo Prison and the Tokyo trials by a US participant, see Ginn, *Sugamo Prison*.

7. These statistics are cited in *SSKS*: 48. *Kokushi daijiten* gives a different figure: "Five thousand and several hundred found guilty and 937 death sentences." See the entry for *sensō hanzainin* in *Kokushi daijiten* (accessed March 15, 2017).

8. Roos, *In a Prison Called Sugamo*, ix–x.

9. Thought criminals were concentrated in certain prisons. According to Sasaki Masaya, Sugamo Prison did not house inmates convicted for Peace Preservation Law violations as of 1934. For a chart with distribution statistics for thought criminals and chaplains, see Sasaki, "Shihōshō no tenkō yūhatsu seisaku," 3.

10. SKK 1: 6.

11. The order is reproduced in Woodard, *Occupation of Japan and Japanese Religions*, 295–99, Appendix B:5 "Abolition of Governmental Sponsorship, Support, Perpetuation, Control, and Dissemination of State Shinto (*Kokka Shinto, Jinja Shinto*), SCAPIN 448 (CIE) 15 Dec 45 (AG 000.3)."

12. One important Japanese study of the Occupation's impact on the spectrum of Japanese religions is Ikado, *Senryō to Nihon shūkyō*.

13. See Thomas, *Faking Liberties*, chapter 5, "State Shintō as a Heretical Secularism," 141–65.

14. Woodard, *Occupation of Japan and Japanese Religions*, 68.

15. Woodard, *Occupation of Japan and Japanese Religions*, 69.

16. Woodard, *Occupation of Japan and Japanese Religions*, 297 ("Shinto Directive," clause 2.a).

17. The Religions Division was subsequently renamed the Religions and Cultural Resources Division.

18. Woodard writes: "Bunce's unique contribution in drafting the Directive was his expansion of the idea of disestablishing Shinto into the universal principle of the separation of 'all religions, faiths, and creeds from the state.' Thus the Directive had a universal character not envisioned by the Department of State policy makers" (*Occupation of Japan and Japanese Religions*, 69). On Bunce, the Shinto Directive, and the scholarship that informed it, see Thomas, *Faking Liberties*, 149–65. On postwar shrine life, see Creemers, *Shrine Shinto after World War II*.

19. *KKHN* 1: 77–79.

20. Order 2349 is discussed in Woodard, *Occupation of Japan and Japanese Religions*, 137–38. The original text is reproduced in *SSKS*: 48–49. On the history of the correctional system during the war, see Kyōsei Kyōkai, *Senji gyōkei jitsuroku*.

21. *SSKS*: 50.

22. The most comprehensive account in English of these trials is Totani, *Tokyo War Crimes Trial*.

23. See MacArthur's writings about Christianity in Japan, cited in Woodard, *Occupation of Japan and Japanese Religions*, 355–59 (Appendix G:4).

24. For his account of meeting the American military chaplains, see Hanayama, *Sugamo no sei to shi no kiroku*, 14–17.

25. See Hanayama, *Sugamo no sei to shi no kiroku*, 40.

26. See Hanayama, *Sugamo no sei to shi no kiroku*, 39. The official charged with locating a chaplain was Nakao Bunsaku (1903–1991), who later became the head of the Corrections Office.

27. For a brief discussion of Hanayama from the perspective of the National Chaplains' Union, see *SSKS*: 50–51.

28. See Hanayama, *Sugamo no sei to shi no kiroku*, 41.

29. Hanayama, *Heiwa no hakken* (1949) was reprinted as Hanayama, *Sugamo no sei to shi no kiroku* (1995). I rely on the 1995 edition here.

30. Curley, "Prison and the Pure Land," 151.

31. Hanayama, *Sugamo no sei to shi no kiroku*, 10–11.

32. Tanabe Hajime's work *Philosophy as Metanoetics* (*Zangedō to shite no tetsugaku*, 1946) is one notable example of an argument for repentance. Calls for collective repentance were ubiquitous in postwar discourse. For a general survey, see Dower, *Embracing Defeat*, 496–504.

33. Hanayama, *Sugamo no sei to shi no kiroku*, 20.

34. In Shin Buddhism, the term *tariki* refers to salvation through faith in Amida Buddha. It is contrasted with self-power (*jiriki*), which refers to methods for obtaining salvation through one's own religious practice.

35. Hanayama, *Sugamo no sei to shi no kiroku*, 35.

36. See Woodard, *Occupation of Japan and Japanese Religions*, 68. Woodard notes, "Because of the name by which the Directive became popularly known, [its] universality was not generally recognized, and shrine Shinto became the whipping boy of the Occupation. Moreover, in spite of the fact that the shrine priests were no more ultranationalistic as a class than were many of the leaders of the other religions, including Christianity,

this fact was also ignored by the general public." Shinto shrines were not the only group to face antagonism from SCAP. Dorman discusses SCAP's policies toward certain new religions in this light ("SCAP's Scapegoat?").

37. Monbushō, *Kokutai no hongi*. The text is readily available in reprints such as Kure PASS Shuppan, *Senzen no kokumin kyōiku: Kokutai no hongi*.

38. Klautau, *Kindai Nihon shisō to shite no Bukkyō shigaku*, 153–59.

39. Klautau, *Kindai Nihon shisō to shite no Bukkyō shigaku*, 156.

40. Hanayama published a second memoir in 1982, *Eien e no michi* (The path to eternity). In this account, he minimizes his prewar career and focuses on his time as a chaplain and his subsequent career as an international Buddhist intellectual. However, he maintained his interest in Shōtoku Taishi (see Hanayama, *Shōtoku Taishi to kenpō jūshichijō*). More recently, Kobayashi Hirotada has published a nonfiction account of Hanayama's work with the war criminals (*Sugamo Purizun: Kyōkaishi Hanayama Shinshō to shikei senpan no kiroku*).

41. See the criticism in Hamada, "Hanayama kyōkaishi no mondai." The title of this book review translates roughly to "The Problem with Chaplain Hanayama."

42. Shinshūren Chōsashitsu, *Sengo shūkyō kaisōroku*, 123.

43. Morita, *Sugamo Purizun no kaisō*, 295–97. Correctional officer Morita Ishizō's story contains some obvious errors. For example, he mistakenly claims that Hanayama was a Shingon priest (Hanayama was a Shin priest). Nonetheless, Morita's record is of interest because it sheds light on tensions between Hanayama and rank-and-file correctional staff. Hanayama was an elite professor who managed to become a minor celebrity by publishing his version of events at Sugamo Prison. By contrast, Morita privately distributed a handful of copies of his own self-published book to people in his professional network (including chaplains). I am thankful to chaplain Hirano Shunkō for letting me borrow his copy.

Also, it seems worth noting here that one senior chaplain I met at the *Chaplain's Manual* committee meetings—himself a recognized expert on the history of chaplaincy—voiced concern about my declared intention to write about Hanayama. In this chaplain's view, "Hanayama was not really a prison chaplain. He just took care of the famous war criminals and then left to write his book." In other words, this contemporary prison chaplain seemed to think of Hanayama as a sellout who leveraged his position at the University of Tokyo to gain access to prisoners primarily as a means to a mainstream literary career. I take no position on the matter, but I found it remarkable that a negative view of Hanayama appeared to have been preserved in some quarters of the chaplaincy from the 1940s into the 2010s.

44. See an American view of Hanayama presented in Roos, *In a Prison Called Sugamo*, 39–48.

45. Hanayama, *Sugamo no sei to shi no kiroku*, 51–52. He uses two phrases for "mercy." The first is a Japanese rendering of the English term in katakana as *māshī*, and the second is the traditional Buddhist term for compassion (*jihi*).

46. *KKHN* 1: 272–73.

47. *KKHN* 1: 276–77. See also Tajima's own memoir, *Waga inochi hateru hi ni* (On the day I die), published in 1953. For a biography of Tajima covering his time at Sugamo, see Tajima and Yamaori, *Sugamo no chichi*, 74–104.

48. Sugamo Isho Hensankai, *Seiki no isho*. For a discussion of the documents included in this collection, see Dower, *Embracing Defeat*, 515–21. For Tajima's role in publishing these "testaments," see Tajima and Yamaori, *Sugamo no chichi*, 99–102.

49. Takizawa, *Nihon Shūkyō Renmei shōshi*, 13–14. The 1940 Religious Organizations Law set the number of officially recognized religions at forty-three sects: twenty-eight Buddhist groups were permitted along with the thirteen sectarian Shinto groups; the Catholic church was permitted, and all thirty-four major Protestant branches were merged into the United Church of Christ in Japan (Nihon Kirisuto Kyōdan). Shinto shrines were officially defined as nonreligious, so they fell outside the purview of this law. From 1940, all forty-three recognized religious groups were placed under the Ministry of Education's direct authority so that they could be mobilized to support Japan's war in China.

50. In addition to the original member organizations, the newly formed Jinja Honchō umbrella organization of Shinto shrines also joined. This addition reflected the fact that under the Occupation, Shinto shrines lost their status as nonreligious public institutions and were instead forced to reorganize as private religious organizations.

By the 1960s, all prison chaplains were being appointed through JARO, but not all religious organizations joined JARO. For example, the enormous Buddhist new religious movement Sōka Gakkai has never been a member of JARO. To this day, there are no Sōka Gakkai prison chaplains in Japan. This exclusion can be traced to historical tensions between the religious organizations participating in JARO and Sōka Gakkai.

51. Takizawa, *Nihon Shūkyō Renmei shōshi*, 29.

52. Takizawa, *Nihon Shūkyō Renmei shōshi*, 45. The Constitution of the United Nations Educational Scientific and Cultural Organization was signed on November 16, 1945. The opening lines read: "The Governments of the States Parties to this Constitution on behalf of their peoples declare: That since wars begin in the minds of men, it is in the minds of men that the defenses [*sic*] of peace must be constructed." Available on the UNESCO website, http://portal.unesco.org/en/ev.phpURL_ID=15244&URL_DO=DO_TOPIC&URL_SECTION=201.html, accessed September 23, 2018.

53. Takizawa, *Nihon Shūkyō Renmei shōshi*, 47.

54. Takizawa, *Nihon Shūkyō Renmei shōshi*, 48. Bunce's speech is cited in Japanese only.

55. The order is known in Japanese as Sengo gyōkei sengen. Its official title is Corrections Order No. 1 (Keisei kō dai ichi gō). This declaration states the three guiding principles for the postwar correctional system: human rights (*jinken songen*), correctional rehabilitation (*kōsei hogo*), and self-sufficiency (*jikyū jisoku*). See the order in *SSKS*: 50. For a historical overview of corrections during the war itself, see Kyōsei Kyōkai, *Senji gyōkei jitsuroku*.

56. *SSKS*: 50.

57. Despite SCAP's employment of Hanayama at Sugamo Prison, the general question of prison chaplains' legal status remained unresolved for some time after the war. Outside of Sugamo Prison, Shin Buddhist prison chaplains continued to work within the Japanese prison system as salaried employees, but changes were made to deemphasize the religious nature of their work so as to avoid running afoul of SCAP policies separating religion from state. On March 6, 1946, a draft of the Postwar Constitution,

written by Americans, was presented to the Japanese public. The draft guaranteed religious freedom and the separation of religion from state. One month after the constitution was presented to the people, the Corrections Office revised the official title of "prison chaplain" to "correctional instructor" (*shihō kyōkan*), and their numbers were reduced to 115 persons. The new constitution was scheduled to be implemented in 1947, and so, like other sectors of the Japanese government, the Corrections Office began to implement reforms to bring itself into line with the new law of the land. On the development of the constitution, see Dower, *Embracing Defeat*, chaps. 12 and 13. On the parallel developments in the prison system, see *SSKS*: 51–56.

58. Shūkyō Renmei et al., *Shūkyō benran*, 307. The title can also be read as *Shūkyō binran*. The book exemplifies public-private collaboration between religions and the post-war state.

59. *SSKS*: 56.

60. Religious preference has become one type of data maintained by the Japanese correctional system, and such data is routinely exchanged with chaplains' groups. *SSKS* is an example of a training document produced by and for chaplains that relies heavily on Corrections Office data. Surveys on inmates' religious preferences have been conducted periodically until the present day. For other examples of this trend, see Hōmushō Kyōseikyoku, *Kyōsei shiryō dai nijūnana gō: Kyōsei shisetsu hishūyōsha no shūkyō chōsa* (1960); and Akaike and Ishizuka, *Kyōsei shisetsu ni okeru shūkyō* (2011).

61. *SSKS*: 75. Under Japanese law, a foundation (*zaidan hōjin*) was a type of public interest corporation (*kōeki hōjin*) until legal reforms in 2008 established a difference between ordinary foundations (*ippan zaidan hōjin*), which may serve private interests, and public interest foundations (*kōeki zaidan hōjin*), which must demonstrate their contributions to the public good. Under the new system, the National Chaplains' Union belongs to the latter category, retaining government recognition as a public interest corporation. Public interest corporations are defined as nonprofit groups that promote rituals, religion, welfare, scholarship, and the arts for the public benefit. The Japanese Sumo Wrestling Association (Nihon Sumō Kyōkai) is a public interest corporation and so is the Red Cross of Japan. On public interest corporations, see Kaneko et al., *Hōritsugaku shōjiten*, 331.

62. *SSKS*: 74–75.

63. *SSKS*: 77.

64. Kyōkai Hikkei Henshū Iinkai, ed. *Kyōkai hikkei*. This is the first version of the National Chaplains' Union's vocational guide. Updated editions were published in 1993 and 2017 by Kyōkai Manyuaru Henshū Iinkai and titled *Kyōkai manyuaru*. I use the English-language title *Chaplain's Manual* to refer to all of these works.

65. In addition to sectarian chaplains' unions, there are trans-sectarian groups associated with the Corrections Office's eight administrative districts. These district unions include the Kantō Chaplains' Union, the Hokkaido Chaplains' Union, the Tokyo Chaplains' Union, and even a group in Okinawa. Finally, there are chaplains' groups attached to particular penal institutions, like the Tachikawa Jail Chaplains' Group and the Fuchū Prison Chaplains' Group. Chaplains from various sects participate together in the regional and institutional groups. A typical prison chaplain is likely to be a member of three or more of these unions. For example, one chaplain will typically belong to

a sectarian group, the regional group, and at least one institutional group (more for those who work at more than one institution). Each group incurs obligations on its members to attend periodic training sessions and to contribute financially to the organization's upkeep.

66. Jōdoshū Chaplains' Union (founded in 1962) is an exception. This group never published a manual. Personal communication (email) with Jōdoshū prison chaplain on March 30, 2017.

67. *KKHN* 1: 4.

68. See the introductory doctrinal chapter of *One Hundred Years of Prison Chaplaincy*. *KKHN* 1: 3–30. The chapter moves through the following topics: salvation of the evil person (not suitable for preaching in prison); the problem of karma (better suited to prison chaplaincy); hell in Pure Land thought; and *gedō* (like purgatory) in Pure Land thought. The purpose of each section is essentially to affirm that Shin is socially beneficial and to apply basic doctrinal concepts to the prison context. The sections offer the following ideas: the doctrine of the salvation of the evil person can be problematic for teaching in prison, but Shin is not antisocial (in other words, the section asserts that Shin offers a social benefit). The doctrine of karma is a subjective truth that must be grasped by experience (and this doctrine can be an expedient means to encourage the prisoners' moral development). Shinran and Hōnen (1133–1212, founder of the Pure Land, or Jōdo, sect and Shinran's mentor) thought of hell as a place to spread the dharma (the unstated implication here appears to be that the prison is akin to a hell). Finally, Prison is *gedō* (a purgatorial path of purification).

69. Shinshū no Kyōkai Hensan Iinkai, *Shinshū no kyōkai*, 47.

70. Fukkyō Kenkyūsho, *Kyōkaishi kyōhon*. For more on Shingon prison chaplaincy, see Miyazaki, *Kyōkai kōwashū*. For examples of Buddhist prison chaplaincy materials from other sects, see Sōtōshū Kyōkaishi Rengōkai, *Sōtōshū kyōkaishi manyuaru*; and Nichirenshū Kyōkaishikai, *Kyōkaishi hikkei*, and *Nichirenshū kyōkaishi hikkei hoshū*.

71. Fukkyō Kenkyūsho, *Kyōkaishi kyōhon*, 144–46.

72. Fukkyō Kenkyūsho, *Kyōkaishi kyōhon*, 145.

73. Fukkyō Kenkyūsho, *Kyōkaishi kyōhon*, 148. On Kūkai's teachings, see Hakeda, *Kūkai*; and Abé, *Weaving of Mantra*.

74. Fukkyō Kenkyūsho, *Kyōkaishi kyōhon*, 145.

75. Fukkyō Kenkyūsho, *Kyōkaishi kyōhon*, 144

76. Fukkyō Kenkyūsho, *Kyōkaishi kyōhon*, 145

77. Jinja Honchō Kyōkaishi Kenkyūkai, *Kyōkai no tebiki*.

78. "In the words of Kami-sama [the founder Nakayama Miki], it is taught that this world is a path to extinguish one's store of past-life causes and connections (*innen nasshō no michi*). The aim of correctional education in our doctrine is to extinguish a past of crime, to help people to change for the better and become *yōboku* [full members of Tenrikyō], and through our efforts to help others we can cultivate people who will make a contribution to society." See Tenrikyō Kyōkai no Tebiki Henshū Iinkai, *Tenrikyō kyōkai no tebiki*, 50. For the official history of the Tenrikyō prison chaplaincy, see Tenrikyō Kyōkaishi Renmei, *Tenrikyō Kyōkai no ayumi*. Of the new religions, aside from Tenrikyō, Konkōkyō has also been particularly active in prison chaplaincy. On their activities, see Konkōkyō Kyōkaishi Renmei, *Tomo ni kokoro o hiraite*.

79. For a Protestant chaplain's manual, see Nihon Kirisuto Kyōdan Kyōkaishikai, *Kyōkai manyuaru.*

80. See Sullivan, *Ministry of Presence.*

81. Kyōkai Manyuaru Henshū Iinkai, *Kyōkai manyuaru* (2017), 39–40.

6. The Spirit of Public Service and the Social Role for Religions

1. The lack of clarity about the chaplain's role is perhaps related to the absence of standardized training for chaplains. As of 2020, there was still no equivalent to clinical pastoral education and thus no unified curriculum nor formal educational requirements. As a result, most training was conducted on an ad hoc basis, through shadowing sessions with senior chaplains, attending conferences, and reading journals, chaplain's manuals, casebooks, and sectarian circulars. A survey of this literature reinforces the sense that the chaplain's role has entailed potentially conflicting obligations. In the annual proceedings of the National Chaplains' Union (published in the primary vocational journal *Chaplaincy*), for example, the chaplaincy's objectives are everywhere framed with reference to two poles. On the one hand, the chaplaincy adopts the language of rights and freedoms to describe its responsibilities to the incarcerated. On the other hand, the literature continually refers to the efficacy of religious instruction for correctional reform. This latter theme reflects the responsibilities that chaplains owe to the prison institutions who host them.

2. ZHZK 31: 81–84.

3. ZHZK 31: 88–90.

4. ZHZK 31: 93.

5. See Hardacre, "Religion and Civil Society." The Civil Code (Minpō) was promulgated as Regulation 89 of 1896 (Meiji 29), and it came into effect in 1898. Article 33 establishes regulations for the formation of public benefit corporations (including groups devoted to scholarship, the arts, charity, rituals, religion, and other public benefit activities). Article 34 addresses the functions (*nōryoku*) of these corporations simply by referring to their articles of incorporation and "other fundamental terms" (in other words, such corporations must function to serve the public benefit in accord with Article 33). For the full text of the Civil Code and its subsequent amendments in Japanese, see e-Gov Japan (website), Minpō.

6. e-Gov Japan (website), Shūkyō hōjin hō [Religious Corporations Law]. On the postwar Religious Corporations Law, see Garon, *Molding Japanese Minds,* 208–9. See also Thomas, *Faking Liberties,* 188–89.

7. Hardacre, "After Aum," 148. Religious organizations receive tax benefits in part because it is assumed that they contribute to the general public good; on this point, see Ishimura, *Shūkyō hōjinsei to zeisei no arikata,* 4–5.

8. Garon, "From Meiji to Heisei," 56–57.

9. Hardacre, "After Aum," 141.

10. Hardacre, *Shinto,* 511.

11. Aum Shinrikyō has become a field of study. A partial sampling of some major works in English includes: Baffelli and Reader, "Editors' Introduction"; Hardacre, "After

Aum," and "Aum Shinrikyō and the Japanese Media"; McLaughlin, "Did Aum Change Everything?"; Reader, *Poisonous Cocktail*, and *Religious Violence in Contemporary Japan*; and Shimazono, "In the Wake of Aum."

 12. Hardacre, *Shinto*, 511–12, 515–19.

 13. Hardacre, "After Aum," 148.

 14. Garon, *Molding Japanese Minds*, 213–15.

 15. For examples of the immediate scholarly responses to the revised Religious Corporations Law, see Mullins, "Political and Legal Response to Aum-Related Violence"; and Yuki, "Problems with the Revisions to the Religious Corporations Law." For a translation of the revisions, see Lo Breglio, "Revisions to the Religious Corporations Law." Hardacre discusses the worsening public perceptions of religions (*Shinto*, 512).

 16. Cited in Garon, *Molding Japanese Minds*, 214. Garon added the italics to the original quote from the *Los Angeles Times*, October 16, 1995, part A, p. 1.

 17. On Kōmeitō, see Ehrhardt et al., *Kōmeitō*. On Sōka Gakkai, see McLaughlin, *Human Revolution*. The topic of Sōka Gakkai's political activism is related to the wider conversation about engaged Buddhism in modern societies on the one hand (see Stone, "Nichiren's Activist Heirs") and to the debate about the relationship between religions and civil society on the other (see Hardacre, "After Aum," 141–42).

 18. Hardacre, "After Aum," 136.

 19. Established religions competed with one another to ally with the bureaucracy in government-backed "social management" projects, particularly in areas like social work (Garon, *Molding Japanese Minds*). However, what about marginal religious groups aspiring to attain a position closer to the religious mainstream? The prewar system did not assume associations aspiring to the status of state-recognized religion would inevitably yield some form of public benefit. To the contrary, *associations seeking to attain state recognition as a religion were required to demonstrate their capacity to contribute to the public benefit.* This amounted to a system of *accreditation* for religions (see Ishimura, *Shūkyō hōjinsei to zeisei no arikata*, 11–23). The history of Tenrikyō's campaign for sectarian independence (*ippa dokuritsu undō*) offers a clear example of these principles in operation (see Tenri Daigaku Fuzoku Oyasato Kenkyūsho, *Tenrikyō jiten*, 47). Tenrikyō applied unsuccessfully to register as an independent sect of Shinto four times between 1898 and 1908 before finally gaining government approval upon its fifth attempt. In order to receive this coveted recognition, the group was forced to compromise its core theology and practices to bring itself in line with the state's vision of Shinto. Its leaders hired outside scholars to edit their scriptures to meet the government's requirements, but this alone was insufficient. They next had to show that they had an education system for training their clergy and that their churches were actually teaching the scriptures (the curriculum) they submitted to the authorities for review. This, too, was insufficient. Finally, Tenrikyō needed to prove that it was willing and able to perform public benefit work. Tenrikyō leadership agreed to open the Yōtokuin orphanage in 1909 as part of an effort to demonstrate the sect's value to the nation. On this point, see the Yōtokuin official history (Yōtokuin Hyakunenshi Hensan Iinkai, *Yōtokuin*). Only with the added stipulation that Tenrikyō would invest in social work and contribute to the public good on terms set by the state was the group granted legal standing as a religion and classified as a sect of Shinto. On the subsequent history of Tenrikyō's work for the public good, see Nagaoka, *Shin shūkyō to sōryoku sen*.

20. The most convenient way to survey this material is to look through the latest scholarly volumes on religions and social welfare. On Buddhism, see the *Buddhist Social Welfare Dictionary* (Nihon Bukkyō Shakai Fukushi Gakkai, *Bukkyō shakai fukushi jiten*). On Christianity, see *History of Japanese Christian Social Welfare* (Nihon Kirisutokyō Shakai Fukushi Gakkai, *Nihon Kirisutokyō shakai fukushi no rekishi*). On the social welfare activities of the new religion Tenrikyō, see Tenrikyō Shakai Fukushi Hyakunenshi Henshū Iinkai, *Yōki yusan e no michi*. The study of the social welfare activities of Shinto shrines is less developed than research on other groups, but Fujimoto Yorio's pioneering study of prewar Shinto social work (*shakai jigyō*) provides a detailed introduction to the topic (Fujimoto, *Shintō to shakai jigyō no kindaishi*).

21. ZHZK 1: 10.

22. Ōtani Kōshō retired as leader of the Honganji sect at the age of sixty-five in 1977. He continued to serve as honorary president of the National Chaplains' Union until he was eighty-two years old. See Zaidan Hōjin Zenkoku Kyōkaishi Renmei, *Ayumi tsuzukeru shūkyō kyōkai*, 37.

23. ZHZK 1: 70.

24. Georgeou, "Hōshi to Borantia," 469.

25. Zaidan Hōjin Zenkoku Kyōkaishi Renmei, *Ayumi tsuzukeru shūkyō kyōkai*, 37.

26. Garon, *Molding Japanese Minds*, 52–56.

27. Avenall, "Facilitating Spontaneity."

28. Garon, *Molding Japanese Minds*, 219–20, 227–28.

29. Garon, *Molding Japanese Minds*, 228.

30. The three categories of "volunteers" or "persons of good will" (*tokushika*) who work with the prison system are commonly recognized. They are discussed briefly in ZHZK 4: 29.

31. See the website of the Union of Volunteer Prison Visitors: Kōeki Zaidan Hōjin Zenkoku Tokushi Mensetsu Iin Renmei, http://tokumen.server-shared.com/list1002.html, accessed May 28, 2020.

32. For a comprehensive official history of the probation system in two volumes, see Kōsei Hogo Gojūnenshi Henshū Iinkai, *Kōsei hogo gojūnenshi*. For biographies of major figures in the history of the Japanese probation system, see Hōmushō Hogokyoku Kōsei Hogoshi Henshū Iinkai, *Kōsei hogo seido shikō*. For a general introduction to the probation system, see Imafuku and Konagai, *Hogo kansatsu to wa nanika*.

33. See the chart in Kōsei Hogo Gojūnenshi Henshū Iinkai, *Kōsei hogo gojūnenshi* 1: 434.

34. Zaidan Hōjin Zenkoku Kyōkaishi Renmei, *Ayumi tsuzukeru shūkyō kyōkai*, 68–69.

35. During the civil service years, most clerics who served as chaplains were on rotating, temporary appointments, but there were also a minority of lifers who made a career of chaplaincy. See the list of chaplains (and their terms) at Fuchū Prison in *KKHN* 1: 358–60. Fujii Eshō was one of the lifers during the civil service period. He worked with thought criminals and over 200 death row inmates. Fujii wrote a memoir, and he begins the story by clarifying the difference between the temporary chaplains and the lifers like himself. See Fujii Eshō, *Shikeishū monogatari*, 2.

36. ZHZK nijūgo shūnen kinen gō (1982), 136.

37. Zaidan Hōjin Zenkoku Kyōkaishi Renmei, *Ayumi tsuzukeru shūkyō kyōkai*, 40. By 2006, Watanabe had been a prison chaplain for forty-seven years. As for the history of Tokyo Jail, the central structure of what once was Kosuge Prison now sits abandoned on the grounds of the current Tokyo Jail. The connection to Sugamo Prison is more tenuous, but when I visited Tokyo Jail during the course of fieldwork, the warden maintained that the institution under his watch was the institutional successor to Sugamo. Interestingly, on a subsequent visit to Fuchū Prison, a correctional officer in the prison's education department (overseeing chaplaincy) asserted that in fact Fuchū Prison was the true successor to Sugamo Prison.

38. Horikawa, *Kyōkaishi*, 272.

39. *KKHN* 2: 539.

40. Kyōkai Manyuaru Henshū Iinkai, *Kyōkai manyuaru* (1993), 11.

41. The manual takes up religious freedom and religion-state separation as central themes of prison chaplaincy. See Kyōkai Manyuaru Henshū Iinkai, *Kyōkai manyuaru* (1993), 19–24.

42. The full text of the verdict in the the *Tsu City Shinto Groundbreaking Ceremony Case* is available online in English. Courts in Japan (website), 1971 (Gyo-Tsu) 69, section b.i.

43. It is thought that this framework was made with reference to the "Lemon test" of Lemon v. Kurtzman, 403 U.S. 602 (1971). The Lemon test consists of three stipulations designed to test whether a particular statute with bearing on religion-state involvement is constitutional: (1) The statute must have a secular legislative purpose; (2) the principle or primary effect of the statute must not advance or inhibit religious practice; and (3) the statute must not result in excessive government entanglement with religious affairs. On the *mokuteki kōka kijun*, see Kaneko et al., *Hōritsugaku shōjiten*, 1199.

44. See Kaneko et al., *Hōritsugaku shōjiten*, 883–84 (for *Tsu jichinsai jiken*), 1199 (for *mokuteki kōka kijun*).

45. Courts in Japan (website), 1971 (Gyo-Tsu) 69, section b.i.

46. Nakao, "Jigan hishin," 4–5.

47. Kyōkai Manyuaru Henshū Iinkai, *Kyōkai manyuaru* (1993), 393. The history of this bill is complex. It was intended as a complete revision of the Prison Act of 1908, and it was submitted to the Diet several times between the 1960s and the 1980s without passing. Ultimately, the Prison Act was not revised until 2005—after scandalous incidents in 2001 and 2002 involving the death and injury of Nagoya Prison inmates at the hands of guards spurred reforms. On the history of the Prison Act and its revision, in English, see Lawson, "Reforming Japanese Corrections."

48. Personal communication with Ishizuka Shin'ichi, *Chaplain's Manual* committee meeting, November 2015.

49. Interview with Hirano Shunkō, October 3, 2014.

50. *ZHZK* 1: 71.

51. *ZHZK* 1: 50.

52. The *Chaplaincy* journal discusses the multiple chapels at Fuchū Prison and Yokohama Prison. *ZHZK* 18: 83.

53. *KKHN* 1: 3.

54. Zaidan Hōjin Zenkoku Kyōkaishi Renmei, *Ayumi tsuzukeru shūkyō kyōkai*, 12–13.

55. Zaidan Hōjin Zenkoku Kyōkaishi Renmei, *Ayumi tsuzukeru shūkyō kyōkai*, 12.

56. Zaidan Hōjin Zenkoku Kyōkaishi Renmei, *Ayumi tsuzukeru shūkyō kyōkai*, 10–23.

57. ZHZK 1: 45–49.

58. On the history of Tenrikyō's prison chaplaincy, see Tenrikyō Kyōkaishi Renmei, *Tenrikyō kyōkai no ayumi*.

59. On communal living in Tenrikyō, see the entry for *sumikomi* in Tenri Daigaku Fuzoku Oyasato Kenkyūsho, *Tenrikyō jiten*, 474.

60. Kyōkai Manyuaru Henshū Iinkai, *Kyōkai jireishū* (2017), 71.

61. ZHZK 18: 121–23.

62. When I interviewed two Shinto chaplains between 2014 and 2016, both claimed that shrine Shinto "has no doctrines."

63. Jinja Honchō Kyōkaishi Kenkyūkai, *Kyōkai no tebiki*, 42.

64. Jinja Honchō Kyōkaishi Kenkyūkai, *Kyōkai no tebiki*, 45.

65. Jinja Honchō Kyōkaishi Kenkyūkai, *Kyōkai no tebiki*, 77.

66. ZHZK 18: 113–16.

67. Kyōkai Manyuaru Henshū Iinkai, *Kyōkai jireishū* (2017), 93–102.

68. Kyōkai Manyuaru Henshū Iinkai, *Kyōkai jireishū* (2017), 102.

69. Kyōkai Manyuaru Henshū Iinkai, *Shūkyō kyōkai jireishū* (1993), 60.

70. See Sullivan, *Ministry of Presence*.

71. On this topic, see Harding et al, *Religion and Psychotherapy in Modern Japan*.

72. Shimazono, *From Salvation to Spirituality*.

73. One may note that the tradition of death row chaplaincy focused on "emotional stability" provided chaplains with the opportunity to innovate practices of counseling and attentive care focused on the problem of suffering. Under this rubric, death row chaplains shifted from remonstrating with offenders toward comforting them. Some prison chaplains seem to have effectively performed the functions associated with spiritual care chaplaincy despite a lack of its formal concept. However, death row chaplaincy remained cut off from society outside the prison and so did not influence the development of spiritual care as a social phenomenon in Japan. For one death row chaplain's memoir, see Fujii Eshō, *Shikeishū monogatari*. For a biography of the death row chaplain Watanabe Fusō, see Horikawa, *Kyōkaishi*. Both works contain moving passages about the death row chaplains' commitments to caring for their clients.

74. Chilson, "Naikan," 4–5.

75. Chilson, "Naikan," 1.

76. On the religious roots of *naikan*, see Shimazono, "From Salvation to Healing."

77. Ozawa-de Silva, *Psychotherapy and Religion in Japan*, 1.

78. For an overview of the relationship between *naikan* and spirituality movements, see Chilson, "Naikan"; and Ozawa-de Silva, *Psychotherapy and Religion in Japan*, chap. 7.

79. Chilson, "Naikan," 5.

80. Yamamoto, "Naikan ni kan suru shiryōshū," 11.

81. Yamamoto, "Naikan ni kan suru shiryōshū," 13.

82. Yamamoto, "Naikan ni kan suru shiryōshū," 14.

7. The Dilemmas of Bad Karma

1. Jackson, *Politics of Storytelling*, 183.

2. Recent English-language ethnographic studies of Japanese temple Buddhism have provided a window into the lived experience of Buddhist temple families and temple parishioners. See Covell, *Japanese Temple Buddhism;* Rowe, *Bonds of the Dead;* and Starling, *Guardians of the Buddha's Home.*

3. Interview with a chaplain conducted on November 25, 2014.

4. Interview with shrine Shinto priest and Fuchū Prison chaplain, June 6, 2016.

5. Group interview with three sect Shinto prison chaplains, May 8, 2015.

6. Group interview with three sect Shinto prison chaplains, May 8, 2015.

7. Interview with Fukai Miyoko, June 2, 2016.

8. Interview with Fuchū Prison Education Department staff member, January 10, 2016.

9. Research on spiritual care work in Japan has developed in the wake of the 3.11 disaster, the earthquake and tsunami that devastated the Tōhoku region in 2011. Scholars have examined the role of religionists in the recovery effort, and recently a body of literature has developed around the theme of *kokoro no kea.* On spiritual care after the disaster, see Takahashi, "Ghosts of Tsunami Dead"; on religions' contributions to the recovery efforts after the disaster, see McLaughlin, "In the Wake of the Tsunami." I was aware of the trend toward spiritual care discourse in scholarship when I started interviews, and I expected the discourse of spiritual care to be important to prison chaplains. I found that it was not. The history of prison chaplaincy in Japan is disconnected from this line of thinking. This may be changing, as one chaplain acknowledged that the Corrections Office had recently invited a speaker to a chaplains' training retreat to discuss the topic of *kokoro no kea.* However, the spiritual care issue was by no means a central topic in prison chaplaincy discourse when I conducted fieldwork.

10. On hospice chaplaincy in Japan, see Benedict, "Practicing Spiritual Care in the Japanese Hospice." On chaplaincy and spiritual care in Japan, see Kasai, "Introducing Chaplaincy to Japanese Society"; and Kasai and Itai, *Kea to shite no shūkyō.*

11. Interview with Dōyama Yoshio, September 25, 2014. The Ōedo Branch Church is in the lineage of the Senba Grand Church of Osaka.

12. On volunteer prison visitors and volunteer probation officers, see chapter 6.

13. Such activities appear to have the government's tacit approval according to an "unspoken agreement" or *anmoku no ryōkai*—a phrase that implies "turning a blind eye."

14. Interview with shrine Shinto priest and Fuchū Prison chaplain, June 6, 2016.

15. Shrine Shinto chaplaincy sessions sometimes feature rites of purification (*oharai*) intended to cleanse the pollution associated with crime. I observed one such session in June 2015.

16. The work is *Tegami* by Higashino Keigo.

17. Many chaplains voiced similar concerns. The lack of aftercare programs for people released from prison is a commonly recognized problem.

18. The group chaplaincy session was for ordinary inmates. There are no group sessions for death row inmates, and death row is totally closed to outsiders.

19. Interview with Hirano Shunkō conducted on October 3, 2014.

20. Interview with journalist Horikawa Keiko, April 19, 2015.

21. *Katsu* is a word used during ascetic training to encourage a practitioner to focus. Horikawa, *Kyōkaishi*, 194–96.

22. Berger, *Invitation to Sociology*, 181–82.

23. This line of thinking draws from Michael Jackson's "existential anthropology." See Jackson, *Existential Anthropology*; *The Palm at the End of the Mind*; *Politics of Storytelling*; and *How Lifeworlds Work*.

24. For more on death row families and disenfranchised grief, see Beck et al., *In the Shadow of Death*.

25. This is not the same thing as saying, "I have no personal opinion." Chaplains have a range of views about the death penalty. I met one who declared, straightforwardly, "I support capital punishment." He did not serve on death row. I encountered another who said, "We are not supposed to say anything about it, but I am opposed to the death penalty." This latter was serving on death row. For more perspectives on the death penalty in Japan, see Fuse Tatsuji, *Shikeishū jūichiwa*; Fuse Yaheiji, *Nihon shikeishi*; Kaibara, *Keidan ni kiyu*; Maesaka, *Nihon shikei hakusho*; Mukai, *Shikeishū no haha to natte*; Saki, *Kōya e: Shikeishū no shuki kara*; Satō Daisuke, *Dokyumento: Shikei ni chokumen suru hitotachi*; Satō Hiroshi, *Miyazawa Kenji to aru shikeishū*; Sawachi and Kaga, *Shikeishū monogatari*; and Takamizawa, *Mujitsu no shikeishū*.

26. See Hirano Shunkō, "Shikei to shūkyō kyōkai," 49–51.

27. The Japanese title of the symposium is *Shūkyō kyōkai no genzai to mirai: Nihonjin no shūkyō ishiki*. A publication emerged from this symposium: Akaike and Ishizuka, *Shūkyō kyōkai no genzai to mirai*. Participants included law professor and human rights lawyer Ishizuka Shin'ichi, the president of Ryukoku University Akamatsu Tesshin, emeritus professor of Nagoya University Hirakawa Munenobu, and former chairman of the National Chaplains' Union and death row chaplain Hirano Shunkō.

28. Ōtani Kōshin speaking at the Ryukoku University Symposium, July 11, 2015. I attended the symposium and thank Ishizuka Shin'ichi for a transcript of the proceedings.

29. Horikawa, *Kyōkaishi*, 253.

30. Horikawa, "Kyōkaishi shuzai o tōshite kanjita koto," 99–117 (see 107 for the reference to "murder"). See also Horikawa, *Kyōkaishi*, 221.

A. Tenrikyō Group Chaplaincy Session Field Notes

1. I received this text from the chaplain after the session. This translation is based on the written document.

2. I also received this text from the chaplain after the session. This translation is based on the written document.

3. I took notes throughout, and the chaplain also provided me with a draft version of his sermon later. Here I have largely translated his draft, but I have also included things that he said on the day (as recorded in my own notes) that did not appear in the written text I received later.

Bibliography

List of Abbreviations

Full bibliographic information for the abbreviated sources is included under either "Prison Chaplaincy Periodicals" or "Other Sources" below. Abbreviations refer either to the author/editor or to the title of the work (italicized). Where the abbreviated title is for a work in the Other Sources list, the author/editor is also given. The Other Sources list arranges works alphabetically by author/editor. For example, to find *KF* (abbreviation for *Kirishitan no fukkatsu*) in the Other Sources list, look under Urakawa Wasaburō.

HSK   Honganji Shiryō Kenkyūsho, ed. *Honganji shi*, vol. 3. 1969.

ISSK   *Ishin seiji shūkyōshi kenkyū*. By Tokushige Asakichi.

KF   *Kirishitan no fukkatsu*. By Urakawa Wasaburō.

KGKK   *Kangoku kyōkai* [Prison chaplaincy]. *See* Periodicals.

KK   *Kyōkai kenkyū* [Chaplaincy studies]. *See* Periodicals.

KKHG   *Kyōkai to hogo* [Chaplaincy and probation]. *See* Periodicals.

KKHN   *Kyōkai hyakunen*. Ed. Kyōkai Hyakunen Hensan Iinkai.

NKGS   *Nihon kinsei gyōkei shi kō*. Ed. Zaidan Hōjin Keimu Kyōkai.

NKKS   *Nihon kangoku kyōkai shi*. Ed. Nishi Honganji and Higashi Honganji.

SBK   *Shūkyōgaku no shobun'ya no keisei*. Ed. Shimazono Susumu, Takahashi Hara, and Hoshino Seiji.

SKK   Shisō no Kagaku Kenkyūkai, ed.

SSKS   *Shiryō shūkyō kyōkaishi*. Ed. Chūgoku Chihō Kyōkaishi Renmei.

STK   *Shūkyō to kokka*. Ed. Yasumaru Yoshio and Miyachi Masato.
ZHZK   Zaidan Hōjin Zenkoku Kyōkaishi Renmei, ed. *See* Periodicals.

Prison Chaplaincy Periodicals

Kangoku kyōkai [Prison chaplaincy]. Watanabe Kakumu, ed. Tokyo: Dai Nihon Kangoku Kyōkai Tsūshinsho, 1892–1893.
Kyōkai kenkyū [Chaplaincy studies]. Keimu Kyōkai Jigyō Kenkyūsho, ed. Tokyo: Keimu Kyōkai Jigyō Kenkyūsho, 1926–1939.
Kyōkai to hogo [Chaplaincy and probation]. Keimu Kyōkai Shihō Hogo Jigyō Kenkyūsho, ed. Tokyo: Keimu Kyōkai Shihō Hogo Jigyō Kenkyūsho, 1939–1943.
Zaidan Hōjin Zenkoku Kyōkaishi Renmei, ed. *Kyōkai* [Chaplaincy]. Tokyo: Zaidan Hōjin Zenkoku Kyōkaishi Renmei, 1963–2007.

Other Sources

Abé, Ryūichi. *The Weaving of Mantra: Kūkai and the Construction of Esoteric Buddhist Discourse*. New York: Columbia University Press, 1999.
Akaike Kazumasa and Ishizuka Shin'ichi, eds. *Kyōsei shisetsu ni okeru shūkyō ishiki katsudō ni kan suru kenkyū: Sono genzai to mirai*. Tokyo: Nihon Hyōronsha, 2011.
———, eds. *Shūkyō kyōkai no genzai to mirai: Kyōsei hogo to shūkyō ishiki*. Kyoto: Honganji Shuppansha, 2017.
Akamatsu Kaion. *Buppō tsūron jūroku-dai kōkai*. 2 vols. Kyoto: Kawashima Bunkadō, 1875.
Akamatsu Toshihide and Kasahara Kazuo, eds. *Shinshū shi gaisetsu*. Kyoto: Heirakuji Shoten, 1963. Reprint, 1995.
Akashi Hirotaka and Matsuura Sōzō, eds. *Shōwa tokkō dan'atsu shi*. 8 vols. Tokyo: Taihei Shuppansha, 1977.
Akashi Tomonori. *Kangoku no kindai: Gyōsei kikō no kakuritsu to Meiji shakai*. Fukuoka: Kyūshū Daigaku Shuppankai, 2020.
Akazawa Shirō. *Kindai Nihon no shisō dōin to shūkyō tōsei*. Tokyo: Kura Shobō, 1985.
Ama, Michihiro. "Shinran as 'Other': Revisiting Kurata Hyakuzō's *The Priest and His Disciples*." *Japanese Journal of Religious Studies* 43, no. 2 (2016): 253–74.
Ama Toshimaro. *Nihonjin wa naze mushūkyō na no ka*. Tokyo: Chikuma Shinshō, 2009.
Ambaras, David. *Bad Youth: Juvenile Delinquency and the Politics of Everyday Life in Modern Japan*. Berkeley: University of California Press, 2005.
Anderson, Ronald. *Nishi Honganji and Japanese Buddhist Nationalism, 1862–1945*. PhD diss., University of California, Berkeley, 1956. ProQuest.
Andō Masazumi. *Sugamo kangoku kyōkaishi funjō tenmatsu*. Tokyo: Shakai Hyōronsha, 1898.
Anesaki Masaharu. *Kirishitan kinshi no shūmatsu*. Tokyo: Kokushokan Kyōkai, 1976.
———. *Kirishitan shūmon no hakugai to senpuku*. Tokyo: Dōbunkan, 1925.
Arendt, Hannah. *The Human Condition*. 2nd ed. Introduction by Margaret Canovan. Chicago: University of Chicago Press, 1998.
Asad, Talal. *Formations of the Secular*. Stanford, CA: Stanford University Press, 2003.

———. *Genealogies of Religion: Discipline and Reasons of Power in Christianity and Islam.* Baltimore: Johns Hopkins University Press, 1993.

Auerback, Micah. "Paths Untrodden in Japanese Buddhist Chaplaincy to the Imperial Military." In *Military Chaplaincy in an Era of Religious Pluralism: Military-Religious Nexus in Asia, Europe, and USA,* edited by Torkel Brekke and Vladimir Tikhonov, 62–80. New Delhi, India: Oxford University Press, 2017.

Avenall, Simon. "Facilitating Spontaneity: The State and Independent Volunteering in Contemporary Japan." *Social Science Japan Journal* 13, no. 1 (2010): 69–93.

Baffelli, Erica, and Ian Reader. *Dynamism and the Ageing of a Japanese "New" Religion: Transformations and the Founder.* London: Bloomsbury Academic, 2019.

———. "Editors' Introduction: Impact and Ramifications: The Aftermath of the Aum Affair in the Japanese Religious Context." *Japanese Journal of Religious Studies* 39, no. 1 (2012): 1–28.

Bandō Tomoyuki, Gatō Satoshi, Murai Toshikuni, Akaike Kazumasa, Ishizuka Shin'ichi, Satō Yoshihiko, Tateishi Kōji, and Higashiyama Tetsu. "Keiji shisetsu ni okeru shūkyō isshiki, katsudō ni kan suru chōsa." In *Kyōsei shisetsu ni okeru shūkyō isshiki, katsudō ni kan suru kenkyū: Sono genzai to mirai,* edited by Akaike Kazumasa and Ishizuka Shin'ichi, 1–54. Tokyo: Nihon Hyōronsha, 2011.

Barnlund, Dean C. *Public and Private Self in Japan and the United States: Communicative Styles of Two Cultures.* 1st ed. Tokyo: Simul Press, 1975.

Becci, Irene. *Imprisoned Religion: Transformations of Religion during and after Imprisonment in Eastern Germany.* Farnham, UK: Taylor and Francis, 2016.

———. "Religion's Multiple Locations in Prisons." *Archives de Sciences Sociales des Religions* 153 (2011): 65–84.

Beck, Elizabeth, Sarah Britto, and Arlene Andrews. *In the Shadow of Death: Restorative Justice and Death Row Families.* Oxford: Oxford University Press, 2007.

Beckford, James, Benjamin Berger, and Ilona Cairns. "Prison Chaplaincy: A Selective Bibliography." Religion and Diversity Project. http://religionanddiversity.ca/media/uploads/prison_chaplaincy_bibliography_final.pdf. Accessed July 30, 2020.

Beckford, James, and Sophie Gilliat-Ray. *Religion in Prison: Equal Rites in a Multi-Faith Society.* New York: Cambridge University Press, 1998.

Beckford, James, Danièle Joly, and Farhad Khosrokhavar. *Muslims in Prison: Migration, Minorities, and Citizenship.* London: Palgrave Macmillan, 2005.

Beckman, George, and Genji Okubo. *The Japanese Communist Party: 1922–1945.* Stanford, CA: Stanford University Press, 1969.

Bellah, Robert Neelly. "Civil Religion in America." *Daedalus* 96, no. 1 (1967): 1–21.

Benedict, Timothy O. "Practicing Spiritual Care in the Japanese Hospice." *Japanese Journal of Religious Studies* 45, no. 1 (2018): 175–99.

Berger, Peter L. *Invitation to Sociology: A Humanistic Perspective.* New York: Penguin, 1963. Reprint, 1986.

———. *The Sacred Canopy: Elements of a Sociological Theory of Religion.* Garden City, NY: Doubleday, 1967.

Berger, Peter L., and Thomas Luckmann. *The Social Construction of Reality.* Garden City, NY: Doubleday, 1967.

Blum, Mark, and Robert Rhodes. *Cultivating Spirituality: A Modern Shin Buddhist Anthology.* Albany: State University of New York Press, 2011.

Blum, Mark, and Yasutomi Shin'ya, eds. *Rennyo and the Roots of Modern Japanese Buddhism.* New York: Oxford University Press, 2006.

Botsman, Daniel. *Punishment and Power in the Making of Modern Japan.* Princeton, NJ: Princeton University Press, 2005.

Brekke, Torkel, and Vladimir Tikhonov, eds. *Military Chaplaincy in an Era of Religious Pluralism: Military-Religious Nexus in Asia, Europe, and USA.* New Delhi, India: Oxford University Press, 2017.

Bukkyō Shisō Kenkyūkai, ed. *Kokoro. Bukkyō shisō,* vol. 10. Kyoto: Heirakuji Shoten, 1984.

Burkman, Thomas W. "The Urakami Incidents and the Struggle for Religious Toleration in Early Meiji Japan." *Japanese Journal of Religious Studies* 1, nos. 2–3 (1974): 143–216.

Catholic Weekly. "Pilgrims Visit Site of Nagasaki Christians' Exile." October 26, 2008. https://web.archive.org/web/20081219125907/http://www.cbcj.catholic.jp/eng/jcn/nov2008.htm. Accessed July 30, 2020.

Chappel, James, *Catholic Modern: The Challenge of Totalitarianism and the Remaking of the Church.* Cambridge, MA: Harvard University Press, 2018.

Chikazumi Jōkan. *Zangeroku.* Tokyo [?]: Morie Shoten, 1905.

Chilson, Clark. "Naikan: A Meditation Method and Psychotherapy." In *Oxford Research Encyclopedia of Religion* (online edition). https://doi.org/10.1093/acrefore/9780199340378.013.570. Accessed July 17, 2020.

Chūgoku Chihō Kyōkaishi Renmei, ed. *Shiryō shūkyō kyōkaishi.* Hiroshima: Chūgoku Chihō Kyōkaishi Renmei, 1986.

Chūō Shakai Jigyō Kyōkai, ed. *Zenkoku shakai jigyō dantai meikan.* Tokyo: Chūō Shakai Jigyō Kyōkai, 1927.

Courts in Japan (website). 1971 (Gyo-Tsu) 69 (*Tsu City Shinto Groundbreaking Ceremony Case*). https://www.courts.go.jp/app/hanrei_en/detail?id=51. Accessed October 28th, 2020.

Covell, Stephen. *Japanese Temple Buddhism: Worldliness in a Religion of Renunciation.* Honolulu: University of Hawai'i Press, 2005.

Creemers, Wilhelmus H. M. *Shrine Shinto after World War II.* Leiden: E. J. Brill, 1968.

Cullen, Jennifer. "A Comparative Study of Tenkō: Sata Ineko and Miyamoto Yuriko." *Journal of Japanese Studies* 36, no. 1 (2010): 65–96.

Curley, Melissa. "Prison and the Pure Land: A Buddhist Chaplain in Occupied Japan." *Journal of Buddhist Ethics* 25 (2018): 147–80.

———. *Pure Land, Real World: Modern Buddhism, Japanese Leftists, and the Utopian Imagination.* Honolulu: University of Hawai'i Press, 2017.

de Bary, Wm. Theodore, Carol Gluck, and Arthur E. Tiedemann. *Sources of Japanese Tradition, Volume 2: 1600 to 2000.* 2nd ed. Introduction to Asian Civilizations. New York: Columbia University Press, 2005.

Dobbins, James. *Jōdo Shinshū: Shin Buddhism in Medieval Japan.* Honolulu: University of Hawai'i Press, 2002.

Dorman, Benjamin. *Celebrity Gods: New Religions, Media, and Authority in Occupied Japan.* Honolulu: University of Hawai'i Press, 2012.

―――. "SCAP's Scapegoat? The Authorities, New Religions, and a Postwar Taboo." *Japanese Journal of Religious Studies* 31, no. 1 (2004): 105–40.

Dower, John W. *Embracing Defeat: Japan in the Wake of World War II.* New York: W. W. Norton & New Press, 1999.

Dubler, Joshua. *Down in the Chapel: Religious Life in an American Prison.* New York: Farrar, Straus and Giroux, 2013.

Durkheim, Émile. *The Elementary Forms of the Religious Life: A Study in Religious Sociology.* Glencoe, IL: Free Press, 1947.

e-Gov Japan (website). Minpō [Civil Code]. https://elaws.e-gov.go.jp/search/elawsSearch/elaws_search/lsg0500/detail?lawId=129AC0000000089. Accessed June 19, 2020.

―――. Shūkyō hōjin hō [Religious Corporations Law]. https://elaws.e-gov.go.jp/search/elawsSearch/elaws_search/lsg0500/detail?lawId=326AC0000000126#2. Accessed June 18, 2020.

Ehrhardt, George, Axel Klein, Levi McLaughlin, and Steven R. Reed. *Kōmeitō: Politics and Religion in Japan.* Japan Research Monograph 18. Berkeley, CA: Institute of East Asian Studies, University of California, Berkeley, 2014.

Eurel Project. "Chaplaincy." http://www.eurel.info/spip.php?rubrique674&lang=en.

Ezure Takashi. "Sugamo kyōkaishi jiken to sono ato no bukkyōkai no dōkō." *Tokyo shakai fukushi kenkyū* 7 (May 2013): 39–54.

Fuchū Keimusho, ed. *Fuchū Keimusho rakusei kinen shashinshū.* Tokyo: Fuchū Keimusho, 1935.

Fujioka Ryōkū. *Kangoku kyōkaigaku teiyō sōan.* Hyōgo: Fujioka Ryōkū, 1892.

Foucault, Michel. *The Birth of the Clinic.* Translated by Alan Sheridan. Routledge Classics. Electronic version. Taylor and Francis, 2012.

―――. *Discipline and Punish: The Birth of the Prison.* 2nd ed. Translated by Alan Sheridan. New York: Vintage Books, 1995.

―――. *Security, Territory, Population: Lectures at the Collège De France, 1977–78.* Translated by Graham Burchell. Edited by Michel Senellart. New York: Palgrave Macmillan, 2007.

Fujii Eshō. *Shikeishū monogatari.* Kyoto: Hyakkaen, 1969.

Fujii Takeshi. "Shinzoku nitairon ni okeru shintō no henka: Shimaji Mokurai no seikyōron no motarashita mono." In Inoue and Sakamoto, *Nihon-gata seikyō kankei no tanjō,* 199–244.

Fujimoto Yorio. *Shintō to shakai jigyō no kindaishi.* Tokyo: Kōbundō, 2009.

Fujitani, Takashi. *Splendid Monarchy: Power and Pageantry in Modern Japan.* Berkeley: University of California Press, 1996.

Fujiwara Satoko. "Introduction." *Journal of Religion in Japan* 5 (2016): 93–110.

Fukkyō Kenkyūsho. *Kyōkaishi kyōhon.* Wakayama: Kōyasan Shingonshū Kyōgakubu, 1994.

Fukushima Tsuneo. *Hokkaidō Kirisutokyōshi.* Tokyo: Nihon Kirisuto Kyōdan Shuppankyoku, 1982.

Fuse Tatsuji. *Shikeishū jūichiwa.* Tokyo: Santōsha, 1930.
Fuse Yaheiji. *Nihon shikeishi.* Tokyo: Gannandō, 1983.

Garon, Sheldon M. "From Meiji to Heisei: The State and Civil Society in Japan." In Schwartz and Pharr, *The State of Civil Society in Japan,* 42–62.
———. *Molding Japanese Minds: The State in Everyday Life.* Princeton, NJ: Princeton University Press, 1997.
———. "State and Religion in Imperial Japan, 1912–1945." *Journal of Japanese Studies* 12 no. 2 (Summer 1986): 273–302.
Georgeou, Nichole. "From 'Hōshi to Borantia': Transformations of Volunteering in Japan and Implications for Foreign Policy." *Voluntas: International Journal of Voluntary and Nonprofit Organizations* 21, no. 4 (2010): 467–80.
Gibson, Mary. "Global Perspectives on the Birth of the Prison." *The American Historical Review* 116, no. 4 (2011): 1040–63.
Ginn, John L. *Sugamo Prison, Tokyo: An Account of the Trial and Sentencing of Japanese War Criminals in 1948, by a U.S. Participant.* Jefferson, NC: McFarland, 1992.
Gluck, Carol. *Japan's Modern Myths: Ideology in the Late Meiji Period.* Princeton, NJ: Princeton University Press, 1985.
Goldsmith, Larry. "History from the Inside Out: Prison Life in Nineteenth-Century Massachusetts." *Journal of Social History* 31, no. 1 (1997): 109–25.
Gómez, Luis. *Land of Bliss: The Paradise of the Buddha of Measureless Light: Sanskrit and Chinese Versions of the Sukhāvatīvyūha Sutras.* Honolulu: University of Hawai'i Press, 1996.
Gottfredson, Michael R., and Travis Hirschi. *A General Theory of Crime.* Stanford, CA: Stanford University Press, 1990.
Graber, Jennifer. *The Furnace of Affliction: Prisons and Religion in Antebellum America.* Chapel Hill: University of North Carolina Press, 2011.
Grapard, Allan. "Institution, Ritual, and Ideology: The Twenty-Two Shrine-Temple Multiplexes of Heian Japan." *History of Religions* 27, no. 3 (1988): 246–69.
———. "Japan's Ignored Cultural Revolution: The Separation of Shinto and Buddhist Divinities in Meiji (*"Shimbutsu Bunri"*) and a Case Study: Tōnomine." *History of Religions* 23, no. 3 (1984): 240–65.

Hakeda, Yoshito. *Kūkai: Major Works.* New York: Columbia University Press, 1972.
Hamada Hon'yū. "Hanayama kyōkaishi no mondai." *Shūkyō kōron* 7 (1949): 16–17.
Hanayama Shinshō. *Eien e no michi: Waga hachijūnen no shōgai.* Ohtemachi Books. Tokyo: Nihon Kōgyō Shinbunsha, 1982.
———. *Heiwa no hakken: Sugamo no sei to shi no kiroku.* Tokyo: Asahi Shinbunsha, 1949.
———. *Shōtoku Taishi to kenpō jūshichijō.* Tokyo: Ōkura Shuppan, 1982.
———. *Sugamo no sei to shi no kiroku.* Tokyo: Chūkō Bunkō, 1995.
Hardacre, Helen. "After Aum: Religion and Civil Society in Japan." In Schwartz and Pharr, *The State of Civil Society in Japan,* 135–53.
———. "Aum Shinrikyō and the Japanese Media: The Pied Piper Meets the Lamb of God." *History of Religions,* vol. 47, no. 2 (2007): 171–204.

―――. "Creating State Shinto: The Great Promulgation Campaign and the New Religions." *Journal of Japanese Studies* 12, no. 1 (1986): 29–63.
―――. *Kurozumikyō and the New Religions of Japan.* Princeton, NJ: Princeton University Press, 1986.
―――. *Lay Buddhism in Contemporary Japan: Reiyūkai Kyōdan.* Princeton, NJ: Princeton University Press, 1984.
―――. "Religion and Civil Society in Contemporary Japan." *Japanese Journal of Religious Studies* 31, no. 2 (2004): 389–415
―――. *Shinto: A History.* New York: Oxford University Press, 2017.
―――. *Shinto and the State, 1868–1988.* Princeton, NJ: Princeton University Press, 1989.
Harding, Christopher, Fumiaki Iwata, and Yoshinaga Shin'ichi, eds. *Religion and Psychotherapy in Modern Japan.* Routledge Contemporary Japan Series. London: Routledge, 2015.
Hasegawa Kei. *Tenkō no meian: Shōwa jūnen zengo no bungaku.* Tokyo: Inpakuto Shuppankai: Hatsubaimoto Izara Shobō, 1999.
Hayashida Shigeo. "Bukkyō to tenkō no mondai." In *Kōza kindai Bukkyō,* vol. 5, edited by Hōzōkan, 119–32. Kyoto: Hōzōkan, 2013.
Heisig, James W., and John C. Maraldo. *Rude Awakenings: Zen, the Kyoto School, and the Question of Nationalism.* Nanzan Studies in Religion and Culture. Honolulu: University of Hawai'i Press, 1995.
Hirano Shunkō. "Shikei to shūkyō kyōkai." In Akaike and Ishizuka, *Shūkyō kyōkai no genzai to mirai,* 41–52.
Hirano Takeshi and Honda Jintai. *Honganji hō to kenpō: Honganji-ha no jihō, shūsei, shūkyō no rekishi to tenkai.* Kyoto: Kōyō Shobō, 2011.
Hirata Atsushi. *Shinshū shisōshi ni okeru "shinzoku nitai" ron no tenkai.* Kyoto: Ryūkoku Gakkai, 2001.
Hirota, Dennis, ed. *The Collected Works of Shinran.* 2 vols. Shin Buddhism Translation Series. Kyoto: Jodo Shinshu Hongwanjiha, 1997.
Hokkaidō Kyōkaishi Renmei, ed. *Kaidō hyakunen: Hokkaidō shūkyō kyōkai shoshi.* Tokyo: Zenkoku Kyōkaishi Renmei Shuppan, 1968.
Hōmushō. *Hanzai hakusho 2018.* http://hakusyo1.moj.go.jp/jp/65/nfm/n65_2_2_4_1_1 .html. Accessed July 30, 2020.
Hōmushō Hogokyoku Kōsei Hogoshi Henshū Iinkai, ed. *Kōsei hogo seido shikō gojū shūnen kinen: Kōsei hogo shi no hitobito.* Tokyo: Kōsei Hogo Hōjin Nihon Kōsei Hogo Kyōkai, 1999.
Hōmushō Kyōseikyoku, ed. *Kyōsei shiryō dai nijūnana gō: Kyōsei shisetsu hishūyōsha no shūkyō chōsa.* Tokyo: Hōmushō Kyōseikyoku, 1960.
Honda Shūgo. *Tenkō bungaku ron.* Tokyo: Miraisha, 1964.
Hong Chong-uk. *Senjiki Chōsen no tenkōshatachi.* Tokyo: Yūshisha, 2011.
Honganji Shiryō Kenkyūsho, ed. *Honganji shi,* vol. 3. Kyoto: Jōdo Shinshū Honganji Shūmusho, 1969.
―――, ed. *Honganji shi,* vol. 3. Kyoto: Honganji Shuppansha, 2019.
Horikawa Keiko. *Kyōkaishi.* Tokyo: Kōdansha, 2014.
―――. "Kyōkaishi shuzai o tōshite kanjita koto." In Akaike and Ishizuka, *Shūkyō kyōkai no genzai to mirai,* 99–117.

Hoseikai, ed. *Shisōhan hogo kansatsu hō taii.* Hoseikai sosho dai roku shū. Tokyo: Hoseikai, 1936.

———, ed. *Shisōhan no hogo o chūshin to shite.* Hoseikai sosho dai yon shū. Tokyo: Hoseikai, 1935.

Hoshino Seiji. *Kindai Nihon no shūkyō gainen: Shūkyōsha no kotoba to kindai.* Tokyo: Yūshisha, 2012.

Hoston, Germaine. "Emperor, Nation, and the Transformation of Marxism to National Socialism in Prewar Japan: The Case of Sano Manabu." *Studies in Comparative Communism* 18, no. 1 (1985): 25–47.

———. "*Tenkō*: Marxism and the National Question in Prewar Japan." *Polity* 16, no. 1 (1983): 96–118.

Hur, Nam-lin. *Death and Social Order in Tokugawa Japan: Buddhism, Anti-Christianity, and the Danka System.* Cambridge, MA: Harvard University Asia Center, 2007.

Hurd, Elizabeth Shakman. *Beyond Religious Freedom.* Princeton, NJ: Princeton University Press, 2015.

Ikado Fujio, ed. *Senryō to Nihon shūkyō.* Tokyo: Miraisha, 1993.

Imafuku Shōji and Konagai Kayo. *Hogo kansatsu to wa nanika: Jitsumu no shiten kara toraeru.* Kyoto: Hōritsu Bunkasha, 2016.

Inaba Keishin and Sakurai Yoshihide. *Shakai kōken suru shūkyō.* Kyoto: Sekai Shisōsha, 2009.

Inagaki, Hisao, and Harold Stewart, trans. *The Three Pure Land Sutras.* Moraga, CA: Bukkyō Dendō Kyōkai, 2003.

Inoue Nobutaka. *Kyōha Shintō no keisei.* Tokyo: Kōbundō, 1991.

———, ed. *Shinshūkyō jiten.* Tokyo: Kōbundō, 1990.

Inoue Nobutaka and Sakamoto Koremaru. *Nihon-gata seikyō kankei no tanjō.* Tokyo: Daiichi Shobō, 1987.

Inoue Tetsujirō. *Kyōiku to shūkyō no shōtotsu.* Tokyo: Keigyō Shatō, 1893.

Ishii Shirō and Mizubayashi Takeshi, eds. *Hō to chitsujo. Nihon kindai shisō taikei,* vol. 7. Tokyo: Iwanami Shoten, 1992.

Ishimura Kōji, ed. *Shūkyō hōjinsei to zeisei no arikata: Shinkyō no jiyū to hōjin un'ei no tōmeisei no kakuritsu.* Kyoto: Hōritsu Bunkasha, 2006.

Itō Akira. *Tenkō to tennōsei: Nihon kyōsan shugi undō no 1930 nendai.* Tokyo: Keisō Shobō, 1995.

Itō Chōjirō, ed. *Shinzoku nitai kan shū.* Kobe: Guroria Sosaete, 1927.

Ito Masami. "I Became an Accessory to Legal Murder." *The Japan Times,* April 25, 2004. https://www.japantimes.co.jp/life/2004/04/25/to-be-sorted/i-became-an-accessory -to-legal-murder/. Accessed July 30, 2020.

Ives, Christopher. "The Mobilization of Doctrine: Buddhist Contributions to Imperial Ideology in Modern Japan." *Japanese Journal of Religious Studies* 26, no. 1 (1999): 83–106.

Ivy, Marilyn. "Modernity." In *Critical Terms for the Study of Buddhism,* edited by Donald S. Lopez, 311–31. Chicago: University of Chicago Press, 2005.

Iwata Fumiaki. *Kindai Bukkyō to shōnen: Chikazumi Jōkan to sono jidai.* Tokyo: Iwanami Shoten, 2014.

Iwata Mami and Kirihara Kenshin, eds. *Kami to hotoke no bakumatsu ishin: Kōsaku suru shūkyō sekai.* Kyoto: Hōzōkan, 2018.

Jackson, Michael. *Existential Anthropology: Events, Exigencies and Effects.* New York: Berghahn Books, 2005.
———. *How Lifeworlds Work: Emotionality, Sociality, and the Ambiguity of Being.* Chicago: University of Chicago Press, 2017.
———. *The Palm at the End of the Mind: Relatedness, Religiosity, and the Real.* Durham, NC: Duke University Press, 2009.
———. *The Politics of Storytelling: Violence, Transgression, and Intersubjectivity.* 2nd ed. Copenhagen, Denmark: Museum Tusculanum Press, University of Copenhagen, 2013.
Jaffe, Richard M. *Neither Monk nor Layman: Clerical Marriage in Modern Japanese Buddhism.* Princeton, NJ: Princeton University Press, 2001.
Jansen, Marius B., John Whitney Hall, and Madoka Kanai. *The Cambridge History of Japan: Volume 5, The Nineteenth Century.* Cambridge: Cambridge University Press, 1989. Reprint, 2008.
Jinja Honchō Kyōkaishi Kenkyūkai, ed. *Kyōkai no tebiki.* Tokyo: Jinja Honchō, 1999.
Jōdo Shinshū Honganji-ha Kyōkaishi Hikkei Hensan Iinkai, ed. *Jōdo Shinshū Honganji-ha kyōkaishi hikkei.* Kyoto: Jōdo Shinshū Honganji-ha Shakaibu, 2003.
Jōdo Shinshū Honganji-ha Sōgō Kenkyūsho, ed. *Jōdo Shinshū seiten.* Kyoto: Jōdo Shinshū Honganji-ha Honganji Shuppan, 2013.
Johnson, David T. "Crime and Punishment in Contemporary Japan." *Crime and Justice* 36 (2007): 371–423.
———. *The Japanese Way of Justice: Prosecuting Crime in Japan.* New York: Oxford University Press, 2002.
———. "Japan's Secretive Death Penalty Policy." *Asia-Pacific Law & Policy Journal* 7, no. 2 (2006): 62–124.
Josephson, Jason A. *The Invention of Religion in Japan.* Chicago: University of Chicago Press, 2012.

Kaibara Taku. *Keidan ni kiyu: Tengoku Takahashi Yoshio to jūninin no shikeishū.* Tokyo: Nihon Keizai Hyōronsha, 2015.
Kaneko Hiroshi, Shindō Kōji, and Hirai Yoshio, eds. *Hōritsugaku shōjiten.* 4th ed. Tokyo: Seikōsha, 2008.
Kangakuryō, ed. *Jōdo Shinshū to shakai: Shinzoku nitai o meguru shomondai.* Kyoto: Nagata Bunshōdō, 2008.
Kantei (website). Constitution of Japan [Postwar constitution of 1947]. http://japan.kantei.go.jp/constitution_and_government_of_japan/constitution_e.html. Accessed July 30, 2020.
Kasai Kenta. "Introducing Chaplaincy to Japanese Society." *Journal of Religion in Japan* 5, nos. 2–3 (2016): 246–62.
Kasai Kenta and Itai Masanari, eds. *Kea to shite no shūkyō.* Tokyo: Meiseki Shoten, 2016.
Kashiwahara Yūsen. *Shinshū shi Bukkyō shi no kenkyū: Kindai*, vol. 3. Kyoto: Heirakuji Shoten, 2000.

Kataoka Yakichi. *Fumie, Kakure Kirishitan.* Tokyo: Chishobō, 2014.

———. *Nagasaki no Kirishitan.* Nagasaki: Seibo no Kishisha, 2007.

———. *Nihon Kirishitan junkyōshi.* Tokyo: Chishobō, 2010.

———. "Urakami isshūtō ikken kaidai." In *Minkan shūkyō,* edited by Tanigawa Ken'ichi, 761–62. *Nihon shomin seikatsu shiryō shūsei,* vol. 18. Tokyo: San Ichi Shobō, 1972.

———. *Urakami yonban kuzure.* Tokyo: Chishobō, 2019.

Kataoka Yūko. *Hara Taneaki no kenkyū: shōgai to jigyō.* Hyogo: Kwansei Gakuin Daigaku Shuppankai, 2011.

Ketelaar, James. *Of Heretics and Martyrs in Meiji Japan: Buddhism and its Persecution.* Princeton, NJ: Princeton University Press, 1990.

Kiely, Jan. *The Compelling Ideal: Thought Reform and the Prison in China, 1901–1956.* New Haven: Yale University Press, 2014.

Kikuchi Jin'ichi. *Hanzai shinri.* Tokyo: Shōkadō Shoten, 1934.

———. *Shisō hanzai no sho mondai.* Tokyo: Nihon Hanzai Gakkai Shuppanbu, 1934.

Kisala, Robert. "Contemporary Karma: Interpretations of Karma in Tenrikyō and Risshō Kōseikai." *Japanese Journal of Religious Studies* 21, no. 1 (1994): 73–91.

———. *Prophets of Peace: Pacifism and Cultural Identity in Japan's New Religions.* Honolulu: University of Hawai'i Press, 1999.

Klautau, Orion. *Kindai Nihon shisō to shite no Bukkyō shigaku.* Kyoto: Hōzōkan, 2012.

Kobayashi Hirotada. *Sugamo Purizun: Kyōkaishi Hanayama Shinshō to shikei senpan no kiroku.* Tokyo: Chūō Kōron Shinsha, 2007.

Kobayashi Morito. [Ono Yōichi, pseud.]. *Kyōsantō o dassuru made.* Tokyo: Daidōsha, 1932.

———, *Tenkōki no hitobito: Chian iji hō ka no katsudōka gunzō.* Tokyo: Shinjidaisha, 1987.

———, ed. *Tenkōsha no shisō to seikatsu.* Tokyo: Daidōsha, 1935.

Kojima Nobuyuki. "Tokubetsu kōtō keisatsu ni yoru shinkyō no jiyū seigen no ronri: Kōdō ōmoto to hito no michi kyōdan 'fukei jiken' no haikei ni aru mono." *Shūkyō to shakai* 14 (2008): 69–86.

Kojima Yuki. "Daihi no mite ni sugaru made." In *Tenkōsha no shuki,* edited by Saotome Yūgorō, 43–73. Tokyo: Daidōsha, 1933.

Kokushi daijiten. Accessed through the JapanKnowledge Database, www.japanknowledge .com.

Kondō Shuntarō. "Kindai Nihon ni okeru Marukusu shugi to Bukkyō (jō)." *Bukkyō shi kenkyū* 53 (March 2015): 53–86.

———. *Tennōsei kokka to seishinshugi: Kiyozawa Manshi to sono monka.* Kyoto: Hōzōkan, 2013.

Konkōkyō Kyōkaishi Renmei, ed. *Tomo ni kokoro o hiraite: Kyōkaishi hikkei.* Konkōchō, Okayama: Konkōkyō Kyōkaishi Renmei, 2005.

Kōsei Hogo Gojūnenshi Henshū Iinkai, ed. *Kōsei hogo gojūnenshi: Chiiki shakai to tomo ni ayumu kōsei hogo.* 2 vols. Tokyo: Zenkoku Hogoshi Renmei, Zenkoku Kōsei Hogo Hōjin Renmei, Nihon Kōsei Hogo Kyōkai, 2000.

Koyasu Nobukuni. *Tannishō no kindai.* Tokyo: Hakutakusha, 2014.

Krämer, Hans Martin. *Shimaji Mokurai and the Reconception of Religion and the Secular in Modern Japan.* Honolulu: University of Hawai'i Press, 2015.

Kure PASS Shuppan, ed. *Senzen no kokumin kyōiku: Kokutai no hongi.* Tokyo: Kure PASS Shuppan, 1985.

Kuroda Toshio. *Ōbō to buppō: Chūseishi no kōzu.* Kyoto: Hōzōkan, 2001.

Kuroda Toshio and Jacqueline Stone. "The Imperial Law and the Buddhist Law." *Japanese Journal of Religious Studies* 23, nos. 3–4 (Fall 1996): 271–85.

Kyōkai Hikkei Henshū Iinkai, ed. *Kyōkai hikkei.* Nagoya: Dai Jūnikai Zenkoku Kyōkaishi Taikai Jimukyoku, 1966.

Kyōkai Hyakunen Hensan Iinkai, ed., *Kyōkai hyakunen.* 2 vols. Kyoto: Jōdo Shinshū Honganji-ha and Ōtani-ha, 1973–1974.

Kyōkai Manyuaru Henshū Iinkai, ed. *Kyōkai jireishū.* Tokyo: Kōeki Zaidan Hōjin Zenkoku Kyōkaishi Renmei, 2017.

———, ed. *Kyōkai manyuaru.* Tokyo: Zaidan Hōjin Zenkoku Kyōkaishi Renmei, 1993.

———, ed. *Kyōkai manyuaru.* Tokyo: Kōeki Zaidan Hōjin Zenkoku Kyōkaishi Renmei, 2017.

———, ed. *Shūkyō kyōkai jireishū.* Tokyo: Zaidan Hōjin Zenkoku Kyōkaishi Renmei, 1993.

Kyōsei Kyōkai, ed. *Senji gyōkei jitsuroku.* Tokyo: Kyōsei Kyōkai, 1966.

Kyōseikyoku, ed. *Kyōsei no genjō.* Tokyo: Hōmushō Kyōseikyoku, 2014.

Lawson, Carol. "Reforming Japanese Corrections: Catalysts and Conundrums." In *Who Rules Japan?: Popular Participation in the Japanese Legal Process*, edited by Leon Wolff, Luke Nottage, and Kent Anderson, 128–63. Cheltenham, UK: Edward Elgar, 2015.

Lo Breglio, John. "The Revisions to the Religious Corporations Law: An Introduction and Annotated Translation." *Japanese Religions* 22 (1997): 38–59.

Lyons, Adam. *Karma and Punishment: Prison Chaplaincy in Japan from the Meiji Period to the Present.* PhD diss., Harvard University, 2017.

MacArthur, Douglas. *Reminiscences.* McGraw Hill: New York, 1964.

Maesaka Toshiyuki. *Nihon shikei hakusho.* Tokyo: San Ichi Shobō, 1982.

Maxey, Trent. *The "Greatest Problem:" Religion and State Formation in Meiji Japan.* Cambridge, MA: Harvard University Asia Center, 2014.

McLaughlin, Levi. "Did Aum Change Everything? What Soka Gakkai Before, During, and After the Aum Shinrikyō Affair Tells Us About Persistent 'Otherness' of New Religions in Japan." *Japanese Journal of Religious Studies* 39, no. 1 (2012): 51–75.

———. "In the Wake of the Tsunami: Religious Responses to the Great East Japan Earthquake." In *Cross-currents: East Asian History and Culture Review* 61, no. 3 (2011): 290–97.

———. *Soka Gakkai's Human Revolution: The Rise of a Mimetic Nation in Modern Japan.* Honolulu: University of Hawai'i Press, 2018.

McMahan, David L. *The Making of Buddhist Modernism.* Oxford: Oxford University Press, 2008.

Mills, C. Wright. "The Professional Ideology of Social Pathologists." *American Journal of Sociology* 49, no. 2 (1943): 165–80.

———. *The Sociological Imagination.* New York: Oxford University Press, 2000.

Mitchell, Richard H. *Thought Control in Prewar Japan*. Ithaca, NY: Cornell University Press, 1976.

Miyachi Masato. "Shūkyō kankei hōrei ichiran." In *Shūkyō to Kokka*, edited by Yasumaru Yoshio and Miyachi Masato, 423–88. Tokyo: Iwanami Shoten, 1988.

Miyachi Naokazu and Saeki Ariyoshi, eds. *Shintō daijiten*. Shukusatsuban. Kyoto: Rinsen Shoten, 1986.

Miyake Moritsune, ed. *Sanjō kyōsoku engisho shiryōshū*. 2 vols. Tokyo: Meiji Seitoku Kinen Gakkai, 2007.

———. *Sanjō kyōsoku to kyōiku chokugo: Shūkyōsha no sezoku rinri e no apurōchi*. Tokyo: Kōbundō, 2015.

Miyazaki Shikiei, ed. *Kyōkai kōwashū*. Osaka: Zen Shingonshū Kyōkaishi Renmei, 1973.

Miyoshi Akira. *Arima Shirosuke*. Edited by Nihon Rekishi Gakkai. Tokyo: Yoshikawa Kōbunkan, 1967.

Monbushō. *Kokutai no hongi*. Tokyo: Monbushō, 1937.

Morita Ishizō. *Sugamo Purizun no kaisō*. Saitama: Kan'etsu Seihan Sentā, 2005.

Morris, Norval, and David J. Rothman, eds. *The Oxford History of the Prison: The Practice of Punishment in Western Society*. New York: Oxford University Press, 1995.

Mukai Takeko. *Shikeishū no haha to natte: Kono yamai wa shi ni itarazu*. Tokyo: Shinkyō Shuppansha, 2009.

Mullins, Mark. "The Political and Legal Response to Aum-Related Violence in Japan." *Japan Christian Review* 63 (1997): 37–46.

Murai Sanae. *Kirishitan kinsei to minshū no shūkyō*. Tokyo: Yamakawa Shuppansha, 2008.

Murakami Shigeyoshi. *Kokka Shintō*. Tokyo: Iwanami Shoten, 1970.

———. *Shinshūkyō: Sono kōdō to shisō*. Tokyo: Iwanami Shoten, 2007.

Murase Masamitsu, Higashiguchi Takashi, Sekine Ryūichi, Itō Takaaki, and Taniyama Yōzō. "Kanwa kea byōtō ni okeru shūkyōka no katsudō no genjō ni tsuite no shitsuteki kenkyū." 2012. http://www.hospat.org/assets/templates/hospat/pdf/report_2012/2012-c1.pdf. Accessed July 1, 2020.

Murota Yasuo. *Kindai Nihon no hikari to kage: Jizen, hakuai, shakai jigyō o yomu*. Hyogo: Kwansei Gakuin University Press, 2012.

———. *Tomeoka Kōsuke no kenkyū*. Tokyo: Fuji Shuppan, 1998.

Nabeyama Sadachika. *Watakushi wa Kyōsantō o suteta: Jiyū to sokoku o motomete*. Tokyo: Daitō Shuppansha, 1949.

Nagaoka Takashi. *Shinshūkyō to sōryokusen: Kyōso igo o ikiru*. Nagoya: Nagoya Daigaku Shuppankai, 2015.

Nagasaki Shinbunsha, ed. *Wakaru wakaran: Shin Nagasaki shishi fukyū ban*. Nagasaki: Nagasaki Shinbunsha, 2015.

Nagata Shin'ya. "Fashizumuki no shisō, shūkyō tōsei to kōminka seisaku: Shokuminchi Chōsen ni okeru kyōkaishi, hogoshi no katsudō o chūshin ni." *Minshūshi kenkyū* 49 (1995): 61–75.

Nakamura Hajime, ed. *Bukkyōgo daijiten*. Shukusatsuban. Tokyo: Tokyo Shoseki, 1985.

Nakanishi Naoki. *Bukkyō to iryō fukushi no kindaishi*. Kyoto: Hōzōkan, 2004.

Nakao Bunsaku. "Jigan hishin: Jo ni kaete." In *Jigan hishin: Kyōkaishi rokujūnen no ayumi*, by Otoyama Nyoun. Ichinyoan: Urawa, 1987: 1–7.

Nara, Yasuaki. "May the Deceased Get Enlightenment! An Aspect of the Enculturation of Buddhism in Japan." *Buddhist-Christian Studies* 15, no. 19 (1995): 19–42.

Narita Satoshi. *Kangoku bēsubōru: Shirarezaru kita no yakkyūshi.* Sapporo, Hokkaido: Arisusha, 2009.

National Diet Library (website). The Constitution of the Empire of Japan [Meiji constitution of 1889]. Translated by Itō Miyoji. http://www.ndl.go.jp/constitution/e/etc/c02 .html. Accessed July 30, 2020.

Nichirenshū Kyōkaishikai, ed. *Kyōkaishi hikkei.* Tokyo: Nichirenshū, 1990.

———. *Nichirenshū kyōkaishi hikkei hoshū.* Tokyo: Nichirenshū, 2000.

Nihon Bukkyō Shakai Fukushi Gakkai. *Bukkyō shakai fukushi jiten.* Kyoto: Hōzōkan, 2006.

Nihon Kirisuto Kyōdan Kyōkaishikai, ed. *Kyōkai manyuaru.* Unpublished manuscript. n.d.

Nihon Kirisutokyō Rekishi Daijiten Henshū Iinkai, ed. *Nihon Kirisutokyō rekishi daijiten.* Tokyo: Kyōbunkan, 1988.

Nihon Kirisutokyō Shakai Fukushi Gakkai, ed. *Nihon Kirisutokyō shakai fukushi no rekishi.* Kyoto: Mineruva Shobō, 2014.

Nihon Shūkyō Konwakai, ed. *Gotaiten kinen Nihon shūkyō taikai kiyō.* Tokyo: Nihon Shūkyō Konwakai, 1928.

Nilsson, Roddy. "The Practise of Pastoral Power: The Swedish Prison Chaplains in the 19th Century." *Crime, Histoire & Sociétés / Crime, History & Societies* 17, no. 1 (2013): 53–76.

Nishida Tenkō. *Zange no seikatsu.* Tokyo: Shunjūsha, 1921.

Nishi Honganji and Higashi Honganji, eds. *Nihon kangoku kyōkai shi.* 2 vols. Kyoto: Shinshū Honganji-ha Honganji, Shinshū Ōtani-ha Honganji, 1927.

Niwa Fumio. *The Buddha Tree.* Translated by Kenneth Strong. Rutland, VT: Tuttle, 1968.

Nosco, Peter. "The Experiences of Christians during the Underground Years and Thereafter." *Japanese Journal of Religious Studies* 34, no. 1 (2007): 85–97.

Obeyesekere, Gananath. *Imagining Karma: Ethical Transformation in Amerindian, Buddhist, and Greek Rebirth.* Comparative Studies in Religion and Society 14. Berkeley: University of California Press, 2002.

O'Brien, David M., and Yasuo Ohkoshi. *To Dream of Dreams: Religious Freedom and Constitutional Politics in Postwar Japan.* Honolulu: University of Hawai'i Press, 1996.

Odanaka Toshiki. *Chian seisaku to hō no tenkai katei.* Kyoto: Hōritsu Bunkasha, 1982.

Ogawara Masamichi. *Daikyōin no kenkyū: Meiji shoki shūkyō gyōsei no tenkai to zasetsu.* Tokyo: Keiō Gijuku Daigaku Shuppankai, 2004.

———. *Kindai Nihon no sensō to shūkyō.* Tokyo: Kōdansha, 2010.

———. *Nihon no sensō to shūkyō, 1899–1945.* Tokyo: Kōdansha, 2014.

Ogino Fujio. *Shōwa tennō to chian taisei.* Tokyo: Shin Nihon Shuppansha, 1993.

———. *Tokkō keisatsu.* Tokyo: Iwanami Shoten, 2012.

———. *Tokkō keisatsu taiseishi: Shakai undō yokuatsu torishimari no kōzō to jittai.* Tokyo: Sekita Shobō, 1984.

Ohara Shigechika. *Kangoku soku zu shiki.* Tokyo: Kyōsei Kyōkai, 1976.

Okudaira Yasuhiro, ed. *Chian iji hō. Gendaishi shiryō*, vol. 45. Tokyo: Misuzu Shobō, 1973.
Okuyama, Michiaki. "'State Shinto' in Recent Japanese Scholarship." *Monumenta Nipponica* 66, no. 1 (2011): 123–45.
Ōmi Toshihiro. *Kindai Bukkyō no naka no Shinshū: Chikazumi Jōkan to kyūdōshatachi.* Hōzōkan: Kyōtō, 2014.
Ōnishi Osamu. *Senji kyōgaku to Jōdo Shinshū: Fashizumu-ka no Bukkyō shisō.* Tokyo: Shakai Hyōronsha, 1995.
Ono Yasuhiro, Shimode Sekiyo, Sugiyama Shigetsugu, Suzuki Norihisa, Sonoda Minoru, Nara Yasuaki, Bitō Masahide, Fujii Masao, Miyake Hitoshi, Miyata Noboru, eds. *Shukusatsuban: Nihon shūkyō jiten.* Tokyo: Kōbundō, 1994. Reprint, 2001.
Ono Yōichi. *See* Kobayashi Morito.
Orwell, George. *Nineteen Eighty-Four.* New York: Houghton Mifflin Harcourt, 2017.
Ōsawa Ayako. "Kokodō dōjin ni yoru *Tannishō* no dokkai to Shinran zō: Kurata Hyakuzō no shukke to sono deshi e no keishō to sōi." *Shūkyō kenkyū* 90, no. 3 (2016): 497–520.
Ōta Aito. *Kaika no Tsukiji, minken no Ginza: Tsukiji bando no hitobito.* Tokyo: Tsukiji Shokan, 1989.
Ōtani Eiichi, Yoshinaga Shin'ichi, and Kondō Shuntarō, eds. *Kindai Bukkyō sutadīzu: Bukkyō kara mita mō hitotsu no kindai.* Kyoto: Hōzōkan, 2016.
Ozawa-de Silva, Chikako. *Psychotherapy and Religion in Japan: The Japanese Introspection Practice of Naikan.* Japan Anthropology Workshop Series 6. London: Routledge, 2006.

Pew Research Center. "Religion in Prisons: A 50-State Survey of Prison Chaplains." March 12, 2012. https://www.pewforum.org/2012/03/22/prison-chaplains-exec/. Accessed July 30, 2020.
———. "Religious Landscape Study." https://www.pewforum.org/religious-landscape-study. Accessed July 30, 2020.

Reader, Ian. *A Poisonous Cocktail? Aum Shinrikyō's Path to Violence.* Copenhagen: Nordic Institute of Asian Studies, 1996.
———. *Religious Violence in Contemporary Japan: The Case of Aum Shinrikyō.* Richmond, Surrey, U.K.: Curzon, 2000.
———. "Secularisation, R.I.P.? Nonsense! The 'Rush Hour Away from the Gods' and the Decline of Religion in Contemporary Japan." *Journal of Religion in Japan* 1, no. 1 (2012): 7–36.
Reader, Ian, and George Tanabe. *Practically Religious: Worldly Benefits and the Common Religion of Japan.* Honolulu: University of Hawai'i Press, 1998.
Roemer, Michael K. "Religion and Subjective Well-Being in Japan." *Review of Religious Research* 51, no. 4 (June 2010): 411–27.
Rogers, Minor, and Ann Rogers. "The Honganji: Guardian of the State (1868–1945)." *Japanese Journal of Religious Studies* 17, no. 1 (1990): 3–28.
Rolston, Simon. "Conversion and the Story of the American Prison." In "Reading and Writing in Prison," special issue, *Critical Survey* 23, no. 3 (2011): 103–18.
Roos, John G. *In a Prison Called Sugamo.* Lexington, KY: John. G. Roos, 2014.
Rostaing, Corinne, Céline Béraud, and Claire de Galembert. "Religion, Reintegration and Rehabilitation in French Prisons." In *Religious Diversity in European Prisons: Chal-*

lenges and Implications for Rehabilitation, edited by Irene Becci and Olivier Roy, 63–79. Cham, Switzerland: Springer, 2015.

Rowe, Mark. *Bonds of the Dead: Temples, Burial, and the Transformation of Contemporary Japanese Buddhism.* Chicago: University of Chicago Press, 2011.

Ruch, Barbara, ed. *Engendering Faith: Women and Buddhism in Premodern Japan.* Ann Arbor: Center for Japanese Studies, University of Michigan, 2002.

Ruppert, Brian. "Sin or Crime? Buddhism, Indebtedness, and the Construction of Social Relations in Early Medieval Japan." *Japanese Journal of Religious Studies* 28, nos. 1–2 (2001): 31–55.

Ryūkoku Daigaku, ed. *Bukkyō daijirui.* 5 vols. Tokyo: Fuzanbō, 1972.

Sagara Tōru. *Kokoro (ichigo no jiten).* Tokyo: Sanseidō, 1995.

Said, Edward. *Orientalism.* 25th anniversary ed. New York: Vintage Books, 2003.

Sakamoto Hideo. *Shisōteki hanzai ni taisuru kenkyū.* Tokyo: Shihōshō Chōsa-ka, 1928.

Sakamoto Koremaru, ed. *Kokka Shintō saikō: Saisei ichi kokka no keisei to tenkai.* Tokyo: Kōbundō, 2006.

———. "Nihon-gata seikyō kankei no keisei katei." In Inoue and Sakamoto, *Nihon-gata seikyō kankei no tanjō*, 5–82.

Saki Ryūzō. *Kōya e: Shikeishū no shuki kara.* Tokyo: Kōdansha, 1979.

Sango, Asuka. *The Halo of Golden Light: Imperial Authority and Buddhist Ritual in Heian Japan.* Honolulu: University of Hawai'i Press, 2015.

Sano Manabu. "Gokuchū koten ni yorite kokoro o arahu." In *Sano Manabu chosakushū*, vol. 1, edited by Sano Manabu Chosakushū Kankōkai, 41–55. Tokyo: Meitoku Insatsu Shuppansha, 1957.

———. *Kyōsanshugi to Bukkyō.* Kōya, Wakayama: Kōyasan Shuppansha, 1953.

———. *Shinran to Rennyo.* Kyoto: Chōjiya Shoten, 1949.

Sano Manabu and Nabeyama Sadachika. "Kyōdō hikokudōshi ni tsuguru sho." In *Sano Manabu chosakushū*, vol. 1, edited by Sano Manabu Chosakushū Kankōkai, 3–20. Tokyo: Meitoku Insatsu Shuppansha, 1957.

Sano Shō, ed. *Dai Nihon keigoku enkaku ryakushi.* Tokyo: Dai Nihon Kangoku Kyōkai, 1895.

Saotome Yūgorō, ed. *Tenkōsha no shuki.* Tokyo: Daidōsha. 1933.

Sasaki Masaya. "Shōwa shoki shihōshō no tenkō yūhatsu seisaku to chiteki jōhō tōsei: Shihō kenryoku ni yoru yomi-kaki no shōaku katei." In *Rekishigaku kenkyū* 965 (2017): 1–16.

Satō Daisuke. *Dokyumento: Shikei ni chokumen suru hitotachi, nikusei kara mita jittai.* Tokyo: Iwanami, 2016.

Satō Hiroshi. *Miyazawa Kenji to aru shikeishū.* Tokyo: Yōyōsha, 1965.

Sawachi Kazuo and Kaga Otohiko. *Shikeishū monogatari: Gokuchū nijūnen to shikeishū no nakamatachi.* Tokyo: Sairyūsha, 2006.

Schroeder, Jeff. *After Kiyozawa: A Study of Shin Buddhist Modernization, 1890–1956.* PhD diss., Duke University, 2015.

———. "Historical Blind Spots: The Overlooked Figure of Chikazumi Jōkan." *Religious Studies in Japan* 3 (2016): 67–82. http://jpars.org/online/wp-content/uploads/2016/01/RSJ-vol-3-Schroeder-JAN-19.pdf. Accessed July 22, 2019.

Schull, Kent. *Prisons in the Late Ottoman Empire: Microcosms of Modernity*. Edinburgh: Edinburgh University, 2014.

Schwartz, Frank J., and Pharr, Susan J., eds. *The State of Civil Society in Japan*. Cambridge: Cambridge University Press, 2003.

Senji Kyōgaku Kenkyūkai, ed. *Senji kyōgaku to Shinshū*. 3 vols. Kyoto: Nagata Bunshōdō, 1988.

Shields, James. *Against Harmony: Progressive and Radical Buddhism in Modern Japan*, New York: Oxford University Press, 2017.

Shigematsu Kazuyoshi. *Shiryō: Hokkaidō kangoku no rekishi*. Tokyo: Shinzansha; Abashiri, Hokkaido: Abashiri Kangoku Hozon Zaidan Komon, 2004.

Shigeta Shinji. *Aku to tōchi no Nihon kindai: Dōtoku, shūkyō, kangoku kyōkai*. Kyoto: Hōzōkan, 2019.

———. "Hōhō to shite no Kiyozawa Manshi no kanōsei: Aku to kindai e no toi." *Gendai to Shinran* 35 (2017): 176–94.

———. "Yoshida Kyūichi: Kindai Bukkyō shi kenkyū no kaitaku to hōhō." In *Sengo rekishigaku to Nihon Bukkyō*, edited by Orion Klautau, 249–75. Kyoto: Hōzōkan, 2016.

Shimazono Susumu. "From Salvation to Healing: Yoshimoto Naikan Therapy and Its Religious Origins," In *Religion and Psychotherapy in Modern Japan*, edited by Christopher Harding, Iwata Fumiaki, and Yoshinaga Shin'ichi, 150–64. Routledge Contemporary Japan Series. London: Routledge, 2015.

———. *From Salvation to Spirituality: Popular Religious Movements in Modern Japan*. Melbourne, Australia: Trans Pacific, 2004.

———. "In the Wake of Aum: The Formation and Transformation of a Universe of Belief." *Japanese Journal of Religious Studies* 22, nos. 3–4 (1995): 381–415.

———. *Kokka Shintō to Nihonjin*. Tokyo: Iwanami Shoten, 2010.

———. "State Shinto and the Religious Structure of Modern Japan." *Journal of the American Academy of Religion* 73, no. 4 (2005): 1077–98.

Shimazono Susumu and Regan Murphy. "State Shinto in the Lives of the People: The Establishment of Emperor Worship, Modern Nationalism, and Shrine Shinto in Late Meiji." *Japanese Journal of Religious Studies* 36, no. 1 (2009): 93–124.

Shimazono Susumu, Takahashi Hara, and Hoshino Seiji, eds. *Shūkyōgaku no shobun'ya no keisei*. 9 vols. *Shirīzu Nihon no shūkyōgaku*, vol. 5. Tokyo: Kuresu Shuppan, 2007.

Shinshū no Kyōkai Henshū Iinkai, ed. *Shinshū no kyōkai*. Kyoto: Shinshū Ōtani-ha Shūmusho, 2011.

Shinshūren Chōsashitsu, ed. *Sengo shūkyō kaisōroku*. Tokyo: PL Shuppansha, 1963.

Shisō no Kagaku Kenkyūkai, ed. *Tenkō*. 3 vols. Tokyo: Heibonsha, 2000.

Shōtokukai, ed. *Tokushū: Shisōhan hogokansatsu hō jisshi isshūnen kinen*. *Shōtokukai hō* 2, no. 12 (1937).

Shūkyō Renmei, Monbushō-nai Shūkyō Kenkyūkai, and Jiji Tsūshinsha, eds. *Shūkyō benran*. Tokyo: Jiji Tsūshinsha, 1947.

Sonoda Minoru and Hashimoto Masanori, eds. *Shintō shi daijiten*. Tokyo: Yoshikawa Kōbunkan, 2004.

Sōtōshū Kyōkaishi Rengōkai, ed. *Sōtōshū kyōkaishi manyuaru*. Tokyo: Sōtōshū Shūmuchō, 1974.

Staemmler, Birgit, and Ulrich Dehn, eds. *Establishing the Revolutionary: An Introduction to New Religions in Japan*. Berlin: Lit, 2011.

Stalker, Nancy. *Prophet Motive: Deguchi Onisaburo and the Transformation of Religion in Modern Japan*. Honolulu: University of Hawai'i Press, 2008.

Starling, Jessica. *Guardians of the Buddha's Home: Domestic Religion in the Contemporary Jōdo Shinshū*. Honolulu: University of Hawai'i Press, 2019.

Steinhoff, Patricia G. *Tenkō: Ideology and Societal Integration in Prewar Japan*. Harvard Studies in Sociology. New York: Garland, 1991.

Stone, Jacqueline. "Nichiren's Activist Heirs: Sōka Gakkai, Risshō Kōseikai, Nipponzan Myōhōji." In *Action Dharma: New Studies in Engaged Buddhism*, edited by Christopher Queen, Charles Prebish, and Damien Keown, 63–94. New York: Routledge Curzon, 2003.

Suetake Yoshiya, ed. *Taishō shakai to kaizō no chōryū. Nihon no jidaishi*, vol. 24. Tokyo: Yoshikawa Kōbunkan, 2004.

Sugamo Isho Hensankai, ed. *Seiki no isho*. Tokyo: Sugamo Isho Hensankai Kankō Jimusho, 1953.

Sullivan, Winnifred Fallers. *The Impossibility of Religious Freedom*. Princeton, NJ: Princeton University Press, 2005.

————. *A Ministry of Presence: Chaplaincy, Spiritual Care, and the Law*. Chicago: University of Chicago Press, 2014.

————. *Prison Religion*. Princeton, NJ: Princeton University Press, 2009.

Suzuki Iwayumi. "Rinshō shūkyōshi no tanjō." In *Tasharonteki tenkai*, edited by Isomae Jun'ichi and Kawamura Satofumi, chapter 8. Tokyo: Nakanishiya Shuppan, 2016.

Tajima Ryūjun. *Waga inochi hateru hi ni*. Tokyo: Kōdansha, 1953.

Tajima Shin'yū and Yamaori Tetsuo, ed. *Sugamo no chichi: Tajima Ryūjun*. Tokyo: Bungei Shunjū, 2020.

Takahashi Hara. "The Ghosts of Tsunami Dead and *Kokoro no Kea* in Japan's Religious Landscape." *Journal of Religion in Japan* 5 (2016): 93–110.

Takamizawa Shōji. *Mujitsu no shikeishū: Mitaka jiken, Takeuchi Keisuke*. Tokyo: Nihon Hyōronsha, 2009.

Takizawa Kiyoshi, ed. *Nihon Shūkyō Renmei shōshi*. Tokyo: Nihon Shūkyō Renmei, 1966.

Tanabe Hajime. *Zangedō to shite no tetsugaku*. Tokyo: Iwanami Shoten, 1946.

Tanigawa Ken'ichi, ed. *Minkan shūkyō. Nihon shomin seikatsu shiryō shūsei*, vol. 18. Tokyo: San Ichi Shobō, 1972.

Tenri Daigaku Fuzoku Oyasato Kenkyūsho, ed. *Tenrikyō jiten*. Tenri: Tenrikyō Dōyūsha, 1997.

Tenrikyō Kyōkai no Tebiki Henshū Iinkai, ed. *Tenrikyō kyōkai no tebiki*. Tenri: Tenri Jihōsha, 1993.

Tenrikyō Kyōkaishi Renmei, *Tenrikyō kyōkai no ayumi*. Tenri: Tenri Jihōsha, 2009.

Tenrikyō Shakai Fukushi Hyakunenshi Henshū Iinkai, ed. *Yōki yusan e no michi: Tenrikyō shakai fukushi no hyakunen*. Tenri: Tenri Jihōsha.

Thomas, Jolyon Baraka. *Faking Liberties: Religious Freedom in American Occupied Japan*. Chicago, IL: University of Chicago Press, 2019.

Tokushige Asakichi. *Ishin seiji shūkyōshi kenkyū*. Tokyo: Meguro Shoten, 1935.

————. *Meiji Bukkyō zenshū*, vol. 8. Tokyo: Shun'yōdō, 1935.

Tomeoka Kōsuke. *Jizen mondai*. Tokyo: Keiseisha Shoten, 1898.

Tonohira Yoshihiko. "Tenkō to Bukkyō shisō: Keimusho kyōkai nado to kanren shite." In *Senjika no Bukkyō*, edited by Nakano Kyōtoku, 249–79. *Kōza: Nihon kindai to Bukkyō*, vol. 6. Tokyo: Kokushokan Kyōkai, 1977.

Totani, Yuma. *The Tokyo War Crimes Trial: The Pursuit of Justice in the Wake of World War II*. Cambridge, MA: Harvard University Asia Center, 2008.

Toyohara Ryūen. *Daikyō goakudan no ohanashi*. Kyoto: Ōyagi Kōbundō, 1981.

Tsuchiya Senkyō and Tsuji Zennosuke. *Meiji Bukkyōshi gaisetsu: Haibutsu kishaku to sono go no saisei*. Tokyo: Shoshi shinsui, 2017.

Tsukada Nobutoshi. "Meiji shoki no shūkyō kyōkaishi kō." *Kyōsei Kenkyū* 4 (March 1968): 73–81.

Turnbull, Stephen R. "Diversity or Apostasy? The Case of the Japanese 'Hidden Christians.'" *Studies in Church History* 32 (1996): 441–54. https://doi.org/10.1017/S0424208400015552.

———. *The Kakure Kirishitan of Japan: A Study of Their Development, Beliefs and Rituals to the Present Day*. Richmond, UK: Japan Library, 1998.

UK Freedom of Information Request 112352 [regarding prison chaplains]. https://assets.publishing.service.gov.uk/government/uploads/system/uploads/attachment_data/file/640126/foi-112352-religious-affiliation-by-grade-of-prison-chaplains-and-of-prisoners.docx. Accessed July 30, 2020.

Umemori Naoyuki. "The Modern Penitentiary System in Meiji Japan." In *New Directions in the Study of Meiji Japan*, edited by Helen Hardacre and Adam Kern, 734–68. Leiden: Brill, 1997.

———. "Shingaku to iu tekunorojī: Ninsoku yoseba ni okeru jissen o chūshin ni." *Waseda seiji keizai gaku zasshi* 328 (1996): 228–60.

Uno Enkū, ed. *Hanshūkyō undō no hihan*. Tokyo: Kindaisha, 1932.

Urakawa Wasaburō. *Kirishitan no fukkatsu*. 2 vols. Tokyo: Kokusho Kankōkai, 1979.

———. *Tabi no hanashi*. Nagasaki: Nagasaki Kōkyō Shingakkō, 1938.

Victoria, Brian Daizen. *Zen at War*. War and Peace Library. Lanham, MD: Rowman & Littlefield, 2006.

Waggoner, Edward. "Taking Religion Seriously in the U.S. Military: The Chaplaincy as a National Strategic Asset," *Journal of the American Academy of Religion* 82, no. 3 (September 2014): 702–35.

Wakabayashi, Bob Tadashi. *Anti-Foreignism and Western Learning in Early-Modern Japan: The New Theses of 1825*. Cambridge, MA: Council on East Asian Studies, Harvard University Asia Center, 1986.

Ward, Max. *Thought Crime: Ideology and State Power in Interwar Japan*. Durham, NC: Duke University Press, 2019.

Washington, Garrett. "Fighting Brick with Brick: Chikazumi Jōkan and Buddhism's Response to Christian Space in Imperial Japan." *Cross-currents: East Asian History and Culture Review* 6 (2013): 95–120. https://cross-currents.berkeley.edu/sites/default/files/e-journal/articles/Washington.pdf. Accessed July 22, 2019.

Whelan, Christal. *The Beginning of Heaven and Earth: The Sacred Book of Japan's Hidden Christians*. Honolulu: University of Hawai'i Press, 1996.

Woodard, William P. *The Allied Occupation of Japan 1945–1952 and Japanese Religions*. Leiden: Brill, 1972.

Yamaguchi Teruomi. *Shimaji Mokurai: "Seikyō bunri" o motarashita sōryo*. Tokyo: Kabushiki Kaisha Yamakawa Shuppansha, 2013.

Yamamoto Haruo. "Naikan ni kan suru shiryōshū." Unpublished manuscript, September 30, 1965. Notes distributed at a lecture (?).

Yamaori Tetsuo, ed. *Nihon shūkyōshi nenpyō*. Tokyo: Kawade Shobō Shinsha, 2004.

Yamazaki Ryūmyō. *Shinshū to shakai: "Shinzoku nitai" mondai o tou*. Tokyo: Daizō Shuppan, 1996.

Yasumaru Yoshio. *Ikki, kangoku, kosumoroji: Shūensei no rekishigaku*. Tokyo: Asahi Shinbunsha. 1999.

———. *Kamigami no Meiji ishin: Shinbutsu bunri to haibutsu kishaku*. Tokyo: Iwanami Shoten, 2013.

———. "Kindai tenkanki ni okeru shūkyō to kokka." In *Shūkyō to kokka*, edited by Yasumaru Yoshio and Miyachi Masato, 490–540. *Nihon kindai shisō taikei*, vol. 5. Tokyo: Iwanami Shoten, 1988.

———. *Nihon no kindaika to minshū shisō*. Tokyo: Heibonsha, 1999.

Yasumaru Yoshio and Miyachi Masato, eds. *Shūkyō to kokka. Nihon kindai shisō taikei*, vol. 5. Tokyo: Iwanami Shoten, 1988.

Yoshida Kyūichi. *Gendai shakai jigyōshi kenkyū. Yoshida Kyūichi chosakushū*, vol. 3. Tokyo: Kawashima Shoten, 1990.

———. *Kiyozawa Manshi*. Tokyo: Yoshikawa Kōbunkan, 1961.

———. *Nihon kindai Bukkyō shakaishi kenkyū*. 2 vols. *Yoshida Kyūichi chosakushū*, vols. 5 and 6. Tokyo: Kawashima Shoten, 1991.

———. *Nihon kindai Bukkyō shi kenkyū. Yoshida Kyūichi chosakushū*, vol. 4. Tokyo: Kawashima Shoten, 1992.

———. *Nihon shakai fukushi shisōshi. Yoshida Kyūichi chosakushū*, vol. 1. Tokyo: Kawashima Shoten, 1989.

Yoshida Kyūichi and Hasegawa Masatoshi. *Nihon Bukkyō fukushi shisōshi*. Kyoto: Hōzōkan, 2001.

Yoshimoto, Takaaki, and Hisaaki Wake. "On Tenkō, or Ideological Conversion." *Review of Japanese Culture and Society* 20 (2008): 99–119.

Yōtokuin Hyakunenshi Hensan Iinkai. *Yōtokuin hyakunenshi*. 2 vols. Tenri: Tenri Jihōsha, 2010.

Yuki, Hideo. "Problems with the Revisions to the Religious Corporations Law." *Japanese Religions* 38, nos. 1–2 (2013): 25–36.

Zaidan Hōjin Keimu Kyōkai, ed. *Nihon kinsei gyōkei shi kō*. 2 vols. Tokyo: Kyōsei Kyōkai, 1943. Reprint, 1978.

Zaidan Hōjin Zenkoku Kyōkaishi Renmei, ed. *Ayumi tsuzukeru shūkyō kyōkai*. Tokyo: Zaidan Hōjin Zenkoku Kyōkaishi Renmei, 2006.

Zenkoku Kyōka Dantai Rengōkai, ed. *Zenkoku kyōka dantai meikan*. Tokyo: Zenkoku Kyōka Dantai Rengōkai, 1929.

Index

Page numbers for figures and tables are in italics.

Union, 34, 168, 170; and Occupation, 35, 148–49, 151, 154–60, 162, 166, 167, 171, 177, 264, 269; political activism of, 117–21; in postwar period, 146, 166, 171, 174, 206, 207, 238; and probation system, 140–41; vs. Protestantism, 39, 100, 148–49; and the public good, 12, 33, 34, 38, 68, 98, 113, 123, 124; and religion-state relations, 34, 74, 75, 97, 100, 105–14, 141, 300n95; 310n4; and religious freedom, 120, 126–27, 310n6; on salvation of evil person, 171, 287, 327n68; and Shingaku preachers, 301n2; and Shinto Directive, 151; and *tenkō*, 123, 132, 136, 138, 142, 143–44; terms in, 293n16; and thought criminals, 133–34; and two domains of law, 13, 28, 34, 41, 73–79, 95, 99, 114–15, 120, 123–24, 167, 220, 269, 305n16, 306n17; universalization of, 162, 166. *See also* Honganji sect; Ōtani sect

Shingon Buddhism, xi–xiii, 24, 91, 92, 173–74, 206

Shingon Chaplain's Manual, xiii

Shingon Chaplains' Union, 170

Shinoda Tatsuo, 190, 251–52, 259

Shinran, 171, 306n17, 313n34, 317n14, 327n68; and death row inmates, 247, 248, 282, 286, 287

Shinshū Takada-ha (sect), 90, 311n10

Shinto: vs. Buddhism, 27, 33, 38, 76, 95, 158, 183; chaplains from, 11, 24, 36, 37, 88, 89, 90, 204, 214; vs. Christianity, 57, 60, 183; and civil service, 119, 151; constitutions for sects of, 98; on crime as pollution, 174, 240, 264, 333n15; evangelists of, 72–73, 76, 77; and Great Promulgation Campaign, 57, 69, 71, 77, 87, 149; group chaplaincy session, *204*; on the heart, 299n79; hereditary transmission in, 222; and illegal Christians, 50, 53, 72; and imperial ideology, 97, 150, 310n4; and Imperial Rescript on Education, 149, 209, 309n4; and Kami worship, 45, 47,

74–75; vs. Marxism, 129; in Meiji period, 27, 50, 53, 72; and militarism, 158, 309n4; and National Chaplains' Union, 169–70; and nationalism, 51, 125, 208–9, 323n36; and Occupation, 149–51, 309n4, 323n36; officially recognized sects of, 325n49; organizations of, 180, 206, 208–9, 325n50; in postwar period, 157–58, 164, 168, 264; and private vs. public domains, 295n38, 309n4; and the public good, 113, 304n8; and public service, 186; purification in, 240, 260, 333n15; and Shin Buddhism, 21, 37; shrine, 97, 119, 174, 179, 207, 208, 214, 224, 239, 241, 323n36, 332n62, 333n15; State (Kokka), 7, 97, 149, 157–58, 159, 292n8, 309n4, 315n70; and *tenkō*, 135; and Tenrikyō, 276, 329n19

Shinto Directive (Shintō shirei), 149–51, 176, 220, 323n18, 323n36

Shōtokukai, 321n65

Shōtoku Taishi, 159, 324n40

Siddhartha Gautama, 246

Sino-Japanese War (1894–1895), 32

Social Christianity Movement (SCM), 319n36

socialism, 125, 128, 137, 319n36

social order: and Buddhism, 41–42, 95; and change of heart, 64–68, 70, 94, 107, 108, 134, 237–38, 257, 262, 264; vs. Christianity, 120, 141; and Great Promulgation Campaign, 71–73; and prison chaplaincy, 87, 94, 95, 166, 174, 186; and religion, 141, 206, 262, 266; and spiritual transformation, 163–67; and *tenkō*, 124, 132, 134, 142; and two domains of law, 75, 78, 95, 287

social welfare work (*shakai jigyō*): Buddhist, 9, 111, 124; Christian, 16, 30, 115; in Meiji period, 29, 31; and moral suasion, 317n9; and New Buddhism, 292n12; organizations for, 125, 126; and purpose and effects standard, 194; and religion, 179, 184; and the state, 105, 111; volunteer, 188–89

Harvard East Asian Monographs
(most recent titles)

Harvard East Asian Monographs